THE MADMAN'S MIDDLE WAY

BUDDHISM AND MODERNITY

A series edited by Donald S. Lopez Jr.

DONALD S. LOPEZ JR.

The

Madman's

Middle

Way

REFLECTIONS

ON

REALITY

OF THE

TIBETAN

MONK

GENDUN CHOPEL

THE UNIVERSITY OF CHICAGO PRESS · CHICAGO AND LONDON

Donald S. Lopez Jr. is the Arthur E. Link Distinguished University
Professor of Buddhist and Tibetan Studies in the Department of Asian
Languages and Cultures at the University of Michigan. He is the author or
editor of a number of books, including *Critical Terms for the Study of
Buddhism; Curators of the Buddha: The Study of Buddhism under
Colonialism;* and *Prisoners of Shangri-La: Tibetan Buddhism and the West.*
He is editor of the series Buddhism and Modernity.

The University of Chicago Press, Chicago 60637
The University of Chicago Press, Ltd., London
© 2006 by The University of Chicago
All rights reserved. Published 2006
Printed in the United States of America

15 14 13 12 11 10 09 08 07 06   1 2 3 4 5
ISBN: 0-226-49316-4 (cloth)

The University of Chicago Press gratefully acknowledges the generous
support of the Institute for the Study of Buddhist Traditions at the
University of Michigan toward the publication of this book.

Library of Congress Cataloging-in-Publication Data
Lopez, Donald S., 1952–
    The madman's middle way : reflections on reality of the Tibetan monk Gendun Chopel /
Donald S. Lopez, Jr.
        p.   cm — (Buddhism and modernity)
    Includes English translation of Tibetan text.
    Includes bibliographical references and index.
    ISBN 0-226-49316-4 (hardcover : alk. paper)
    1. Dge-'dun-chos-'phel, A-mdo, 1905?–1951? Dbu ma'i zab gnad sñiṅ por dril ba'i legs bśad
klu sgrub dgoṅs rgyan. 2. Mādhyamika (Buddhism).   I. Dge-'dun-chos-'phel, A-mdo, 1905?–
1951? Dbu ma'i zab gnad sñiṅ por dril ba'i legs bśad klu sgrub dgoṅs rgyan. English.   II. Title.
III. Series.
BQ7455.D483L67 2006
294.3'923'092—dc22   2005011087

⊗ The paper used in this publication meets the minimum requirements of
the American National Standard for Information Sciences—Permanence
of Paper for Printed Library Materials,

ANSI Z39.48-1992.

Contents

Preface

In January 1979, I was visiting Sarnath in northern India, the site of the Buddha's first teaching, the place where he first "turned the wheel of the dharma." The Buddha is said to have encountered his five fellow ascetics in the Deer Park at Sarnath, and to have taught them the four noble truths. Today the area is still a park, with the ruins of a large stūpa and the remnants of a monastery.

There was a dense morning fog, and as I walked into the park the huge stūpa loomed suddenly out of the mist. The fog began to burn off after several clockwise circumambulations of the stūpa, and the monastery came into view. There is archaeological evidence of a monastery from the third century BCE; the visible ruins date for the most part from the twelfth century. As I walked through the ruins, I stopped in front of what appeared to be the remains of a door, framed in white stone, with the lintel missing. A young Tibetan monk was standing nearby, and we exchanged greetings. He then said, in Tibetan, "This is the place where the Buddha stood when he first turned the wheel of the dharma." I was skeptical; although I knew little about the archaeological record, I was unaware of any identification of the precise site of the first teaching, but I politely responded with the Tibetan equivalent of "Oh, really?" The monk said, "Yes, Dge 'dun chos 'phel said so." I was vaguely aware of who Dge 'dun chos 'phel was. In my graduate courses at the University of Virginia, Jeffrey Hopkins once mentioned that Dge 'dun chos 'phel had written that if the pure lands had been designed by the Tibetans, they would have been awash in buttered tea. I knew that Dge 'dun chos 'phel had written a sex manual. I knew that he had spent some time in India in the first half of the twentieth century. And I knew that he had written a book on Madhyamaka philosophy entitled *Adornment for Nāgārjuna's Thought* (*Klu sgrub dgongs rgyan*), but I knew little more about it than its title. I took a photograph of the door, thanked the monk, and continued on my way.

I was in India at that time on a Fulbright fellowship, doing dissertation research on a school of Madhyamaka philosophy, especially as it was understood in the Dge lugs sect of Tibetan Buddhism. I was reading two famous doxographies of the school, one from the seventeenth century, one from the eighteenth, with Tibetan monks residing in the refugee Dge lugs monasteries in southern India.

I thought little about Dge 'dun chos 'phel for the next decade as I published my dissertation and then wrote a book about the *Heart Sūtra*. In 1985, Heather Stoddard published a biography of Dge 'dun chos 'phel in France entitled *Le Mendiant de l'Amdo*. In a review essay published in 1989 in the *Journal of the Royal Asiatic Society*, David Seyfort Ruegg, the doyen of Madhyamaka studies, wrote,

> A judgement as to whether GCh was a powerful and penetrating thinker or simply a gifted scholastic will have to await a detailed study of his controversial study on the Madhyamaka compiled by his disciple Zla ba bzang po, the above mentioned *Klu sgrub dgongs rgyan*. . . . An assessment of this work will be no easy undertaking because it will be necessary to determine what belongs in this text to GCh himself and what might have been added by his disciple and editor (the compiler Zla ba bzang po), because of the inherent difficulty of such a work that exploits the resources of Tibetan Mādhyamika dialectics, because of the extensive Indo-Tibetan philosophical background that it presupposes, and because of the critical responses and refutations it has already called forth. An evaluation of this work will no doubt be of some importance for our understanding of the rôle of Middle Way philosophy in modern times.[1]

This description led me to want to study and perhaps translate the text. My friend Elizabeth Napper kindly gave me her copy, and I began to read it. I made references to the text in an article for Professor Ruegg's Festschrift, where I considered the views of Tsong kha pa, famous "founder" of the Dge lugs sect, and Dge 'dun chos 'phel on the vexed question of whether the Madhyamaka holds any philosophical position. I became intrigued by the text; the author clearly knew the Dge lugs scholastic tradition very well, but wrote about it in a way I had never encountered, either in substance or in style. It lacks the ploddingly systematic structure of most Tibetan scholastic literature ("With regard to the

---

1. D. Seyfort Ruegg, "A Tibetan's Odyssey: A Review Article," *Journal of the Royal Asiatic Society* 2 (1989): 309.

first topic, there are three parts, the first of which has five sections"). Instead, upon initial reading, it had very much the sense of being disconnected statements, perhaps uttered over a number of sessions, jumping from one topic to another without warning. Indeed, its style reminded me more of the *Philosophical Investigations* than of any Buddhist text I had read. Adding to the difficulty of the work, both for the reader and the translator, is that it assumes a complete knowledge of Dge lugs scholastic vocabulary, especially in the areas of *pramāṇa* and *madhyamaka*, as well as the logical choreography of the debating courtyard.

During my years at the University of Virginia, I had been trained to read Dge lugs scholastic philosophy, but had for the most part lost interest in it during the decade after I earned my degree there. Dge 'dun chos 'phel's text seemed to provide an opportunity for me to once again make use of the training I had received in Dge lugs scholasticism, albeit to translate a text that mocked that scholasticism. It seemed like the perfect project. I received a fellowship from the National Endowment for the Humanities in 1992 and completed a translation of the text over the next year. In conversations with friends and colleagues in Tibetan Buddhist studies, I learned that a number of people, both in Europe and the United States, had set out to translate the text, but had given up for one reason or another. They said it was difficult, that it was cryptic in places, that whether Dge 'dun chos 'phel even wrote it was in dispute. All these things were quite true; the text was replete with mind-bending philosophical points, and I was uncertain about numerous points in my translation. It was also an awkward size: the translation was about one hundred pages in typescript, too long for an article, too short for a book. And then there were the refutations. Two prominent Dge lugs scholars had written detailed refutations of the text, each far longer than the text itself. These works were models of high Dge lugs scholasticism, exactly the kind of literature I was hoping to put behind me with the translation.

And so my mind turned to other things, and to other works in the oeuvre of this most fascinating figure, especially his travel journals and his poetry (both of which are cited in chapter 1). In 2003, the centennial of Dge 'dun chos 'phel's birth, I received another fellowship and returned to the project in earnest. In November of that year, I was invited to participate in a conference to celebrate his life, which brought together scholars from India, Tibet, Europe, and America as well as a number of Tibetans who had actually known him. It was a fascinating and inspiring event, held in the stylish premises of the Latse Contemporary Tibetan Cultural Library in New York. There were translators for English and Tibetan, as well as for the dialect of Dge 'dun chos 'phel's beloved homeland of A mdo. And there was an exhibition of dozens of his paintings and drawings, most on display for the first time.

The conference began with the lighting of a butter lamp upon an altar, where a portrait of Dge 'dun chos 'phel, recently painted in Lhasa, had been placed. A woman who had come all the way from Tibet, and who may be his only child, bowed down before the altar while five Tibetan monks chanted two prayers that he had found especially moving. Apparently thinking of his storied irreverence, someone in the audience was overheard to whisper, "He would be spinning in his grave if he could see this." To which someone else whispered, "If he hadn't been cremated." But this person identified often as the slender figure with the sly smile at the edge of the faded group photograph, this person who felt so neglected and misunderstood, especially by his countrymen, also would have been delighted to be the subject of a symposium in New York, a city he had always wanted to visit, with people coming from around the world to both debate and celebrate his life, his art, and his work. Members of the audience would stand to recite unpublished poems that had suddenly been remembered years after his death, like a treasure being discovered in the mind. By the end of the symposium, everyone was speaking Tibetan.

In 2004, I was finally able to finish the project I had begun a decade earlier. It became this book, which begins with a brief account of Dge 'dun chos 'phel's life, liberally interspersed with passages from his writings. This is followed by a translation of his most controversial work, the *Adornment for Nāgārjuna's Thought*. The text deserves commentary, and that is provided in the next chapter. There are many ways in which the text could, and should, be approached: as philosophy, as a work of Tibetan literature, as a product of one of the most fraught moments in Tibetan history. All these approaches remain to be pursued; although I allude to each briefly, the purpose of the commentary is above all to provide the doctrinal context of the work and a paraphrase of its arguments. Following the commentary is an appraisal of the evidence for and against the claim that Dge 'dun chos 'phel is the author of the text. The vociferous and vicious responses to the text, themselves a worthy topic for a separate study, are considered briefly in the next chapter. The book then concludes with the question of modernity, of how the *Adornment for Nāgārjuna's Thought* might best be understood.

The *Adornment* is a text that requires and rewards repeated reading. One of the reasons this book has taken so long to complete is that every time I read the text I see something new, and I know that there are many things I have yet to see. I offer this study with the hope that its rendering in English will allow its readings to multiply.

I have named the book *The Madman's Middle Way*. When Dge 'dun chos 'phel joined Sgo mang College of 'Bras spungs monastery in Lhasa in 1927, he attended the lectures of Geshe Shes rab rgya mtsho, one of the most prominent scholars of the day. He and Dge 'dun chos 'phel would often get into shouting matches over the interpretation of a point of doctrine, and Shes rab rgya mtsho is said to have become so frustrated that he began to address Dge 'dun chos 'phel as "the madman," refusing to call him by name. The term *madman* (*smyon pa*) has many connotations in Tibetan, not all of them negative, and one can only wonder whether Dge 'dun chos 'phel was the least bit bothered by the epithet; he is said to have referred to himself as the madman in his last words.

The middle way, of course, is one of the terms most associated with Buddhism, and was said to have been set forth by the Buddha in that same Deer Park in Sarnath, where he described in his very first sermon a middle way between the extremes of self-indulgence and self-mortification, both of which he had experienced prior to his enlightenment. Some centuries after the Buddha's passing, the term was reinterpreted, most famously by Nāgārjuna, in a more philosophical sense, as a middle way between the extremes of existence and nonexistence.

The philosophical school that the Tibetans credit Nāgārjuna with founding is called the Madhyamaka, or middle way. Consequently, in a prosaic sense, this book is about Dge 'dun chos 'phel's interpretation of Nāgārjuna's philosophy and is thus "the madman's middle way." But Dge 'dun chos 'phel was a person who explored other extremes, knowing both fame and disgrace, praise and blame, gain and loss, happiness and sorrow. He traveled between the antipodes, from northeastern Tibet to Sri Lanka, and wandered the length and breadth of India. As he moved from monk to libertine, his erotic life and his indulgence in cigarettes, drugs, and alcohol were regarded as licentious in the Tibetan society of his day. And his politics were regarded as revolutionary by the Tibetan government and the British Raj alike, and he was punished for them.

The *Adornment for Nāgārjuna's Thought*, his last work before his untimely death, has itself been regarded as extreme from the moment of its publication, and remains so today. But in it, Dge 'dun chos 'phel presents his own middle way, one between wisdom and ignorance, certainty and doubt, faith and skepticism—a middle way that calls everything we know into question because, rather than in spite of, the enlightenment of the Buddha.

～

Over the course of the past decade, I have become increasingly fascinated with Dge 'dun chos 'phel, and I hope to write another book about him. The reasons for the fascination are not entirely clear to me. I have always regarded the great figures of Tibetan literature as distant, almost mythical figures, so far away in time and place. But Dge 'dun chos 'phel is of my time, almost. He died in October 1951, seven months before I was born. And as I write these words, I am already two years older than he was when he died. If he had not been thrown into prison, if he had not become an alcoholic, he might have lived to escape with so many others to India in 1959, and might have been alive when I first went there in 1978, and I may have had a chance to meet him, and offer him a white scarf. But I imagine a different encounter. My father was a pilot in the Second World War, flying P-40s in China against the Japanese. Additional planes for the squadron had to be flown in from India, so in 1944 my father flew from China to India to pick up a new P-40, which he would fly "over the hump" of the Tibetan plateau and back to China. During this respite from war, he spent a few days in Calcutta. As he walked through the streets in the uniform of a lieutenant in the Army Air Corps, I wonder if he might have seen a slightly built, nondescript Tibetan and that their eyes might have met for an instant as they went on their way.

Acknowledgments

I would like to thank three institutions for their generous support of this project. The initial translation of the text was made with the support of a fellowship from the National Endowment for the Humanities. In the spring and summer of 1997, I was the Leverhulme Research Professor at the Institute for Advanced Studies at the University of Bristol and during that time refined and improved the translation. The book was completed while I was the Helmut F. Stern Distinguished Professor of Humanities at the Institute for the Humanities at the University of Michigan. I am especially grateful to Professor Paul Williams, who invited me to come to Bristol, and Professor Daniel Herwitz, director of the Institute for the Humanities at the University of Michigan, who provided a most congenial setting for the book's completion.

In the interest of brevity, I will not list the names of all those who, over the past decade, have asked me when I was going to finish this book. However, I want to acknowledge the support of a number of colleagues around the world, many of whom kindly provided me with newly published texts from Tibet or with photocopies of rare materials. In England, Paul Williams, with whom I read the draft translation during my stay in Bristol, deserves my thanks. The current translation is very different from the one we discussed, but our conversations were very helpful in identifying some of the key elements of the argument. Also while in England, I was able to consult with Geshe Thupten Jinpa, at that time completing his doctorate at Cambridge. His extensive knowledge of Madhyamaka philosophy and his vast vocabulary provided invaluable assistance in clarifying many difficult points in the text. From Germany, I have benefited from the work of friends and colleagues interested in GC: Toni Huber, David Jackson, Irmgard Mengele, and Isrun Engelhardt. I have enjoyed long conversations with Luc Schaedler, a Swiss documentary filmmaker, as he made his film about GC. In France, Heather Stoddard, GC's biographer, has been very supportive over the years and graciously provided me with a copy of her translation of the first pages of the *Adornment*, made many years ago. Katia Buffetrille has always brought me back another book about GC during her annual ethnographic pilgrimages to A mdo. Losang Shastri of the Library of Tibetan Works and Archives in Dharamsala, India, provided me with detailed information about the library's editions of the text. Tashi Tsering of the Amnye Machen Institute, also in Dharamsala, has generously shared his great knowledge about GC's life and work. Elizabeth Napper of the Tibetan Nuns Project in Dharamsala gave me her copy of the Kalimpong edition many years ago, and it was this copy that I first read and translated. In the United States, a number of friends and colleagues have kindly provided me with copies of texts and of their unpublished work, including Georges Dreyfus, José Cabezón, Guy Newland, Daniel Cozort, and Derek Maher. A special thanks to E. Gene Smith for mercilessly prodding me to finish the book while at the same time informing me of the title of yet one more text that I absolutely must read. Finally, I thank Jeffrey Hopkins. As my teacher at the University of Virginia thirty years ago, he set me on the path that has led to this project. As my friend thirty years later, as he retires from his position at Virginia, it has been a source of great pleasure for me to revisit with him the profound and the vast.

chapter

1

THE LIFE

FIRST BEGINNING Should they make his life into a movie, the film would begin with a panoramic shot of the Potala, the palace of the Dalai Lamas, on a brilliantly sunny morning in the autumn of 1950. The camera would pan down to the cluster of buildings known as Shol at the foot of the Potala, zooming slowly to the notorious prison there, where a group of prisoners is being released in a general amnesty proclaimed in the name of the fifteen-year-old Dalai Lama. The inmates emerge one by one into the sunlight, some staggering, some limping, all unshaven, with long unkempt hair, emaciated bodies, and tattered garments. The camera focuses on the last man to emerge, undistinguished from the rest. He appears disoriented as he is approached by a small group of obviously well-born monks and laypeople. But instead of greeting them, he turns to look behind and above, to stare up at the massive edifice of the Potala looming over him. The sight sends him into a reverie (cinematically rendered as a flashback), back to 1927, the year he first arrived in Lhasa from his homeland in the far northeastern region of the Tibetan cultural domain and first beheld the Potala. He is unaware that his gaze is met by that of the teenage Dalai Lama, the young lord who looks down at the prisoners from a window of his palace, peering through a telescope that had been presented to his previous incarnation by a foreign potentate.

But students of his life would immediately note evidence of artistic license in this single scene. It is unclear precisely when he was released from prison; his release may have occurred as much as a year earlier. Although he had been incarcerated at Shol during part of his sentence, he was released not from the prison at the foot of the Potala but from the courthouse in Lhasa. And there are conflicting reports about the state of his health at the time of his release. Some say that he emerged a broken man. Others say that his health was good, that he only began drinking heavily later.

SECOND BEGINNING On December 1, 1951, the following obituary appeared on the front page, center column, of *Melong* (English title, *The Tibet Mirror*). Founded in 1925 by the Tibetan Christian Khunu Tharchin (1890–1976), *Melong* was the first, and at the time the only, Tibetan-language newspaper. It was published not in Lhasa but in Kalimpong in northern India, in the borderland between Nepal, Sikkim, and Bhutan.

ADMONITION TO REMEMBER THE UNCERTAINTY OF DEATH

We have been saddened ever since hearing the most distressing news of the passing from this lifetime on the fifteenth day of the eighth month, due to water sickness, of the supreme being renowned as a spiritual friend skilled in the outer and inner sciences, Dge 'dun chos 'phel. Earlier, he had gone to India, the Land of the Noble Ones, and although he only stayed there for twelve years, he carefully examined the various Tibetan treatises and histories concerning the holy places and cities of India, and while visiting the holy places along the way, he studied the Devanagari script of Sanskrit and the English script, and he translated various Sanskrit books into Tibetan. He performed many auspicious deeds to benefit others, such as composing a pilgrimage guide in order to assist those who go on pilgrimage. In the foreign year 1947, he went to Tibet via Bhutan. During that very year, the Tibetan government, for whatever reason, ordered his imprisonment. Last year, after being released from prison, he was writing a chronicle of Tibet on the orders of the government. Nowadays, if one needed to acquire the learning of the likes of this excellent spiritual friend, even if one spent several hundred thousand coins, it would be difficult for such a scholar to appear. Alas, such a loss, such a loss. I do not know whether or not anyone is publishing the book that he wrote about his long stay in India as well as whatever he had finished of his newly written chronicle of Tibet.

One notes here the tone of personal loss; the obituary was presumably written by Tharchin himself. Also notable is the lack of the kind of specific information that one would expect to find in an obituary. The only dates provided are the date of his return to Tibet, which is inaccurate (he returned to Lhasa in 1946) and the date of his death, and this date, although occurring just a few months before, is disputed by other sources. Of his numerous writings, only his pilgrimage guide is mentioned. And the lament ends on a note of uncertainty, wondering what might have become of his books.

THIRD BEGINNING It is one of the pious conventions of Tibetan Buddhist literature not to immediately mention the name of a great religious figure, .

especially if it is one's teacher, but to write instead, "The name of this exalted being cannot be expressed in words, but if it is necessary to do so, he might be called _____." I have not mentioned his name thus far, not out of any particular piety, but because I do not know how to write it in English. Among the various European-language sources I have consulted, his name has appeared as Gedun Chopel, Gendun Chophel, Gendun Chöphel, Gedun Choephel, Gedün Chompel, Gendun Chomphel, Gedun Chöpel, Gedün Chöpel, Gendün Chöphel, Gedun Chos-'phel, Gedhun Chonphel, Dge 'dun chos 'phel, dGe-'dun-chos-'phel, Dge-vdun Chos-vphel, Dge chos, dGe-hdun Chos-hphel, Gedun Ch'omp'el, and Gytun Chhephel (as he himself first spelled his name). This remarkable range of renderings results from the fact that, despite its vast literature, no one—Tibetan, Chinese, Japanese, European, or American—has devised a standardized system for the phoneticization of Tibetan words in the Latin alphabet. In the generally accepted transliteration system, it is dGe 'dun chos 'phel, but how is that pronounced? Faced with yet another uncertainty about his identity, if I must express his name, I will call him GC.

He was arguably the most important Tibetan intellectual of the twentieth century. Born at the beginning of that century and dying in the middle (his birth and death dates are variously reported), he lived a life bracketed by two of the defining moments in modern Tibetan history, the entry of British troops into Lhasa in 1904 and the entry of Chinese troops into Lhasa in 1951. He thus witnessed decades of profound upheaval in Tibetan society, an upheaval only exceeded by that which followed shortly after his death.

After excelling in the traditional monastic curriculum in his youth, GC would become a philosopher, a poet, an essayist, an artist, a linguist, a translator, a geographer, a historian, a social critic, a sexologist, a botanist, a journalist, an ethnographer, and a sometimes tantric yogin. For some combination of these activities—the precise reasons are unclear—he would be imprisoned by the government of the young Fourteenth Dalai Lama. Sometime shortly before his imprisonment or shortly after his release—the date is uncertain—he gave teachings on the middle way to a group of students. Shortly after his death, although some say before, a text was published that purported to contain those teachings. But the authorship of the text was immediately questioned, and remains a point of sometimes impassioned contention today. One can say with some degree of conviction that the overriding theme of the work is the question of the possibility of knowledge. That is, it is a work of uncertain authorship, attributed to a man about whose life so little can be said with confidence, which calls into question the possibility of certainty. This is a study of that text.

That text, whoever its author, was composed near the end of GC's life. To what extent that text, which we shall call the *Adornment*, represents the culmination of that life is a question worthy of consideration, a consideration that can occur only when one has some sense of the events of that life. I shall begin, therefore, with a survey of GC's life. This will not be a conventional biography, however. Too many questions remain concerning the most basic events of his life. Employing the broad chronology of his life and travels, I shall offer instead a literary life of GC, providing as much of the narrative as possible from his own words, especially his writings from his time in India and Sri Lanka, in an attempt to give some sense of his interests, concerns, and perspectives in the possibly vain hope that these might allow us to better understand the *Adornment*.[1]

1. The events of GC's life presented in this chapter are drawn from a number of European-language and Tibetan sources. The most complete biography is found in Heather Stoddard, *Le mendiant de l'Amdo* (Paris: Société d'ethnographie, 1985). Among English-language works, I consulted Irmgard Mengele, *dGe-'dun-chos-'phel: A Biography of the 20th Century Tibetan Scholar* (Dharamsala, India: Library of Tibetan Works and Archives, 1999); K. Dhondup, "Gedun Chophel: The Man Behind the Legend," *Tibetan Review* 21, no. 10 (October 1978): 10–18; Toni Huber, *The Guide to India: A Tibetan Account by Amdo Gendun Chöphel* (Dharamsala, India: Library of Tibetan Works and Archives, 2000); Jeffrey Hopkins *Tibetan Arts of Love: Sex, Orgasm, and Spiritual Healing* (Ithaca, NY: Snow Lion Publications, 1992); and Hor-khang bsod-nams dpal-vbar, "The Tibetan Scholar Dge-vdun Chos-vphel," *Tibet Studies* 1 (June 1989): 156–67, where GC's close friend was presumably compelled by the editors to describe GC as "a patriot who upheld the unification of the country and opposed imperialist aggression against Tibet. But he was cruelly persecuted by imperialists and the Tibetan reactionary local government and died in the prime of life" (p. 156); moreover, GC "consistently considered that Tibet was the inalienable territory of China an undeniable historical fact. He deemed it an irresistible historical trend to carry out reunification with China" (p. 162).

I also consulted the following Tibetan sources: Bkras mthong thub bstan chos dar, *Dge 'dun chos 'phel gyi lo rgyus* (Dharamsala, India: Library of Tibetan Works and Archives, 1980); Shes rab rgya mtsho, "Dge 'dun chos 'phel," in *Biographical Dictionary of Tibet and Tibetan Buddhism*, vol. 4, *The Rñiṅ-ma-pa Tradition (Part Two)*, ed. Khetsun Sangpo (Dharamsala, India: Library of Tibetan Works and Archives, 1973), 634–57, reprinted in Tashi Tsering and Ven. Ngawang Lungtok, eds., *Go 'jo bla chung thub bstan shes rab rgya mtsho'i gsung thor phyogs bsdud: Collection of Miscellaneous Writings of Go 'jo Bla chung Apho Thub bstan shes rab rgya mtsho (1905–1975)* (Dharamsala, India: Library of Tibetan Works and Archives, 2002), 202–34; Hor khang bsod nams dpal 'bar, "Mkhas pa'i dbang po dge 'dun chos 'phel gyi rtogs pa brjod pa dag pa'i snang ba zhes bya ba," *Bod ljongs zhib 'jug* 2 (1983): 3–31; Tshe ring dbang rgyal and Lcang zhabs pa 'gyur med tshe dbang, *Mkhas dbang dge 'dun chos 'phel skor la dpyad pa tshang pa'i drang thig* (Chengdu, China: Si khron mi rigs dpe skrun khang, 2000); Rdo rje rgyal, *'Dzam gling rig pa'i dpa' bo rdo brag dge 'dun chos 'phel gyi byung ba brjod pa bden gtam rna ba'i bcud len* (Kansu, China: Kan su'u mi rigs dpe skrung khang, 1997); Kirti rin po che Blo bzang bstan 'dzin, *Dge 'dun chos 'phel gyi rab byed zhabs btags ma* (Dharamsala, India: Kirti byes pa grwa tshang, 2003); Hor gtsang 'jigs med, *Drang bden gyis bslus pa'i slong mo ba* (Dharamsala, India: Youtse Publications, 1999); Zho ra bstan pa dar rgyas, "Mkhas dbang dge 'dun chos 'phel mchog gi mdzad rjes rags bsdus," in *Dge 'dun chos 'phel: Mkhas dbang dge 'dun chos 'phel sku 'khrangs nas bgrang bya brgya 'khor bar rjes dran rtsom yig*, ed. Dorjee Wangchuk and Tenpa Dergey (Sidhpur, India: Norbulingka Institute, 2002), 1–28; and an unpublished brief biography of

A MDO   He was born in A mdo, the northeast province of the Tibetan cultural domain. Although dates as disparate as 1895 and 1905 have been suggested
for the year of his birth, recent consensus has placed his birth on August 14,
1903. (Among others born in 1903, one could list Yasujirō Ozu, Bing Crosby,
Benjamin Spock, Claudette Colbert, George Orwell, Bob Hope, Evelyn Waugh,
Mark Rothko, Anais Nin, Yevgeny Mravinsky.) His father, A lags rgyal po (also
known as A lags dpal ldan and Snags 'chang rdo rje), was an incarnate lama
(*sprul sku*, pronounced *tulku*) and *sngags pa* or *māntrika* of the Rnying ma or
"ancient" sect of Tibetan Buddhism, which traced its heritage to the mythically
potent but historically problematic visit of Padmasambhava to Tibet at the end
of the eighth century. Prior to his birth, a prominent Rnying ma lama known as
Rdo brag sprul sku (or "the tulku of Rdo rje brag Monastery"; his name was Rig
'dzin 'jigs med bsod nams rnam rgyal) had visited GC's parents and announced
that he, the lama, would be reborn as their son, leaving behind his ceremonial
hat as an omen. GC's parents subsequently set out on a long pilgrimage from
their home in A mdo to the holy city of Lhasa, a journey of many months.
GC had been conceived by the time they reached Rdo rje brag monastery near
Lhasa, where the monks believed that the unborn child was the next incarnation of the tulku who had visited them; the monks urged the future parents to
remain until the birth. The parents decided to return home, however, knowing
that if the child were a girl, it would be considered inauspicious, and if it were
a boy, the monastery would insist that the child remain there for his education.
They thus set off on the long trek to A mdo, but did not reach their village
before the child was born, near the birthplace of Tsong kha pa (1357–1419), the
famous "founder" of the Dge lugs sect. GC's parents took their new son to their
home in the village of Zho phung in Gser mo ljong, "Golden Valley," in the Reb
gong region of A mdo.

GC was apparently something of a prodigy, learning to read and write by
the age of four. He was regarded, at least locally, as the incarnation of Rdo brag
sprul sku and was known by that name. His birth name, however, was Rig 'dzin
rnam rgyal. When he was seven years old, he was invested as an incarnate lama

---

GC by Hor khang bsod nams dpal 'bar, dated 1990, entitled "Mkhas pa'i dbang po dge 'dun chos
'phel gyi rnam thar yang zhun gser gyi thigs pa."

   For a very useful listing of GC's writings, both published and rumored, see Mengele, *dGe-'dun-
chos-'phel: A Biography of the 20th Century Tibetan Scholar*, 85–113. This should now be supple-
mented by Rdo rje rgyal, ed., *Mkhas dbang dge 'dun chos 'phel gyi gsar rnyed gsung rtsom* (Zi ling,
China: Zi ling mi rigs par khang, 2002), although the attribution of a lengthy pilgrimage guide to
India reprinted in this volume as a work by GC is mistaken.

in a ceremony at the Rnying ma monastery of G.ya' ma bkra shis 'khyil. He continued to study, both with his father and other local lamas, gaining particular recognition for his skills as a poet. Sometime during this period, his father seems to have died or otherwise departed from the scene, for reasons that are unclear. At age fourteen GC entered a local Dge lugs monastery of five hundred monks, called Rdi tsha, where he studied Buddhist logic for three or four years and developed a reputation as an excellent debater. It was from his time at this monastery that he came to be known as "Rdi tsha Slim" (Rdi tsha skam po), a nickname he would carry among his A mdo countrymen throughout his life. It was at Rdi tsha that he was ordained as a Buddhist monk and was given the ordination name Dge 'dun chos 'phel. *Dge 'dun* is the Tibetan translation of saṅgha, the order of monks; *chos 'phel* means "spreading the dharma." He would enjoy a complicated relationship with the Buddhist saṅgha throughout his life. Many would come to question whether he indeed spread the dharma, although *dharma* is notoriously difficult to translate. He would probably point out that one of its ten traditional meanings is "truth."

At the age of seventeen, in 1920, he moved to one of the two major Dge lugs monasteries in the region, Bla brang bkra shis 'khyil, with 2,500 monks, where he completed his studies of logic and epistemology, and began the study of the structures of the Buddhist path.

The standard Dge lugs curriculum was the vehicle of GC's monastic education, an education that he came to stridently criticize. It is probably useful, therefore, to describe its general contours.[2] After learning to read and write (usually beginning between the ages of seven and twelve, although GC learned at a younger age), a monk would study the elementary textbooks on logic called *Collected Topics* (*bsdus grwa*), which introduced basic philosophical categories drawn largely from the works of Dharmakīrti and which provided numerous examples of the mechanics of logical statements that are roughly the equivalent of the syllogism (technically closer to an enthymeme). This was followed by the study of basic epistemology through textbooks called "types of awareness" (*blo rigs*) and more advanced study of the mechanics of argumentation through works called "types of reasons" (*rtags rigs*).

The formal curriculum involved the study of five main texts. The first is the *Ornament of Realization* (*Abhisamayālaṃkāra*) attributed to Maitreyanātha, a poem in eight chapters from which numerous commentators in India, and later

2. For a more detailed description of the curriculum, especially as it survives in exile, see Georges B. J. Dreyfus, *The Sound of Two Hands Clapping: The Education of a Tibetan Buddhist Monk* (Berkeley and Los Angeles: University of California Press, 2003).

in Tibet, extracted a complex taxonomy of the Buddhist paths to enlightenment, via both the Hīnayāna and Mahāyāna. It is highly detailed, employing the famed eight subjects (beginning with the Buddha's omniscient consciousness and ending with the *dharmakāya* of the Buddha) and seventy topics to reveal the so-called hidden teaching of the perfection of wisdom (*prajñāpāramitā*) sūtras.

After completing the study of this text, which took about six years, the curriculum moved next to Candrakīrti's *Entrance to the Middle Way* (*Madhyamakāvatāra*), which is regarded as a supplement to Nāgārjuna's famous *Treatise on the Middle Way* (*Madhyamakaśāstra*) in that it provides what can be termed the religious context to Nāgārjuna's exposition of emptiness. Candrakīrti's text is devoted to setting forth how the understanding of emptiness is to be integrated with the practice of each of the ten perfections (*pāramitā*), virtues cultivated by bodhisattvas on a ten-staged path to enlightenment. Over half of Candrakīrti's text is devoted to the sixth perfection, wisdom. This long discussion of the seminal topics of Madhyamaka philosophy, including emptiness, the two truths, a critique of the Yogācāra, and proofs for the selflessness of persons and other phenomena, is regarded by the Dge lugs as the locus classicus of Prāsaṅgika-Mādhyamika. GC quotes from it frequently in the *Adornment*.

Throughout the long course of study, there was time taken each year (often in the form of a communal winter retreat at 'Jang of monks from several monasteries) for the topic of logic and epistemology, represented by Dharmakīrti's *Commentary to [Dignāga's "Compendium on] Valid Knowledge"* (*Pramāṇavārttika*). This text contains arguments for the existence of rebirth, for liberation from rebirth, and for the omniscience of a buddha; discussions of the two valid sources of knowledge (direct perception and inference); classifications of proof-statements; and an analysis of the operations of thought. Written in a cryptic poetic style, this is considered one of the most difficult Indian śāstras. It was one in which GC excelled.

The final two texts of the Dge lugs curriculum are the *Discourse on Monastic Discipline* (*Vinayasūtra*) by Guṇaprabha, which is the Tibetans' primary source for the rules and regulations governing monastic life, and the *Treasury of Knowledge* (*Abhidharmakośa*) by Vasubandhu, a compendium of Vaibhāṣika and Sautrāntika tenets dealing with all the major categories of Hīnayāna doctrine, encompassing philosophy, soteriology, and cosmology.

The successful completion of the entire curriculum commonly took some twenty years of study. During this time, the chief educational techniques were limited to memorization and debate. In addition to the Indian texts listed above, the monk would study extensive commentaries or textbooks (*yig cha*) on each work. Each college of the major monastic universities had its own textbooks on the Indian root texts. There were two types of these textbooks. The first, called general meaning (*spyi don*), was a relatively straightforward prose commentary that followed the sequence of the Indian text, offering what the college considered the correct interpretation. The other form of textbook was the analysis (*mtha' dpyod*), which set forth the meaning of the text in the form of debates on each of the important points. Each section of the analysis had three subsections: the refutation of wrong interpretations, the presentation of the correct position, and the dispelling of any objections that might be raised about the correct position. The most famous of the *yig cha* were those used by the six scholastic colleges of the three great Dge lugs monasteries around Lhasa, Dga' ldan, 'Bras spungs, and Se ra. Composed between the sixteenth and eighteenth centuries, these texts, and various allegiances to them, led eventually, among other effects, to a concentration on them instead of the Indian and Tibetan texts that they sought to synthesize. Some would also say that such a concentration, even a fixation, resulted in a heightened degree of sectarianism, both among the Dge lugs colleges and especially between Dge lugs and the non-Dge lugs sects of Tibetan Buddhism.

For those monks engaged in the scholastic curriculum (a minority in the major Dge lugs monasteries), it was customary over the course of his study for a monk to memorize the five Indian texts, his college's textbooks on the Indian text, and Tsong kha pa's major philosophical writings; it was not uncommon for an accomplished scholar to have several thousand pages of Tibetan texts committed to memory.

This repository of doctrine was mined in debate, the second educational technique of the monastic university. The debate tradition in Tibet is said to have originated with Phya pa chos kyi seng ge in the twelfth century and was adopted by all of the major sects. Debate took place in a highly structured format in which one monk defended a position that was systematically attacked by his opponent. Skill in debate was essential to progressing to the highest rank of academic scholarship and consequently was greatly admired. Particular fame was attached to those monks who were able to hold the position of one of the lower schools in the doxographical hierarchy against the higher. These debates were often quite spirited, and certain competitions between highly skilled opponents are remembered with the affection not unlike that which some attach to important sporting events in the West. However, it is commonly the case that a monk, adept at the skills of memorization and debate, would achieve scholastic prominence without ever writing a single text; only a small percentage of the highly trained scholars of the Tibetan sects ever wrote anything. The motivations of those who did are not always clear. Judging from their colophons, texts were often written at the request of a student who wished some record of his teacher's views on a particular topic.[3] Texts were also written, of course, as a response to doctrinal controversies that occurred throughout Tibetan history, both within and between sects.

GC read very widely, even in settings in which reading was not deemed appropriate. A common ceremony for generating merit in a Tibetan monastery is to have the entire canon of the word of the Buddha (*bka' 'gyur*) recited. The 108 volumes are taken from their place in the temple and distributed among the monks. They are then all read, not in chorus but in cacophony: each monk takes a different portion of a volume and reads it aloud at the top of his lungs as his fellows read other portions, until every word of every page of the canon has been spoken. During one performance of this ceremony, GC was observed silently reading the text that had been distributed to him.

GC gained notoriety as a particularly skillful debater while at Rdi tsha and Bla brang; as noted, such skill is often measured by the ability to successfully defend positions that are traditionally refuted by what is regarded as the orthodox position. GC was once able to defend the Jaina position, rejected by Buddhists, that plants have consciousness. At Bla brang he met an American missionary, Marion Griebenow, and his family, from whom he may have learned some English.[4] It was also while at Bla brang that he apparently learned of steam engines and airplanes and became fascinated by the wonders of modern science, which he would later describe in his travel journals.

GC remained at Bla brang until 1926. Some sources suggest that he was asked to leave the monastery for critical remarks about the positions set forth in its textbooks, while others say that he was expelled for making mechanical toys. He writes bitterly of his expulsion in a poem describing how a diligent young scholar is forced to leave while corrupt monks are allowed to remain. Addressing the protector deity of the monastery, he writes,

> Alas! After I had gone elsewhere
>> Some lamas who can explain nothing

3. On colophons, see José Ignacio Cabezón, "Authorship and Literary Production in Classical Buddhist Tibet," in *Changing Minds: Contributions to the Study of Buddhism and Tibet in Honor of Jeffrey Hopkins*, ed. Guy Newland (Ithaca, NY: Snow Lion Publications, 2001), 233–63.

4. On Griebenow, see Paul Kocot Nietupski, *Labrang: A Tibetan Buddhist Monastery at the Crossroads of Four Civilizations* (Ithaca, NY: Snow Lion Publications, 1999).

Said that Gnas chung, king of deeds [the protector of the
    monastery]
Did not permit me to stay due to my excessive pride.

If there were a dharma protector who was pure
How could he permit those muddle-headed [monks] to stay,
Wandering everywhere, the familiar and the unfamiliar
Selling tea, beer, and dried mutton?

. . . .

Destroyers of the auspicious teaching with [opulent] hats,
    robes, and boots
And destroyers of the teaching who eat the worst of food;
When we look at them, there is a great difference,
But when the king above [i.e., the protector] looks at them,
    there is no difference.

Rather than expelling to distant mountain passes, valleys, and
    towns
One who takes pride in studying the textbooks of Rva and Bse
Would it not be better to expel to another place
Those who take pride in selling meat, beer, and smoke?[5]

LHASA   Whatever the reason, after returning briefly to his home village, he left A mdo in March 1927 for the four-month journey to Lhasa, the necessary destination for any Dge lugs monk who wished to pursue scholastic training at the highest level. He enrolled in Sgo mang College of 'Bras spung monastery, one of the "three seats" of the Dge lugs sect in the vicinity of Lhasa and the largest Buddhist monastery in the world, with some twelve thousand monks at that time. For the Dge lugs sect, Lhasa was regarded as the intellectual center of Inner Asia, drawing monks from as far away in the west as the Kalmyk region of the former Soviet Union located between the Caspian Sea and the Black Sea, from as far east as Sichuan Province in China, from as far north as the Buryiat region near Lake Baikal in Siberia, and from as far south as the Sherpa regions of Nepal.

5. From "Bla brang la bskur ba'i ka rtsom." In *Dge 'dun chos 'phel gyi gsung rtsom*, vol. 2 (Gangs can rig mdzod 11), ed. Hor khang bsod nams dpal 'bar (Lhasa, Tibet: Bod ljong bod yig dpe rnying dpe skrun khang, 1990), 389–90.

The monastic colleges of the Dge lugs monasteries were divided into houses (*kham tshan*), which provided living quarters, meals, and instruction to monks from a particular geographic region. GC joined one of the A mdo houses, called Klu 'bum ("100,000 Dragons"). There, he studied with the most famous scholar of the house, and one of the most prominent Dge lugs scholars of the day, Shes rab rgya mtsho (1884–1968). Their relationship apparently began well, but deteriorated when GC criticized the positions taken in the monastic textbooks of the college, which were the same that he had studied, and criticized, at Bla brang. When he attended Shes rab rgya mtsho's lectures, the two would fall into heated arguments; Shes rab rgya mtsho eventually refused to address him by name, calling him only "the madman." GC seems to have eventually stopped attending classes, but would frequent the debating courtyard to confound his fellows, often challenging the best students while disguised as one of the illiterate *ldab ldob*—a subgroup within the monastery that lacks a precise analog in Christian monasticism, but shares certain of the characteristics of college fraternity brothers and the Hell's Angels. GC devoted much of his time to studying painting and was eventually able to earn a comfortable living making paintings (thangkas) of various deities. Whatever his reputation may have been among his fellows, he seemed to have been a favorite of Pha bong kha pa, the most powerful Dge lugs lama of the day.

Although there are conflicting reports about the degree of his participation in the monastic curriculum, he seems to have continued to live at Klu 'bum House until 1934. He seems certainly to have completed the curriculum in Madhyamaka (*dbu ma*), and may have finished the last two courses in Vinaya and Kośa as well. He did not, however, sit for the geshe examination, but in later years would refer to himself as a geshe; several of his essays in *The Maha-Bodhi* are signed "Lama Geshe Chömpell."

In 1934, GC met the Indian scholar Rahul Sankrityayan (1893–1963), who was making his second visit to Tibet. Sankrityayan, although only forty at the time, was already a distinguished Sanskritist and an active figure in the Indian independence movement. After a six-month prison term at the hands of the British, he had become a member of the Indian Communist party and a founder of the All India Kisan Sabha. Sankrityayan was seeking a Tibetan scholar to accompany him as he visited the monasteries of southern Tibet in search of Sanskrit manuscripts that been brought there during the disseminations of Buddhism from India to Tibet, and he invited GC to join his expedition. GC ended up accompanying Pandit Rahul to Nepal and then on to India, where he was to spend the next twelve years.

INDIA GC wrote little while in Tibet. Instead, his primary means of expression was that of the Dge lugs monk: the verbal sparring of the debating courtyard. Yet even in this most traditional form of discourse he took on a different guise, sometimes appearing as an illiterate monk to defeat the brightest scholars, sometimes defending a non-Buddhist position against all opponents. It was during his time in India that he began to write in a serious way, in a range of genres, cultivating a distinctive style. He also developed as an artist, moving far beyond the traditional Tibetan thangka style he had learned in Lhasa.

A serious assessment of GC as an artist deserves a separate study that would include the publication of his extant drawings and paintings. My focus here is his thoughts as they are preserved in his writings. Thus, rather than attempt the difficult task of tracing his myriad encounters during his time abroad, here we will examine some of the things that he wrote during those years. His most important work by his own estimation is his travel journal, *The Golden Surface, the Story of a Cosmopolitan's Pilgrimage* (*Rgyal khams rig pas bskor ba'i gtam rgyud gser gyi thang ma*). His longest work, its seventeen chapters in 611 pages constitute approximately half his surviving writings.[6] While in India he also

---

6. The chapter titles give a sense of the breadth of the work:
   1. Initial departure from Lhasa (*Thog mar lha sa nas phebs thon mdzad pa'i tshul*)
   2. General description of the land of India and how it received its name (*Rgya gar gyi yul spyi'i chags tshul dang ming btags tshul*)
   3. How the land was named [in the past] (*Yul gyi ming btags tshul*)
   4. The northern mountains and analysis of questions concerning them (*Byang phyogs kyi gangs ri dang de las 'phros pa'i dogs dpyod*)
   5. What the famous regions of the past were like (*Sngon gyi gnas yul grags can rnams ji ltar yod tshul*)
   6. Concerning the men, women, food, drink, and possessions (*Skyes pa bud med bza' btung yo byad sogs kyi skor*)
   7. Identification of flowers and trees and how to recognize them (*Shing dang me tog sogs kyi ngos 'dzin dang ngos ji ltar 'phrod tshul*)
   8. The orthography of various regions from ancient times to the present (*Sngon dang da lta'i bar yul so so'i yig rigs*)
   9. Concerning the letters of the Tibetan alphabet (*Bod yig gi sgra sbyor skor*)
   10. The edicts of the dharma king Aśoka inscribed on the stone surface of Mount Nagare (*Chos rgyal mya ngan med kyi yi ge ri na ga re'i brag ngos la brkos pa*)
   11. The Gupta Dynasty (*Gupta'i rgyal brgyud*)
   12. The period of the Pāla Dynasty (*Pā la'i rgyal brgyud skabs*)
   13. From 1600 years after the passing of the Buddha to the present (*Sangs rgyas 'das rjes kyi lo brgya phrag bcu drug nas da bar*)
   14. Concerning the history of Sri Lanka (*Singgala'i lo rgyus skor*)
   15. Concerning the life of Tibetans in ancient times (*Sngon dus bod pa rnams kyi gnas skabs dang tshul lugs ci ltar yod lugs skor*)
   16. The religions of non-Buddhists (*Mu stegs kyi chos lugs*)
   17. Conclusion (*Mjug rtsom*)

wrote a guidebook to the Buddhist pilgrimage sites and a work on erotica. He studied several Dunhuang manuscripts on the Tibetan dynastic period as well as Tang historical records, which he used as the basis for his unfinished history of early Tibet, the *White Annals* (*Deb ther dkar po*), a work important for its attempt to demythologize the history of the Yar lung dynasty in Tibet and to discuss Tibet's role as a major military power in inner Asia during the sixth and seventh centuries. In collaboration with other scholars he translated various works from Sanskrit into Tibetan, from Pāli into Tibetan, from Tibetan into English. He wrote newspaper articles in Tibetan and in English; he also wrote poetry in Tibetan and in English. In Tibetan, he developed a distinctive prose style, highly erudite but conversational in tone, employing a rich vocabulary but an informal presentation, never missing an occasion for irony even amid the most sober subjects. GC explains his style at the beginning of the chapter on Sri Lanka in his travel journal: "What I have written, however, is not a treatise, an essay, or a text. I have written down in letters a conversation that is difficult to have because my mouth is separated from your ear by many yojanas [a unit of distance of approximately 5 miles]."[7] Yet his writing has none of the infelicities of the transcription of conversation; it is instead a highly studied and artful composition.

GC writes for a large audience, the Tibetan people, often chastising them for their narrow-mindedness or extolling them to consider seriously what it is that he has to say. Although he seems to have found some success in India (being offered, for example, a position as professor of Tibetan at Shantiniketan by Rabindranath Tagore himself), he often found himself in financial straits, and consistently adopts the persona of the wandering beggar (sometimes calling himself *sprang po dpyod ldan*, a "discerning beggar"), the stranger in a strange land; he writes often of being in a land that is *rgyus med*, a word that can be translated as "unaccustomed," but carries a sense of the unknown and the unrecognized, where nothing is familiar because one has no family.

GC's time in South Asia can be regarded as a series of encounters with the interlocking facets of a certain modernity. He encounters, and writes about, modern scholarship, modern travel, modern geography, modern archaeology, modern science, modern religion, and modern love. The setting for all of this is colonial India and Sri Lanka. And so he also writes of colonialism in the final chapter of his travel journal:

7. Dge 'dun chos 'phel, *Rgyal khams rig pas bskor ba'i gtam rgyud gser gyi thang ma* (*smad cha*). In *Dge 'dun chos 'phel gyi gsung rtsom* 2:3.

About 1959 years after the teacher passed away, the Europeans crossed the ocean, setting out to cover long distances. In particular, the people of Portugal, a small country located in a remote corner of the western foreign lands, were emboldened. By crossing the distant ocean, they discovered many lands, such as Africa. Before long they also controlled the maritime routes of India. 1943 years after the passing of the Buddha, a ship captain named Wa li ko arrived at the coast called Ki la ka rnga.

It is generally the case that in every kind of worldly custom, the intelligence of Europeans is superior to ours in a thousand ways. They could easily spin the heads of the peoples of the East and the South, who, honest but naive, had no experience of anything other than their own countries. And thus they came to many lands, large and small, accompanied by their armies. Their hearts were filled with only self-interest, in their sexual behavior their lust was even greater than a donkey's. Sponsored by kings and ministers who disregarded others' welfare, they trod upon the happiness of others like a turnip on the ground, sending out a great army of bandits, calling them "traders." The timid peoples who subsisted in the forests of the small countries, terrified to hear even the braying of donkeys, were caught like sheep and taken to the [foreigners'] own countries. With feet and hands shackled in irons and given only enough food to wet their mouths, they were made to perform the most difficult work until they died. It is said that due to this severe hardship, even the young were unable to last more than five years. Young women were captured, and to arouse the desires of the gathered customers, were displayed naked in the middle of the marketplace and then sold. If thoughtful people heard how they treated the bodies of humans like cattle, their hearts would bleed. It is in this way that the foundations were laid for all the wonders of the world, railroads stretching from coast to coast and multi-storied buildings whose summits cannot be seen from below. From Africa alone the people thus captured numbered more than one million, and uncountable numbers of the unusable were put in huge boats and abandoned at sea.[8]

In this passage, probably composed in 1940 or 1941, just six years after his departure from Tibet, GC describes the origins of European colonialism, beginning with the first Portuguese explorers; the "a ship captain named Wa li ko" is presumably Vasco da Gama, who arrived at Calicut (Ki la ka rnga) on the west coast of India in 1498. He is writing for a Tibetan audience and measures time in the traditional Buddhist way, from the year in which the Buddha entered

8. Ibid., 2:156–57.

nirvāṇa. GC seems to place the Buddha's nirvāṇa in 544 BCE, a date which he presumably learned while in Sri Lanka. Although as we shall see below, GC's identity as a Tibetan is something that he repeatedly maintains, in the passage above he evinces a clear sense of solidarity with a rather undifferentiated "peoples of the East and the South," the victims of the most inhuman exploitation at the hands of the Europeans. He goes on to describe the activities of Catholic missionaries and then the Dutch, but focuses particularly on the activities of the British in India. Although he praises the British for banning the practice of *sati* (the burning of widows on their husbands' funeral pyres), his evaluation of their rule in India is ultimately damning: "They introduced the new ways of the modern world, such as railroads, schools, and factories. Their law is only good for the educated and the wealthy families. If one has money and knowledge, anything is permitted. As for the lowly, their small livelihoods that provide the necessities of life are sucked like blood from all their orifices. The marvelous land of India appears to be filled with hungry ghosts."[9] At the same time, there was much that he admired among the Europeans (whom he often refers to simply as foreigners [*phyi gling pa*]), perhaps nothing more than their scientific knowledge.

In addition to his posthumously published travel journals, GC wrote for journals and newspapers, including the only Tibetan-language newspaper, *Melong*. Published in Kalimpong by the Tibetan Christian Khunu Tharchin (1890–1976), *Melong*'s full title in Tibetan was *Yul phyogs so so'i gsar 'gyur me long*, "Mirror of the News from Various Homelands." In its June 28, 1938, issue, GC published an essay entitled "The World is Round or Spherical" under the pseudonym Honest Dharma (Drang po Dharma). Above the essay is a map of the world (azimuthal equidistant) presumably drawn by GC himself, showing latitude and longitude, with the names of the continents written in Tibetan cursive script. There are two circles, with North America and South America in one and Africa, Europe, Asia, and Australia in the other. Below is a single globe, perhaps meant to show that the earth is not two globes but one. Above the maps, one reads in Tibetan "Map of the Round World" (*'jig rten ril mo'i sa khra*). I translate the essay in its entirety here:

THE WORLD IS ROUND OR SPHERICAL

In the past, in the lands of the continent of Europe, it was only said that this world is flat, just as it appears to the non-analytical mind; there was not

9. Ibid., 2:161.

a single person who said that it was round. All the ancient religions in the various lands said only that the world is flat; there was not one that said that it was round. Thus, when some intelligent people first said that it is round, the only method to keep it from spreading was to order that they be burned alive. However, in the end, unable to withstand the light of true knowledge, everyone came to believe that it is round. Today, not only has the fact that it is round been determined, but also the size all of the islands in the world just four or five yojanas long have been measured down to spans and cubits. Therefore, in the great lands there is not a single scholar who has even a doubt.

Among all of the Buddhists in Singhala, Burma, Ceylon [presumably, he meant Siam], Japan, and so forth, there is not one who says that it is untrue that it is round. Yet we in Tibet still hold stubbornly to the position that it is not. Some say mindless foolish things, such as that the foreigners' sending of ships into the ocean is a deception. I have also seen some intelligent persons who understand [that it is round] but, fearing slander by others, remain unable to say so. When even the most obstinate European scholars, who do not believe in anything without seeing the reason directly, were not able to maintain the position that it is not round and accepted it completely, then there is no need to talk about this stubbornness of ours not coming to an end.

[Saying that the world is not round] because the Buddha stated that is flat is not accepted as authoritative in other [non-Buddhist] schools and thus does not do a pinprick of damage [to their assertion that it is round]. Even with regard to the scriptures of our own [Buddhist] school, which does accept [the Buddha's statement] as authoritative, because the majority of the sūtras were set forth by the Buddha in accordance with the thoughts of sentient beings, even in this case, we do not know what is provisional and what is definitive. If he set forth even matters of great importance, such as emptiness and the stages of the path to liberation, in various types of provisional meaning in accordance with the thoughts of sentient beings, what need is there to discuss these presentations of environments and their inhabitants? During the lifetime of the Buddha, when it occasionally happened that the way that the monks ate their food did not accord with [the customs] of the time and place, causing slight concern among the laity, he would make a rule that it is was unsuitable. At that time, throughout all the world, the words "[the world] is flat" were as famous as the wind. Thus, even if the Buddha had said, "it is round," whose ear would it have entered? Even if he had said so emphatically, it would have had no purpose, even if he had demonstrated it with his miraculous powers. Nowadays, at a time when [the fact that the world is round] has become evident to billions of beings, there are still those of us who say, "This is your deception." In the same way, I am certain that they would not have believed it, saying, "This is the magic trick of Gautama." If all of us would believe in this world that we see with our eyes rather than that world that we see through letters, it would be good.[10]

Without seeking to overstate the frequently overstated isolation of Tibet, we can note that in 1938, the year that this essay was published in Kalimpong, Hitler annexed Austria; Otto Hahn produced the first nuclear fission of uranium; Howard Hughes, flying a twin-engine Lockheed, set a new record for the circumnavigation of the globe; color television was first demonstrated; the first Xerox image was produced; Teflon was discovered; the ballpoint pen was patented; the first "Superman" episode appeared in *Action Comics*; Disney's *Snow White and the Seven Dwarfs* premiered; Benny Goodman's orchestra performed "Sing, Sing, Sing" at Carnegie Hall. In this same year, GC was attempting to prove to his countrymen that the world was not flat.

It is not possible to consider this fascinating essay in detail here; only a few comments can be made. In the traditional Buddhist cosmology, our world is composed of a great circular ocean enclosed by a ring of mountains. At the center of the ocean stands Mount Meru, upon whose slopes and summit dwell the demigods and two of the types of gods. Four great islands surround Mount Meru in the cardinal directions, the southern of which, called Jambudvīpa, is inhabited by humans and is regarded as our world. This cosmology was widely accepted in Tibet in GC's day, and it is still held by some Tibetan lamas, who argue, when shown photographs of the earth taken from space, that the world that we see is the product of our own past karma, and that those with pure karma see the world as it is: Mount Meru surrounded by the continents. This is the view of the world that GC is trying to dispel.

Significantly, GC does not seek to prove that it is round; he simply declares that it is so. It is so because the Europeans, who once believed that the world is flat, now all say that it is round. Thus, everyone knows that it is round, including the inhabitants of the various Buddhist lands, who also once accepted the Mount Meru cosmology. It is only the narrow-minded and stubborn Tibetans who refuse to see the truth. (This is a theme to which he would repeatedly return in his writings.)

10. Dge 'dun chos 'phel, "'Jigs rten ril mo 'am zlum po," in *Mkhas dbang dge 'dun chos 'phel gyi gsar rnyed gsung rtsom*, ed. Rdo rje rgyal (Zi ling, China: Zi ling mi rigs par khang, 2000), 289–90.

GC next turns to the most potent argument in defense of Mount Meru: that the "flat world" was described by the omniscient Buddha. He imagines a debate in which someone says, "The subject, the world, is not round, because the Buddha said that is flat." Can this be considered a valid argument? GC notes that for the non-Buddhist, the fact that the Buddha said that the world is flat is utterly inconsequential to any discussion of its true shape. Thus, there is no point in arguing with a non-Buddhist from that perspective. However, GC also says that the Buddha's declaration that the world is flat is also insufficient to prove its true shape to a Buddhist, because it is impossible to know whether the Buddha made the statement from a provisional or a definitive perspective. The Buddha is renowned for his skillful pedagogical methods, by which he teaches what is most appropriate for his audience, often saying things that are ultimately inaccurate. Unlike the current Dalai Lama, who is prepared to concede that the Buddha was simply wrong about the cosmology (although he was right about more important things), GC argues that the Buddha knew quite well that the world is round. Yet because he taught in accordance with the culture of ancient India (where everyone thought the world was flat), he did not challenge that view, so that he could more effectively teach the dharma. If he had said that the world was round, or even demonstrated that it was using his magical powers, no one would have believed him. GC will return to the question of the Buddha's conformity to worldly convention in the *Adornment*. What is perhaps more interesting in this context is the confidence he places in European knowledge, a knowledge which, as he implies in his last sentence, is an empirical knowledge derived from observation, and therefore is superior to the knowledge derived from books, by which he seems to mean religious texts, including Buddhist scriptures.

GC provides a much more detailed discussion of European science and its marvels in his travel journals, where he describes the radio, the X-ray machine, slow-motion photography, and color spectrography. Two passages from his discussion can be provided here:

Now I offer a sincere discussion for those honest and far-sighted friends who are members of my religion. The views of the system of the new reasoning called "science" are spreading and increasing in all directions. In the great countries, after scattered disagreements among many people, both intelligent and stupid, who say, "It is not true," they all have become exhausted and must remain silent. In the end, even the Indian brahmins, who care more about the literal interpretation of scriptures than their own lives, have had to powerlessly accept it.

These assertions of the new reasoning are not established through disputation alone. For example, a spyglass constructed by new machines sees across thousands of miles as if it were the palm of one's hand, and similarly, a glass that sees what is close by makes even the smallest atoms appear the size of a mountain; one can analyze the myriad parts, actually seeing everything. Therefore, apart from closing their eyes, they [the opponents of science] had nothing else to try. At first, the adherents of the Christian religion in the foreign lands joined forces with the king, casting out the proponents of the new reasoning, using whatever methods to stop them, imprisoning them and burning them alive. In the end, just as one cannot hide the sunshine in one's hands, so also the parts of their religion that were unacceptable within the new system were defeated and they had to admit that they were utterly false. The glorious Dharmakīrti said [at *Pramāṇavārttika* I:221], "Those who are mistaken about the truth cannot be changed, no matter how one tries, because their minds are prejudiced." The rejection of reason is the most despicable act.

Even so, when we [Tibetans] hear the mere mention of the new system, we look wide-eyed and say, "Oh! This is heretical!" There is the danger that if we come eventually to believe baselessly in the new reasoning, we will lose all faith in the Buddha, like some Mongolian of the Tā khu ral region [that is, Communists], and thus become non-Buddhists. Therefore, whether one either stubbornly says "No!" to the new reasoning or believes in it and utterly rejects the teaching of Buddhism, one is prejudiced; this is nothing more than recalcitrance and will not take you far.

No matter what aspect is set forth in this religion taught by our teacher [the Buddha], whether it be the nature of reality, how to progress on the path, or the good qualities of the attainment, there is absolutely no need to feel ashamed in the face of the reasoning of science. Furthermore, any essential point [in Buddhism] can serve as a foundation for science. Among the foreigners, some of the many scholars of science have acquired a faith in the Buddha, becoming Buddhists, and have even become monks.[11]

This passage shares a number of characteristics with the essay on the shape of the world: the same brief history of European superstition followed by universal acceptance, the same criticism of the narrow-mindedness of Tibetans. And, significantly, there is the same claim that there is no ultimate contradiction

---

11. Dge 'dun chos 'phel, *Rgyal khams rig pas bskor ba'i gtam rgyud gser gyi thang ma* (*smad cha*). In *Dge 'dun chos 'phel gyi gsung rtsom* 2:166–68.

between the discoveries of modern science and the insights of the Buddha. Here, GC's arguments are very much of a piece with the claims of other Buddhist thinkers of the late nineteenth and early twentieth centuries.

The more positive portrayals of Buddhism during the Victorian period saw the Buddha as the greatest philosopher of India's Aryan past and Buddhism as a complete philosophical and psychological system, based on reason and restraint, opposed to ritual, superstition, and sacerdotalism, and thus standing in sharp contrast with the spiritual and sensuous exoticism perceived by the British in colonial India. The Buddha was called a rationalist, and his four noble truths—suffering, the cause of suffering, the cessation of suffering, and the path to that cessation—were said to anticipate the medical model of sickness, diagnosis, prognosis, and cure.

In Asia, despite (or perhaps because of) the European disparagement of the contemporary state of Buddhism in Asia, Buddhist elites very quickly adopted arguments for the compatibility of Buddhism and science and made them their own. By the time that the claims of affinity between Buddhism and science began to be made at the end of the nineteenth century, science had come to carry connotations of authority, validation, and truth separate from, and in some cases in conflict with, those of the Christian church. It is therefore unsurprising that Buddhist leaders in Asia would point to the scientific aspects of Buddhism in an effort to trump the charges of idolatry and superstition leveled at them by Christian missionaries. They argued that the Buddha knew long ago what the science of the Christian West was only now discovering, whether it be the mechanisms of causation that rely on no god, the analysis of experiences into their component parts, the disintegration of matter that is subtle impermanence, or the existence of multiple universes. GC makes many of these points, but does not limit his discussion to the triumphal proclamation of Buddhism's prescience. Indeed, he notes that there may be cases in which the Buddhists might be wrong. He writes, "Yet, to be excessively proud, that is, to continually assert that even the smallest parts of all the explanations in our scriptures are unmistaken, only seems beautiful temporarily; it is [in fact] pointless recalcitrance. There is no point in your becoming angry at me."[12] And he gives as an example the very thing that he had successfully debated back in Tibet, that plants have consciousness, providing what is presumably the first reference to the Venus flytrap in Tibetan literature.[13]

12. Ibid., 2:171.
13. Ibid., 2:171–72.

Here, as in much of his poetry, there is both a certain bitterness and a certain poignancy in his words: he is neglected; he speaks, but he is not heard, although he has something important to tell his people, both for their sake and the sake of the dharma.

I have a great desire to write a separate book on what the advantages are in considering things from the perspective of this new reasoning, but because of great difficulty and because it would become a source of disillusionment [for others], I have set the task aside.

Do not think that I am a dullard, believing immediately in whatever others say. I too am rather sharp-witted. In serving the teaching, I do not find disciples to whom I can explain the dharma. Founding a monastery requires the accumulation of many conditions. I am incapable of these great acts. [My] sympathy for the dharma is not less than yours. For that reason, do not dismiss my statements, seeking only to refute and reject me. If one does not want the tree-trunk of the teachings and these roots of our Buddhist knowledge to be completely destroyed, one must be far-sighted.

Having become an open-minded person who sees the important and unimportant, you should strive to ensure the survival of the teaching, so that it remains together with the ways of the new reasoning. Otherwise, if, fearing complaints by others, one acts stubbornly, then one may gain great profit and many friends, [but only] for a short while. As it says on the pillar at Zon de above Gro tshang, "Like the light-rays of the sun and moon in the vastness of space, may the teachings of the Buddha and my reign remain equally for tens of thousands of years." Please pray that the two, this modern reasoning of science and the ancient teachings of the Buddha, may abide together for tens of thousands of years.[14]

The most important Buddhist organization in India during the first half of the twentieth century was the Maha Bodhi Society. Presumably at the suggestion of Rahul Sankrityayan, himself a member, GC joined the society, founded in 1891 by the Sinhalese nationalist and Buddhist leader Anagārika Dharmapāla (1864–1933). Dharmapāla had been shocked to read Sir Edwin Arnold's description of the sad condition of Bodh Gayā, the site of the Buddha's enlightenment, and had established the society to restore Bodh Gayā as place of Buddhist worship and pilgrimage. GC came to admire Dharmapāla's efforts and urged his fellow Tibetans to join this world Buddhist movement. He wrote in 1939,

14. Ibid., 2:172–73.

Then, because of the troubled times, the place [Bodh Gayā] fell into the hands of *tīrthika* [that is, Hindu] yogins. They did many unseemly things, such as building a non-Buddhist temple in the midst of the stūpas, erecting a statue of Śiva in the temple, and performing blood sacrifices. The lay disciple Dharmapāla was not able to bear this. He died as a result of his great efforts to bring lawsuits in order that the Buddhists could once again gain possession [of Bodh Gayā]. Still, despite his efforts in the past and the passage of laws, his noble vision has not yet come to fruition. Therefore, Buddhists from all of our governments must unite and make all possible effort so that this special place of blessings, which is like the heart inside us, will come into the hands of the Buddhists who are its rightful owners.[15]

GC's appeal is made to his fellow Tibetans, but he writes from a stance of solidarity with the Buddhists of the world, who must work together to reclaim Bodh Gayā. This solidarity seems to have evolved during his time in Sri Lanka. During the 1920s, Rahul Sankrityayan had spent eighteen months in Sri Lanka studying Pāli under the sponsorship of the Maha Bodhi Society. After living some four years in India, GC accompanied Pandit Rahul on a brief trip to western Tibet, once more in search of Sanskrit manuscripts, in 1938. Upon their return to India, he may have encouraged GC to now travel south, and probably in 1940 or 1941 (again, the sources are inconsistent), with travel documents provided by the Maharaja of Sikkim, permanent president of the Maha Bodhi Society, he went to Sri Lanka, where he would spend sixteen months.

It was there that GC learned of the attacks on Buddhism by Christian missionaries, and of Buddhist responses. He writes, for example, about the famous debate held at Pānadure in 1873 between the Buddhist monk Guṇānanda, founder of the Society for the Propagation of Buddhism, and the Methodist minister Rev. David de Silva. An audience of five thousand attended the two-day debate, during which each side sought to demonstrate the fallacies of the other's sacred scriptures. The debate continued over two days, with Guṇānanda eventually being declared the winner by audience acclamation.[16] GC describes the debate in the chapter on Sri Lanka in his travel journals, although he erroneously reports both the date and the name of the Buddhist victor: "Only

15. Dge 'dun chos 'phel, *Rgya gar gyi gnas chen khag la bgrod pa'i lam yig*, in *Dge 'dun chos 'phel gyi gsung rtsom*, vol. 3 (Gangs can rig mdzod 12), ed. Hor khang bsod nams dpal 'bar (Lhasa, Tibet: Bod ljongs bod yig dpe rnying dpe skrun khang, 1990), 319.
16. For a detailed study of the debates, its antecedents, and aftermath, see R. F. Young and G. P. V. Somaratna, *Vain Debates: The Buddhist-Christian Controversies of Nineteenth-Century Ceylon* (Vienna: de Nobili Research Library, 1996).

fifty years ago a great debate took place between a Christian and a Buddhist in Sri Lanka. On that occasion, a monk called Guṇaratna annihilated the opponents and admitted many thousands who had converted to Christianity back to Buddhism."[17]

Since Buddhism had long since disappeared from India, the Theravāda monks of Sri Lanka were the first Buddhist monks that GC encountered outside the Tibetan cultural realm. His attitude toward them and their Buddhism was ambivalent. When he followed the Sinhalese monks on their daily alms-rounds, he felt as if he had been transported back in time and was in the presence of the first disciples of the Buddha: "I thought, 'I alone am seeing this legacy of our compassionate teacher.' On many occasions, my eyes filled with tears and I had to sit on the ground for a moment."[18] Indeed, he concluded the long chapter on Sri Lanka in his travel journals with this poem:

> Although the dress of a monk has long ago disappeared
>> And the practice of monastic discipline was entirely left
>>> behind,
>> This meeting with the assembly of *sthavira* monks
>> Is certainly the fruition of a deed in a former life.[19]

And despite the great historical and doctrinal differences that separated Tibetan from Sinhalese Buddhism, he sought to find common ground. Thus, when he translated the *Dhammapada* from Pāli into Tibetan in collaboration with the monk Dhammānanda, he described the team in a poem:

> A Sthaviravādin of Singhala
>> And a Sarvāstivādin of the Snowy Range
>> Disciples protected by the same teacher
>> Sole remnants of the vanished eighteen schools.[20]

17. Dge 'dun chos 'phel, *Rgyal khams rig pas bskor ba'i gtam rgyud gser gyi thang ma* (*smad cha*). In *Dge 'dun chos 'phel gyi gsung rtsom* 2:172.

18. Quoted in the biography of GC by his friend Bla chung a pho, also known as Shes rab rgya mtsho. See Shes rab rgya mtsho, "Dge 'dun chos 'phel," in *Biographical Dictionary of Tibet and Tibetan Buddhism, Volume 4: The Rñiṅ-ma-pa Tradition (Part Two)*, ed. Khetsun Sangpo (Dharamsala, India: Library of Tibetan Works and Archives, 1973), 639–40. The biography has been translated into English by Mengele in her *dGe-'dun-chos-'phel: A Biography of the 20th Century Tibetan Scholar*. The translation is my own, but I have relied on Dr. Mengele's excellent rendering of *mdzad rjes* as "legacy."

19. Dge 'dun chos 'phel, *Rgyal khams rig pas bskor ba'i gtam rgyud gser gyi thang ma* (*smad cha*). In *Dge 'dun chos 'phel gyi gsung rtsom* 2:73–74.

20. Dge 'dun chos 'phel, *'Phags pa gnas brtan pa rnams kyi mdo sde'i sde snod bsdus pa las phran tshegs kyi mdo phran gnyis pa chos kyi tshigs su bcad pa*. In *Dge 'dun chos 'phel gyi gsung rtsom* 2:270.

The non-Mahāyāna schools of Indian Buddhism are often referred to as "the eighteen schools" (although there were certainly more). One of these was the Sthaviravāda, the "school of the elders," which according to traditional histories became established in Sri Lanka as the Theravāda (Pāli for Sthaviravāda). Thus, Dhammānanda, from the Tibetan perspective, is a Sthaviravādin. These eighteen schools were distinguished more by their monastic codes than by their doctrines. The monastic code of one of the schools, the Sarvāstivāda, "the school [that asserts that] everything exists" (in fact, a branch of that school, called the Mūlasarvāstivāda), was adopted in Tibet. Thus, although he had given up his monk's vows by then, GC calls himself "a Sarvāstivādin of the Snowy Range," thus going to considerable lengths to establish kinship with his collaborator; they are "sole remnants of the vanished eighteen schools."

But such kinship was in many ways forced, and although he admired the Sri Lankan monks for their monastic discipline and was grateful to them for the kindness they showed him, from his perspective they were nonetheless followers of the Hīnayāna, those who rejected the Mahāyāna sūtras as the word of the Buddha and who eschewed the path of the bodhisattva. He writes,

In general, all the monks of Sinhala hold only their own system to be supreme. Without clearly distinguishing between what is good and what is bad in other systems, they reject it all completely. However, there are many who have some interest in the philosophical perspective of the Mahāyāna; some have memorized Nāgārjuna's *Treatise on the Middle Way*. Regarding the other [part of the Mahāyāna], the presentation of the vast, such as the *saṃbhogakāya*, they say that it is something to be rejected, like the Mahābrahmā of the *tīrthikas*. . . . Apart from referring to them as the *śrāvaka* group or the Theravāda, that is, Sthaviravāda, if one calls them Hīnayāna [*theg dman*, "inferior vehicle"], they start to explode, saying things like "Who uses that name? Then you have to call the Buddha the inferior teacher." Moreover, they consider the Vajrayāna to be a dangerous thing and call it *pañcamakara*, or the "five m's." When I tell them that even monks such as Bu ston and Tsong kha pa believed in mantra, it does not go into their ears. When they hear the story of the monk Mi la ras pa, they are well disposed, thinking, "He was a good layman." When I tell

---

GC's translation of the *Dhammapada* has been translated into English by the Dharma Publishing staff as *Dhammapada* (Berkeley, CA: Dharma Publishing, 1985). The poem above is not included in the translation.

them that he was also a follower of secret mantra, they do not listen to this shift in the conversation and get up to leave.[21]

GC is confronted here with the human embodiment of what in Tibet is merely a scholastic category. The Dge lugs monastic curriculum dwells at length on the structure of the Hīnayāna path, but there are no followers of the Hīnayāna. He thus knows the Theravāda monks through what he has learned about their doctrinal positions. And in this respect they do not disappoint him. They object to being called followers of the Hīnayāna, of the "inferior vehicle," they dismiss such fundamental Mahāyāna doctrines as the three bodies of the Buddha as just so much Hinduism. Finally, they have nothing but scorn for tantra, which Tibetans regard as the Buddha's highest teaching. They refer to it using a term that GC does not know, the "five m's," derived from Hindu tantra, in which five substances that all begin with the letter *m* in Sanskrit (beer, meat, fish, *mudrā*, and sexual union) are prescribed. Thus, when he mentions that respected scholar-monks like Tsong kha pa and Bu ston were practitioners of tantra, the Theravāda monks are incredulous. When GC tells them stories about Mi la ras pa's practice of solitary meditation in the caves of southern Tibet, they are delighted to learn that such pious Buddhist laymen lived in Tibet. When GC mentions that Mi la ras pa was a great tantric master, they get up and walk away.

These were not GC's only frustrations. In Tibetan Buddhism, the island of Laṅkā figures as the formidable abode for the preservation of many of the most potent of the tantric Buddhist teachings. GC knows the various accounts, and goes off in search of one of Padmasambhava's disciples, who was said to have lived a very long life in Laṅkā. "I wandered around in that region for more than a fortnight, but I did not meet anyone who had heard of him. It is said that he would live for seven hundred years; now he would be more than nine hundred, or else he has certainly passed away. Otherwise, I wondered why he would not grant an audience to a Mahāyāna person who had come from Tibet."[22]

Thus, the Buddhist solidarity that GC encountered in Sri Lanka only ran so deep, a fact that he acknowledged with a certain sense of irony in the conclusion of the Sri Lanka chapter in his travel journals. He offers the following thoughts, speaking, as he says, as the first Tibetan (or at least the first Tibetan not endowed with yogic powers) to set foot on the island of Sri Lanka:

---

21. Dge 'dun chos 'phel, *Rgyal khams rig pas bskor ba'i gtam rgyud gser gyi thang ma* (*smad cha*). In *Dge 'dun chos 'phel gyi gsung rtsom* 2:25–26.
22. Ibid., 27.

Connecting the Mahāyāna of the north and the Hīnayāna of the south are the four seals that designate a view as being the word [of the Buddha]. All of these weighty and profound connections must be taken into account by everyone. However, those of the black begging bowl [the Sinhalese] worry about everything. Those of the human thighbone flute [the Tibetans] stomp on everything. Moreover, no one surpasses these two in stubborn obstinacy. Therefore, for the time being, we will abide in a state of affection and yearning for one other from our respective lands; the most important thing is that our counting each other as friends, who have the same teacher and the same teaching, not disappear.[23]

GC writes not only about Buddhism in his travel journals, but also about what he calls "new religions" that have appeared in British India:

One amazing thing is that even at this time of the development of the foreigners' traditions in India, there arose a new religion. Its teacher, named Rāmakrsna, "Delightful Black One," was born 2380 years after the Buddha's passing in a place called Kamala in the land of Bengal, the son of a mother named Candradevī. From the time of his youth, he saw that samsāra was without essence. When he was twenty-four years old, in accordance with local custom, he married a five-year-old girl named Shadhadevi [Saradadevī]. Later she also became a renunciant, becoming a wondrous yoginī. Having respected all women as if they were his mother since his youth, Rāmakrsna took Mahākali as his *yi dam*. He went to the temple of Kali called Daksinesvar near Calcutta. He became a renunciant and lived there for his entire life. He had no possessions other than a bag of sesame. He went before the image of Kali and sat every day, crying, "Mother! Why don't you appear to me?" One day, he thought, "If I don't see her face now, I will kill myself," and just as he was holding a sword to his heart, he saw Kali's body filling the sky. From then on a great and authentic compassion for all beings was born. . . .

At its heart, in this religion [it is said that], although at first glance they seem to be in disagreement, just as all rivers flow to the sea or hundreds of roads enter one great city, just so the final resting place [of all religions] appears to be the same. For Brahmins, Brahman; for Muslims, Allah; for Buddhists, the place of refuge that is known as the Buddha. [Rāmakrsna] thought, "In reality, nothing exists apart from this great sphere called 'I' pervading all inanimate and animate objects." A great certainty was born in him and he

23. Ibid., 73.

taught it earnestly to others. In reality, the majority of people are pleased by such words, and before long countless followers gathered, and it became a large separate religious sect. In a short time it pervaded the entire land of India. Even in the continents on the other side of the ocean, like America, they have built monasteries of this system. All the principal disciples, numbering more than ten, such as Vivekanasha [Vivekānanda] and Abheranasha [Abhedānanda], became very famous throughout the land. Of all the students who personally knew that guru, Abhek [Abhedānanda] was the last. He died on the seventh day of the ninth month of this Hare year [=1939]. His students wear saffron robes and yellow hats and care for the sick and for the orphans, and they work persistently to stop religious sectarianism. They have respect for all—the Buddha, Rāma, Allah, and so on. Because they do not irritate the other religions, today their teachings are still spreading like the flocks of a rich man. However, most scholars who uphold a religious tradition regard each other as opponents on the fine points of their particular tenets. After the scholars are gone, after those subtle reasons dissolve, the dividing lines will be mixed into one taste and there will be a blissful unification of everything. This appears to be the supreme virtue for these fools.[24]

GC provides here a brief biography of Śrī Rāmakrishna (1836–86), the great Bengali saint whose teachings have been so influential for modern Hinduism. A devotee of the goddess Kali, he experienced a vision of her as the Divine Mother. He went on to practice other religious traditions—including other forms of Hinduism as well as Christianity, Buddhism, and Islam—claiming in each case to experience the highest state, and finding them all to be the same. GC notes that his teachings became very popular, with his claims for the unity of all religions providing a foundation for a new religion. GC provides the names of two of his most famous disciples, Swami Vivekānanda (1863–1902) and Swami Abhedānanda (1866–1939), and notes the charitable work of the Rāmakrishna Mission on behalf of the indigent. However, GC attributes much of the popularity of Rāmakrishna's teaching to its uncritical embrace of all religions. As a scholar trained in debating the fine points of philosophical positions, he has little patience with a view that "all religions are one," as his final sentence makes acerbically clear. It is also notable that he regards Rāmakrishna's teachings as a new religion that has arisen under the British, rather than as a form of Hinduism; he devotes a separate chapter of his travel journals to a detailed exposition of the tenets of the classical Hindu schools.

24. Ibid, 162–64.

GC's knowledge of the Rāmakrishna Mission may have derived from his collaboration with Swami Prabhandānanda in translating several chapters (the second, third, fourth, and twelfth) of the *Bhagavad Gītā* from Sanskrit into Tibetan. The translation of the twelfth chapter, on the discipline of devotion (*bhakti yoga*) to the Lord, was published by the Swami Bhadheshananda Ramakrishna Vedanta Ashram in Darjeeling in 1941.

The other new religion that he encountered in India and described in his travel journals was Theosophy. In New York City in 1875, Madame Helena Petrovna Blavatsky, a Russian émigré, and Colonel Henry Steel Olcott, a veteran of the American Civil War, founded the Theosophical Society. The goals of their society were "to diffuse among men a knowledge of the laws inherent in the universe; to promulgate the knowledge of the essential unity of all that is, and to determine that this unity is fundamental in nature; to form an active brotherhood among men; to study ancient and modern religion, science, and philosophy; and to investigate the powers innate in man."

Madame Blavatsky claimed to have spent seven years in Tibet as an initiate of the Brotherhood of the White Lodge, a secret order of enlightened masters who watch over and guide the evolution of humanity, preserving the ancient truths. These masters—the two most prominent were named Koot Hoomi and Morya—whom she called Mahatmas ("great souls"), lived in Tibet but were not themselves Tibetan. (In fact, the very presence of the Mahatmas in Tibet was unknown to ordinary Tibetans.) They had instructed her in the ancient truths of the mystic traditions of Theosophy, which her disciple A. P. Sinnett referred to as "Esoteric Buddhism"; the Buddhism being practiced in Asia, including Tibet, was a corruption.

Theosophists have long sought evidence of Madame Blavatsky's studies in Tibet. The following description of her by GC may be the first reference to her in the Tibetan language. And he does not dismiss her claims out of hand.

Another new religion like that [of Rāmakrishna] has appeared. Its founder is a Russian woman named Blavatsky. I think that she is some kind of incredible self-made yoginī. In any case, she attained magical powers. When she was a child, she was blessed in a dream by two Tibetan lamas named Mu ra and Sku thu med. Then, occasionally she would see a kind of vision, until in the end she actually met with them, like one person talking to another. They instructed her in everything, matters both subtle and coarse. When I carefully read her extensive stories about them, sometimes it reminds me of when Guhyapati appeared to Las kyi rdo rje; sometimes I think it is like when a demon king appeared to the venerable translator Rga. I don't know whether [the stories] can be judged unequivocally. She also continuously communicated with these two masters through letters. It is said that a great many people have actually seen their [the two masters'] letters fall in front of her out of empty space and that sometimes they are in Lanza and Tibetan script written on birch bark. However, I have not seen this myself. In any case, all of the foreigners believe this woman's magic. Some wonder whether they are tricks, but I think it would be difficult for her to deceive all of the fully trained foreign magicians. Her distinguishing features are: under one of her breasts is a large scar and no one knows how she got it, and sometimes it will drip blood; she summons things she needs just by looking at them; she can light a lamp or blow it out with thought alone; by looking at another person's body they freeze; what sounds like the tune of a silver bell constantly rings in empty space; when she needs to send letters, clothing, and so forth to another country, she burns them in a fire in front of her and by turning them into ashes, they arrive at the very place and can actually be received. Most of the things that she needs she takes out of trees, water, or air. Among all those things, it is said that her second mental powers, sending letters, and hearing answers are most amazing.

When she arrived in India, the foreigners did not like her and said she was a magician. They sent for the army, but as much as they searched, they could not expose her deception. In any case, among all the foreigners today, some follow her and some haughtily attack her, like the faith in the Buddha of the brahmin Gnam gyi skar ma. These are the main ideas of the new system of this woman.

The minds of the Sinhalese monks are more narrow than the eye of a needle, but nowadays many of them praise her. Dharmapāla, the restorer of Ṛṣipatana [Sarnath], is said to have initially become interested in the Buddha through her. It fascinates all the Westerners because she explains her religion by stitching it to the views of the new reasoning (science). In particular, there were foreigners who in the past did not believe in the supernatural. Not only did she demonstrate magic to them, but the way she transformed matter through magical powers was combined with the principles of the new reasoning. That mode of explanation seemed to impress everyone. However, if it were explained to us [Tibetans] who are not familiar with the assertions of science, it would only confuse us.[25]

25. Ibid., 164–66.

A number of noteworthy points occur in this passage, only a few of which can be pursued here. First, GC identifies the Mahatmas as Tibetans, and attempts to render their names in a feasible Tibetan form. Morya becomes Mu ra, the name of a medicinal herb that sometimes appears in Tibetan personal names; Koot Hoomi is Sku thu med, "the cloakless one." GC does not seem to doubt that Madame Blavatsky met with these masters; he is, however, unsure of their true nature. Was it like the meeting of Las kyi rdo rje with the bodhisattva Vajrapāṇi (Guhyapati), or was it like the meeting of the translator Rga with a demon? Both incidents are mentioned in the *Blue Annals* (*Deb ther sngon po*), a massive history of the lineages of Tibetan Buddhism composed in 1476 that GC had come to know well. It is more difficult to say where he first learned about Madame Blavatsky; here, he writes about her with respect, and he seems disposed to believe the stories about her, although he makes clear that he has not witnessed anything himself.

GC may have first heard about her during his visit to Sri Lanka. Determined to join the Buddhists of the British colony of Ceylon in their battle against Christian missionaries, Blavatsky and Olcott had sailed from America to India, arriving in 1879 in Bombay, where they proclaimed themselves to be Hindus. In 1880 they proceeded to Ceylon, where they both took the vows of lay Buddhists. Madame Blavatsky's commitment to Buddhism was not as great as that of Colonel Olcott, but she initiated the young Anagārika Dharmapāla into the Theosophical Society in 1884, and he accompanied her to the society's headquarters in India that same year.

As we have seen, although GC was impressed by the Sinhalese monks' devotion to monastic discipline, he criticized their rejection of Mahāyāna and tantric Buddhism. Consequently, he is impressed that Madame Blavatsky had gained their respect. He also mentions her influence on Dharmapāla, whom, as we have seen, GC revered for his efforts to wrest control of Bodh Gayā, the site of the Buddha's enlightenment, from Hindus and restore it to Buddhist hands. GC ends with a typical note of skepticism concerning how effective Blavatsky's appeals to science would be to a Tibetan audience.

Through his many travels and collaborations, GC became well known in the small community of European and American scholars and enthusiasts of Tibetan Buddhism. Indeed, his fame as a scholar and his knowledge of English led to his being invited to the United States. In the introduction to a group of poems published in English in the August 1941 issue of *The Maha-Bodhi*, we read, "Lama Geshe Chompell, with whom our readers are already acquainted, has returned from his sojourn in Ceylon. . . . He has an invitation from an

American Tibetan Scholar to visit New York, which journey, though not without danger, he seems willing to undertake."[26] The invitation came from Theos Bernard (1908–47), the self-styled "first white lama" and the first American to write a doctoral dissertation (at Columbia University) on Tibetan Buddhism.[27] GC was apparently prevented from accepting the invitation by World War II. One can only imagine how the landscape of Tibetan studies and Tibetan Buddhism in the West may have been transformed had he come to America.

In addition to collaborating with Sinhalese monks and Hindu swamis in the translation of Pāli and Sanskrit works into Tibetan (projects that he presumably undertook on his own initiative), GC worked with European scholars during his years abroad. After his return to India from Sri Lanka, he collaborated with a Russian Tibetologist, George Roerich. He was the son of Nicholas Roerich (1874–1947), a poet and artist who designed the costumes and sets for the scandalous first performance of Stravinsky's *Rite of Spring* in Paris in 1913. The senior Roerich and his wife, Elena Ivanovna (1879–1955), were ardent Theosophists; she had translated Madame Blavatsky's *The Secret Doctrine* into Russian and was the author of such works as *Leaves of Morya's Garden*. It is possible that GC's description of Madame Blavatsky was written while he was living at the Roerich home, where Elena Ivanovna had a large library of Theosophical texts; we know from other sources that GC's reading knowledge of English was good by this time, such that he would have been able to read the "extensive stories" about her.

Like Blavatsky, Nicholas Roerich believed that the king of Shambhala was destined to appear on earth for the final destruction of the wicked, the renovation of creation, and the restoration of purity. Shambhala was located in central Asia, he suspected, perhaps in the Gobi Desert; and from 1925 to 1928 he led an expedition, which included his son George, that traversed 15,000 miles and crossed thirty-five mountain passes. It made its way through Chinese Turkestan, Mongolia, and Tibet, searching for evidence of the hidden kingdom of Shambhala, the abode of the spiritual masters of all religions.

26. See "Lama Geshe Chompell," *The Maha-Bodhi* (August 1941): 291.

27. On Bernard and his possible plans for GC in America, see David Jackson, "The Elusive American Tibetologist in Gendun Chöphel's Life: 'The First White Lama' (Theos Bernard) and Their Dream of Tibetland, California," *Lungta*, forthcoming. Paul G. Hackett (personal communication) has located a letter from Theos Bernard to GC dated September 12, 1944, in which Bernard invites GC to America. However, by that time Bernard, who received his doctorate from Columbia University in New York in 1943, was established in Santa Barbara, California. Also, Bernard's letter dates three years after the reference to the invitation in *The Maha-Bodhi*. An earlier letter of invitation presumably exists among Bernard's uncatalogued papers, held at the University of California, Berkeley.

While in India, Roerich founded the Urusvati Himalayan Research Institute (in Kulu, Himachal Pradesh), and it was there that GC worked with George Roerich on the laborious translation of the *Blue Annals*, written by 'Gos lo tsa ba gzhon nu dpal in 1476. It is a worked filled with the names of persons, places, and texts that would have been impossible to identify without the assistance of an erudite Tibetan scholar. GC provided such assistance, which Roerich noted in a single sentence in the preface: "It has been a source of much satisfaction to me that I was able to discuss the entire translation with the Rev. dGe-'dun Chos-'phel, the well-known Tibetan scholar, and I gratefully acknowledge here his very helpful guidance."[28] By portraying GC both as a collaborator with whom to discuss the work and as a teacher who would guide it, Roerich's brief acknowledgment suggests his own ambivalence concerning the appropriate form in which to recognize GC's role. Given both the technical difficulty and the extent of the text (the translation and scholarly apparatus fill almost thirteen hundred pages of fine print), it is difficult to imagine that GC's name should not have appeared on the title page, perhaps as coauthor.

The Roerich family was wealthy by the standards of the day, and GC was paid for his work. But he suffered periods of great poverty during his years in India, especially while in Calcutta, immediately after his work with Roerich. According to his friend Rak ra bkras mthong, a portion of a poem that GC wrote at this time describes his experience of collaborating with Roerich. The relevant stanzas may include the following:

> Made to compile all the games of lies and deception,
>> Because my worldly aspirations were accomplished with so much toil,
>> After waiting such a long time, it turned into nothing, just deceit.
> So three years of miserable labor have finally come to an end.
>
> When you are rich, they slink up close;
> When you are poor, they scorn you with pointed fingers from afar.
> To consider the nature of bad friends who do not know how to be kind to the kind
> Is an occasion for tears and laughter.

28. George N. Roerich, *The Blue Annals* (Delhi: Motilal Banarsidass, 1976), xxi.

The abilities of a humble scholar, seeking only knowledge
Are crushed by the tyranny of a fool, bent under the weight of
his wealth.
The proper hierarchy has been reversed;
How sad that the lion is made servant to the dog.[29]

GC also pursued a number of his own research projects. He spent a good deal of time studying Sanskrit erotica and frequenting Calcutta brothels, using his studies and his experiences as the basis for one of his most famous works, the *Treatise on Passion* (*'Dod pa'i bstan bcos*).[30] He clearly had given up his monk's vow of celibacy by this point. It is unclear, however, how long before his days in Calcutta he had renounced his monkhood, with some sources indicating that he did so even before his departure from Tibet.

Treatise on Passion was only the second erotic manual to appear in the long history of Tibetan literature, the first having been composed by the famous Rnying ma scholar, and monk, 'Ju Mi pham (1846–1912) and also entitled *'Dod pa'i bstan bcos*. At the end of his text, written entirely in verse, GC explains that he is no longer a monk (the last two lines in the first stanza below may mean that he stopped considering himself a monk long ago, but had only recently broken the vow of celibacy), and then he compares the two authors:

With small shame for myself and great faith in women
    I am the kind who chooses evil and abandons good.
    For some time I have not had the vows in my head
    But recently I stopped the pretense in my bowels.

---

29. The poem appears in its entirety twice. It appeared first in Bkras mthong thub bstan chos dar, *Dge 'dun chos 'phel gyi lo rgyus* (Dharamsala, India: Library of Tibetan Works and Archives, 1980), 71–74, with the stanzas translated here appearing on pp. 72–73. The same poem has appeared more recently under the title "Mi rtag pa dran pa'i gsung mgur," or "Song of Remembering Impermanence," in *Dge 'dun chos 'phel gyi gsung rtsom* 2:395–99. This version differs in several places from Rak ra's version, most significantly in the omission of the stanza about the lion and the dog. In my translation of the first stanza, I followed the second version, reading *rtsed mo* instead of *rtse mo* and *'dun mas* instead of *mdun mas*. Two stanzas, with still other variants, and including the stanza about the lion and the dog, appear as "Fragment Six" (*thor bu drug pa*) in the same volume of the collected writings, pp. 409–10.

For a partial translation of the poem and a convincing argument in support of Rak ra's claim that at least part of the poem is directed at George Roerich, see Benjamin Bogin and Hubert Decleer, "Who Was 'this Evil Friend' (the 'dog,' the 'fool,' the 'tyrant') in Gedün Chöphel's Sad Song," *Tibet Journal* 22, no. 3 (1997): 67–78.

30. The text has been translated into English by Jeffrey Hopkins under the title *Tibetan Arts of Love: Sex, Orgasm, and Spiritual Healing* (Ithaca, NY: Snow Lion Publications, 1992).

The venerable Mi pham wrote from what he studied.
The promiscuous Chos 'phel wrote from what he experienced.
The difference in the power of their blessings
Will be understood when a passionate man and woman put
them into practice.[31]

A fascinating work, *Treatise on Passion* enumerates the varieties of bites and scratches, as in the *Kāma Sūtra*; offers various physiognomical and regional classifications of women; advises males to do the multiplication tables in order to postpone ejaculation; and speculates on the profound nature of desire. It is based on GC's studies of a variety of Sanskrit treatises (he cites eight) and his experiences with various lovers, to whom he gives due credit. In an ironic adaptation of the traditional Tibetan Buddhist convention of dedicating the merit derived from composing a text to the welfare of all beings and identifying the disciples who urged its composition, he writes,

By this virtue, may all like-minded friends
Cross the dark road of frantic desires
And see the sky of the meaning of reality
From the summit of peak of the sixteen pleasures.

May G.yu sgron, Gangā, Asali, and the others,
The women who joined with my body,
Continue on the path, from bliss to bliss
To arrive at great bliss, the place of the *dharmakāya*.

May all the lowly people who live on the broad earth
Be delivered from the pit of merciless laws
And be able to indulge, with common freedom,
In those humble enjoyments, so useful and right.[32]

GC's other famous work from his time in India is his *Guide for Traveling to Various Great Sites of India* (*Rgya gar gyi gnas chen khag la 'grod pa'i lam yig*), his guidebook to the Buddhist pilgrimage places there. This work has already been translated and analyzed by Toni Huber,[33] so I will translate only a brief passage found at the end, in which GC describes his credentials with typical irony:

31. Dge 'dun chos 'phel, *'Dod pa'i bstan bcos*, in *Dge 'dun chos 'phel gyi gsung rtsom*, vol. 2, ed. T. G. Dhongthog (Bir, India: Dzongsar Institute, 1991), 357–58.
32. Ibid., 2:359.
33. See Huber, *The Guide to India*.

Furthermore, I am not some gullible fool who believes everything he hears. I am a discerning beggar who is naturally intelligent and who has spent this human life in learning. Thus, one need not have any of the three qualms about anything that I say here: that is it mistaken, that it has no textual source, or that it is confused. For the majority of the human race, if you explain something that is difficult in an easy way, they do not believe you and are dismissive. If you explain something easy in a difficult way, you are counted as a scholar and they believe you. Thus, there is nothing to be done.[34]

GC's poetry, like his painting, deserves a full study. We can only note in passing here his consummate skill as poet, adopting a wide variety of styles on a wide variety of subjects. He was fond of wordplay and excelled particularly at alphabetical poetry (*ka rtsom*), in which the first word of the first line of the poem begins with *ka*, the first letter of the Tibetan alphabet, and the first letter of the first word of each line that follows continues in alphabetical order (obviously difficult to render in translation). He also delighted in the use of numbers, as three poems below illustrate. The first is a stanza from the *Treatise on Passion*:

Unfitting for a third person to see
　Unfitting for a fifth ear to hear
　Those who share special secrets
　Become the best of heart-friends in this world.[35]

Elsewhere, GC exploits Buddhism's famous penchant for lists. In the original, the first word of each line in the first stanza is a number. In the second stanza, the first word of each of the four lines is one of the four directions.

The one door of entry into the realm of peace is
　The two truths, the stainless path to the profound mode of
　　phenomena.
　The assembly of disciples of the three lineages are taught by
　The Buddha whose nature is the four bodies, to which I bow.
　All beings included in the five lineages
　Rely on the path of the six perfections.
　Through relying continually on all the qualities of the seven
　　jewels

34. Dge 'dun chos 'phel, *Rgya gar gyi gnas chen khag la bgrod pa'i lam yig*, in *Dge 'dun chos 'phel gyi gsung rtsom* 3:349–50. See also Huber, *The Guide to India*, 104–5.
35. Dge 'dun chos 'phel, *'Dod pa'i bstan bcos* in *Dge 'dun chos 'phel gyi gsung rtsom* 2:319.

May they attain a body free of the eight extremes of
  elaboration.

At the ends of the oceans of east and west
I have journeyed to land of India in the south.
This lamp raised in the darkness of the west
Was written for the beings of Tibet in the north.

GC also wrote a type of numerical poetry in English, perhaps with less success:

Look at God by two small eyes
  Listen to him by two small ears
  Serve him by two small hands
  Go to the church by two small feet
  Tell the truth by a small tongue
  Be loved by a small heart
  Praise God for ever and pray to him.

The poem is dated November 1, 1943, and is signed "G. Chomphel, Y.M.B.A. [Young Men's Buddhist Association], Dorjeeling."[36] Two years earlier, he had published some of his poetry in *The Maha-Bodhi*, the journal of the Maha Bodhi Society. "Oh Where?" appeared in the August 1941 issue and is a good deal more accomplished than the poem above, suggesting that GC may have received some assistance:

A city there is which lone does stand
  In ruins mid bamboo trees
  Hot blows the burning desert sand
  Where dry shrubs sigh on the thirsting land
  Where monkeys cry, and with these
  Joins the shrill cry of the jungle cock
  Where a maiden drives her scattered flock
  To the tune of an ancient lay.
  Where an ox-cart moves on its lazy way
  And halts for shade neath a jutting rock;
  Oh, City, where is the day,
  When on thy golden Throne sat Kings

36. Reprinted in the front matter of Rdo rje rgyal, ed., *Mkhas dbang dge 'dun chos 'phel gyi gsar rnyed gsung rtsom* (Zi ling, China: Zi ling mi rigs par khang, 2000).

Of a mighty name and a mighty race,
Who held the Sceptre high in this place?
Hark, heareth thou Time's fleet wings?[37]

GC traveled extensively through South Asia during his twelve years there. Throughout this period, he seems to have remained an outsider, a foreigner far from home. At the same time, his studies in Tibet had provided him with a textual familiarity with Buddhist India, and he now visited many of it sites. Indeed, when extolling the virtues of Sri Lanka as a country that remains Buddhist, he speaks of northern India (Magadha) as "the home of our forefathers," where today one must contend with "a Hindu wife and a British soldier."[38] That he must wander through India is his fate, a result of his past karma, but he is ambivalent as to whether he regards this karma as good or bad. From one perspective, it has brought him home. As he writes at the end of his translation of the *Dhammapada*,

> Recognizing my own home, familiar from so long ago
>> And finding the remnants of my deeds from former lives,
>> How can I express my joy in translating anew, at long last
>> This scripture of the perfect Buddha?
>
> It has been 800 human years since
> A translator, endowed with freedom, has arrived in India.
> I say, "Now, there is in Magadha
> Someone who can actually read the Sanskrit treatises."[39]

Thus, GC's description of modern India is not an unmitigated lament. Unlike so many others who mourned the death of the dharma in the land of its birth, he insisted that the true practice of Buddhism had never disappeared; it was always there, if one only knew where to look:

> One evening I was wandering in the forest when I saw a naked woman with many different bones tied to her body. By following her I arrived at a cave. By hiding myself, I could watch. Male and female yogins sat face to face and practiced samādhi. I saw them kiss and embrace and perform many rites. It is said that at times they laugh so loudly, "Ha ha," that the rocks in the

37. Geshé Chompell, "Oh Where?" *The Maha-Bodhi* (August 1941): 294.

38. Dge 'dun chos 'phel, *Rgyal khams rig pas bskor ba'i gtam rgyud gser gyi thang ma (smad cha)*. In *Dge 'dun chos 'phel gyi gsung rtsom* 2:73.

39. Dge 'dun chos 'phel, *'Phags pa gnas brtan pa rnams kyi mdo sde'i sde snod bsdus pa las phran tshegs kyi mdo phran gnyis pa chos kyi tshigs su bcad pa*. In *Dge 'dun chos 'phel gyi gsung rtsom* 2:269.

cave might fall. They are apparently yogins who practice the path of desire. They said that they were Buddhists, because in that region there actually is an unbroken tradition of instruction in Buddhist mantra. I saw this recently, this very year.[40]

This is another example of his solitary vision, traveling in the land where nothing is familiar in order to find his home. He sees what others have not seen and thus cannot see, what is invisible to others. He sees the practice of secret Buddhist tantric rites in an India where Buddhism was long dead, he sees through the telescope, he sees through the microscope, he sees that the world is round. And, as he says in the *Adornment*, "To think that the earth, stones, mountains, and rocks that we see now are still to be seen vividly when we are buddhas is very much in error." He proclaims this vision to the world, but no one seems to listen. There is thus a profound loneliness that pervades much of his writing. He walks across the Indian Subcontinent alone (with occasional traveling companions), unknown to those he meets and forgotten by his homeland, driven to carry out the work that it is his karmic lot to do. The following verses appear at the end of his travel journal, *The Golden Surface*, which he regarded as the most important of his many projects, yet unpublished and unread during his lifetime:

> Walking with weary feet to the plains of the sandy south,
> > Travelling the circumference of a land surrounded by the pit of
> > the deep black sea,
> > By pulling the thread of my life—precious and
> > abandoned—across the sharp blade of a sword,
> > Consuming long years and months of hardship, I have finished
> > this book in any way I could.

> Although there is no one to make supplications [to me]
> With quotations from great [scriptures] and mandalas of gold,
> I myself have taken on the burden of hardship and written this,
> Concerned that the treasury of knowledge will be lost.

> Although I am terrified by the orange eye of envy
> In the burning flame of those bloodthirsty for power,
> My mind is attached to the talk of reason,

40. Dge 'dun chos 'phel, *Rgyal khams rig pas bskor ba'i gtam rgyud gser gyi thang ma* (*smad cha*). In *Dge 'dun chos 'phel gyi gsung rtsom* 2:181–82.

Accustomed to the habit of gathering a little of what I have
heard.

If [what I have written] somehow enters the door of a wise
person, intent on learning,
Then the fruit of my labor will have been achieved.
For the smiles of the stupid and the approval of the rich,
I have never yearned even in my dreams.

If I have scattered everything from a family that had lost hope
for profit and fame
To become a mass of ink whose necessities of food and drink
are exhausted,
Then may the forms of these letters, a pile of much learning
amassed through hardship
Reveal the path of vast benefit in the presence of my unseen
friends.[41]

GC spent the last two years of his stay in India, from 1945 to 1946, in the
Kalimpong-Darjeeling area near Sikkim. As a major conduit for trade and travel
in and out of Tibet, Kalimpong seems to have been the center for a wide range
of political discussion among the Tibetan community there as the Indian independence movement and attendant anti-British sentiment grew with the defeat
of Germany, and the civil war in China again flared with the defeat of Japan.
GC became involved in discussions with a small group of Tibetans who would
become the ill-fated Tibet Improvement Party. The very name of the group
raises issues concerning its purpose. Its logo, designed by GC, featured a sickle,
a sword, a loom, and the name of the organization in both Chinese and Tibetan. In Chinese, it was Xizang gemingdang. *Xizang* is a standard Chinese
name for Tibet, literally translated as "western treasury." *Gemingdang* usually
is translated as "revolutionary party." In Tibetan, however, the name was much
less threatening: Nub bod legs bcos kyi skyid sdug, the "Association for the
Improvement of Western Tibet." In Tibetan, it is thus a friendly organization
rather than a political party, dedicated to improvement rather than revolution.
However, the otherwise innocuous Tibetan name is betrayed by the term *nub
bod*, "western Tibet," which connotes nothing in Tibetan other than the Chinese
designation of the country.

41. Ibid., 2:184–86.

The founder of the group, Rab dga' spom mda' tshang, was a great admirer of Sun Yatsen and his political philosophy and had translated some of Sun's writings into Tibetan. He sought the same changes in Tibet that had occurred in China with the fall of the Qing, believing that the present form of government in Tibet was unsuited for the modern world. He sought the help of the Kuomintang (National People's Party) in creating an autonomous Tibetan republic, organized along democratic lines and under the overall control of the Republic of China. Article 2 of the party agreement states,

> Recently President Chiang has declared to allow autonomy of Tibet. According to this we must exert our efforts mainly for Liberation of Tibet from the existing tyrannical Government. Also we must act in the light of other progressive and democratic nations of the World and especially democratic Central Government of China for which all members of our party must work as men on the same boat.[42]

GC had become increasingly critical of the government of Tibet and of the corruption and political machinations of the Dge lugs pa monasteries, and so found kindred spirits in the Tibet Improvement Party. He believed that major reforms, if not revolution, were necessary in Tibet and proposed that monks be paid salaries rather than being allowed to own estates; he also thought that they should be required to study and prohibited from engaging in commerce. However, the degree of his involvement in the party, like so many other elements of his biography, is in doubt. Although he wrote on a wide range of topics, no overtly "political" writings have emerged, apart from the critique of European colonialism translated above.

TIBET   Late in 1945, apparently against the advice of some of his Tibetan and European friends, GC began the journey back to Tibet. He did not travel by the usual route but through Bhutan and then east and north along the Anglo-Tibetan border, making maps requested by Rab dga'. Apparently, he did not know that the maps and notes he had made were intended ultimately for the Kuomintang and so sent them through the British postal service to India rather than by personal messenger. Some sources contend that the package was intercepted by Hugh Richardson, the British trade representative in Gyantse, who in turn alerted the police in Kalimpong.

---

42. Cited in Melvyn C. Goldstein, *A History of Modern Tibet: The Demise of the Lamaist State* (Berkeley and Los Angeles: University of California Press, 1989), 459.

GC arrived in Lhasa after twelve years abroad (interrupted by the brief trip to western Tibet in 1938) by early January 1946. While in India, he had had the opportunity to study several Dunhuang manuscripts related to the Tibetan monarchy as well as some Tang annals (both in English translation and, with the help of bilingual scholars, in Chinese). With access to sources unknown to previous Tibetan historians, and perhaps inspired by the nationalism he encountered in the Indian independence movement, he had decided to write a history of Tibet that would demonstrate the vast dominion of the ancient kings and their armies, in whose exploits he seems to have taken a certain delight. In the poem that opens this unfinished work, which he would call *The White Annals* (*Deb ther dkar po*), he wrote,

> Through compiling the available ancient writings
>> That set forth dates in a manner certain and clear
>> I have generated a small degree of courage
>> To measure the dominion and power of the first Tibetan
>>> kingdom.
>
> The Tibetan army of red-faced bloodthirsty demons,
> Who pledged their lives with growing courage to
> The command of the wrathful Hayagriva,
> Are said to have conquered two thirds of the circle of the
>> earth.[43]

Upon his arrival in Tibet, he continued his research for this history, traveling to the sites of ancient castles and temples to record the inscriptions on the pillars (*rdo ring*) that remained there.

GC seems to have become something of a celebrity upon his return to his homeland, meeting with various members of the aristocracy and the occasional European (including Heinrich Harrer) and gathering a circle of young disciples to whom he taught poetry and grammar. The latter included two Rnying ma lamas, Bla chung a pho (1905–75) and Zla ba bzang po (1916–58). Bla chung a pho reports in his biography of GC, written in 1972, that GC came to visit him when he was recovering from a serious illness: "One day, when I was somewhat more lucid, he gave me a small book of Elephant brand paper in which were

---

43. Dge 'dun chos 'phel, *Bod chen po'i srid lugs dang 'brel ba'i rgyal rabs deb ther dkar po.* In *Dge 'dun chos 'phel gyi gsung rtsom* 3:210. The text has been inadequately translated into English by Samten Norboo as *The White Annals (Deb-ther dkar po)* (Dharamsala, India: Library of Tibetan Works and Archives, 1978). For a review of the translation, see Hugh Richardson, "Gedun Chophel's 'Unfinished' *The White Annals (Deb-ther dkar-Po),*" *Tibetan Review* (October 1978): 19–22.

written the words, beginning with, 'All of our decisions about what is and is not' and ending with the verse, 'I am uncomfortable about positing conventional validity.' He said, 'Look at this; it will keep you from sleeping.' It was a great help to me."[44] He reports that he and Zla ba bzang po later received instruction in Sanskrit poetics from GC, as well as in Madhyamaka philosophy:

> Then he gave Zla ba bzang po instruction in Madhyamaka. He had him take notes to supplement the small book he had given to me earlier. . . . At the end, when it had been completed and printing blocks had been carved by [the sponsorship of] Ka shod pa, he said to Zla ba bzang po, "Later, there is going to be controversy about this. The controversy will not occur until after I am already dead. If it occurs, it is all right. You must be careful. Do not forget the essential points I explained."
>
> He also said, "In order for human birth to have real meaning in this world, one must leave some imprint. In my own opinion, I thought that I must draw out some of the distinctive features of Madhyamaka and Pramāṇa. Now, I have done what is appropriate to suffice for Madhyamaka."[45]

What GC did, according to this account of his friend, was to compose the *Adornment for Nāgārjuna's Thought*.

In addition to his work on *The White Annals* and his teachings to his students, GC assisted his former 'Bras spungs classmate, Geshe Chos grags, in the compilation of a Tibetan-Tibetan dictionary, and he gave English lessons to the son of the government minister Ka shod pa.

Some time in the latter half of 1946 (perhaps late July or August), GC returned from the home of Khri byang rin po che, tutor to the young Dalai Lama, to find two magistrates waiting at his door. They arrested him on charges of distributing counterfeit currency and took him to the jail in the courthouse of Lhasa, the Snang rtse shag. A search of his rooms yielded a black box containing notes and papers connected with a number of projects. There were also various papers around the room, including information on the border area and a list of members of the government. Upon his arrest, GC told his captors that when they searched his room, they would find scraps of paper and cigarette wrappers

---

44. See Shes rab rgya mtsho, "Dge 'dun chos 'phel," in Khetsun Sangpo, ed., *Biographical Dictionary of Tibet and Tibetan Buddhism, Volume 4: The Rñiṅ-ma-pa Tradition (Part Two)* (Dharamsala, India: Library of Tibetan Works and Archives, 1973), 644. See also Mengele, *dGe-'dun-chos-'phel*, 33, 62.

45. Shes rab rgya mtsho, "Dge 'dun chos 'phel," 647–48. See also Mengele, *dGe-'dun-chos-'phel*, 36–37, 65–66.

with notes on them that were the basis of a history of Tibet. He asked that these not be disturbed. Although his room was sealed after his arrest, when he eventually returned to it, all of his papers and his black box were gone and were never recovered. The fate of the black box has been yet another of the enduring mysteries about his life.

At the city jail, he was given a separate room on an upper floor and was allowed to receive food and bedding from friends, but he was interrogated repeatedly and on one occasion received some fifty lashes. After a number of months, he was transferred to the prison at Zhol at the base of the Potala. Although the physical conditions there were worse, he was given writing materials. He continued his work on *The White Annals* and also wrote letters and poetry. Requests from Sankrityayan and George Roerich that he be released went unheeded, perhaps because of the tenor of their argument: they pleaded for clemency by explaining that a Communist takeover of Tibet was inevitable, at which time GC's friendship with China would prove useful.

He was released in 1949 (some say 1950), probably in the summer. His arrest and release dates are uncertain, and thus the exact length of his prison term is unknown. He is said to have received a three-year sentence, but some sources report that he served more than three full years, others somewhat less. Above all, more than when, it is uncertain why he was imprisoned. In addition to the apparently fabricated charge of counterfeiting currency, it has been suggested that he was imprisoned because of his membership in the Tibet Improvement Party, because he was a Russian spy, because he was a Kuomintang spy, because he was a Fascist, because he was a Communist, because of his philosophical views, and because he had embarrassed the government minister Ka shod pa. Recent Tibetan biographers suggest that Hugh Richardson, the British trade representative, played a role. GC is said to have left this poem on the wall of his cell:

> May the wise regard as an object of compassion
>> The small truthful child left all alone
>> In the wilderness where the frightening roar resounds
>> Of the stubborn tiger drunk on the blood of envy.[46]

46. The story appears in Bla chung a pho's biography of GC. See Shes rab rgya mtsho, "Dge 'dun chos 'phel," 651; and Mengele, *dGe-'dun-chos-'phel*, 40, 69. The poem appears with a number of variants. For example, in Bla chung a pho's account, it reads, "phrag dog khrag gis myos pa'i u btsug stag l 'jig pa'i nga ro sgrog pa'i tshang tshing nang l gcig pur lus pa'i bden pa'i bu chung la l shes rab spyan gyis thugs rje'i dbyings nas dgongs." For corrections of the misspellings, see Mengele, *dGe-'dun-chos-'phel*, 40. The version translated here is found in GC's collected writings. It is "phrag

The regent of Tibet at the time of GC's arrest was Stag brag rin po che, whose name means "tiger rock."

The actions of the government, though perhaps paranoid in retrospect, were taken at a time when the political situation in Lhasa was unstable. GC was arrested less than a year before the so-called Rwa spreng affair. Upon the death of the Thirteenth Dalai Lama in 1933, a prominent Dge lugs incarnate lama named Rwa spreng rin po che (1910–47) had been appointed as regent, to lead the nation during the search for the next Dalai Lama and to rule during his minority. Rwa spreng used the position to significantly increase his already substantial wealth and to place his supporters in positions of power within the government. Although a monk, he was widely reported to have had both male and female lovers, an indiscretion that would have ordinarily been ignored except for the fact that the time was approaching for him to administer the vows of a novice to the seven-year-old Dalai Lama. The thirty-six vows included one of celibacy, and it seems that there was a certain insistence that this vow be given by a celibate monk.

As a result, Rwa spreng abdicated in 1941, turning the regency over to his own teacher, an elderly monk named Stag brag rin po che (1874–1952), explaining that he would immediately go on retreat and devote the rest of his life to the pursuit of the dharma. But not long after the ordination, Rwa spreng began sending signals that he wanted the regency back, signals that the Tibetan cabinet attempted to ignore. In 1947, shortly after GC's imprisonment, a package containing a hand grenade was sent to Stag brag rin po che and exploded upon being opened by a servant. An investigation revealed documents identifying

---

dog khrag gis myos pa'i u tshugs stag | 'jigs pa'i nga ro sgrogs pa'i tshang tshing nang | gcig pur lus pa'i bden pa'i bu chung la | shes rab can gyis snying rje'i yul du dgongs." See "'Thor bu gsum ba," in Dge 'dun chos 'phel gyi gsung rtsom, 2:408–9.

Significantly, a slightly different version of this poem also appears in the eighth chapter of GC's travel journals, composed probably no later than 1941. It reads, "chags sdang phrag gi myos pa'i u tshugs stag | 'jigs pa'i nga ro sgrog pa'i tshang tshing du | gcig pur lus pa'i bden pa'i bu chung 'di | shes rab can gyis snying rje'i yul du mdzod." See Dge 'dun chos 'phel, Rgyal khams rig pas bskor ba'i gtam rgyud gser gyi thang ma (stod cha), in Dge 'dun chos 'phel gyi gsung rtsom, 1:270–71. This might be translated as follows:

> May the wise take as an object of compassion
> This small truthful child left all alone
> In the wilderness where the frightening roar resounds
> Of the stubborn tiger drunk with desire, hatred, and envy.

That GC wrote this poem almost a decade before his imprisonment does not preclude the possibility that he also wrote it on the prison wall. It does, however, cast doubt on its status as a spontaneous expression of rage against the regent.

the sender as Rwa spreng, who was preparing to take back the regency. Other letters indicated that he had sought the aid of the Kuomintang. Rwa spreng's arrest provoked a violent response from the monks of his monastic college, Se ra bye, who took up arms and began a revolt intended to overthrow the government and restore Rwa spreng to power. They were subdued only when their monastery was surrounded by the Tibetan army and shelled with artillery. With the Se ra monks defeated, Rwa spreng was imprisoned in the Potala, where he died three weeks later, probably by poison.[47] All of this occurred while GC was serving his prison term.

There is, again, uncertainty about GC's condition upon his release. He had been known to enjoy both alcohol and cigarettes before his imprisonment. According to some, he developed symptoms of alcoholism while in prison and had to receive regular deliveries of liquor from his students to avoid suffering severe withdrawal symptoms. Others say that he drank little during his incarceration. There is little doubt that he began to drink heavily upon his release and showed little interest in returning to his various projects, especially when he returned to his room to find all of his books and notes gone. He lived with a woman from Chab mdo who cared for him, and was supported by friends, who provided him with a place to live for the first months after his release. The government eventually provided him with rooms behind the Jo khang, above the Ministry of Agriculture, along with a stipend of money and grain, with the instruction that he resume work on *The White Annals*. He did not do so. Anecdotes from this period deal for the most part with his heavy drinking, interrupted by occasional visits from dignitaries and rare moments of the old brilliance. Troops of the People's Liberation Army entered Lhasa on September 9, 1951. At the beginning of October, GC developed a severe cough and his body began to retain fluids, causing acute swelling (edema is one of the symptoms of advanced cirrhosis of the liver). Eventually unable to walk, he asked Bla chung A pho to read him two poems, Tsong kha pa's *Praise of Dependent Origination* (*Rten 'brel bstod pa*) and Mi pham's *Prayer to the Indivisible Basis, Path, and Fruit of the Great Perfection of Mañjuśrī* (*'Jam dpal rdzogs pa chen po gzhi lam 'bras bu dbyer med pa'i don la smon pa*). After commenting on their beauty, he said, "The madman Dge chos has already seen all the sights of the world. Now, I have heard talk of a famous land down below. If I went to have a look, I wonder what it would be like?" He died shortly after that, at four in the afternoon of

47. On the "Reting Incident," see Goldstein, *A History of Modern Tibet*, 464–521.

October 12, 14, or 15, 1951. He was 48. His body was cremated three days later. Also in 1951, Akira Kurosawa's *Rashomon* won an Academy Award for Best Foreign Film.

Having given an account of the uncertainties of his life, I now turn to his text on uncertainty.

chapter

2

THE TEXT

Eloquent Distillation of the Profound Points of the Madhyamaka An Adornment for Nāgārjuna's Thought

Compiled as notes by Zla ba bzang po according to the oral instructions of Dge 'dun chos 'phel.[1]

¶1 To the sharp weapons of the demons, you offered delicate flowers in return. When the enraged Devadatta pushed down a boulder [to kill you], you practiced silence. Son of the Śākyas, incapable of casting even an angry glance at your enemy, what intelligent person would honor you as a friend for protection from the great enemy, fearful saṃsāra?

¶2 You are the eye of the world who displayed precise subtlety unerringly through your aspiration to the path of liberation, the source of the ambrosia of excellent virtue and soothing peace. The assembled philosophers ever respect you without waxing or waning, saying, "This is the lord of the dharma, the supreme lion of speakers."

¶3 From the maṇḍala of the sun of your wisdom in the sky of Samantabhadra, in the lotus garden of my heart of meager knowledge, innate or acquired, (274) [grows] the glory of the smiling stamen of eloquent explanation, surrounded a thousandfold by the rays of reasoning. May the bees of scholars of the three realms enjoy the sweet honey of the true transmission.

¶4 All of our decisions about what is and is not are just decisions made in accordance with how it appears to our mind; they have no other basis whatsoever. Therefore, when we ask, "Does it exist or not?" and the other person answers,

---

1. This statement is added by Hor khang bsod nams dpal 'bar, the editor.

"It exists," in fact, we are asking, "Does this appear to your mind to exist or not exist?" and the answer is simply, "It appears to my mind to exist." In the same way, everything that one asks about—better or worse, good or bad, beautiful or ugly—is in fact merely asked about for the sake of understanding how the other person thinks. That the other person makes a decision and answers is in fact just a decision made in accordance with how it appears to his or her own mind; there is no other reason whatsoever. Therefore, as long as the ideas of two people are in disagreement with each other, they will argue. When they agree, the very thing that they agree upon will be placed in the class of what is, what exists, what can be known, and what is valid, and so on. Thus, the more people there are who agree, the more the point they agree upon becomes of great significance and importance. Contrary views are taken to be wrong views, mistaken perceptions, and so on. (275)

¶5 Regarding the mode of agreement furthermore, occasionally agreement is based just on some scripture. For example, two Muslims argued about whether or not it is permissible to eat camel meat. Finally, when they saw that the Qur'an grants permission to eat camel meat, they agreed that it is permissible to eat it. Occasionally, the agreement of two people is based on the reasoning of the two disputants. For example, if there is an argument about whether or not there is a fire beyond a mountain pass, they agree when they see smoke at the summit of the pass. Whatever it may be, if they both see it directly, they agree without argument. This is the case for all common beings. Now someone may wonder whether it is infallible to accept a presentation of what can be known that is based on some universal agreement. It is not. For example, if one arrives in a place in which the eyes of all the people in the land are afflicted by bile disease, all the people of that land will agree that a white conch is yellow, that there is no white. However, one cannot hold that a white conch is yellow due merely to that. Thus, the existence of that object is not decided by the mere agreement of some hundred people. It is not decided by the agreement of a thousand or ten thousand. It is not decided if all humans agree. It is not decided even by the agreement of all the common beings of the three realms. Therefore, all of our decisions about what exists and does not exist, what is and is not (276), are merely decisions in accordance with how it appears to our respective minds. When many hundreds of thousands of common beings to whose minds [things] appear similarly gather together, then the thing that they decide upon becomes firmly grounded and unchangeable, and those who speak in disagreement are proclaimed to be denigrators, nihilists, and so on.

¶6 Therefore, our statements about what does and does not exist are in fact classifications of what appears before our mind. Our statements that something does not exist or is impossible are classifications of what cannot appear before our mind. The reality [*dharmatā*] that is neither existent nor nonexistent does not belong to the former class, it belongs to the latter.

¶7 An amazing example of a majority in agreement dismissing the minority as false is set forth by the master Candrakīrti. Āryadeva's *Four Hundred* (*Catuḥśataka*) says: "Therefore, why is it incorrect to say that the whole world is insane?" The commentary on that [by Candrakīrti] says: "Once, in a country, there was an astrologer who went before the king and said, 'Seven days from now a rain will fall. All those whose mouths the water enters will go insane.' When the king heard that he carefully covered the mouth of his well of drinking water and none of the rain fell into it. His subjects were unable to do the same and so the water went into all of their mouths and they all went insane. The king was the only one whose mind remained normal. (277) In that country the way of thinking and the way of speaking of all the people did not agree with the way of thinking and the way of speaking of the king. Therefore, they all said, 'The king is insane.' In the end, not knowing what else to do, the king drank the water, whereby he came to agree with everyone else."[2]

¶8 Thus, due to the single great insanity from our having continually drunk the crazing waters of ignorance from time immemorial, there is no confidence whatsoever in our decisions concerning what exists and does not exist, what is and is not. Even though a hundred, a thousand, ten thousand, or a hundred thousand of such insane people agree, it in no way becomes more credible.

¶9 One may think: "We concede that our decisions are unreliable, but when we follow the decisions of the Buddha, we are infallible." Then who decided that the Buddha is infallible? If you say, "The great scholars and adepts like Nāgārjuna decided that he is infallible," then who decided that Nāgārjuna is infallible? If you say, "The Foremost Lama [Tsong kha pa] decided it," then who knows that

---

2. The verse "Therefore, why is it incorrect to say that the whole world is insane?" (de nyid phyir na 'jig rten kun I smyon pa yin zhes cis mi 'thad) does not appear in Āryadeva's *Catuḥśataka*. GC may therefore have misremembered its source. The story of the king, however, does appear in Candrakīrti's commentary on the text at III.22 (Derge edition, *dbu ma, ya,* 73b6–74a1). GC provides a paraphrase of the story here rather than a direct quotation from Candrakīrti.

This and all subsequent citations from Madhyamaka and *pramāṇa* texts are taken from the Derge (Sde dge) edition of the Tibetan *bstan 'gyur* published by the Faculty of Letters of Tokyo University in the series Sde dge Tibetan Tripiṭaka Bstan Hgyur (Tokyo: Sekai Seiten Kanko Kyokai, 1977, 1978, 1981).

the Foremost Lama is infallible? If you say, "Our kind and peerless lama, the excellent and great so and so decided," then infallibility, which depends on your excellent lama, is decided by your own mind. In fact, therefore, it is a tiger who vouches for a lion, it is a yak who vouches for a tiger, it is a dog who vouches for a yak, it is a mouse who vouches for a dog, it is an insect who vouches for a mouse. Thus, an insect is made the final voucher for them all. Therefore, when one analyzes in detail the final basis for any decision, apart from coming back to one's own mind, (278) nothing else whatsoever is perceived.

¶10 But is it not appropriate to place one's confidence in that very decision which has been made by one's own mind? It is not the case. Sometimes this mind of ours seems mistaken, sometimes it seems correct. It is established by experience that it is always deceptive, like the divination of a bad soothsayer. Who can trust it? Many things that are decided to be in the morning are decided not to be in the evening. Things that are decided to be early in life are decided not to be later in life. Things that 100,000 Muslims decide are true are decided to be false by 100,000 Buddhists. Each is firmly based in their own scripture and reasoning, which are as immutable as a diamond. Each of them asserts that their teacher is the infallible final refuge.

¶11 But then who should decide what is true? Someone may say, "Since the mere agreement of the majority is not sufficient, it must be decided from the point of view of valid knowledge [*pramāṇa*]." Then what sort of thing is this so-called valid knowledge? Is this pillar that one vividly sees with the eyes established by valid knowledge, and is the awareness that sees it in such a way a valid consciousness? If it is, how should one decide that this awareness is infallible? Until one decides whether or not the pillar exists, one does not know whether or not this awareness is a valid consciousness. Until one decides whether or not this awareness is a valid consciousness, one does not know whether or not the pillar exists. Therefore, when does one decide?

¶12 Someone may think, "The reason the pillar exists is that it can be seen by the eyes, touched by the hands, (279) and can also be seen when looked at by a friend." As was said before, it is decided because the eye and the hand agree and, in addition, the friend agrees. What confidence is there in something like that? If it is possible for the eye to be mistaken, what is the reason it would be impossible for the hand and the friend to be mistaken as well? For two people with bile disease, a yellow conch can be seen with their eyes and touched with their hands, and they both agree that it is yellow. In fact, are they not all in error?

¶13 Therefore, having made hundreds of presentations of what exists and does not exist, what is and is not, you go on to make various grandiloquent statements that the person who decides these things is not me, it is the Buddha, it is Nāgārjuna, it is the Great Charioteers, and so on. However, in the final analysis the Buddha, Nāgārjuna, the Great Charioteers, and so on are decided by just this mind of ours, and no scholar asserts that our own mind is unmistaken. Hence, is not the root of everything now rotten?

¶14 Therefore, as long as we remain in this land of saṃsāra, it is true that there is no other method than simply making decisions, having placed one's confidence in this mind in which one can have no confidence in any of the decisions that it makes. However, is it not going too far by virtue of merely this to concoct a system of thought for the nature of the final reality [dharmatā] and for each and every one of all the inconceivable and unnameable supramundane qualities and, having given a name to each and every one of them, to then make decisions? (280)

¶15 Therefore, regarding these conventional phenomena that have the nature of fictions, it comes down to the fact that there is nothing suitable other than a mere decision by this mind of ours, which is itself a source of fictions. However, those who strive wholeheartedly in search of the ultimate truth must understand at the outset that this fiction-making mind does not take you very far.

¶16 In brief, if a final reason for the unmistakenness and infallibility of this mind of ours could be demonstrated, then it would be possible to posit many other unmistaken and infallible things. However, the reason one's mind is unmistaken is nothing other than mere stubbornness and arrogance. Candrakīrti's *Commentary on the Entrance to the Middle Way* (*Madhyamakāvatārabhāṣya*) says: "Saying simply, 'It is true because it is true,' does not make it true." In the same way, even if one would exert the greatest stubbornness in saying, "It is unmistaken because it is unmistaken," how could that make it unmistaken?

¶17 What is there to say about the mistaken mind of a vulgar fool? The venerable Buddhaghosa decided that external objects are truly established, but the master Asaṅga took them to be fictions. And Asaṅga himself decided that the imaginary lacks truth and that the dependent is truly established. The Madhyamaka masters, however, placed it in the category of fictions. Therefore, if there can be no confidence even in the minds of those scholars, in whose mind can there be confidence? Even in the case of someone like us, I would say:

¶18 If one analyzes with one's own experience, one can understand how much our attitudes change[3] from the time we are children until we are old and decrepit. (281) How can one have confidence in today's conceptions?

¶19 But if there is no confidence in anything at all, what should one do? As stated before, as long as one abides in this world, there is nothing to do other than to remain believing in fictions, placing one's trust in fictions, making various presentations on the basis of fictions.

¶20 However, to think that the earth, stones, mountains, and rocks that we see now are still to be seen vividly when we are buddhas is very much in error. As long as consciousness remains in the body of a donkey, one is able to experience the delicious flavor of grass, but when it has left [the body of the donkey], the flavor is also completely lost. The knowledge of the rooster that the night has passed is completely lost when consciousness departs from the rooster's body. In our case as well, if we had some additional sense organs other than these present five, all external objects of knowledge also would increase. If these two eyes were stacked one on top of the other rather than on the right and left, it is certain that the shapes and colors of all external forms would be different. In whatever we decide, we have no means whatsoever other than deciding in dependence on these five sense organs. If it is not seen within these two eyes on the forehead, there is no other method to see forms. It is impossible to hear any sound that does not fit within this small hole of the ear. (282) And so on. Therefore, to decide that all objects of knowledge are included within just this measure, based on these five weak senses, with the mistaken mind summoned to assist, and to remain content, saying that the mode of being which does not appear before our mind is nonexistent and impossible, is the door to all trouble.

¶21 That our sensory valid consciousnesses cannot be the criteria was also stated clearly by the Bhagavan himself. As it says in the *King of Meditations* (*Samādhirāja* IX:23): "The eye, the ear, the nose are not valid; the tongue, the body, the mind are not valid. If these senses were valid, what could the noble path do for anyone?"

¶22 Therefore, the ultimate purpose for cultivating the noble path is in order to newly understand what the mind did not perceive and the eyes did not see before. When we carefully examine all of these assumptions that we hold about supramundane qualities, they are merely fabrications from examples taken

3. The block-print edition reads *brjes byur* rather than *brjes gyur*.

from the world and, within that, from the human realm alone. For example, due to the fact that we like jewels, the ground, houses, and so on in Akaniṣṭha are made of jewels. Similarly, the auspicious marks of a *saṃbhogakāya* are in fact things that are pleasing to our human eye.

¶23 It is known through detailed analysis that the attire of the *saṃbhogakāya* and of the gods is the attire of ancient Indian kings. (283) These are not merely our concoction but are stated in the sūtras. Indeed, they are merely set forth with skillful methods so that the qualities of the buddha level, which in reality cannot appear to our mind, can appear to our mind in order to create admiration and delight within us. For example, if the Buddha had been born in China, it would certainly be the case that the *saṃbhogakāya* of Akaniṣṭha would have a long shiny beard and would wear a golden dragon robe. Similarly, if he had been born in Tibet, there is no doubt that in Akaniṣṭha there would be fresh butter from wish-granting cows in a golden tea churn five hundred yojanas high, and there would be tea made from the leaves of the wish-granting tree. Therefore, all of this is merely the way that we common beings think. Regarding the actual domains of the Buddha himself, the master Candrakīrti said [at *Madhyamakāvatāra* XII.39d], "However, this secret of yours cannot be told." It is certain that it is not suitable to be spoken in our presence, or that even though it were spoken, it is something that we could not understand. If one has just a little faith toward the inconceivable secret of the Buddha, then one should have some slight belief in all these deeds by the Buddha of making an aeon equal to an instant and an atom equal to a world.

¶24 But if this mind of ours is a valid consciousness, we conclude that an atom is the smallest material form and we conclude that a world is extremely vast. We conclude that the great does not fit inside the small. (284) Therefore, no matter how great the magical powers and abilities of the Buddha may be, how is he able to destroy principles that are established by valid knowledge? If he is able to do so, is the power of the Buddha able to make all phenomena become truly established and capable of making all sentient beings into buddhas? If there is no reason why he cannot, other than because sentient beings are not buddhas and because all phenomena are not truly existent, then why can't they be transformed? If, when we say that an atom and a world do not differ in size, we denigrate the conventional and fall into nihilism, then could there be a sin more heavy than the Buddha's putting that very nihilism into practice when he actually makes them the same size? To decide that in general an atom and a world differ in size, but then to have to make many exceptions, such as saying that the Buddha's doing so is a special case, is in fact proof that the bag of our valid knowledge[4] is leaking in all directions.

¶25 If this is understood well, the Buddha's making an atom and a world equal in size is not a case of making the unequal equal by reason of the immense power of the Buddha. Is it not because the mind of the Buddha, which has the nature of nondual wisdom, cannot be bound by this decision based on a conception that sees large and small to be contradictory for our mind? The Buddha sees large and small as of the same taste; large and small are in fact of the same taste. (285) Therefore, it is an act of making what is, is. How could it be a magical display of turning what is not into what is?

¶26 To our conceptions, existence and nonexistence, is and is not, large and small, good and bad, and so on are all simply mutually exclusive. Therefore, a world not fitting into an atom is a great feat of magic conjured by this very misconception of ours, which we choose to call valid knowledge. Thus, one must understand that we, and not the Buddha, are the real magicians.

¶27 In the colophon to the *Entrance to the Middle Way* (*Madhyamakāvatāra*), it says that the master Candrakīrti "reversed attachment to things as being true by milking a picture of a cow . . ." If this appearance is established by valid knowledge, then because it is impossible for a picture of a cow to have intestines, lungs, udders, and so on, if he could milk some real milk from something like that, Candrakīrti would have greatly denigrated dependent origination. How would that reverse [attachment to] true establishment?

¶28 In the *Book of the Bka' gdams* (*Bka' gdams glegs bam*), it says that Atiśa displayed various miracles, such as placing his entire body inside a small *tsha tsha* mold, after which he said: "Everything we did today is counted as a contradiction by reason-advocating logicians. But if they count it [as such], let them count. I am ready to roam through India and Tibet, swearing that: 'The mode of being of phenomena is certainly not like that.'"

¶29 Therefore, we proclaim with a great roar such things as if something is not nonexistent it must be existent, (286) if it is not existent, it must be nonexistent, that those two are explicitly contradictory, and that something that is neither of those two is impossible. Similarly, [we proclaim that] if something is small it must not be large, if something is large it must not be small, that if there is

---

4. Following the block print, which reads *tshad ma*, rather than the Hor khang edition, which reads *rgya da ma*.

no difference between them, then all categories of dependent origination will be destroyed. Statements like "The view that reality [*dharmatā*] is free from the eight extremes of elaboration is great nihilism" are made because nothing can appear to our mind other than existence and nonexistence and because our mind does not recognize anything other than existence and nonexistence. But how can the inability of something to appear to our mind prove that it is impossible and does not exist?

¶30 For example, if you arrived in a region of the Northern Plain where the people had no familiarity with anything sweet other than milk, they would be stubbornly certain that "if something is sweet it must be milk; if it is not milk it is not sweet." To the sight of the people from that region, not being milk and being sweet is an ultimate explicit contradiction, and those who said something [to the contrary] are great nihilists who denigrate the conventional. Similarly, for example, if someone does not know anyone other than Rnam rgyal and Tshe ring, then, in deciding that there is someone in a house, when he decides that Rnam rgyal is absent, he decides that the person is Tshe ring. Because of not recognizing people other than those two, he would insist, "If it is not one, it must be the other." (287)

¶31 It is true that, in the same way, our mind continually oscillates between existence and nonexistence. There is no method for abiding in something that is other than those two.

¶32 However, referring to the middle path as that which is in the center of existence and nonexistence is very clearly set forth by the Buddha himself. For example, in the *Kāśyapa Chapter* (*Kāśyapaparivarta*) there are such statements as "Kāśyapa, 'existence' is one extreme; 'nonexistence' is the second extreme. That which is in the center of those two is the inexpressible and inconceivable middle path." And it is stated very clearly in the *Pile of Jewels* (*Ratnakūṭa*): "Existence and nonexistence are disputed. Pure and impure are also disputed. Suffering is not pacified by disputes. Being without dispute is the end of suffering." However, when scholars these days hear a scripture that refers to neither existence nor nonexistence, they first seek out the identity of the speaker of the scripture. If the scripture is a statement of an earlier Tibetan scholar, they dismiss it [saying]: "One who says something like that is a nihilistic fool." If the scripture is identified as a statement of the Buddha, Nāgārjuna, and so on, they patch it with words like "The statement 'does not exist' means 'does not truly exist'" and "'Is not nonexistent' means 'is not conventionally nonexistent,'" so that it fits with their own desires. In fact, the only difference is that if they direct refutations at the Buddha, (288) they fear being labeled evil persons with evil views, [whereas] if they are able to refute earlier Tibetans, they are labeled heroic scholars. Apart from that, there is no difference in the frequency of occurrence of expressions like "does not exist," "does not not exist," "inexpressible," and "free from elaboration" in the sūtras and Nāgārjuna's Collections of Reasoning [on the one hand] and the scriptures of the earlier Tibetan scholars [on the other]. Therefore, some refute the statements of the earlier Tibetan scholars that the mode of being is inexpressible and inconceivable, saying that they are fools and nihilists, and some show some slight respect, saying that there are no great errors in the thinking of those earlier Tibetan scholars and adepts— it is just that at the time that they spoke, the fine points of someone like the Foremost Lama [Tsong kha pa] had not yet appeared. If that is true, there are no errors in the thinking of the Bhagavan himself, yet when he spoke he simply said such things as "the perfection of wisdom, inexpressible by words or thoughts"[5] and "When you use 'it is,' you use signs; when you use 'it is not,' you use signs." Those beautiful patches of the system of those of us from Dga' ldan[6] Mountain, such as "When you use that which is truly established, you use signs" and "When you use what does not exist, you use signs," do not appear. [The Buddha] left them out. Thus, the way that the Buddha himself taught the doctrine is something that lacks fine points.

¶33 Therefore, if the earlier Tibetans and the Buddha are to be refuted, refute them equally. If they are to be affirmed, affirm them equally. (289) Please do not be deceitful, turning your tongue in various ways and worrying about whether or not people will criticize you.

¶34 Thus, if one takes pains in analyzing the ultimate, one must accept that all our decisions are mere fabrications of the mind, with no basis whatsoever. When one thinks about things like this, a great fear is created, and this is the onset of the arising of fear of the view of emptiness. Otherwise, we leave our ideas of existence and nonexistence, is and is not, purity and filth, good and bad, buddha and sentient being, heaven and hell, and so on just as they are, saying that they are all infallible dependent arisings, and it would not be proper to refute those. If they are refuted, it is decided that one falls to such things as nihilism. Saying that one must refute some so-called true establishment which is not that, is just the talk of some scholars who are skilled in dry words.

5. See note 12.
6. Following the block print. Hor khang reads *dge ldan*.

¶35 According to their system, this mind of ours that ordinarily thinks "I" is not the conception of self and therefore is not to be refuted. Therefore, this is how they identify the innate conception of I: For example, when someone says, "You are a thief," you say, "How am I a thief?" The appearance of a freestanding I is the innate conception of I. That is what they say.

¶36 If this ordinary mind that thinks "I" is valid, then the mind thinking "I" that is produced when someone says "You are a thief" would simply be more valid. How could this mean that it becomes the conception of true existence? If it is the conception of true existence, then when someone says [something equally false, such as], "The Buddha is not a refuge," (290) then why is the mind which thinks, "How can he not be a refuge?" not the conception of true existence? Similarly, when someone says, "This is not a pot," then the mind that decides, "If it is not a pot, what else is it? It is a pot" is also a conception of the true existence of the pot. How is it valid? Therefore, according to their system, it seems that weak thoughts are valid, and when that very mind becomes stronger, like a shift in the wind, it turns into a conception of true existence. How strange!

¶37 "In order to understand the view, it is very important to identify the object of negation" is as well known in the mouths of everyone as breath. If this is true, how is it possible to identify true establishment separately before understanding the view? For the Foremost Lama [Tsong kha pa] himself said, "Until one has understood emptiness, it is impossible to ever distinguish mere existence from true existence and, similarly, one cannot distinguish non-true existence from mere nonexistence"[7] and "That is the final reason why there is no commonly appearing subject for Prāsaṅgika and Svātantrika." Thus, how can one rely on that pretense of the identification of the object of negation?

¶38 Moreover, some say that when a valid form of awareness is produced that thinks, "A pot exists," a conception of true existence is simultaneously produced, which thinks, "The pot exists as truly established," but that it is difficult to identify them separately.

¶39 Now, the so-called valid knowledge is the primary cause of attaining buddhahood, and the so-called conception of true existence is the root of all faults.

7. GC seems here to be paraphrasing a statement from the *lhag thong* section of Tsong kha pa's *Lam rim chen mo*, which reads: "de la rang bzhin med pa'i lta ba ma snyed gong du gang zag de dag gis yod pa tsam dang rang gi mtshan nyid kyis grub pa'i yod pa gnyis so sor phyed pa mi srid de." See Tsong kha pa, *Mnyam med tsong kha pa chen pos mdzad pa'i byang chub lam rim che pa* (Xiling, China: Mtsho sngon mi rigs dpe skrun khang, 1985), 705.

It is very strange that they cannot be identified separately by reason of their being so similar to each other. (291) If one is certain to arrive whenever the other arrives, then when they are refuted, they should be refuted equally. How is it possible to distinguish between them?

¶40 The mind that thinks, "It is dawn" is valid. The mind that thinks, "I am tying my belt" is valid. In the same way, if all the thoughts like "I am drinking tea" and "I am eating tsampa" are simply valid, then among all the thoughts that fill a day, there is not even one thing to refute. Thus, when is this object of negation, the so-called conception of true existence, produced? If it is the case that the mind which is the conception of true existence, grown accustomed to from time immemorial, does not occur more than a couple of times a day, then it is most amazing.

¶41 Thoughts of whatever you are most accustomed to are produced first. For example, as is stated in the treatises on valid knowledge, when you see your father coming, who is also a brahmin and a teacher, the first thought produced is, "My father is coming." Such thoughts as "The teacher is coming" or "A brahmin is coming" do not appear to the mind. Because we have become accustomed from time immemorial to this mind which is the conception of true existence, we must decide that when we see a pot, the mind that is produced first is the conception of the true existence of the pot. Therefore, no matter how much one verbally specifies the object of negation by reasoning, in fact, what is to be negated is that the pot must be negated, the pillar must be negated, existence must be negated, nonexistence must be negated. Leaving the pot aside, how could there be something to negate separately called a truly established pot? This approach is not simply that of the scholars of old. (292) It was also clearly understood by scholars and adepts on the Dge lugs side who had [meditative] experience. There are unpleasant statements, like that of Lcang skya rin po che: "Leaving this vivid appearance where it is, they search for something protruding to refute." Gung thang bstan pa'i sgron me and Paṇ chen Blo bzang chos rgyan also said the same thing.

¶42 Some fear that if pots and pillars are refuted by reasoning, it will create nihilism, the view that nothing exists. This is a pointless worry. How is it possible that the nihilistic view that this pot that he sees in front of him is utterly nonexistent will be produced in an ordinary common being?

¶43 Even if such an idea were produced, because he knows explicitly that the pot is something to be seen and something to be touched, the thought is spontaneously produced that "this pot is something that appears to me. However, it does not exist at all in the way that it appears." Such a thought is the Madhyamaka view of the composite of appearance and emptiness, which understands that although things appear, they do not exist in the way that they appear. How is this nihilism?

¶44 In brief, when one thinks that a pot is utterly nonexistent and sees it directly with the eyes, the illusionlike awareness is produced automatically. Thus, what danger is there of falling into nihilism? Thus, I would say:

> ¶45 When one decides that it does not exist with one's mind and sees that
> it exists with one's eyes, even though the yellow hat abbot does not teach it,
> (293) what can arise other than the awareness of illusion?

¶46 For example, if gold, earth and stones, plants, and so on are simultaneously and without differentiation burned in a fire, the flammable things will burn and the nonflammable things will remain. In the same way, even though all appearances are refuted by reasoning without differentiation, the illusory things are what is left. Being left, they are certain to remain. What need is there to separate out the illusionlike dependent arisings right from the very beginning, placing them where harm will not be inflicted upon them by reasoning?

¶47 "Without asserting that conventions are validly established, how is it that you do not lack confidence in dependent origination?" In general, this so-called establishment by valid knowledge is synonymous with what scholars call "establishment by the reasoning of the three modes," with their great need to construe coarse conventional appearances subtly and minutely. In fact, for the sake of the great need for there to be some distinction among the objects of the artificial ignorance, the logical reasoning of scholars construes [the conventional] with exceeding clarity. In general, apart from the difference of merely adding or not adding through logical reasoning expressions such as "validly established," "trustworthy," "infallible," "undeniable," and so on, there is nothing other than what merely appears through the changing orientations of this conventional consciousness, which occurs instinctively in the minds of all six types of transmigrators. We assert that it is infallible and undeniable that a child says "Ouch!" when its hand meets fire. To give a reprimand that uses reasons, like the father saying, "Fire is hot. The hand is flesh. (294) Therefore, if it touches the fire, why would it not be hot?" is the system of proving it with the valid knowledge of scripture and reasoning. Therefore, as long as these appearances of earth, stones, mountains, rocks, and so on do not vanish, there is no purpose in appearances such as the three jewels, cause and effect, and dependent origination also vanishing. If the necessary appearances vanish first and the unnecessary appearances remain behind, how could it be appropriate for anyone other than common beings of base nature who lack religion?

¶48 When one has arrived at the level which the tantric masters of the past described in their vocabulary as "Phenomena have ceased, the mind has been transcended," these conventionalities of good, bad, and everything in between —like earth and stones, dependent origination, and the three jewels—completely vanish, and I wonder whether many things—like the union of body and mind, the union of the two truths, the union of good and bad, the union of virtue and sin—will not come in their place. At that time, I think that those billions of parts of the knowledge that sees the multiplicities all become the nature of the single knowledge that sees the mode of being.

¶49 In general, for us common beings, there are many beliefs, things that we believe willingly, things we believe unwillingly, and things that we believe with no choice, but their basis is nothing other than merely our own belief in our own perceptions. What is meant by "belief" is the mind being required to engage in a particular object involuntarily through the force of habit.

¶50 No one would assert that what appears in a dream is a validly established truth. (295) However, we must believe involuntarily in the appearances and feelings of things like happiness, suffering, and fear that occur in a dream. For example, when dreaming that you are falling from the peak of a great rocky mountain down into an abyss, if you analyze with the reasoning of the three modes, there is no possibility other than death. But you fall into the abyss and then return. Again, with regard to all those appearances that are not proved by reasoning, such as flying in the sky, it is undeniable that a variety of experiences occur, such as fear when you fall into an abyss and joy when you are flying through the sky. In brief, a fish is carefree in water and a human dreads sinking in water. In both cases, the fish and the human must undeniably and involuntarily believe [this about water].

¶51 Therefore, regarding the difference in what is asserted for oneself and for others in the unique system of the Prāsaṅgikas, these things that must be asserted involuntarily by common beings who have not turned away from dualistic appearances are assertions for others. The fact that a yogin who understands reality [dharmatā] does not assert as his own system even one among all objects in the way that they are perceived and conceived by a common being is the meaning of the Prāsaṅgikas not taking their own position. When one opponent who has assertions debates using scripture and reasoning with an opponent without assertions who abides in a state of meditative equipoise, free from verbalization, whatever answers the latter gives all become mere assertions. Thus, there is no place to fit this view of having no assertions within words, sounds, and, particularly, the reasoning of logicians. (296)

¶52 In summary, if one asserts from the depths of the heart that earth exists, it is an assertion of one's own system. If one is compelled to assert, "Earth exists," it is an assertion for others. That the Tathāgata remained under the Bodhi tree for a week without closing his eyes is his own system, which is without assertions. His turning of the wheel of doctrine of the four truths so that this very view [of reality] could be understood is a presentation of assertions for others, which he entered into through the power of compassion. This way of understanding is not limited to the Prāsaṅgikas. It is not different in the other tenet systems that assert a presentation of the provisional and definitive and the two truths. [Dharmakīrti's] *Commentary on Valid Knowledge* (*Pramāṇavārttika* III.219) says, "Thus, [the buddhas], endowed with equanimity on the meaning of reality, having gazed like elephants, posited external deeds."[8] It seems to be clear in the Indian commentaries that this is how the Bhagavan asserted how external objects exist when he explained the doctrine.

¶53 Each human has two ways of thinking, two ways of asserting, two ways of explaining—for oneself and for others. Who would believe in something like all the ways of perception and the ways of explanation of buddhas and sentient beings being wrapped up in one intention and one voice?

¶54 If one is frightened merely of being injured in the ordinary debates of today's debating courtyards, then one does not need any other answer [than "I have no assertion"] to whatever consequence that is presented. This mere answer of "I have no assertion, I have no assertion" (297) can turn into a joke.

¶55 Logical reasoning of the three modes that takes as its foundation the misconceptions of common beings, when used simply as a method to destroy itself by itself, is good. But when it is used as a tool to damage the view of having no

---

8. The Derge edition reads slightly differently, with two variants that could be ascribed to homophony. In addition, the *Adornment* omits the third line of the stanza. The Derge reads: "des de nyid don btang snyom can I glang chen gzigs stangs nyid mdzad nas I 'jig rten thugs ni 'ba' zhig gis I phyi rol spyod la 'jug par mdzad II" The Tibetan might be translated as "Thus, [the buddhas], endowed with equanimity on the meaning of reality, having gazed like elephants, engaged in external deeds in keeping with the world's understanding alone."

assertion, then there is no method for entering the *dharmadhātu*. This is very clearly stated by the master Dignāga in his *Compendium on Valid Knowledge* (*Pramāṇasamuccaya*). So I would say:

¶56 Objects of knowledge posited by the mind as existent and nonexistent; valid forms of knowledge dependent on objects true and false; having seen that the source of falsity in one is entrusted to the other, I am uncomfortable about positing conventional validity.

¶57 The presentation of the unexamined, unanalyzed world; the traditions of tenets that examine and analyze; having seen that the foundation of one rests on the other, I am uncomfortable about positing conventional validity.

¶58 Illusions that are mere appearances to the mind; the mode of being determined to be real; having seen that if one is true, the other is false, I am uncomfortable about positing conventional validity.

¶59 The first opponent hides the mountain of his own faults; (298) the second opponent searches for the faults of the other with a needle; having seen that they take turns defeating each other, I am uncomfortable about positing conventional validity.

¶60 The nonobservation of the suitable to appear negates the extreme of existence; the nonobservation of what does not appear abandons the extreme of nonexistence; having seen that the presentation of one is destroyed by the other, I am uncomfortable about positing conventional validity.

¶61 Because there is no difference in the attachment produced by the conception of true existence that holds a friend to be real and by the valid knowledge which understands that friends are helpful, I am uncomfortable about positing conventional validity.

¶62 Having seen no difference in the hatred produced by the conception of real existence that holds an enemy to be true, and the valid knowledge which determines that enemies are harmful, I am uncomfortable about positing conventional validity.

¶63 Inferential valid knowledge is produced from direct awareness; inference analyzes whether direct perception is true or false; because the child is serving as the father's witness, I am uncomfortable about positing conventional validity. (299)

¶64 Analysis by reasoning depends on the founders; the founders are established [as such] by the power of reasoning; if I can decide on my own, whom should I follow? If I cannot decide, whom should I believe?

¶65 Correct reasoning is found in the definitive scriptures; the provisional and definitive are differentiated by stainless reasoning. If one understands with reasoning, why search for the definitive meaning? If one does not understand with reasoning, how does one find the definitive meaning?

¶66 Because of this way in which Maitreyanātha was seen as a female dog, I do not believe in the unanalyzed, innate mind. Because of this way in which the views and tenets of Madhyamaka and Cittamātra abbots contradict each other, I do not believe in the minds of analytical scholars.

¶67 Vulgar people, having repeatedly followed what is right, find the innate conception of true existence; it is the root of all downfall. Scholars, having repeatedly followed what is right, find the artificial conception of true existence; it is worse than that.

¶68 In this world in which the noise of debate about existence and nonexistence, is and is not, true and false resounds, whatever is constantly seen appears as an object of knowledge. (300) Whatever one has become continually accustomed to appears to be valid.

¶69 Whatever most people like appears as the truth; whatever most mouths agree on appears as a philosophical tenet. Inside each person is a different valid form of knowledge, with an adamantine scripture supporting it.

¶70 Beyond each mountain pass is a different religious sect with thousands of scholars and fools who follow it, saying, "Just this is true; this will not deceive you." This self-authorization of one's own truth delights a group of similar beings; when told to a group who does not agree, they are scornful.

¶71 Here in the capital of the six types of transmigrators who do not agree, what is asserted by ten is not asserted by a hundred, and what is seen by humans is not seen by gods. Therefore, who makes the laws for validating truth and falsity?

¶72 If even the mind of an abbot of tenets who has consumed his human life by training in wisdom can be mistaken, then it is mistaken to place confidence in the false perceptions of the fools of the world as conventionally valid. (301)

¶73 All the things that appear to the mind to be useful and good are separated out and asserted to be valid. Therefore, in the ruins of a magical city in an empty plain, an illusory pile of jewels is often found.

¶74 This reflection of objects of knowledge, inconstant and changing—by changing the face slightly, it changes, by changing the mirror slightly, it also changes—is certain to vanish completely in the end.

¶75 Because analysis comes to this, I wonder whether it does not exist. Because the hand touches a needle, I wonder whether it exists. Because it is[9] a direct experience, I wonder whether it happened. Because perceptions can be mistaken, I wonder whether it did not happen.

¶76 Because we seek the root of existence, I wonder whether it does not exist. Because we see the peak of nonexistence, I wonder whether it exists. When we plant the seed of truth, we know it to be false. When we taste the fruit of the false, it seems to be true.

¶77 That which is referred to as the Madhyamaka's having no assertion does not mean that a Madhyamaka does not speak for his entire life. Even Candrakīrti certainly made assertions such as "This is Nālandā monastery," "I am Candrakīrti," "These are my monk's robes," (302) and [*Madhyamakāvatāra* I.1,] "Buddhas are born from bodhisattvas." However, it is necessary to distinguish the contexts of ultimate and conventional analysis. Some say such things as that the statement "I have no assertion in the context of ultimate analysis" is itself an assertion. If you say, "Don't say anything, I'm sleeping," someone without heeding what you said will make a joke and say, "The very fact that you said, 'Don't say anything' is a sign that you are not sleeping. Thus, [to say that '"I have no assertion" is itself an assertion'] is like that. What is the point? Long ago, when a flock of cranes was flying, the leader of cranes said, "Don't talk. If we talk, we will be killed." So they all said, "Don't talk, don't talk" [*mi grags mi grags*, pronounced *mi dak mi dak*], and they have been very famous from long ago for the sound "*mi dang mi dang*" [*mi grang mi grang*]. This is like that.

¶78 In brief, if the vow of silence during a fast is possible, and the Bhagavan's not indicating anything whatsoever about the fourteen unindicated views is possible, then the view of having no assertion is also possible. Otherwise, because it is explained [at *Madhyamakakārikā* XI.1] that "[w]hen asked whether

9. Following the block print, *lags pas*, rather than Hor khang, *lag pas*.

the beginning could be known, the great sage remained silent"[10] and [because] it is explained in the *Scripture on Discipline* (*Vinayāgama*) that "[t]o be without an answer is the ultimate of all defeats," you should not be proud of the fact that you carry around in your hand this kind of argument that would utterly defeat the Bhagavan. The Ārya [Nāgārjuna] praised the very fact that he did not answer [at *Ratnāvalī* I.74]: "Thus, he did not speak of the profound doctrine to transmigrators who were not vessels. Therefore the wise know the teacher to be the omniscient one." (303)

¶79 If one has understanding, the very fact that he had no assertion will itself be able to create the correct view in one's mind. The Ārya [Nāgārjuna] said, "the discipline of not speaking"; what more need be said about it being an essential point of profound meaning? Anāthapiṇḍada asked the Bhagavan, "May I invite you to my grove for tomorrow's noon meal?" Because the Bhagavan did not say anything, he [Anāthapiṇḍada] understood that he [the Buddha] had accepted. It is simply that [others] have not seen such explanations.

¶80 Therefore, as long as someone says, "I have no thesis," it is in the context of analyzing the ultimate. From the point at which that very lack of a thesis is made into a subject [for debate] and analyzed as to whether or not it is a thesis and so on, this is then a case of analyzing the conventional. From that point on, what other method is there than this set forth by the Sugata himself: "Whatever the world says exists, I also say exists. What they say does not exist, I also say does not exist"?

¶81 Saying to Nyag sked bu long ma,[11] "You are a *cakravartin* king" is an assertion. If Bu long ma asks, "Do you really believe that, [literally, "Do you assert

10. Two significant variants occur in the *Adornment*'s version of *Madhyamakakārikā* XI.1ab. The Sanskrit reads: "pūrvā prajñāyate koṭir nety uvāca mahāmuniḥ." *MMK* XI.1a appears in the Derge edition (*dbu ma, tsa,* 7a7) as "sngon mtha' mngon nam zhes zhus tshe." The *Adornment* reads: "sngon mtha' sngon rnams zhus pa'i tshe," replacing *mngon nam* with the homophonic *sngon rnams,* making the passage read something like "When he was asked about the beginning by the ancients." This error would suggest that the passage was dictated to someone who did not understand what was being said. In translating the passage here, I have taken it as a scribal error and translated the passage according to the Derge. The second variant is a more creative misreading. The *Adornment* reads "thub pa chen pos mi gsungs bzhugs" (The great sage remained without speaking.). The Derge, following the Sanskrit, says "thub pa chen pos min zhes gzungs" ([When asked whether the beginning could be known,] the great sage said that it could not). Here GC seems intentionally to modify the passage to make it serve as an example of the Buddha's silence. I have therefore translated *MMK* XI.1b following his reading.

11. Nyag sked bu long ma, better known as Nyag rong mgon po rnam rgyal (died 1865), was a feared and powerful warlord from the Nyag rong area of Khams in the midnineteenth century. Among his reported pastimes was force-feeding infants milk and yogurt and then dropping them from an upper-story window in order to observe the colorful results. See Tashi Tsering, "Nag-roṅ

that as your own system?"] or are you just flattering me?" there is no other recourse but to say, "I am not flattering you at all; it is my own belief [literally, "my own system"]." Such an assertion is made involuntarily out of fear of Bu long ma, without believing it in the least in one's own mind. In the same way, such things as being burned by fire, cooled by water, and moved by wind (304) are like Bu long ma; although it is true that these external capacities must be asserted powerlessly, one must distinguish them from what one must not assert in one's own system. Since this point is made very clearly in the Foremost Lama [Tsong kha pa]'s answers to Red mda' ba's questions, be honest and look there.

¶82 In brief, of all the thoughts in this present way of thinking, there does not appear to be even one that is not rooted in desire, hatred, and delusion. And if by chance there were a single correct reason amid these ordinary thoughts of ours, there is nothing more amazing than that we still have not progressed beyond this, although we had grown accustomed [to that reason] for countless aeons from beginningless saṃsāra. All of the thoughts experienced by cats and dogs are expressed within no more than three or four modulations of their feline and canine voices. Apart from that, they have no other method. In the same way, we common beings, relative to bodhisattvas who have attained power [that is, one of the bhūmis], do not even reach the level of dogs and cats. How is one able to formulate within the tiny hole of our thoughts [the question of whether] the great sky of the dharmadhātu, free from extremes and seen by the knowledge of all aspects, is a nonaffirming negative or an affirming negative?

¶83 To say that the very absence of assertion is itself an assertion is to be stubborn, like the people in the land of the northern nomads, mentioned above, who have no acquaintance with sugar; they determine that the sweet taste of sugar, which in fact is neither yogurt nor milk, is milk. (305) Also, the size of a reflection is proportional to the size of the mirror; it is nothing more than that. To assert that everything that does not fit inside that mirror is merely an object for negation by reasoning should be understood to be an impediment to creating a genuine understanding of all profound phenomena.

¶84 Furthermore, if it is a hypocritical lie for one opponent to take the position that he has decided that he has no assertions mentally yet he will assert various presentations verbally, then is it not also a lie for the other opponent to prove that all phenomena lack true existence when he has not damaged a corner of the

Mgon-po rnam-rgyal: A 19th Century Khams-pa Warrior," in Soundings in Tibetan Civilization, ed. Barbara Nimri Aziz and Matthew Kapstein (Delhi: Manohar Publications, 1985), 196–214.

conception of true existence in his own mind? Thus, even in the tiny activities of the world, in order to behave skillfully when you meet people, whether strong or weak, whose way of thinking differs from your own, you must differentiate between your physical and verbal manner on the outside and the way you think on the inside. If this is the case, what need is there to talk about the difference between the way that the Bhagavan Buddha—who has buried the conceptions of common beings under the ten bodhisattva stages—understands things himself and the way he leads disciples?

¶85 Therefore, even in the case of the correct view, there is a mode of understanding of yogins themselves [as described in such statements as]: "The perfection of wisdom, inexpressible by words or thoughts" and "The sphere of wisdom of specific knowledge,"[12] and it is also indispensable [to maintain] that "if it is not existent, it must be that it does not exist, and if it is not nonexistent, it must be that it is existent." Whatever it may be, including the *dharmadhātu*, it must be included under the dominion of either existence or nonexistence, thus hoisting the white banner of scholarly reputation until the end of the universe. (306) Certainly it would be unsuitable for it to be otherwise. How you express it, whether as the *dharmadhātu* or scholarly reputation, the unfabricated nature or conceptual reasoning, freedom from unspecified elaborations or the four specified extremes, is simply your choice.

¶86 In general, when one arrives at the final rank of turning an instant into an aeon and an atom into a world, and so on, all categories are unified.

¶87 Everything—this wisdom realizing emptiness, mutually dependent on the vividly appearing son clear light, and the basic clear light; same and different; existence and nonexistence; and so on—is turned, for example, into the single body of the Sow Mother with two faces, that is, the final mother and son clear lights meet irreversibly. This is called "the rank of liberation."

12. These two phrases (the first of which also appears in ¶32) are the first and third lines of a poem traditionally recited at Se ra and 'Bras spung monasteries prior to the recitation of the *Heart Sūtra*. It is said to have been spoken by the Buddha's son Rāhula to his mother. The full poem reads: "smra bsam brjod med shes rab pha rol phyin | ma skyes ma dgag nam mkha' snying po dang | so so rang rig ye shes spyod yul ba | dus gsum rgyal ba'i yum la phyag tshal lo ||" This can be translated as follows:

I bow down to the mother of the conquerors of the three times
The perfection of wisdom, inexpressible by words or thoughts,
Unproduced and unceased [like] the essence of space,
And the sphere of wisdom of specific knowledge.

See Donald S. Lopez Jr., *The "Heart Sūtra" Explained: Indian and Tibetan Commentaries* (Albany: State University of New York Press, 1988), p. 147.

¶88 When it is considered in terms of how they reason on the debating court-yard: "It follows that Mount Meru measures 80,000 yojanas." If you agree to that: "It follows that an atom lacks directional parts." If you also agree to that: "Well then, it follows that [the Buddha] did not place all the worlds equal to the number of atoms [into a single particle, contrary to what Candrakīrti said at *Madhyamakāvatāra* XII.17]: 'Worlds reaching to the limits in a single particle,'[13] because a form the size of 80,000 yojanas does not fit inside an atom that lacks directional parts." When this consequence is presented, the well-known answer today is that this is "a special case." (307) If taking something like this to be a special case is permissible, then what is wrong with giving a special answer also to a reasoning such as "It follows that if it is not the case that it is not existent, then it is the case that it is nonexistent because you have understood the true nature of the two negations"?

¶89 In brief, all those who believe in the Mahāyāna must also believe in the inconceivable. Otherwise: "In the midst of a mass of extremely hot fire [like that at the end of an] aeon, on a limpid lotus cushion with a very cool moon underneath a cushion of the sun, brandishing most wrathful weapons, embrac-ing a consort who is most desirable," and so on—these are seen as merely to be included among contradictions when analyzed with the reasoning of logi-cians. Therefore, saying that those are merely different types of emanation [of the same deity] in fact entails that this simply cannot be differentiated from a painting on a thangka. However, one should know that the union which non-dualistically mixes as one such things as object and subject, desire and hatred, hot and cold, pure and polluted, is the body of great wisdom or the body of union, the mixture of body and mind in one entity.

¶90 If the two form bodies are displayed for the welfare of others, and the major and ancillary marks are fundamentally only for the sake of creating serenity in the minds of others, how is it possible that a body, with the complete major and ancillary marks established as the final imprint of the two collections, has the face of a sow, or the face of a lion, and so on?

---

13. The full passage from Candrakīrti reads as follows in the Derge edition: "dag pa 'di ni bzhed pa 'jug pa yis | rdul gcig yul la mkha' gtugs 'jig rten dang | 'jig rten mtha' yas phyogs khyab rdul ston mod | rdul rags mi 'gyur 'jig rten phra mi 'gyur ||." See Derge, *dbu ma*, 'a, 217a2–3. The *Adornment* cites only the second line, and imprecisely, with *mthas* instead of *mkha'*, although the meaning is not changed. The Derge version might be translated as "Worlds reaching to the sky in a single atom."

¶91 Thus, in general, in the Mahāyāna and also, especially, in all of the Vajra-yāna, from the point when it is suitable to view the lama as a buddha (308) through to meditating on yourself as Vajradhara and believing that you have a fully established body maṇḍala—these are only for the purpose of turning upside down this present valid knowledge. All of this, such as offering the five meats [beef, elephant flesh, horse flesh, dog flesh, human flesh] and the five ambrosias [feces, urine, semen, blood, brains] to the Buddha, are set forth for the purpose of smashing to dust the conceptions of the ordinary, together with the reasoning of logicians. Otherwise, this offering of impure things to an excellent object of worship is contrary to valid knowledge in general, and contrary specifically to the reasoning of logicians, and more specifically, contrary even to the laws of the land. Therefore, is it not as Pho brang Zhi ba 'od said:[14] "Have pity on those who make offerings to the Tathāgata with the mud of filth and [as a result] go to [the hell called] Mud of Corpses"?

¶92 In brief, one should understand that taking the impure as pure and the improper as proper and so on is only set forth for the sake of reversing the conception of the ordinary. The state of the great unsurpassed joining of contradiction, when the earth is Buddhalocana [the goddess who is the perfected earth element] and Buddhalocana is the earth, the central deity [in the maṇḍala] is the peripheral and the peripheral is the central deity, seems to be something to be discovered.

¶93 In brief, the foremost of all of our faults is our blithe verbal explanation of all categories of the conventional and the ultimate. As long as something is able to appear to the mind, we stubbornly persist. Moreover, having taken blithe verbal explanation to be primary, when such an understanding arises, we pride ourselves on having found a final meaning that is found by scripture and reasoning. But, in fact, because one likes meat, one finds meat; (309) because one likes beer, one finds beer. In the same way, it is merely the discovery of an

14. The *Adornment* cites here from the famous ordinance (*bka' shog*) of king Ye shes 'od, who ruled in Pu hrangs in western Tibet in the early eleventh century. However, the author is mistakenly identified as Zhi ba 'od, grandnephew of Ye shes 'od and also author of a famous ordinance. The *Adornment*'s citation is approximate. The ordinance reads: "dri chu khu khrag dag gis mchod 'bul bas I ro myag 'dam du skye ba snying re rje" (Have pity on those who by making offerings of urine, semen, and menses are born in [the hell called] Mud of Corpses). For an edition, translation, and study of Ye shes 'od's ordinance, see Samten G. Karmay, "The Ordinance of lHa Bla-ma Ye-shes-'od," in *Tibetan Studies in Honour of Hugh Richardson*, ed. Michael Aris and Aung San Suu Kyi (Warminster, UK: Aris and Phillips, 1980), 150–60.

object that accords with our own conceptions. How could it be the discovery of the profound sphere of the Conqueror and his children?

¶94 Through seeing this fact, this mind of common beings recognizes the nature of the ultimate from the negative side, the "is not" side and the "does not exist" side. There is no method for it to encounter the mode of being from the positive side, the "is" side and the "exists" side. Having seen that this is the case, anything that is asserted by others is reversed by consequences, and the Tathāgata, who is without any assertion whatsoever in his own system, clearly set forth this very nonlocatability and nonobjectification of the excellent dharma, which is the essence of his teaching.

¶95 Thus, the primary obstacle on the correct path are these "conceptions." Therefore, the master Dharmakīrti said [at Pramāṇavārttika I.A], "He clears away the nets of conceptualization and has a body that is profound and vast." Dignāga said [in the Pramāṇasamuccaya], "If one is led to reality by way of the path of logic, one has gone far from the teaching of the Sugata and so is damaged."[15] At the point of explaining that, the Commentary on Valid Knowledge (Pramāṇavārttika I.85–86) says: "Why are the presentations of object and subject different and not different? In fact, relying only on what is renowned in the world without analysis, all probandums and proofs are posited. The wise do this in order to cause entry into the excellent meaning."

¶96 "To not exist ultimately does not constitute being nonexistent. To exist conventionally, (310) constitutes being existent." This means, in fact, "Not to be found by the wisdom of a noble being [āryan] does not constitute not being found. To be found by the conceptions of a common being constitutes being found." Except for these kinds of empty subjects which are utterly impossible— "Intrinsic establishment does not ultimately exist"; "The horns of a rabbit do not ultimately exist"; and so on—to not ultimately exist is never found to constitute nonexistence. If this is the case, then not only does it just not constitute nonexistence, it therefore constitutes existence. When one affixes the qualification ultimate to the object of negation in the statement "The horns of a rabbit

---

15. This is the penultimate śloka of Pramāṇasamuccaya. The Adornment reads: "rtog pa'i lam nas chos nyid la khrid na | bde gshegs lam nas ches srid nyams par 'gyur." The Derge edition differs considerably in form if not content, suggesting that GC was paraphrasing. The Derge reads: "gang zhig rtog ge'i lam nas chos nyid la khrid na | thub pa'i bstan las cher bsrings nyams par byas ma yin." See Derge, tshad ma, ce, 13a3. This might be translated as "If one is led to reality by the path of logic, one does not reduce the distance from the teaching of the Muni."

do not ultimately exist," one understands implicitly that they conventionally exist. Otherwise, what is the difference in the force of the words in "The horns of a rabbit do not ultimately exist" and the "The horns of a rabbit do not exist"? With this in mind, the master Candrakīrti said that with respect to the application of the qualification *ultimate* in the context of the reasoning "Production from self does not ultimately exist" which refutes the Sāṃkhya, it is not necessary to apply the qualification *ultimate* because with regard to the non-Buddhists who violate the two truths, what is to be refuted is at the level of both of the two truths. Similarly, what need is there to apply the qualification *ultimate* if one is refuting the horns of a rabbit that do not exist at the level of either of the truths? Are the lack of ultimate existence of the horns of a rabbit and the mind which understands that, respectively emptiness and the mind that understands emptiness, or not? The mind that understands that the horns of a rabbit are utterly nonexistent implicitly eliminates superimpositions of existence, such as white and black horns of a rabbit. Therefore, it also eliminates the superimposition of truly established existence.

§97 It is said that when the afflictions are made the object of negation by the path, the corresponding objects of abandonment (311) are utterly destroyed. Therefore, it is not necessary to apply the qualification *ultimate*. But when it is said that there is no sharp and very long black horn on the head of a rabbit, it is permissible to apply qualifications like *sharp* and *long*. One should ask why it is not permissible to apply the qualification *ultimate*, saying, "There is no truly established horn on its head."

§98 What is known as this object of negation by the path is nothing more than the habits of the afflicted mind from long ago being destroyed by later [states of mind]. If there is no need to apply the qualification *ultimate* in that case, what need is there to apply it in the case of the object of negation by reasoning?

§99 In brief, that which exists within the conception of true existence and which is being seen in the presence of the conception of true establishment is left as it is, and then something else is refuted. It does not pass beyond what the foremost Lcang skya rin po che said: "Leaving this vivid appearance where it is, they search for something protruding to refute."

§100 When the great tantric master Sangs rgyas rgya mtsho was asked by the foremost 'Jam dbyangs bzhad pa what the difference of view was between Prāsaṅgika and Svātantrika, he pointed at a pillar in his room and said: "In the Svātantrika system, this wooden thing standing alone is the pillar. In the Prāsaṅgika system, this is the basis of designation of the pillar. It is there that a pillar exists in name alone, merely imputedly existent." The great geshe A rig (1726–1803) met Wa mang Paṇḍita (Dbal mang dkon mchog rgyal mtshan, 1764–1853), who said [to the geshe], "Which of the five books are you versed in?" [The geshe said], "I have studied Madhyamaka the most." [Wa mang] said, "Then, what is this in the Prāsaṅgika system?" (312) and pointed his finger at the table in front of him. [The geshe] said, "That is a table." [Wa mang] said, "It follows that it is not a table because of being the basis of designation of a table," to which he [A rig] was left with no reply. These two stories definitely point to a critical issue concerning the views of Prāsaṅgika and Svātantrika. Thus, one should know that the conception that this square piece of wood which stands in front is a table is the conception of true existence in the Prāsaṅgika system, and is valid conventional knowledge in the Svātantrika system. Similarly, one should know that saying that this four-cornered piece of wood that stands in front is a table is an assertion for others in the Prāsaṅgika system, and is an autonomous assertion in the Svātantrika system. Similarly, when one asks whether this thing which stands in front is four-cornered, [the answer is that] it is the basis of designation of the four-cornered; it is not the four-cornered. Then even this which stands in front is the basis of designation of what stands in front; it is not that which stands in front. At the end of replacing the former basis of designation with the latter, the basis of designation of not having any assertion whatsoever of "this is" lacks anything to be designated. Thus, the good—the freedom from superimposition—and the bad—the nonaffirming negative—become synonyms. Therefore, it seems that arriving at this place is the crucial point on the path that severs the root of saṃsāra. Furthermore, all vulgar worldlings whose awareness of the ordinary has not been affected [by tenets] agree that the thing that stands in front exists as the four-cornered wooden thing, that the four-cornered thing exists as the table, and on top of the table there is a pot, and so on. However, it is extremely difficult to make a dividing line between minds affected by tenets and minds not affected by tenets. (313) From one perspective, even those vulgar beings who do not even know a letter [of the alphabet] are just those whose minds have been affected by tenets, because they follow such statements as "Doing things on Friday is always propitious." But if the dividing line between those whose minds have and have not been affected by tenets is made considering the mode of being of phenomena, then there appears to be no difference in either of [the two schools] as regards what is or is not a tenet. For, as the Foremost Lama [Tsong kha pa] said, based on the reason of dependent origination, Madhyamakas assert the absence of intrinsic existence; others, based on the very same reason, assert intrinsic existence. In brief, no distinguishing feature whatsoever is seen other than making a distinction based simply on the nature of the awareness, such that everything dependent on inference is a tenet, and everything dependent on direct perception is vulgar.

¶101 When it is taken in that way, the I which is the object of the thought "I am" should be taken as the self imagined by the innate ignorance, and that very self which is endowed with three features [of being permanent, partless, and independent] and so on must be taken as the object imagined by the artificial ignorance. But who is able to differentiate the conception of being established from the object's own side without depending on terminological designation—the kind of innate ignorance that arises naturally in the minds of all transmigrators—[on the one hand], and the conception that things intrinsically exist even though they do not truly exist, the artificial ignorance of those whose minds have been affected by the tenets invented by the master Bhāvaviveka, [on the other hand]? (314) Isn't the thought of a child who thinks it is permissible to relieve itself at will an innate mind, and the conception that it is never permissible to relieve itself on the carpet a mind affected by the tenets of the parents?

¶102 In brief, it is certainly possible that not all beings in the world have had their mind affected by the four Buddhist tenet systems or the sixty non-Buddhist tenet systems. However, there is not even one whose intellect is not affected by one's own tenets, because it is impossible for anyone to say, "These objects of knowledge are such and such" without it being connected to authoritative utterances of beings of similar background, such as parents, and to one's own reasoning.

¶103 Even the great Prāsaṅgika masters did not see anything beyond just this as the basis for positing the root of the conventional. Therefore, they assert something renowned to the world as the presentation of the conventional.

¶104 As for these things that appear to us to be undeniable, human appearances are undeniable to humans, ghost appearances are undeniable to ghosts, and dog appearances are undeniable to dogs. However, a house established for the perception of a ghost and a house established for the perception of a human are both established by valid knowledge, and the basis from which the two appearances arise is a house which is neither a ghost house nor a human house. It is something which is not seen by either the demon or the human. This assertion in no way differs from the way in which the Sāṃkhyas assert permanent and functional generalities. It is a little closer to the tenets of Cittamātra, but the Yogācāra (315) do not say that on that basis which gives rise to a common visual object there is a cup filled with liquid. They merely explain the way the habitual potencies that abide in the foundational consciousness [*ālayavijñāna*]—the single basis from which the different consciousnesses of the six types of beings arise—are awakened. Thus I say:

¶105 What is there to say about six types of appearance arising for the six types of those who have six fruitional bodies? There are six appearances without a common basis even for the bodies of humans who have six sense organs.

¶106 In brief, it seems that what appears to us vulgar beings, as well as all these irrefutable appearances—even though the chariot is broken into a thousand fragments by the seven-fold reasoning—are all obstructions to omniscience themselves or their potency. It is for this reason that we do not see forms on the other side of a wall, but the Buddha does see forms on the other side of a wall. Therefore, the master Candrakīrti said that if one utterly destroys in the face of reasoning all of these presentations of appearances, the afflictive obstructions are abandoned, and that the utter destruction of them in the face of perception is the abandonment of the obstructions to omniscience; [according to him] it seems that such [appearances] no longer exist for the Buddha who has exhausted the two obstructions.

¶107 Seeing a table wholeheartedly is an afflictive obstruction, and merely seeing it to exist with one's eyes is an obstruction to omniscience. Śāntideva said [at *Bodhicaryāvatāra* IX.30–31] that the way in which people at a magic show lust for an illusory woman is an example of the afflictive obstructions, and the way in which the magician himself lusts for the illusory woman is an example of the obstructions to omniscience. (316)

¶108 On the far side, where these nets of conceptualization such as "If it is one, it must not be the other" have been cleared away and severed, identity and difference are united into one. Therefore, he is endowed with aspects like a body that is profound because it is beyond objects of thought, and vast because it pervades all that is the same and different. Because he ensures the presence of a full diffusion of pure rays of light of the speech of the always auspicious to the minds of superior and inferior disciples, I bow down to him.

¶109 The final point is this: When you have understood the lack of intrinsic existence, then the way in which earth and stones, mountains, and rocks appear to you and the way they appear to others come to be very different. Therefore, when someone else speaks of a stone, in fact they are speaking about a truly established stone, and when you yourself assert that "it is," you are talking about a stone that is not intrinsically established. Therefore, the two ways of thinking—if it is not intrinsically established, it must not be a stone [on the one hand]; and if it is a stone, it must not be intrinsically established [on the other]—never communicate about the same thing. This is why there is no commonly appearing subject for the Prāsaṅgikas and the proponents of true existence. Even when there is communication, when an Indian and a Chinese who have no acquaintance with each other's countries say together, "Long live the king," the referent of the Chinese person's words (317) is a king who has long hair and a long moustache and is dressed in black, and the referent of the Indian's words is a king who does not have long hair or a moustache and who is dressed in white cotton. Yet even though there are the two words "king," they have become as one. Since there is no need for them to make arguments[16] with each other, there is mere mutual communication.

¶110 In fact, with regard to this "assertion," it is similar whether it is asserted mentally or verbally. Therefore, having asserted or believed in accordance with how it appears to oneself is an assertion in one's own system. An assertion in which the mode of appearance and the mode of being do not accord is an assertion for others. Based on that very appearance, an assertion of the four truths which appear and an assertion of the five paths which appear and so on are in fact assertions of mistaken appearance. However, without depending on this sequence of mistaken appearances, there is no path to the final abode. Therefore, it says, "Having understood that doctrines are like a raft." And Śāntideva [at Bodhicaryāvatāra IX.76] said, "In order to completely pacify suffering, one should not negate the delusion of a fruition." That delusion of what constitutes the fruition appears to mean the same as the raft earlier. It is said that when one arrives at the other shore of the river of saṃsāra, it is abandoned simultaneously with saṃsāra.

¶111 In dependence on the lower step, one climbs to the second step. In dependence on that, and abandoning that, one climbs to the third. The mode

16. Hor khang reads *rtsod lan*. The block print reads *rtsod glan*.

of progressing on the three is like this. If, without exchanging the nature of childish conceptions (318) there is no way to move to the state of middle and old age, then without exchanging the mode of appearance of the conceptions of common beings, how can there be any way to move to the buddha stage?

¶112 The proponents of true existence fling the consequence at the Prāsaṅgikas: "If there is no intrinsic existence, cause and effect are not viable." To say that the Prāsaṅgikas answer, "They do not intrinsically exist, but they are not nonexistent, [therefore] there is no fault" is a system of later times. In the system of earlier times, one had to answer, "There is no fault, because in our system we do not assert anything whatsoever about such things as intrinsic existence and nonexistence and about is and is not."

¶113 In brief, one of the most important of the unique features of the Madhyamaka is this: For the proponents of true existence, the very reasoning that negates existence proves nonexistence, and the very reasoning that negates nonexistence proves existence; their idea is that it must be the case that when the opponent's position is negated, one's own position is affirmed. But for the Prāsaṅgikas, not only are all positions of others refuted without exception, even one's own position is refuted by similar types of reasoning. Thus, there are refutations such as the following: [For example] when they refute going on the gone over [at *Madhyamakakārikā* II.1], "Respectively, going is not on the gone over," when someone wonders whether going exists on the not-yet-gone-over, they say, "There is also no going on the not-yet-gone-over." When someone wonders whether going then exists on something other than those two, they refute that also: "Apart from the gone over and not-yet-gone-over, motion is not known."

¶114 When the nothingness in the state of meditative equipoise is connected with the appearances in subsequent attainment, (319) this is the meaning of the unification of the nothingness of the state of equipoise and the appearance of something in subsequent attainment. That should be understood to mean that nothing whatsoever is established ultimately and something is established conventionally.

¶115 The earlier Tibetans asserted that the absence of intrinsic existence was the selflessness of persons, and freedom from the elaborations of the four extremes was the selflessness of phenomena. According to the system of the later period, the two selflessnesses must be divided from the point of view of the subject, the basis which is empty. Therefore, just as they assert that the absence of intrinsic existence of a pot is the emptiness of a pot and the absence of intrinsic existence of a pillar is the emptiness of a pillar, it should be understood that the absence of intrinsic existence of "I" and "mine" is the selflessness of the person and the nonintrinsic existence of a pot is a selflessness of phenomena. According to the system of the earlier Tibetans, there is a very great difference in superiority and inferiority between the two views that understand the selflessness of persons and of phenomena. The mode of placing the mind in the selflessness of persons is to abide in the opposite of this misconception of coarse people who think of true existence. Furthermore, this does not, in fact, pass beyond the appearance of the conventional. For this reason, the most subtle ability for taking conventional appearances as an object of the mind does not pass beyond these four: existence, nonexistence, both, and neither. Therefore, that very absence of all four is called an ultimate not in name only, or a nonconventional ultimate. In brief, it is called an inexpressible ultimate. (320)

¶116 The Entrance to the Bodhisattva Deeds (Bodhicaryāvatāra IX.2) says, "The ultimate is not within the mind's sphere; the mind is said to be the conventional." And, [IX.34] "When the real and the unreal do not remain before the mind, then, because there exists no other possibility, without object it is completely calmed." And, "At that time, the excellent doctrine is without location." And, "The teaching of the Buddha is without abode." Such greatness of the teaching of the Tathāgata is not like that of the others, the non-Buddhists. It is not done in terms of existence and nonexistence, is and is not, and so on, which come to be the objects of the conceptions of saṃsāra. Nor does he make it a method for positing tenets of conceptions that are very dear to and intimate with[17] those. He sets forth a method for passing beyond this fence of conceptions. Even though others talk about how the profound meaning is explained, in fact they are adorning this innate mind itself with their reasonings of direct perception and inference. It merely makes the root firmer. As the Foremost Lama [Tsong kha pa] said [in his Praise of Dependent Origination (Rten 'brel bstod pa)], "Those who oppose your teaching, no matter how long and how hard they try, are like those who repeatedly summon misfortune, because they rely on the view of self."[18] The basic intent of that statement seems to be this.

¶117 There are these debates which are in agreement with the conceptions of common ordinary beings, like "That very expression 'inexpressible' is itself an

17. Reading 'dris rather than 'dres.
18. Tsong kha pa's text reads: "bdag tu lta ba brtan phyir ro." The Adornment reads: "bdag tu 'dzin pa brtan phyir ro," presumably another case of misremembering the passage.

expression." Two disputants who suffer from bile disease debate about "That very thing which appears to be yellow is a conch." In a dream, someone dreams that he is dreaming and thinks, "This is false." Both of these minds are similar in that they are affected by bile disease and sleep. (321) However, as long as they are [not] freed from bile disease and not awakened from sleep, they must be led involuntarily to the position in which one is true and the other is not true. One must know that this is both a fault of ignorance and a quality of dependent origination.

¶118 In general, if as much as one says is taken to be an assertion, then without the one opponent talking, there is nothing to be disputed by the other opponent. "Therefore, if having no assertion is impossible, there is nothing that needs to be refuted. If there is, then having no assertion and not speaking are assertion and speech." "However, being without an assertion is an assertion. Saying that you have no assertion itself is a logical fallacy." It is unavoidable that this debate occur between Prāsaṅgikas and proponents of true existence. In fact, even the very term *absence of intrinsic existence* is intrinsically existent for the proponents of true existence. It is therefore a logical fallacy. It is no different from making the argument [at *Vigrahavyāvartanī* 1] "If nothing intrinsically exists, then your words also do not intrinsically exist." If one argues, "If you have no assertion, then why is having no assertion not an assertion?" it is similar to the former. Therefore, the master Nāgārjuna seems to be saying, "That I have no assertion is just your assertion; that a white conch is yellow is just your assertion." Therefore, the definition of an assertion is that it must be in words and that the meaning of what is expressed must be believed by the speaker himself from the heart. If one accepts such a presentation, there is no place for the provisional statements of the Sugata (322) and the false explanations by vulgar beings. Furthermore, without differentiating discrepancies between the mode of appearance, the mode of being, the mode of explanation, the mode of thought, the mode of assertion, and the mode of intention, it would seem to be difficult to have even the slightest conviction in the excellent dharma. As it says in [the *Samādhirāja*] sūtra, "If these senses were valid, what could the noble path do for anyone?" This seems to mean the same thing as "If [everything] is decided by the individual, what could the noble path do for anyone?"

¶119 Proving that someone is a valid person first and then following his scriptures is the system of others. Proving that the teaching is a valid scripture and then proving that the teacher is a valid person is the standpoint of the king of reasoning [Dharmakīrti]. "Following and not following" is in terms of only [the third] of the three abodes of objects of comprehension, the very hidden meaning. If [a person] is to be followed on that, he is said to be infallible. In general, *fallible* and *infallible* simply mean that when you follow [someone], it leads to either benefit or harm. Therefore, when one follows everything the Tathāgata said, such as "If you do this, it is good," "If you do not do this, it is bad," he is infallible. As [*Catuḥśataka* XII.5] says, "Whoever doubts what the Buddha said about the hidden must have confidence having been taught emptiness; it is the sole method";[19] and [*Pramāṇavārttika* I.217 says,] "Because he is infallible about the primary object, it can be inferred [that he is] about others as well." Because he is infallible about teaching the mode of being of phenomena, the primary aim, he is infallible also in setting forth the presentation of the conventions of high status [in saṃsāra], the ordinary aim. (323) Or [in other words], if one follows him, only benefit will arise; no harm whatsoever will arise. This way is like the example of the way a child follows the mother. In that way of following, it is not necessary to analyze what is provisional and definitive in such things as the mother saying, "If you go outside, there is a tiger"; "If you go far away, [I'll] cut your ears off!" It is not that one should not go outside; it is that [the child] must believe [in the mother's] speech and listen to her.

¶120 Therefore, the Bhagavan Buddha said, "Just as a sly woman[20] looks like a bride, the [Buddha] had the lower garment raised in response to a criticism by householders. When [some monks] swam and were ridiculed, [the Buddha] had them drop the lower garment to the ankle." This skillful method of the Sugata must be applied in the same way from the minute precepts of the vinaya to the final nature of phenomena. It must be understood that there are two: an assertion that must be congruent with the world, and the teacher's own mind. For the mind of the Sugata himself, there was no measure of difference between whether the group of six hitched their lower robe up to just above the knee or dropped it down to the heel. However, he set the measure of the length of the lower robe to accord with the sensibilities of the laymen and laywomen of Śrāvasti. It appears that he made such statements [in the *Śrīmāladevīsiṃhanāda*] as "Even though the sky has no end, it has a center; even though saṃsāra has no beginning, it has an end" to accord with the three

---

19. The *Adornment* introduces several variants without changing the meaning of the passage. It reads: "sangs rgyas kyis gsungs lkog gyur la | gang zhig the tshom za byed pa | de yi stong pa nyid bsten nas | thabs de kho nas yid ches bya." The Derge edition reads: "sangs rgyas kyis gsungs lkog gyur la | gang zhig the tshom skye 'gyur ba | de yis stong pa nyid bsten te | 'di nyid kho nar yid ces bya."

20. Hor khang reads *'chol ma*. The block print reads *chol ma*.

realms of saṃsāra (324) [and within that] the thoughts of the common house-holders of the great city of Śrāvasti.

¶121 As long as the perceptions of conventional reality have not ceased and as long as one has not changed the basis of consciousness, even though emptiness has been directly realized, one must involuntarily assert whatever was asserted earlier. It is not necessary to make effort to prove this with reasoning. Even if it is not asserted, that which is evident to one's own sight, hearing, and experience does not need to be the object of refutation and proof by reasoning. If not as-serting the conventional has the danger of falling into nihilism, then one would be compelled to refute or prove whether or not what is perceived by the eyes and ears exists, but that is not necessary. Even though the mere words *nothing exists* are spoken from the mouth, it does not in any way affect how things are apprehended by the mind. Therefore, I see no reason why the pair, refutation and proof, need to be taken so seriously. On the contrary, when someone who has no such assertions is asked what is out there, he will be bound to say that it is a mountain, it is a tree, and that it is a human. Thus, there is no need of another method to compel [that person] to accept these things through many reasonings.

¶122 When a magician conjures an illusory elephant, the spectators see a real elephant. The magician displays the illusion in order that what is not an ele-phant will be seen as a real elephant. Thus, when the spectators ask the ma-gician, "Is this a real elephant?" he must say that it is. That is the magician's assertion of an elephant for others. (325)

¶123 In brief, if one does not assert the categories of the provisional meaning and definitive meaning, it is not possible also to differentiate the categories of assertions for others and assertions for oneself. Making the refutation that says, "If just this *Treatise on the Middle Way* (*Madhyamakaśāstra*) is not the Madhya-maka's own system, whose system is it?" is like saying the following: "So many sūtras like the *Untying of the Intention* (*Saṃdhinirmocana*) and the *Descent to Laṅka* (*Laṅkāvatāra*) set forth again and again through hundreds of reasonings a foundational consciousness [*ālayavijñāna*] in which external objects do not exist, and a final reality which is the emptiness of duality of object and subject. If this is not their speaker, the Bhagavan's, own system, whose system is it?"

¶124 Therefore, with regard to the reasonings that directly damage this asser-tion for others, in fact, it is very similar to the following: If one were to say to Nyag sked bu long ma that the words "You are a *cakravartin*" are an assertion just for you, one would come to fear being killed. Therefore, there is no other method apart from saying that this assertion for others made in the presence of Nyag sked bu long ma is an assertion for oneself. This approach is stated very clearly by the Foremost Lama [Tsong kha pa] in his answer to Red mda' ba's questions.

¶125 Without this presentation of assertions for others, how can the opportunity arise for the speaking of one word of the dharma between the Buddha who perceives existence as infinite purity, and common beings who perceive everything as impure and contaminated? (326)

¶126 Regarding the differentiation of the contexts of conventional analysis and ultimate analysis, in fact it cannot be other than simply this: Thinking in which the mind is directed toward whether or not something is established by its own nature or mode of being is posited as the context of final analysis; analysis from the perspective of something arising as a mere appearance is posited as the context of conventional analysis. Thus, leave the tenets of the proponents of true existence aside. When vulgar beings whose minds have not been affected by tenets find gold, it is not a case of finding gold which is merely an illusion. Nor is it [gold] which is merely imputed by the mind. It must be a case of finding gold which is established from its own side. It is just this that is the root of creating attachment to gold. The statement that ignorance, the conception of true existence, is the root of the other two root afflictions [desire and hatred] comes down to this. Therefore, the gold which is found by them is furthermore inescapably something that is found by the reasoning that analyzes the final [mode of being] or the nature.

¶127 When one takes to its conclusion the consideration of this view which does not accept a difference between assertion for oneself and for others, there seems to be no difference between this and the statements that what appears to the Buddha appears to sentient beings, and what is known by the Buddha is known by sentient beings. In such a case, who could believe even the scripture about the bodhisattva Vegadhārin with his magical powers not seeing the tip of the Conqueror's crown protrusion?

¶128 In fact, if one has conviction in the dharma, one must have conviction in the inconceivable state. I think that those who say that anything that cannot be conceptualized or cannot be analyzed with thought (327) does not exist are in agreement with the nihilists who are the target of the refutation [at *Pramāṇavārttika* II.83d] "Because it is not seen, it is not that it does not exist."

¶129 "If smoke exists without fire, it must be established by valid knowledge. Therefore, it must be seen with the eyes. Therefore, it must be seen with my eyes. Because one has never seen anything like that before, it is proved that the existence of fire is pervaded by the existence of smoke." These reasonings in fact seem to be a system of analysis that inserts inside a single little hair-pore of reasoning the mode of being of objects of knowledge which come forth as a thousand transformations of happiness and suffering, good and bad, which radiate as a hundred thousand rays of the white and red light of Samantabhadra.

¶130 The *Commentary on the Entrance to the Middle Way* (*Madhyamakāvatāra-bhāṣya*) [in commenting on VI.83] says, "[We have endured] great hardship in order to overcome the conventions [of the world]."[21] The Foremost Lama [Tsong kha pa] says in his commentary that ascetic practice in cultivating the path is not necessary to overcome this. Therefore, it can be understood that when one has completed the ascetic practice of cultivating the path, all of these appearances are overcome. Therefore, the assertion of the presentation of conventions is, in brief, an involuntary assertion. The reason it must be an involuntary assertion is that when this appearance produced from the innate ignorance arises involuntarily, one must involuntarily also make presentations of things such as good and bad, existence and nonexistence, which are based[22] fundamentally on the artificial ignorance; and based[23] on that, there arises this need to remain involuntarily in this triple-realmed saṃsāra. Thus, one must understand that *involuntarily* really means "involuntarily."

¶131 Therefore, it is fitting that what we call "the need to assert involuntarily" causes sorrow; (328) it is not something that causes joy. Hence, the *Madhya-makāvatārabhāṣya* says, "We have endured very great hardship in order that we may overcome the conventions of the world. . . . If the world cannot do you harm, I will accompany you."[24]

21. The *Adornment* cites only a phrase of Candrakīrti's statement, which reads in full: "kho bo cag ni 'jig rten gyi kun rdzob bzlog par bya pa'i phyir shin tu tshegs che bar gnas par 'gyur gyi khyod kyis 'jig rten gyi kun rdzob sol cig." See Derge *dbu ma, 'a,* 276a6–7. This might be translated as "We have endured great hardship in order to overturn the conventions of the world. You must dispel the conventions of the world."

22. Hor khang reads *brten.* The block print reads *brtan.*

23. Hor khang reads *brten.* The block print reads *brtan.*

24. For the Derge version of the first part of the quotation, see note 19. The *Adornment* only omits *ni.* The second part reads in the *Adornment*: "'jig rten gyis gnod par mi 'gyur na ngas kyang khyod la grogs bya'o." The quotation occurs at Derge *dbu ma, 'a,* 276a7 and reads: "gal de khyod la 'jig rten gyis gnod par mi 'gyur na ngas kyang khyod la stongs gdab par bya'o." This might be translated as "If you are not harmed by the world, I offer to accompany you."

¶132 With regard to this being invalidated and not being invalidated by that which is more powerful, Śāntideva said [at *Bodhicaryāvatāra* IX.4], "invalidated by progressively higher levels." That is, he is saying that the reasoning that analyzes the conventional is invalidated by the reasoning that analyzes the ultimate. And even for the reasoning that analyzes the ultimate, the progressively higher stages of a yogin's awareness invalidate the lower. If that which simply has no power must be invalidated by that which simply has greater power, then since there is nothing more powerful in the mind of a common being than the five poisonous afflictions and especially ignorance, then it would have to be asserted that everything taken as an object by the conceptions that follow from these are justified. However, Śāntideva, in stating an example of the lower awareness not invalidating the higher, flings the consequence [at IX.8]: "Otherwise, the determination that a woman is unclean would be invalidated by the world."

¶133 Therefore, it is said that even when the proponents of true existence negate conventions such as external objects by means of analysis with reasoning, it is the case that they have not found it with that reasoning, not that they have negated it. It is most amazing to say on the one hand that not finding external objects and so on for the reasoning consciousness in the system of this or that school of tenets does not mean that they do not exist, and also then to say on the other hand that because true establishment and establishment by [the object's] own character and so on are not found for a reasoning consciousness in the Prāsaṅgika system, [their] existence is refuted. (329) When it is asserted in that way, then even that other emptiness of the Jo nang pa, if taken in accordance with the extreme positions concocted by scholars, is something that is included among conventional phenomena. However, how can the mere fact that it is not found by these subjective conceptions of existence and nonexistence and so on be a case of finding it to be nonexistent?

¶134 In brief, when considered in terms of worldly conventions, if not finding or utterly not finding is posited as the meaning of not existing, then apart from that, there is no dividing line between existence and nonexistence. If one believes that this very nonfinding is the final meaning of not existing, then there is no opportunity whatsoever for entering into the mode of being of phenomena.

¶135 The nonobservation of the suitable to appear is the final proof of nonexistence. However, no one seems to know the dividing line between how much is suitable to appear and how much is not suitable to appear. Thus,[25] someone

25. Reading *pa'i* as *pas*.

endowed with superknowledge does not see a flesh-eating ghost in that house; and therefore, because the suitable to appear is not observed, it is established that there is no flesh-eating ghost. Furthermore, according to a sūtra, a noble being who has attained a bodhisattva level and has great superknowledge sees in the width of the earth [touched] by just the wheel[26] of a chariot sentient beings equal to the particles of the earth. If that is the case, one must differentiate the degrees of this thing being suitable to appear and this thing being unsuitable to appear in accordance with the difference in levels of superknowledge or realization. The nonobservation of the suitable to appear that is agreed upon with one voice by many millions of vulgar common beings is just a portion of the nonobservation of the suitable to appear. (330) Therefore, one must understand that the nonexistence which they prove is just one side of nonexistence.

¶136 When it is nihilistic to refute the object of negation without affixing the qualification *truly established*, then it is certainly nihilistic to refute being truly established without affixing the qualification *intrinsically*. While still not having been able to affix the qualification of being truly established from time immemorial until now, to newly affix some qualification of being truly established and then to refute that here is not a case of identifying the target and shooting the arrow. Rather, it is introducing a different target and then shooting the arrow. If one has not understood from time immemorial until now how to affix the qualification of being truly established to a pot, even though one is trained in it right now, who is able to do so?

¶137 Even ultimate truths exist conventionally; they do not exist ultimately. An ultimate mode of being is unfounded. Even the ultimate is established in a way which is not ultimate. This means that it is conventionally established. Even that is to be established for the mind, and no presentation whatsoever that posits objects of knowledge is seen, apart from being merely established for this merely faultless mind that is not affected by adventitious causes of error.[27] Therefore, none of the Indian and Tibetan scholars of former and later times disagree in their assertion that this mere thing is the basis for positing the conventional.

¶138 In brief, if one does not believe that even though it is refuted by reasoning, it still must be asserted, then in general this is not suitable as the Madhyamaka system, and in particular as the system of Prāsaṅgika. The measure of the object

---

26. Hor khang reads *'phang lo*. The block print reads *'phang lo'i*.
27. Reading *'phral gyi 'khrul rgyus* rather than *'phral rgyu 'khrul rgyus*.

of negation in all refutations by reasoning (331) is able to be made by reasoning itself. Therefore, there appears to be very little need for details like the fact that the awareness which understands that a rabbit has no horns [on its head] should not refute the existence of the head of the rabbit.

¶139 If one accepts that there is no arrangement of contradictions in one's own system, then these words that interrupt with sounds, such as the statement by the followers of Sāṃkhya that "[t]he effect abides in the cause, but it is invisible" and the Cittamātrins saying "Subject and object are the same entity, but external objects appear" and the explanation by the Madhyamakas that "[i]f things are analyzed they do not exist, but they exist for a nonanalytical awareness" are only statements of tenets for the sake of being contradictory. There are two ways of "being contradictory": (1) the two contradictory things are put together in the same place even though they do not go together; and (2) two things that are appropriately contradictory are put together in the same place harmoniously. This too is a case of contradiction. Taking it in the latter of these senses, all of these contradictions, such as the contradiction "Even though it is not the case that it does not exist, it is not necessarily the case that it does exist" and the contradiction "Even though it is not the case that it exists, it is not the case that it does not exist" occur in Madhyamaka. Not only are all these contradictions contradictory for vulgar worldlings, the Madhyamakas also must certainly assert that they are contradictory. However, it is a mere assertion for them. It is a mere assertion for the system of others, and, moreover, it means the same thing as "asserted conventionally."

¶140 The standpoint of the Foremost Lama [Tsong kha pa] is this: forms and so forth appear to the sense consciousnesses to exist, (332) but that existence as it appears is utterly nonexistent. This is the meaning of not asserting an intrinsic nature conventionally.

¶141 How can the system which apprehends something as nonexistent because it is refuted by a reasoning consciousness be similar to the system which apprehends something as nonexistent because it is refuted by another form of reasoning? The awareness which thinks, "If something does not intrinsically exist, it is utterly nonexistent" understands even the nonexistence of what does not exist. Therefore, there is no possibility of falling into nihilism. As Candrakīrti said, the awareness which thinks that cause and effect, dependent arising, and so on do not exist is produced in dependence on some other form of reasoning that proves that they do not exist. Thus, having posited some parts of the conventional as existent and then asserting that some parts do not exist would be nihilism. If one understands that this nonexistence is subsumed within the conventional, the nonexistent itself comes to be within the nonexistent things which are free from the elaborations of the four extremes. Thus, the Sugata's prediction in which he refers to freedom from the two positions of existence and nonexistence—"He will be called by the name Nāga, and having destroyed the positions of existence and nonexistence"—appears to be an opportunity to create conviction in that master and his system.

¶142 Still, not finding the *dharmadhātu* and this inconceivable state is not due to the fault of believing too strongly[28] in existence, but is due to the fault of not believing strongly[29] enough in nonexistence. All the things that common beings of similar status never find are not found when sought among the existent. Therefore, in fact, they exist among the nonexistent. Therefore, all the qualities such as the ten powers, the four unshared capabilities, the union of body and mind (333) seem to exist within this nonexistence of ours.

¶143 The outside of this world of existence appears to be confined by something called "nonexistence." Even things like "If there is no fire, there is necessarily no smoke" are in fact cases of existence being bound by the chains of nonexistence. Therefore, this refutation of the extreme of nonexistence seems to be the most subtle of all the reasonings. The reason for that is that all the final worldly appearances and the final reasonings, that is, the final level, in fact rest on something that does not exist. Furthermore, because, in fact, they rest on a nonfinding, it is not possible to cross beyond that. How is it possible to see the state beyond, to which the Tathāgata went after three periods of countless aeons?[30] The position of the omniscient Go rams pa in brief is this: He says that by understanding the absence of true existence one becomes an arhat; and that by understanding the four signlessnesses, such as that the absence of true existence also is not, one attains the rank of the Mahāyāna [i. e., buddhahood]. Yet he had identified that very conception of the absence of true existence to be the view of those who make the Madhyamaka into a nihilistic view here in the Land of Snow Mountains. How surprising that one can attain the state of an arhat through a nihilistic view!

28. Hor khang reads *drags.* The block print reads *grags.*
29. Hor khang reads *drags.* The block print reads *grags.*
30. The block print inserts a break here.

¶144 In general, no matter which text in the sūtras, tantras, or śāstras one examines, it appears that the afflictive obstructions are something abandoned through view, and the obstructions to omniscience must be abandoned through method. Therefore, the division of afflictive obstructions and obstructions to omniscience in terms of mode of apprehension seems to be the talk of a confused person.

¶145 If one does not make a distinction in the categories of what is seen for oneself and what is seen for others, how can this assertion of all scholars that "[t]he Buddha who has extinguished all imperfect perception sees everything that is imperfect" be correct? (334) I will give a small example that is easy to understand. An opponent with clear sight[31] asserts that the color of a conch is white; it is not yellow. When an opponent with bile disease debates with him, he flings the consequence: "It follows that the subject, the color I see in front of me, is not the color of a conch because of not being yellow." If [the first opponent] does not accept the pervasion, the statement of the reason, and the thesis which is the opposite of that stated by him [the second opponent], then the two people, with and without bile disease, have nothing to analyze about the conch. When [the first opponent] asserts something, he accepts all of the positions of the other person's system, such as the conch is yellow, whatever is the color of a conch is necessarily yellow, that what is not yellow is not the color of a conch. This is the only way that there is for him to explain to the person with eye disease such positions as that the present conch is impermanent, does not truly exist, is an illusion, and so on. In the same way, one should understand that "[t]he Sugata takes care of vulgar common beings."

¶146 Therefore, it is impossible for there to be a commonly appearing property and subject for the two people with and without bile disease. However, within a coarse way of thinking, there is mutual communication about the mere fact of "It is a conch." Based on that fact, there must also be communication about the features of the conch as well. Otherwise, even communicating to the person with bile disease, "This so-called conch is actually white in color" (335) would be extremely difficult. This is because when one says "conch" to him, the conch that appears to his mind is nothing other than a yellow conch. Having made a false yellow conch the basis, there is no other method possible than to listen to reasons seen by the mind even though a white conch is not seen with the eyes.

31. Reading *ming btags* as *mig dwangs*.

¶147 The statement is made in response to saying that the Prāsaṅgikas have no system of their own: "There are so many statements of Nāgārjuna. If they are not the statements of Nāgārjuna, whose statements are they?" There is not the slightest difference [between this] and the argument "There simply are these sūtras which teach that the self exists, and say that external objects and three final vehicles are truly established, and so on. If this is not the statement of the Tathāgata, whose statement is it?"[32] It is stated with very great clarity that even the negation of truth in the ultimate sense is at the level of the conventional. Therefore, even the negation of production from the four extremes must be done conventionally. Yet until one has refuted all of these subtle ideas that conceive things to be true conventionally, how is it possible to refute even one of the various ideas which conceive things to be true ultimately?

¶148 If one becomes a Madhyamaka by asserting a mere production which is not from self or other, then why doesn't the assertion of a mere true establishment which is neither the same nor different also make one a Madhyamaka? Therefore, if it is the case that a pot and a pillar exist without fault even though they do not withstand analysis with the reasoning of the four extremes, then how do you deny that being truly established must also exist without fault and yet not withstand analysis with that reasoning? (336)

¶149 Therefore, if the dividing line between withstanding and not withstanding analysis is analyzed honestly, primordial matter [pradhāna] and the conscious person [puruṣa] and so on are what withstand analysis by the Sāṃkhyas' reasoning. A truly established pot and so on are what withstand analysis by the Sautrāntikas' reasoning, and the lack of external objects and so on are what withstand analysis by the Cittamātrins' reasoning. Thus, with regard to what withstands analysis by them, without positing what is to count as withstanding analysis, all of these presentations of things, like the nonexistence of the foundational consciousness and the existence of external objects, are established with great difficulty. Therefore, if "conventional establishment" was not made for the old men of the world whose minds have not been affected by tenets, and if it is not made for those to whom it is known, such as the Vaibhāṣikas, Sautrāntikas, and Cittamātrins whose learning and wisdom are greater than theirs, then for whom is it made? In this world, no discerning person understands without instruction. Everyone who understands upon been

32. The block print inserts a break here.

instructed is simply someone whose mind has been affected by tenets. Therefore, apart from a mind not affected by tenets being slightly present in dogs and
cats, it is certainly not to be found in anyone else.

¶150 The minds of those who think that there are no former and later lives are
affected by the Cārvākas, and the minds of those who think that there is something that takes rebirth after death have been affected by the tenets of others.
Apart from just this thought that "[n]ow I have been born and in the end I will
die," what mind is there that has not been affected by tenets?

¶151 If by refuting the four extremes of production, mere production is still not
refuted, (337) then because the mode of refuting the four extremes of production is conventional, if there is still a fifth type of production apart from the
four, then it is meaningless to limit it to four types of production and then have
to refute them.

¶152 Therefore, with regard to the system of differentiating what does and does
not exist between truly established production and mere production, the truly
established pot and the mere pot, and so on, what is wrong with dividing the
existent and nonexistent between truly established true establishment and mere
true establishment? If mere production and mere existence are never refuted,
then it is certain that mere obstructions to omniscience and mere afflictive obstructions are also never refuted. Therefore, it is seen that among the thoughts
of ordinary worldlings there is not found even the slightest thing to be refuted.
Thus, the statement [at *Madhyamakāvatāra* VI.36] "Which of your productions
is it?"[33] is commented upon as [advocating] mere production and meaning:
"Which of the four extremes of production is the production that you assert,
proponent of true existence?" However, the reasoning in that context does not
invalidate the thoughts of a stupid worldling. It invalidates the reasoning of a
scholar who holds tenets. There is not the slightest difference between saying
this and saying that the human eye consciousness is invalidated by reason because it can see in the light of day but cannot see at night, whereas the owl's eye
consciousness that sees in the opposite way is not invalidated.

¶153 In brief, if the system of explaining the difference of awareness in which
the higher does not invalidate the lower is like this, there is no opportunity to
create a genuine understanding of the capacity of the afflictions to be abandoned on the path of vision [*darśanamārga*] to be destroyed by the path of

33. GC's text mistakenly reads: "khyod kyi skye ba gang gi yin par 'gyur" rather than "khyod
kyi skye ba gang gis yin par 'gyur."

vision, and these capacities of the objects of abandonment to be abandoned on the nine levels of the path of meditation [*bhāvanāmārga*] to be destroyed by the antidotes. (338) It would be entirely acceptable to make whatever presentations one wished; the Sautrāntika would merely not find the uncommon views and tenets of the Vaibhāṣika; they would not find that they do not exist. The Madhyamaka would simply not find the foundational consciousness of the Cittamātra; they would not find that it does not exist. And so on.

¶154 As for the talk about there being a great difference between not finding and finding not to exist, because the eye consciousness never experiences sounds, terminology was never made for a sound being found or not found by that. A similar point can be made in the case of the ear consciousness, and so on. If a sound not being found means merely that it was not heard by the eye consciousness, then such things as earth and stones, which do not find anything whatsoever—forms and sounds and so on, and being truly established and so on—have already arrived at the final supreme enlightenment.

¶155 Furthermore, when it is understood according to this system, then it is even possible to say that a wrong consciousness does not invalidate valid knowledge, and valid knowledge does not invalidate wrong consciousness. This is because one can make fine points, such as that so long as it apprehends that there is no fire on a smoky pass, it is a case of fire not being found by that wrong consciousness itself; it is not a case of finding that fire does not exist.

¶156 Someone may say, "When we make distinctions by way of [levels of] awareness, then if it is this kind of thing, it must be found by reasoning which analyzes the ultimate; and if it is that kind of thing, it must be found by reasoning which analyzes the conventional. Those two are different objects. Not being found by one does not invalidate being found by the other." Then, if being truly established exists, (339) it must be found by ignorance. Even though it is found by that [ignorance], it is [nonetheless] found. What other reasoning can invalidate the fact that it was found by that? It is incredible that the things found by the six collections of consciousness which are polluted by the deep causes of error are placed in the class of the existent, while the things found by ignorance itself, the ultimate of the deep causes of error, are placed in the class of the nonexistent. Having differentiated not finding and finding not to exist, those who still take nonaffirming negatives seriously have no opportunity that enables them to take the mere negation of the object of negation as a nonaffirming negative. One should think carefully about whether the mere negation of the object of negation is a case of not finding, or of finding that it does not exist.

¶157 With regard to the statement that if something exists, it must be found by this kind of finding mind, according to the system in which each different object is within the purview of its respective awareness [such that] one does not invalidate the other, if being truly established exists, it must be found by the conception of true existence, and because it is found by that, how can it be refuted by a reasoning which analyzes the ultimate? It is explained that the things found by the eye consciousness are not invalidated by the things found by the ear consciousness. However, what does it mean to say that what is found by the conception of true existence comes to be invalidated by the reasoning consciousness? Those two have different objects, and the finders [the awarenesses which find them] are different. Therefore, what is found by one is not found by the other. How is it possible that one has even the slightest capacity to invalidate the other?

¶158 If you think that because a conventional reasoning and an ultimate reasoning are very (340) different, the object of one does not invalidate the other, then it would seem that because the conception of true existence and the reasoning consciousness that analyzes the ultimate are also very different from each other, the object of one is not invalidated by the other.[34] In fact, if something is not found conventionally and not found ultimately, it necessarily does not exist. If it is found by either of those two, it is included among the existent. This assertion is the idea of those who hold that if something is not found by any of the six collections of consciousness, it does not exist, and everything that measures up to being found by them exists. Intending to refute this idea, the Bhagavan Buddha said: "What is there to say about the eye and the ear? Even the mind is not a valid form of knowledge." In fact, if the master Nāgārjuna were still alive, we could ask him about it and be able to learn whether there is a difference between believing in conventional truths from the depths of one's heart, and believing in true establishment from the depths of one's heart.

¶159 With regard to the desire and hatred created in dependence on food and drink, apart from desire and hatred being produced in dependence on the awareness that conceives food and drink to be truly established, there is no place for the arising of desire and hatred. "Conventional existence" does not

34. The block print inserts a break here.

refer merely to "existing for the conception of true existence," but refers instead to what is known by a pure mind, a correct [mind], an understanding of conventions, and conventional reasoning, something that exists even in the mind of the Bhagavan Buddha. This appears to put trust in the essence of the view that these things which beginningless ignorance holds to be correct are correct, and those which it holds to be incorrect are incorrect. (341)

¶160 In the system of those who assert that just the four elements are the basis for progress on the path, this would not be contrary to those also being the causes that generate desire, hatred, and obscuration. Therefore, without depending on either of the two facts—that without relying on the earth there is no method to produce wisdom, and without relying on that [earth] there is no method to produce the afflictions—one comes to be very far away indeed from the system of the Buddhist Madhyamakas.

¶161 Nāgārjuna's view was prophesied by the Bhagavan: "He will destroy the positions of existence and nonexistence." To take existence [in that context] to mean true existence, and nonexistence to mean ultimate nonexistence, is in fact once again to place them in the world's existence and nonexistence. I don't know whether this destroys the essence of Nāgārjuna's teaching or upholds it.

¶162 Very briefly, the view that believes slightly in the way the categories of one's own mind are posited is that of the Svātantrikas, and the view that destroys everything about how they are posited by this [mind] is that of the Prāsaṅgikas.

¶163 Otherwise, what purpose would there be in the Bhagavan saying the words from "no form, no feeling" to "no knowledge of all aspects"?

¶164 The basic difference between the views of Prāsaṅgika and Svātantrika is that the Svātantrikas have assertions in their own system. Because they accept that things ultimately exist but the absence of true existence also exists, (342) this comes to be their assertion of a union of the two truths. For the Prāsaṅgikas, inasmuch as things are seen as not existing truly, to that extent the class of the conventional comes to be like an illusion. Therefore, if the presentation of the ten bodhisattva stages, the *saṃbhogakāya* with its five certainties, and so on are analyzed with valid knowledge, they are very untenable. Yet there are contexts when these are also upheld.

¶165 Therefore, as long as one believes from the depths of one's heart in worldly reasoning, it will never be possible to believe in the reality which is beyond the world. As Candrakīrti [commenting on *Madhyamakāvatāra* XIII.2] said, "It is not reasonable that qualities which are beyond the world could ever be similar to the worldly."[35]

¶166 The reason cultivation of the path is meaningless if one must believe in worldly reasoning is, as the Bhagavan said: "The eye, the ear, [the nose are not valid; the tongue, the body, the mind are not valid. If these senses were valid, what could] the noble path do for anyone?" Therefore, because all presentations have already been settled from beginningless saṃsāra on the basis of these six collections of consciousness, if one must still take this presentation seriously, what is the purpose of an interest in emptiness?

¶167 If one investigates minutely into the differences between (1) factors of appearance, such as form, not being invalidated by reasoning, and (2) the referent object of ignorance, the conception of true existence which is the final cause of that, being invalidated by reasoning, (343) then you will not pass beyond the system in which the referent objects of ignorance are acceptable. It is fitting that those who have already realized emptiness should delineate the difference between the form which is the object of negation and the form which must not be negated. Their understanding is certain. However, for those ordinary people for whom the ideas of[36] truly existent form and existent form are mixed together, to make the case that this much is to be negated and this much is to be left is no different from refuting the legs of an illusory elephant and leaving the trunk. According to the system of those who say that "[t]he analysis as to whether it ultimately exists or not is conventional but is not ultimate," the analysis as to whether the four extremes of production exist or not is also conventional, not ultimate. Thus, the mere production which is not included among the four is found conventionally, it is not found ultimately. Therefore, because it is not found, no matter how much one analyzes conventionally, it does not constitute not finding; because it is not found ultimately, it constitutes not finding. These ideas are a case of believing that genuine presentations of the ultimate are only conventional truths.

¶168 When one must take the refutation of the four types of production in the conventional sense, then if one cannot determine that "production" is the

---

35. The *Adornment* reads: "'jigs rten las 'das pa'i chos ni 'jig rten dang nam yang mtshungs par mi rigs so." The Derge version at *dbu ma, 'a*, 347a6–7, reads: "'di ltar 'jigs rten las 'das pa'i chos ni 'jig rten pa'i chos dang chos mtshung par mi rigs pa'i phyir." This might be translated, "It is thus because it is not reasonable for qualities which are beyond the world to resemble qualities of the world."

36. Reading *pas* as *pa'i*.

four types of production, then there is no point in refuting [production] from the point of view of the four types or the four extremes. To someone who has already understood the view, it does not seem that there is no distinction between (1) the explanation that the mode of being is free from the elaborations of the four extremes, that is, that it is not existent, not nonexistent, and so on, and (2) the explanation that includes "absence of intrinsic existence" in a single term. However, there is no distinction between the way beginners (344) understand "does not truly exist" and the way that they understand "the pot does not exist." In terms of that mode of understanding [of the beginner], there is no choice other than that the very awareness which understood the absence of the pot will in the second moment perceive the basis of negation of the pot. Therefore, one is compelled to maintain that at the time of meditative equipoise [the meditator] is not free of conventional perceptions. If that is the meaning of the union of the two truths, how sad.

¶169 If one must search anew for a true establishment which is other than this truth that appears to the mind of common beings, then it is certain that one must energetically search also for an ignorance which is other than this ignorance, and a desire and hatred which are objects of negation other than this hatred and desire. In the system that thinks that the mind thinking "a pot exists" is not a conception of true existence, but rather is a valid form of consciousness, it is certain that the object of the mind which thinks that the absence of intrinsic existence exists is also established faultlessly. However, just as one must distinguish between the conception of the existence of a pot and the conception of [it] truly existing, one must also distinguish between the conception that emptiness truly exists and the mere existence of emptiness. A person who has not realized emptiness is unfamiliar with emptiness. He is not able to distinguish whether it is truly established. For a person who has understood it, when emptiness appears to his or her mind, it appears in the manner of a nonaffirming negative. Therefore, since that person is not able to differentiate it [nonexistence and nonintrinsic existence], who is? Saying that because even the emptiness of intrinsic existence does not exist at all, there does not exist anything that is not empty of intrinsic existence[37] is certainly a cause of great laughter in the world. (345) However, saying that the Great High One [the Chinese emperor] is not the king of the world and that the queen is unclean is more ridiculous than that. With this point in mind, Śāntideva said [at *Bodhicaryāvatāra* IX.8],

---

37. GC is alluding here to *Madhyamakakārikā* XIII.7: "gal te stong min cung zad yod | stong pa cung zad yod par 'gyur | mi stong cung zad yod min na | stong pa yod par ga la 'gyur."

"Otherwise, the determination that a woman is unclean would be invalidated by the world."

¶170 Therefore, if one must assert only what is not invalidated by the world, then the final thought of the world is the conception of true existence. Therefore, one must assert something which is not invalidated by that, but what benefit is there in asserting that the mere object of the ordinary sense consciousnesses, such as form and sound, exists? When one considers this kind of system [which holds things] such as conventional truths are not invalidated by a reasoning consciousness, conventional reasoning does not invalidate ultimate truths, the objects of the two are different, [and] their ways of thinking are different, then it is certain that the reasoning of a fool who sees a mirage to be water cannot invalidate the reasoning of a wise man who sees a mirage to be a mirage.[38] Regarding the statement "Being sighted is true in the land of the sighted, being blind is true in the land of the blind,"[39] it is not a reasoning that seeks the mode of being of the object; it is a reasoning that seeks merely how things appear to oneself.

¶171 The master Candrakīrti destroyed all presentations of the conventional when he explained the ultimate. When he explained the conventional he disregarded the ultimate truth and merely followed whatever were the most powerful worldly reasonings. But if one is able to determine all the presentations of the objects and subjects that are beyond the world through including them in the reasoning of the world, (346) then why should one seek the middle path?

¶172 Seeking the middle path between the two, not existing conventionally and not lacking ultimate existence, is very similar to understanding that a cooking pot is not unbroken but it is not that it does not exist. It is in very strong agreement with worldly appearance.

¶173 With regard to this so-called union of the two truths, if there were a time when the wisdom of a noble being and the conception of a vulgar worldling could be joined without contradiction, that time certainly would have come; there has never been an opportunity for it to occur elsewhere.

¶174 If it is the case that Vijñaptika scholars do not find external objects but do not find them to be nonexistent, how is it that Madhyamaka scholars do

---

38. The reverse is presumably intended here, that the reasoning of a wise man who sees a mirage to be a mirage cannot invalidate the reasoning of a fool who sees a mirage to be water.

39. Reading *bden* instead of *ldan*.

not find true establishment and find that it does not exist? If you lose a needle and are looking for it, the mind that does not find it anywhere apprehends that the needle does not exist. Upon finding the needle later, if the mind that apprehends that the needle exists has no opportunity to invalidate the earlier mind that apprehended that it did not exist because of their having different objects, then the nature of the needle goes into the category of the occasionally[40] existent and the occasionally nonexistent.[41] Since there is nothing whatsoever other than those two, there is no point in negating them by deciding [that they are not] the four extremes, four possibilities, and so on.

¶175 The objects of the mind that conceives things to be truly established and of the mind that conceives things to lack true existence (347) are very different from each other. Therefore, what need is there that the object of one must be invalidated by the other? If you say that it is invalidated because of a difference in strength, then why doesn't the mind of lustful man who conceives a woman to be clean invalidate the mind of an arhat who sees a woman to be unclean? When we talk about a difference in strength, we base it only on the conceptions of ordinary beings, and that must be posited in dependence on the conventional. Therefore, according to the system of the master Candrakīrti, whether it be the desirable objects of the powerful emotion of attachment, the undesirable objects of the powerful emotion of hatred, or the earth, rocks, mountains, and stones that are the objects of the extremely powerful conception of true existence, for the Buddha down to animals, there is no method other than either accepting them as one's own system or accepting them as the system of others. Therefore, this principle—as much as a butter lamp illuminates, that much is in darkness when it dies out—is very true. However, with regard to this mode of being of objects of knowledge, what opportunity for liberation is there if one takes as one's system an analysis of the two truths in which, in addition to having this mere presentation of what is contradictory, that is, that fire and water are contradictory, hot and cold are contradictory, heavy and light are contradictory, and so on, one says that conventional truths and ultimate truths are not contradictory?

¶176 The way one understands things at the time of childhood and at the time of old age are very contradictory. If this is familiar to everyone, it is most incredible that the object of comprehension of a noble being and the mode of thought of a common being are not mutually contradictory. (348)

---

40. Hor khang reads *res 'ga'*. The block print reads *res 'gal*.
41. Hor khang reads *res 'ga'*. The block print reads *res 'gal*.

¶177 In brief, with regard to the so-called two truths, without understanding what is true for a vulgar being and what is true for a noble being, all the ways of seeing of the noble are mixed into what is true for the vulgar. If[42] this is the case, no one would have the good fortune to come to have the slightest belief in the inconceivable. One must understand that as long as one remains in the abode of the conceivable, one does not in the least pass beyond the world.

¶178 In brief, could it be that the ideas in the tenets of all non-Buddhist and Buddhist proponents of tenets are simply in conflict with the ideas of vulgar worldlings, yet the final ideas of the Prāsaṅgikas, the highest of the tenet systems, do not differ from the mode of thought of vulgar worldlings? The final way to understand this statement that "the conventional is true in the land of the conventional, the ultimate is true in the land of the ultimate"[43] is in no way different from saying that water in the land of water is wet and moistening, and stone in the land of stone is hard and obstructive. According to this system, which holds that the hard and obstructive and the wet and moistening are a noncontradictory union, that "stone in water is dry and water on stone is always wet" is the presentation of noncontradiction itself. When it is taken in that way, since the ignorance that encompasses all worlds and the wisdom of the Buddha that encompasses everything accompany each other, even those two are not contradictory. The sole foundation of the Prāsaṅgika reasoning seems to be to lead one to another path beyond all consciousness, above the disagreement in the way things are perceived by the eye and the ear, and the disagreement in the way they are perceived by the nose and the tongue, (349) and there being no point of contact [between the way things appear to the senses and] even the way they are considered by the final mind. When, because all these modes of thought and modes of recollection do not invalidate each other, a conventional consciousness is taken to be a valid form of knowledge, then there is not the least purpose in distinguishing any of the modes of thought, like those of lice, mice, cats, dogs, and humans; they are all only conventional truths, and the ways that things are perceived by them are conventional truths. However, because what appears to one is simply invalidated by the other, something called conventional truth would be impossible. If what appears to humans does not invalidate what appears to ghosts and, in the same way, what appears to ghosts does not invalidate what appears to gods, there would be no opportunity whatsoever for what appears to the Buddha to invalidate what appears

42. Hor khang reads *na*. The block print reads *ni*.
43. Reading *bden* instead of *ldan*.

CHAPTER TWO ～ 98

to sentient beings. Therefore, all this impure appearance would remain where it is forever.

¶179 This statement [at *Vigrahavyavārtanī* 1] that because words do not intrinsically exist, they are not able to refute that things intrinsically exist[44] is in fact a view which lacks being asserted in his [Nāgārjuna's] own system. [The statement at *Vigrahavyāvartanī* 26], "If one reverses absence of intrinsic existence, it proves intrinsic establishment," is a consequence, not an autonomous thesis. Furthermore, there are such statements as [*Madhyamakakārikā* XIII.7], "If anything that was not empty existed, then something that was empty would also exist." These [statements by Nāgārjuna] are consequences which state that if some object of negation exists a little bit, then the emptiness which is the negation of that and the reasoning which refutes it and so on also exist a little bit. (350) When it is considered in terms of this reasoning, then if a truly established object of negation exists, then that which refutes it must also be something truly established. If the object of negation is something which merely exists, that which refutes it must also be something that merely exists. And if the object of negation is utterly nonexistent, that which refutes it must also be utterly nonexistent. This seems to establish the tenets of the Madhyamaka system.

¶180 In brief, in order to destroy another's position or the position of the world, there is nothing [to be done] other than to destroy these two positions of existence and nonexistence. The Buddha said, "He will be called by the name Nāga and he will destroy the positions of existence and nonexistence." The acceptance of this kind of understanding of the union of the two truths which functions in both the nonexistent category—there is no earth in gold—and the existent category—there is earth in earth—is in fact an assertion of the noncontradictory union of the ideas of a vulgar worldling who is the ultimate of fools, and the wisdom of the Buddha, the ultimate of the wise. When it is taken in that way, what is wrong with asserting that the objects of ignorance and of the reasoning consciousness are also in noncontradictory union?

¶181 By understanding the meaning of light, one knows that darkness is very black. By understanding the meaning of virtue, one determines that sin is very

44. The *Adornment* in fact reads here "tshig rang bzhin med pa nyid kyis dngos po rang bzhin med pa 'gog mi nus par gsungs pa 'di yang," which would be translated as "This statement that because words do not intrinsically exist, they are not able to refute that things intrinsically exist." However, if GC is indeed paraphrasing *Vigrahavyavārtanī* 1cd, "khyod kyi tshig kyang rang bzhin med I rang bzhin bzlog par mi nus so" [(Because) your words do not intrinsically exist, they cannot overturn intrinsic nature], then the second *med* in the *Adornment* would seem to be mistaken and has thus been omitted in the translation.

wrong. If one must take these as presentations of the union of light and dark and the union of virtue and sin, it seems that there is not a single [pair] among all contradictions that is not unified. (351)

¶182 When two vulgar worldlings talk to each other with all of these terms like *true, existence, being,* they conceitedly think that they understand the meaning just because of verbal consensus. When the Buddha says to sentient beings, "Even though things do not ultimately exist, they exist," let us set aside the possibility that they understand the meaning. Even when it was said by someone who has found a little understanding of the Prāsaṅgika view, there is no opportunity to create ascertainment in accordance with his own system. This system that posits the validity of all presentations of conventional reality belittles such creatures as cats and mice, who do not understand conversation, and also dismisses children and fools, who are slightly superior to those [animals]. [Their conventional reality] appears to be posited for the ways of thinking of those who abide in between, who are neither clever like the very learned Prāsaṅgikas nor stupid like vulgar beings.

¶183 No one engages in refutation in the state of equipoise on the complete emptiness of intrinsic nature. If there is to be refutation, there must be refutation in the state of subsequent attainment. According to this way of accepting the union of the two truths, making this presentation is very difficult. However, if having realized the absence of true existence before, there is still some idea that this absence of true existence itself is truly established, what benefit is there in realizing emptiness?[45] As long as one distinguishes the notion of the good and the notion of the bad, there is no choice other than that the conception of the beautiful as beautiful is the notion of the good, and the conception of the beautiful as not beautiful is the notion of the bad. (352) It is amazing that they do not need to make the conception of the truth as truly established the notion of the good and the conception of true establishment as an illusion the notion of the bad. In brief, this acceptance of the two truths as not contradictory is the system of those who hold that no ideas, from those of the Buddha to those of sentient beings, are contradictory.

¶184 The final position of the Foremost One [Tsong kha pa] was that having dismissed the convention "assertion as one's own system," he made "assertion autonomously" and "assertion independently" synonyms. The final meaning of

45. The block print inserts a break here.

this is that the terms *own* and *other* do not apply to the person but to their position, a mode of being of things themselves. Therefore, the assertion that things are established by their own mode of subsistence is taken to be the Svātantrika, and the assertion that they are not established by the mode of subsistence is taken to be the Prāsaṅgika.

¶185 Having taken the so-called own system and others' system to be like a quarrel between vulgar worldlings, the mere agreement of two quarrelers appears to be the foundation of all these presentations. Again, in order to progress to a place beyond the world, it is certain that one must pass beyond the thoughts and expressions of the world. Thus, from a position that does not agree with the entire world and does not accord with its thinking, one must proceed to the level of a noble being. Therefore, except for asserting in all of these presentations that the thoughts of noble beings are superior and the thoughts of sentient beings are base, it appears that this assertion of something as one's own system or as the system of others will not occur. (353)

¶186 In general, unless one speaks to the benighted in a discourse that accords with the thoughts of the benighted, there is no opportunity for communication. Thus, to hold that the very condition for communication is the root of all objects of knowledge is quite amazing. When it is considered in terms of how it actually is, Candrakīrti said, "Just as a barbarian cannot be made to understand with another language, so worldlings cannot understand except with worldly [language]."[46] Thus, just as there is no other method to communicate with barbarians than barbarian language, when the Bhagavan discusses the excellent dharma with worldlings—even concerning how to pass beyond the world—there is no other method than for him to speak, leaving that very presentation of worldlings as it is.

¶187 Regarding *inference* in such statements [paraphrasing Candrakīrti in the *Prasannapadā*] as "Inference is unsuitable,"[47] it is what is well known in Tibet today as a syllogism. When one states a verbal syllogism, everything must be asserted autonomously or as one's own system. Therefore, one must assert the three—the sign, predicate, and meaning—as one's own system. Because there is no difference whatsoever between a "reason that is renowned to others" and a "consequence," through a mere presentation that is renowned to others, the

46. The passage is in fact from Āryadeva, *Catuḥśataka* VIII:19.
47. GC is paraphrasing Candrakīrti in the *Prasannapadā*, "dbu ma pa yin na ni rang gi rgyud kyi rjes su dpag par bya ba rigs pa yang ma yin te." See Derge *dbu ma*, 'a, 6a2.

correctness of the other is merely refuted. Therefore, if there is no commonly appearing subject, this is no different from saying "Autonomous syllogisms do not occur." Thus, there is no opportunity to be able to refute the system of Candrakīrti, who does not assert his own system autonomously. The master Candrakīrti thought that it is unsuitable for even that which is called a pot to be commonly established by two opponents. (354) Similarly, there is no commonly established predicate and reason. However, it was possible to state a mere consequence that is capable of refuting the assertion of the other person.

¶188 If the other person asserts that it exists, one must assert that it does not exist in one's own system. If he asserts that it does not exist, one must assert that it exists in one's own system. Because both of those are assertions of the two extremes, [Candrakīrti] said that if one is a Madhyamaka, it is not suitable to use autonomous [syllogisms].[48]

¶189 Those who assert the presentation of the conventional as their own system are Svātantrikas, and those who assert it as the system of others are Prāsaṅgikas. Therefore, the latter system's very lack of any factor whatsoever that is asserted in common with the world is the meaning of the lack of a commonly appearing subject. The root of all error is calling a mere appearance a conventional truth. When it is taken in this way, because anything that merely appears to a Prāsaṅgika also appears to a vulgar being, it is meaningless for there to be no commonly appearing subject. However, because all appearances and all thoughts are the appearance of true existence and the conception of true existence, there is also no opportunity for there to be a commonly appearing subject.[49] The object of negation is identified by the reasoning which refutes [it]. How could it be identified by some other awareness?[50] The Prāsaṅgikas' system of the conventional is that one must either assert the nihilistic view that conceives a pillar to be utterly nonexistent [as is the case in *samādhi*], or one must assert without believing all appearances polluted by the obstructions to omniscience, leaving them just as they were before, when one rises again from that Madhyamaka *samādhi*—such as that the pillar is something to see with the eye, to be touched with the hand, and even that it performs the function of holding up the roof. (355)

¶190 If the ignorance that is the root of saṃsāra still does not apply the qualification *ultimate* and conceives of the object of negation alone, then there is

48. See previous note.
49. The block print inserts a break here.
50. The block print inserts a break here.

no purpose in wandering in the world of saṃsāra. If there is a need to prepare a new qualification that is not connected with ignorance, then what [object of negation] is there other than an artificial object of negation?

¶191 The way that the worldly mind thinks is just this: form exists, true form exists, truly established form exists, actual form exists. Without negating what is the innermost focal point of the mind, to search for something else and then refute it seems to be a system that believes from the heart in ignorance and the mistaken dualistic appearances it creates.

¶192 Regarding the "reasoning that investigates the mode of being," furthermore [there are questions like]: "Is the color of this yellow?," "Is this gold?," "Is gold good?," "Where did this come from?," "Although I see it, is it really gold?," "Is this true?," "Is this truly established?," and so on. Apart from these analyses, there is nothing else whatsoever to find. All of this, apart from being a mere difference in how much one has been educated in the qualities [valued by] common beings, is in fact just the mind of vulgar worldlings. Therefore, if one considers it in detail, one can understand.

¶193 If one does not find a pot with the reasoning investigating the mode of being of a pot, then where in this world does one find an awareness which finds that a pot is a pot? (356) There is no chance for any proponent of reasoning to accept a way of being that lacks a mode of being. In short, searching for the mode of being is searching for the way in which it itself is it itself. For the likes of those who insist that it still is what it is while utterly not finding the way it is, what need is there for the Madhyamaka view?[51]

¶194 If it is, there must be a way that it is. If it is not, there must be a way that it is not. Having decided that there is nothing to discover about the way that it is or the way that it is not, those who assert that all the presentations of what is and is not are acceptable destroy the power of all Madhyamaka reasonings. As [Nāgārjuna's Madhyamakakārikā II.1] says, "Respectively, going is not on the gone over. There is also no going on the non-yet-gone-over. Apart from the gone over and not-yet-gone-over, motion is not known." To accept motion which lacks a mode of being not included among any of the four extremes is in fact to assert movement that lacks a way of moving and is a system that squanders all the reasonings of the father Nāgārjuna and his sons.

51. Reading lta ba'i for lta bas.

¶195 What it means to refute the way that something is and the way that something is not can be understood even by those of inferior minds. Not even one part of the hundred thousand things that appear to the Bhagavan appears to us.[52] Not even one part of the hundred thousand things that the Bhagavan sees is seen by us. When the very stupid person Cūḍapanthaka and the Bhagavan spoke about the excellent doctrine, apart from using the system of the Prāsaṅgikas, the Bhagavan had no opportunity to assert what was in his own mind. (357)

¶196 Here, the path of the noncontradictory union of the two truths appears in brief to be a system in which the understandings of the Buddha and sentient beings are mixed as one without contradiction. If one believes in such a thing, there is no opportunity for believing even in the words *saṃsāra nirvāṇa*.

¶197 In the system in which there is no commonly appearing subject, even the mere subject is not validly established in one's own system, and the valid establishment of the other system does not constitute valid establishment. Therefore, how is it acceptable for the sign, predicate, probandum, and so on to be validly established from just that?

¶198 Latter-day scholars have divided off the subject of "no commonly appearing subject" and have invented a new type of not commonly appearing. In that system, there is a commonly appearing reason, probandum, and so on. However, for those who believe that conventional truths are ultimate truths, everything is commonly appearing by reason of the fact that appearances to noble beings and appearances to vulgar beings must exist as common appearances. Thus, there is no need to make the distinction between what does and does not appear commonly in the sign, predicate, and subject.

¶199 Otherwise, having expended great effort in the study of the Madhyamaka treatises, they still seek a genuine understanding which is in no way different from the ways of thinking, the ways of seeing, and the ways of recollecting of fools who have not studied anything and scholarly common beings who are learned in artificial tenets. For them, there is a commonly appearing subject, a commonly appearing mode of thought, (358) and a commonly appearing mode of recollection.

¶200 In order to progress to the level of a buddha, one must proceed on a path that is not in common with vulgar appearances. Seeing this, the master

---

52. The block print inserts a break here.

Candrakīrti refuted this so-called commonly appearing subject right from the beginning.

¶201 There is no opportunity for similarity between these two nonaffirming negatives: the nonaffirming negative which is the nonexistence of a pot and the nonaffirming negative which is nonexistence applied to all phenomena. In the former case, there is no opportunity for there not to arise the stains of an affirming negative, such as thinking that even though the pot does not exist, the place [where it would exist] does. Regarding the mind which apprehends both existence and nonexistence as nonexistent, because something other than existence or nonexistence is not possible for the mind, or the observation of the conventional, another possibility which is also established for that mind does not arise. Therefore, it is ascertained definitely to be a mind directed toward the peace of liberation. Śāntideva said [at Bodhicaryāvatāra IX.34], "When the real and the unreal do not remain before the mind, then, because there is no other possibility, being without an object, it is completely calmed." The mind explained in this context was very clearly set forth by the master himself earlier [at Bodhicaryāvatāra IX.2]: "The mind is asserted[53] to be the conventional [literally, 'concealer']." Candrakīrti said [at Madhyamakāvatāra VI.28], "Because delusion obscures the nature, it is a concealer. Its fabrications, perceived to be true, were said by the Muni to be 'conventional truths' [literally, 'truths for a concealer']." Having considered that point well, Padmapāṇi Dge 'dun rgya mtsho said at the end of his commentary on [Tsong kha pa's] Provisional and Definitive (Drang nges legs bshad snying po), "A 'non-affirming negative' (359) is not the non-existence of something protruding; it is that very freedom from the elaborations that you assert."

¶202 Therefore, if one does not manipulate the statements of such great masters, they mean that concealer is the name of the mind, and that what is true for that is called truth for a concealer.[54] If one asserts valid knowledge autonomously, there is no other method than to assert the thinking of others as one's own system. When one uses a consequence, there is no need for anything other than the mere identification of the contradiction in the thinking of others as a contradiction. Therefore, in the context of speaking about reality, even the Buddha's way of speaking is not other than this, and even the Prāsaṅgika's own

---

53. The text reads 'dod, rather than brjod, as in the earlier citation and in Derge.
54. The block print inserts a break here.

system[55] is nothing other than this. From the point of view of the words, *own system* accepts the use of the reasoning of logicians. However, in this system that wishes to refute all other systems, how can the mere name *own system* be similar to the own system accepted by you out of the need to make assertions involuntarily due to the power of the obstructions to omniscience?

¶203 This kind of reasoning from the position of a logician comes to be a joke. Therefore, the Bhagavan said, "The world debates with me, I do not debate with the world." Regarding the way that the world debates, there is no debate about the reason, predicate, and meaning being established as commonly appearing for the Bhagavan. Without there being contradiction of any of their modes of thinking, modes of seeing, or modes of recollection, he must delineate without debate a presentation of everything that is known, or that should be known, (360) or what must be known at higher and higher [levels]. If all of these appearances are objects of faultless valid knowledge, then what purpose would there be in striving with hearing, thinking, and meditating for the sake of finding a path which is other than this?

¶204 In any case, what is called valid knowledge is that mice see everything as something to steal, cats see all mice as something to kill, and humans see both [stealing and killing] as something that is wrong. What kind of valid knowledge is there other than this? If one were to look at the statement "Although the eye consciousness does not find sounds, it does not find that sound does not exist," taking the eye consciousness as an example of the mind analyzing the ultimate and the ear consciousness as an example of the mind analyzing the conventional, then because the object of one is not found by the other and the two objects exist for their respective subjects, it appears that [Tsong kha pa] has developed a method for assisting the process of reasoning to unify the two truths without contradiction. However, the mode of analysis by the reasoning that analyzes the ultimate is parallel to the mode of analysis of sound by the eye consciousness. Therefore, if its mode of investigation is mistaken from the beginning, one can concede that it does not constitute finding that it does not exist. If the mode of investigation is not mistaken, why can't one maintain that the nonfinding is the finding of absence? Furthermore, ultimate analysis is necessarily a conventional consciousness. The Foremost Lama [Tsong kha pa] himself has asserted this. It is pitiable to maintain that there is an existence that

55. The block print reads *rang lugs.* Hor khang reads *gzhan lugs.*

could be found by an "ultimate analysis" which does not constitute a case of absence due to not being found by that [ultimate analysis].

¶205 In the system that does not believe in freedom from elaborations of the four extremes (361), there is analysis of such things as that absence of assertion is an assertion [and] the absence of ultimate existence is an existent. And those who believe in the freedom from elaborations which is the essence of the teaching are certainly neither pleased by nor frightened of whatever benefit or harm may come from the reasoning of coarse worldlings.

¶206 When one relies on these coarse reasonings, the fact that one can see the feet of the Buddha but cannot see his crown protrusion is highly contradictory, and such things as the fact that the *saṃbhogakāya* is newly born but never dies are the ultimate contradiction. Therefore, in brief, these ideas of the world are incapable of going even a little way toward the other side. If one relies upon these series of misconceptions valued by the great ones—such things as the reasoning of the three modes—what is there to say about not finding the final object of the empty class? What opportunity is there to find even the objects of the enlightenment class, which are conventional?[56] In fact, regarding these appearances of the world, deep despair about all reasonings, terms, and conceptions appears to be the view of emptiness.

¶207 The Madhyamaka reasoning, which is beyond existence and nonexistence, is a reasoning that passes beyond the reasoning of vulgar worldlings. Therefore, it is said that no reasoning based on existence and nonexistence is able to defeat it. As Candrakīrti's *Commentary on the Entrance to the Middle Way* (*Madhyamakāvatārabhāṣya*) says, "The proponents of dualism are incorrect. For that very reason, with their refutations and responses based on duality they cannot harm the Madhyamakas in any way."[57] (362)

¶208 If one invests one's trust in such reasonings, who could believe in the mode of being, since it is simply a presentation which transcends reasoning? Not only that, [because they are also simply presentations which transcend reasoning, who could believe] that light radiates from the body of the Buddha, and the story in the sūtra that Ānanda burned a butter lamp at night [although moths flew into the flame], and that Aṅgulimāla after killing 999 people became a chief disciple of the Bhagavan, and just as Aṅgulimāla cast aside his bloody

56. The block print inserts a break here.
57. Commenting on *Madhyamakāvatāra* VI.175. See Derge *dbu ma, 'a*, 311b5.

sword and sat on the seat, so did he destroy the twenty peaks of the mountain of the view of a real person with the diamond of wisdom, and attained the noble path? These systems in brief seem to be systems which accept that the way of thinking of vulgar beings invalidates the reasoning of noble beings. Therefore, it is fitting that they be abandoned by those who desire liberation.

¶209 When the six types of beings look at a cup full of liquid, they do such things as divide it into six parts on account of their disagreement. This assertion that the way in which the Buddha and a sentient being see a pot is similar is most incredible.

¶210 The final way of understanding that there is no commonly appearing subject is this. For those who have not understood emptiness, if one does not observe form as truly established, there is no means of observing form. Therefore, when one observes form, there is no choice but to observe it to be truly established. Thus, although you prove that "[t]he subject, form, does not truly exist, because of being dependently arisen," (363) the subject itself is not established. When one does not observe form, there is no basis for the statement of a syllogism, and just the assertion by the other is the basis for flinging a consequence.

¶211 Therefore, when noble beings of surpassing wisdom talk with the insane people of the world, what is said to be by the insane is not what is said to be in the noble beings' own system. They teach them from the point of view of consequences, saying, "If that is the case for you, then for you to say that it is, entails that it is not otherwise." Therefore, in this case of a reason which is not commonly appearing, there is communication from the point of view of just words. Even the presentation of the conventional is posited from the viewpoint of just words—and the presentation of the insane is posited by the insane. Hence, although it is true that all those presentations are true in their own setting, it is possible that what is gold for the insane is a stone for us. Thus, it is possible that what exists for us does not exist for noble beings. A commonly appearing object of knowledge does not exist among beings with very different types of minds. As long as one is deferential to the perceptions of the world, even though one has already attained the path of vision [*darśanamārga*], there is no choice but to remain in the system of the vulgar. To the extent that the power of the object or the obstructions to omniscience decrease, to that extent there is the consciousness of being freed from the confines of the object, and the fear of external objects subsides. In the end, the knower is mixed with the object of knowledge with which it is of one taste, and one attains the body of union. (364)

¶212 If, having amassed the collections for three periods of countless aeons, you still have perceptions that accord with common beings, then you should have invested in gold, silver, and jewels. What point is there in striving to achieve the rank of a buddha?

¶213 The final purpose of purifying the afflictive obstructions is to purify the obstructions to omniscience. Between the two curtains obstructing us from seeing the final mode of being, having extinguished the curtain of the subject earlier, there is no possibility for abandoning the curtain of the object, or the curtain of objects of knowledge, or what are called the obstructions to objects of omniscience [literally, "obstructions to objects of knowledge"], until one has abandoned the subtle physical obstructions asserted by Stag tshang.[58]

¶214 If the meaning is summarized, the statement that if one is a Madhyamaka, it is not suitable to have one's own system means that if one is a Madhyamaka, it is not suitable to have a mode of assertion based on one's own thoughts.[59] Yet when one considers in detail the artificial conception of true existence, as well as the conception of self and the conception of true existence superimposed by tenets, then the way of thinking about the self at the time of being an ordinary being seems to be a door leading elsewhere. Therefore, I wonder whether all of these so-called artificial conceptions of true existence are not something like the lower rungs of the ladder leading to the path of liberation.

¶215 As it is said [by Tsong kha pa], although one who has turned away from the Conqueror's teaching exhausts himself for a long time, misfortunes recur and increase, and the view of self becomes more stable.[60] If that is the case, then what about this path that creates pride of oneself being Vajrasattva (365) and creates pride thinking: "I am the pure nature of all phenomena"? There is no choice but to say that it makes the view of self more stable. Therefore, by grasping a self that is different from the self of one's earlier ordinary ways of thinking, from that point onward I would think that the door is open to meet the pervasive lord [Vajrasattva] face to face.

¶216 Regarding the way of positing pride, in the type of statements of the Foremost One [Tsong kha pa], it is said that one should take the very I which is held as the object of the conception of self.

58. See Stag tshang lo tsā ba shes rab rin chen, *Grub mtha' kun shes nas mtha' bral sgrub pa zhes bya ba'i bstan bcos rnam par bshad pa legs pa bshad kyi rgya mtsho* (Thimphu, Bhutan, 1976), 142a1 (321).
59. The block print inserts a break here.
60. GC is paraphrasing the statement from the *Rten 'brel stod pa* that was quoted at ¶116. See note 18.

¶217 "This is that; if it is this, it must be that; therefore this is that"—this is the reasoning of the three modes. This kind of reasoning is the very reasoning established for vulgar worldly hunters. Therefore, that something like this should be valued as "valid knowledge analyzing the conventional" is pitiable.

¶218 If one values the valid knowledge of common beings, then the conception that things truly exist, and the conception that a woman is clean, and so on must be taken as valid forms of knowledge. But when those very powerful appearances to which the worldly mind has become accustomed[61] are not taken to be valid, what purpose is there in taking as valid the reasoning of logicians, which is established on the basis of those [appearances]?[62] The earlier translators translated *saṃvṛti* into the religious language as "completely obscuring." It is that which obstructs the real object, or that which is utterly deceptive; it means "mistaken." Therefore, "conventional truth" must be understood as "mistaken truth." (366)

¶219 If one does not negate a chariot with the sevenfold analysis, then how is it possible to negate the obstructions to omniscience and the afflictive obstructions by the cultivation[63] of the five paths? Therefore, when the system is taken in this way, it would appear that there must be many postulates of subtle reasoning, such as ultimately existent desire is an object of abandonment, but desire is not an object of abandonment; that ultimately existent delusion is an object of abandonment, but delusion is not an object of abandonment.

¶220 If one summarizes the meaning of this mixing into one of all the presentations of the two classes—what is seen and not seen by the mind—it is that even the term *conventional truth* [literally, "truth for a concealer"] is not understood. Therefore, [Candrakīrti said at *Madhyamkaāvatāra* VI.28] "Because delusion obscures the nature, it is a concealer. Its fabrications, perceived to be true, were said by the Muni to be 'conventional truths' [literally, 'truths for a concealer']. Things that are fabricated [exist] conventionally." How could one need a source clearer than these words: "Because delusion obscures the nature," and "its fabrications," and "those fabrications were said by the Muni to be 'truths for a concealer'"?

---

61. Hor khang reads *goms*. The block print reads *gom*.
62. The block print inserts a break here.
63. Hor khang reads *goms*. The block print reads *gom*.

¶221 The famous "valid knowledge and reasoning" in fact appear to refer to just a faint comprehending awareness that falls between two uncomprehending awarenesses.

¶222 "Because things do not ultimately exist, they do not qualify as nonexistent, and because things conventionally exist, they qualify as existent"—in this system, I think that there would be no contradiction even if it is explained the other way round: "Because it exists for the reasoning consciousness of a noble being, it does not qualify as existent, but because it does not exist for the mistaken perceptions of the world, it qualifies as nonexistent." (367)

¶223 Thus, because the wise do not find that an illusory horse and elephant are a horse and an elephant, they do not qualify as nonexistent, but because they are found by fools, they qualify as existent.

¶224 The [Buddha] coined the expressions "as much as is found by the mind," "conventional truth," and "the multiplicity." Thus, with regard to "the multiplicity" it appears to mean just as much as is found by the conceptions of very weak common beings. When as much as is found by them is analyzed in rough summary, it includes just what is found in the space from the Peak of Existence to the Naraka hell, and between the eastern peak and the western peak. Therefore, in fact it appears that everything that is found by common beings is found by the Buddha, and is called the "knowledge of the multiplicity."

¶225 However, regarding that multiplicity, it is like finding gold under a familiar hearthstone: although one finds it, one does not know what it is until another person identifies it, saying, "This is gold." In the same way, all of these phenomena of saṃsāra that we find are seen to be without elaboration. That is seeing the mode.

¶226 When it is considered like this, it would seem that one should certainly create slight faith in the explanation by the Rnying ma pas of the principle of the primordial liberation, Samantabhadra.

¶227 The reasoning of dependence is autonomous inference. The reasoning of functionality is effective reasoning, the reasoning of consequences. (368) The reasoning that establishes tenability searches through commonly appearing signs and predicates. The reasoning of reality [dharmatā] is discovery by a reasoning which is not that of logic.

¶228 The everything of *everything* refers to everything that is able to appear as an object of the mind. The view that nothing exists is the view that the object of the mind does not exist. Therefore, if there is denigration, it is the view that nei-ther the denigrated object nor subject exist. Therefore, through understanding this profound excellent dharma, unlocated and ungrounded, having accumu-lated merit for hundreds of aeons, if one understands in this way, why should there be the slightest worry of falling into nihilism?

¶229 Gradually changing both the mind and the object, one arrives at the level of a buddha. But as long as one takes account of how much conventional dirt, stones, mountains, and rocks there are, then one must also take account of such things as women, meat, and beer. Thus, there is no place to go beyond this presentation. Therefore, apart from this presentation which everyone has known about from beginningless saṃsāra, what reason is there for needing to add reasoned proofs on top of that?

¶230 Because we do not understand the beauty of a tigress, we do not feel lust for a tigress. Because a tiger does not understand the beauty of a human girl, he does not feel desire for a human woman. When one reaches the root of this, it is simply that the three modes that are established for a tiger are not established for us, and the three modes that are established for us are not established for the tiger. Therefore, if it seems that this so-called reasoning of the three modes does not exist between animals and humans, (369) it is amazing that it exists from Akaniṣṭha above and from Avīci below.

¶231 Going on without beginning, when there are individual changes in re-birth, there are individual changes in aspect: sometimes it is the fire of hell; sometimes it is the ambrosia of a god; sometimes it is the water of a human; and the pus and blood of a hungry ghost. And so on. Thus, if it is possible to identify even these appearances as water, pus, and so on without having to communicate with each other, then it is amazing that there is this need to newly identify with effort a so-called true establishment, the object of negation, the object of ignorance which has accompanied the mind beginninglessly, without ever changing.

¶232 If one explains that such things as the nonexistence of a pot and the nonexistence of a pillar are nihilistic because they contradict the appearances that are renowned in the world, then wouldn't saying that the true establish-ment that appears commonly to all sentient beings of the six types does not exist be the ultimate of all nihilistic views?

¶233 There is nothing that is more mixed with the mind of the world than the conception of true existence. Therefore, Āryadeva said, "Even when they are ordinary beings, they are seized by the snake of the afflictions."[64] There isn't anyone who, having identified the subject, must still search for the object. Therefore, why is it necessary to newly search for the object of the conception of self which has been mixed [with the mind] without beginning?

¶234 Those who accept the *pradhāna* assert that the *pradhāna* is truly established. Those who accept that there are no former and later lives assert that that very nonexistence is truly established. According to this system, which says with regard to the absence of true existence of the horns of a rabbit, (370) that since the subject which is the basis which is empty does not exist, it is not emptiness, then there is no choice other than to set all nonexistence on one side and everything that exists on another, and then prove the emptiness of true existence. In that case, it is impossible to understand emptiness until one has attained buddhahood. Saying that one does not know how to place emptiness on a nonexistent subject which is the basis which is empty is only to understand that one does not know how to put water in a pot without the pot.

¶235 If in your system you must ascertain the subject, the basis which is empty, in order to prove the absence of true existence with reasoning, then what is wrong with taking true existence to be the basis which is empty and its nonexistence to be emptiness? In the same way, it would also be suitable to take intrinsic existence in "not intrinsically existent" to be the basis which is empty and its nonexistence to be emptiness. There are those who think that true existence and intrinsic nature itself are taken to be empty, [or think that] it is the object of negation by reasoning, but it is not the basis of negation. However, cleaning the stains of true establishment on a pot through washing it with the water of the view of the Six Collections of Reasoning is like the washing of a beautiful woman. It is nothing other than making the face of true establishment even more clear.

¶236 There are those who maintain that with respect to the absence of true existence of the horns of a rabbit, because the basis which is empty does not exist, it does not fit into the category of emptiness, whereas, with respect to the absence of true existence of a pot, because the basis which is empty exists, it is included in the category of emptiness. By this reasoning, it is no different than this analysis: "In the statement 'There is no point on the horn of a rabbit,' because the foundation, the basis which is empty does not exist, it is not included in the category of the non-affirming negative, whereas, in the statement

---

64. The quotation is in fact from Nāgārjuna, *Yuktiṣaṣṭikā* 52cd.

'There is no point on the horn of a yak,' the foundation [of the horn], the basis which is empty; and the object of negation, the tip; and (371) the factor which is the emptiness of that are non-affirming negatives." In fact, this seems to be a system of tenets in which everything that is nonexistent must have something that exists as its basis, and something existent that becomes nonexistent is called nonexistent. It is just as Āryadeva said, "Saying that what arose before does not exist now would therefore be seen as nihilistic."[65] The conception of true existence that has existed beginninglessly, and true establishment that has been nonexistent beginninglessly—these two would be joined in union facing each other. How could this be?[66]

¶237 It is most incredible to assert that there is a difference between those who abide in the Mahāyāna path and those who propound Mahāyāna tenets, on the one hand, and to assert on the other that there is someone who is both a Vaibhāṣika and has generated *bodhicitta*. They have gotten the idea in their mind that one can generate an authentic *bodhicitta* and then enter the Mahāyāna path regardless of which of the four tenet systems one follows. How could one be a bodhisattva simply by thinking, "I will attain the final rank for the sake of all sentient beings" while still not accepting presentations of the ten stages, the five wisdoms, the three bodies, and so on?

¶238 Even Sāṃkhyas and so on have the mere wish to attain the final rank for the sake of oneself and others. However, is it not said that due to erroneous presentations of the basis, path, and fruit, the path that they explain is utterly imperfect? If it is, the Vaibhāṣika bodhisattva will believe both verbally and mentally in all of the tenets unique to the Vaibhāṣika, such as that there are three final vehicles and that an arhat severs the continuum of matter and mind. (372) Whatever buddhahood he seeks is not genuine buddhahood when measured by the Mahāyāna. Therefore, how can the mind seeking the rank desired by him be the Mahāyāna *bodhicitta*? The buddhahood the Vaibhāṣikas assert to be the attainment of the rank of a buddha is asserted by them to be achieved in dependence on the presentation of the basis, path, and fruit explained in the Vaibhāṣikas' own tenets. The higher tenet systems see that all of those presentations are for the most part erroneous. Therefore, how is it possible that

---

65. The quotation is in fact from Nāgārjuna, *Madhyamakakārikā* XV:11. The second line in the *Adornment* reads *des na chad par lta bar 'gyur.* The Derge edition reads *des na chad par thal bar 'gyur.* See Derge, *dbu ma, tsa,* 9a3.

66. Paragraph break inserted following the block print. The paragraph in Hor khang begins above at "The conception of true existence that has existed beginninglessly . . ."

a person on an erroneous path from the start could have a hope for the final fruition which is not false?

¶239 When one is frightened by seeing a coiled rope as a snake, by merely identifying that "it is not a snake," the fear of timid people related to seeing it as a snake is still not completely abandoned. With this in mind, Śāntideva [at *Bodhicaryāvatāra* IX:30] said, "when even the person who made her feels lust for the illusory woman." The magician recognizes that an illusory woman is not a woman, but he feels lust. In the same way, it goes without saying that even though he understands that an illusory tiger is not a tiger, he feels fear. Therefore, for a timid person, an excellent method for dispelling the fear from seeing the coiled rope as a snake is for a hero to throw the coiled rope out of the house. Thereby, both the basis of error, the coiled rope, and the appearance of error, the snake, are gone without a trace. If he carries the coiled rope in front of him saying, "This is not a snake," (373) there is no doubt that it will create fear as before.

¶240 Rainbows and reflections look like something that can be grasped by the hand, but in fact they are not. If this mode of apprehension which understands that they lack[67] obstruction is not even remotely like the mode of apprehending everything to be like an illusion explained in the works of Nāgārjuna, then it is impossible to establish the meaning of *illusionlike* to the proponents of true existence by employing either[68] consequences or autonomous syllogisms. When one states, "The subject, a pillar, is like an illusion because of being dependently arisen, like a rainbow for example," the way that a rainbow's being like an illusion appears to the mind of the other person is utterly different from the way that something illusory is perceived by a Madhyamaka. Therefore, what purpose is there in holding the rainbow as an appropriate example?

¶241 When one's delight in playing[69] with ashes decreases, the mind of childhood is becoming weaker. Therefore, one must strive to create it. When one takes no delight in women, one's mind of manhood is weakening. Therefore, one must strive to create it. When one takes no delight in commerce, home, fields, and money, one's mind of maturity is weakening. Therefore, one must strive to create it. Thus, this taking of the entire teaching as the practice in a single sitting, in one human lifetime, appears to be what is explained as the essential point of the practice of the glorious Atiśa. If it is a system that divides [the

67. Reading *bral ba* rather than *'brel ba.*
68. The block print reads *thal rang gang gis.* Hor khang omits *gang.*
69. Hor khang reads *rtsed mo.* The block print reads *rtse mo.*

practice] into the levels of five paths and ten stages, then when one has attained the path of preparation [*prayogamārga*], strive on the path of accumulation [*saṃbhāramārga*]; when one attains the eighth stage, (374) strive on the first stage; when one attains the buddha stage, strive on the path of accumulation. Having done that, it seems that one should practice the entire teaching on the single lotus throne of the Densely Adorned Realm.

I say:

¶242 The wisdom that is beyond existence and nonexistence is the essential point of the profound thought of Nāgārjuna, the father, and his sons. This eloquent explanation distills into one the traditions of the forefathers, the best of the new and ancient schools of the snowy land.

¶243 When the sun of knowledge from the expanse of my lama's compassionate intention shone in my direction, it devoured the wrong ideas in the heart of one born blind. Yet it causes the calyx of the mind of one with sight to smile.

¶244 It is due to my past karma that I hold in my heart the essence of the intentions of all the conquerors in space and time, the refined, cut, and polished jewel of scripture, reasoning, and instructions, the gold of the inconceivable *dharmadhātu.*

¶245 Yet if in all the water in the mouth of the lama Mañjunātha [Tsong kha pa], the ocean of eloquence turning the wheel of the dharma, there is a part muddied by the swamp of my ignorance, I confess it from the heart to the assembly of the impartial.

¶246 At the instant that the rays of sunlight of the eloquent explanation sought here (375) shine upon the lotus of the minds of those with the power of mindfulness, may the sweet nectar of the drop of honey of the self-arisen wisdom always bear fruit as the nature of peace.

¶247 May I be cared for in all my lives by the lama and understand without error and just as it is the sphere of the profound *dharmatā* free of elaboration, and then proceed to the end of the path of purity.

¶248 Through the strong wind of a thousand virtuous activities, may the autumn cloud [over] the capital of mistaken appearances of the nonexistent become of one taste in the abode of the sky of the *dharmadhātu,* and the sun of the triple-bodied conqueror shine forth.

¶249 Born into a family of *māntrikas* in the land of A mdo, unattached to and unhindered by any doctrine, non-Buddhist or Buddhist, new or ancient, he attained learning and achievement. If one has reason to speak his name, he is the *mahāpaṇḍita* Dge 'dun chos 'phel. At the time when the kind instructions on Madhyamaka had been received by me from his lips, he asked to look over all the scattered notes. Having done this, together with offering a verse of prayer [before] an image of Nāgārjuna, he said that all the notes should be gathered together in one place. While this final testament of the lord himself at the hour of his death was held in my heart, Bdud 'joms rin po che gave the paper on which it was to be written and said, "You must write it in the way [he told you to]." Not bearing to turn away from his exhortation, that lord's stupid student and servant, (376) called Zla ba bzang po of eastern Nyag, performed this task on the auspicious day of the waxing moon of the twelfth month of the Iron Hare year of the sixteenth cycle. May this serve as a cause for all these biased appearances of myself and others to be liberated into the mind-expanse of the unbiased pervasive lord Vajradhara.

¶250 *Svasti.* In the midst of thick darkness of the time of evil views, the friend who radiates the white light of the ambrosia of the definitive meaning, a new moon who is the wondrous second lord of nāgas, shines here today in the sky of the stainless teachings of the Muni.

¶251 Through analysis with the eye of dharma free from dust, the vajra words determine the *dharmatā*. Each part of the eloquent explanation, which did not exist before, revivifies and uplifts the tenets of an earlier time.

¶252 From this merit achieved in the relics of the dharma illustrated in that way, may all those with minds manifest the true meaning of the middle way, the mode of being passed beyond the illusory city of existence and peace.

¶253 This was stated with sincerity by 'Jigs bral ye shes rdo rje of Rgyal Khams [Bdud 'joms rin po che]. Jayantu. Sarvamaṅgalaṃ bhavantu.

A NOTE ON THE TIBETAN TEXT OF THE
KLU SGRUB DGONGS RGYAN

There is some uncertainty concerning the original publication of the text. As noted in chapter 1, GC's friend Bla chung a pho reports that the Tibetan minister Ka shod pa had the blocks of the *Klu sgrub dgongs rgyan* carved before GC's death. It is unclear whether this is accurate and, if so, what relation the Ka shod pa blocks bear to the existing block prints.

It appears that during his regency (1941–50), the Regent of Tibet, Stag brag rin po che (Ngag dbang blo bzang gsung rab mthu stobs bstan pa'i rgyal mtshan, 1874–1952), ordered a survey of Tibetan woodblocks. The date of the compilation is unclear, but it seems to have been completed before 1955. In this survey, the blocks of the *Klu sgrub dgongs rgyan* are listed among those owned or carved by Shel drung ding ri chos kyi rgyal mtshan (1897–1959). We find the following entry: "Adornment for Madhyamaka Nāgārjuna's Thought, critical explanation of A mdo Dge 'dun chos 'phel, compiled from notes by Nyag rong Zla ba bzang po, 78 folios" (A mdo dge 'dun chos 'phel gyi bstings bshad nyag rong pa zla ba bzang pos zin bris su bsgrigs pa dbu ma klu sgrub dgongs rgyan zhes par 78). See *Gangs can gyi ljongs su bka' dang bstan bcos sogs kyi glegs bam spar gzhi ji ltar yod pa rnams nas dkar chag spar thor phyogs tsam du bkod pa phan bde'i pad tshal 'byed pa'i nyin byed* in Ngawang Gelek Demo, ed., *Three Karchacks* (*dkar chag*), with an English introduction by E. Gene Smith, Gedan Sungrab Minyam Gyunphel Series (New Delhi: Ngawang Gelek Demo, 1970), 13:37b1–2 (242). Because the symbols for "8" and "2" are similar in Tibetan, the entry perhaps should read "72 folios," which is the length of the available block prints of the text. I am grateful to Tashi Tsering of the Amnye Machen Institute for this information.

The oldest surviving block-print edition of the text appears to be that from the private collection of the Dalai Lama, donated to the Library of Tibetan Works and Archives in Dharamsala, India (accession number 14452). Seventy-two folios in length, it ends at ¶249 of the translation (adding *sarvamaṅgalaṃ bhavantu*); that is, it lacks the final poem by Bdud 'joms rin po che. No other information is provided to support or refute the possibility that this text was printed from the blocks carved for Ka shod pa. Written in Tibetan on the back of the last page are the words "sixteenth Iron Hare year." This is the same year, 1951, mentioned in Zla ba bzang po's colophon, and it is unclear whether this inscription is simply repeating what is said there or whether it provides some independent evidence of the publication year. I am grateful to Losang Shastri of the Library of Tibetan Works and Archives and to Elizabeth Napper for kindly providing me with a photocopy of this edition.

The Library of Tibetan Works and Archives owns a second block print of the text. This one is identical to the first in page and margin size, number of lines per folio, and number of folios, but adds the poem by Bdud 'joms rin po che, translated here at ¶¶250–52, and the identification of its author at ¶253. Thus, this edition seems to have been printed from the same blocks as the first, with the additional material simply carved into the remaining space of the final block and a new title page carved. This edition has been published as *Dbu ma'i zab gnad sñiṅ por dril ba'i legs bśad klu sgrub dgoṅs rgyan* by D. T. Tashigang and B. P. O. Nemo, Smanrtsis sherig spendzod, vol. 112 (Leh: Ladakh, 1982). The title page carries the statement "Reproduced from a print from the blocks preserved at the Hor-khaṅ House in Lhasa," suggesting that a set of blocks, either the original or a new set, were preserved by GC's friend Hor khang bsod nams dpal 'bar, who would later publish GC's collected writings.

The text was published again in a xylographic format in a letter-press (rather than carved-block) edition, on bluish green paper. It is sixty-seven folios in length, with "Mani Printing Works, Kalimpong" printed in English on the final page. This printing press was owned by GC's friend Babu Tharchin. The edition carries no date but was presumably published in the late 1950s. According to Tashi Tsering, it was published by Bdud 'joms rin po che after having been edited by GC's friend and biographer, Bla chung a pho. If this is the case, Bla chung a pho introduced many errors into the text, most notably mistakenly changing almost all cases of *rigs* to *rig*. This edition carries an additional bene-dictory poem by Bdud 'joms rin po che (not included in the translation here), which reads: "legs bshad ga bur rdul 'dzag 'dzum zer ni I kun rmongs smag la 'khu ba'i ngang tshul gyis I 'phrul spar yar ngo'i phyogs su drangs 'dis kyang I rgyal bstan kun da'i dga' tshal 'phel byed shog." This might be translated as "The eloquent explanation of camphor powder mixed with light, offended by the darkness of complete obscuration, leads in the direction of the waxing moon of burgeoning miracles. May the jasmine garden of the Conqueror's teaching thereby grow." This same edition was reprinted by Shes rab rgyal mtshan in Delhi in 1983, with a three-folio preface by T. G. Dhongthog (Gdong thog Ngag dbang theg mchog bstan pa'i rgyal mtshan).

Beginning in 1990, the *Klu sgrub dgongs rgyan* was published in various col-lections of GC's works. The largest of these was edited by Hor khang bsod nams dpal 'bar as *Dge 'dun chos 'phel gyi gsung rtsom*, in three volumes (Lhasa: Bod ljongs bod yig dpe rnying dpe skrun khang, 1990), with a second edition in 1994.

The text appears in the second volume on pages 271–376. This edition is based on the block-print edition described above, and includes the poem added by Bdud 'joms rin po che. Subsequent versions of the text appear to be reprints of this Hor khang version (although I have not compared them word for word). These are included in the following collections of GC's works: T. G. Dhongthog, ed., *Dge 'dun chos 'phel gyi gsung rtsom* (Bir, India: Dzongsar Institute, 1991), 2:81–186; Bsod nams don grub et al., eds., *Mkhas dbang dge 'dun chos 'phel gyi gsung rtsom phyogs sgrig* (Chengdu, China: Si khron mi rigs dpe skrun khang, 1994), pp. 133–249; Rdo rje rgyal, ed., *Mkhas dbang dge 'dun chos 'phel gyi gsar rnyed gsung rtsom* (Zi ling, China: Zi ling mi rigs par khang, 2002), pp. 172–269. Rdo rje rgyal explains on page 269 that he has included the text in his collection of "newly discovered" (*gsar rnyed*) works of GC because previous editions mistakenly attributed it to Zla ba bzang po.

For the translation that appears here, I have used the 1990 Hor khang edition because it is the most accurate and widely available. It derives from the Lhasa blocks, with only minor variations, each of which is identified in the notes. For those who read Tibetan, the page numbers of the Hor khang edition have been included in parentheses in the body of the translation.

Where to add paragraphs in a translation of a Tibetan text is always a difficult question. In the block-print editions of the *Klu sgrub dgongs rgyan*, marks have been made in the text to indicate section breaks. It is interesting to note that only one appears in the first part of the text (at ¶47), preceding the long poem—possible evidence that this part was indeed written in GC's own hand, as Bla chung a pho states. Numerous breaks occur in the second part of the text, but they are too infrequent to serve as paragraph breaks. In his edition, Hor khang adds paragraphs to the text that generally correspond to the section breaks in the block print, with additional breaks added. I have followed Hor khang's paragraphs, noting where they deviate from breaks in the block print. For ease of reference, each of the paragraphs in the translation has been numbered and marked with ¶.

When the text indicates only the author or only the title of a cited passage, in the translation I have provided the missing element (author or title) of the passage. I have also provided in brackets the sources of the anonymous passages that I have been able to identify.

On the question of authorship, Hor khang bsod nams dpal 'bar writes,

Concerning whether or not the *Adornment for Nāgārjuna's Thought* is an actual composition of that excellent being, there is a difference of opinion between the Dge lugs and the Rnying ma. Some say that it is not the statements of Dge 'dun chos 'phel and that it is a mixture, with a great deal added to Zla ba bzang po's notes. Others identify it as an actual composition of Dge 'dun chos 'phel. Because there are these two [opinions], we have recently allowed it into the category of his compositions. When I consider it myself, I do not know whether or not it is purely the position of the lord of scholars himself. However, because it is undoubtedly a work that inspires qualms and questions about the assertions of others, it should be analyzed by everyone.

See Hor khang bsod nams dpal 'bar, ed., *Dge 'dun chos 'phel gyi gsung rtsom*, vol. 1 (Gangs can rig mdzod 10) (Lhasa: Bod ljongs bod yig dpe rnying dpe skrun khang, 1990), p. 3.

chapter

3

THE COMMENTARY

The full title of GC's text is *Dbu ma'i zab gnad snying por dril ba'i legs bshad klu sgrub dgongs rgyan*, which might be translated literally as *Eloquent Explanation that Combines the Profound Key Points of the Middle Way into Their Essence, An Adornment for Nāgārjuna's Thought*. This kind of grandiloquent title is typical of Tibetan Buddhist texts, and each of its words has connotations that could be explored at some length. In brief, however (and following the order of the Tibetan words), the "middle way" refers here not to the middle way between the extremes of self-indulgence and self-mortification, of which the Buddha spoke in his first sermon, but to the Madhyamaka, the Indian philosophical school said to have originated with Nāgārjuna, who, drawing on the perfection of wisdom (*prajñāpāramitā*) sūtras, set forth a middle way between the ideological extremes of existence and nonexistence. Precisely what constitutes this middle way was the subject of extensive discourse in India, and was elaborated even more extensively in Tibet.[1] There is general agreement among the

---

1. The *Adornment* is written for those well trained in the vocabulary and categories of Madhyamaka philosophy, especially as it is understood by Tsong kha pa and his Dge lugs followers. This chapter seeks to provide some of this background, but a full exposition of the various positions to which GC alludes and his criticisms of them would require an additional volume. For those who seek more detailed background on the Dge lugs interpretation of Madhyamaka, the following works are recommended.

For detailed studies of Tsong kha pa's views on the central problems of Madhyamaka philosophy, with substantial discussion of the Indian masters as well as Tsong kha pa's Tibetan predecessors and followers on these points, see David Seyfort Ruegg, *Three Studies in the History of Indian and Tibetan Madhyamaka Philosophy*, Studies in Indian and Tibetan Madhyamaka Thought, pt. 1 (Wien: Arbeitskreis für Tibetische und Buddhistische Studien Universität Wien, 2000) and David Seyfort Ruegg, *Two Prolegomena to Madhyamaka Philosophy: Candrakīrti's "Prasannapadā Madhyamakavṛttiḥ" on Madhyamakakārika I.1 and Tsoṅ kha pa blo bzaṅ grags pa / Rgyal tshab dar ma rin chen's "Dka' gnad / Gnas rgyad kyi zin bris," Annotated Translations*, Studies in Indian and Tibetan Madhyamaka Thought, pt. 2 (Wien: Arbeitskreis für Tibetische und Buddhistische Studien Universität Wien, 2002). See also Thupten Jinpa, *Self, Reality and Reason in Tibetan Philosophy: Tsongkhapa's Quest for the Middle Way* (London: RoutledgeCurzon, 2002).

sects of Tibetan Buddhism, however, that the Madhyamaka is the "highest" of the schools of Indian Buddhism in the sense that its tenets, albeit widely interpreted, are regarded as authoritative. This authority derives both from the claim that the Madhyamaka can refute the tenets of the other philosophical schools, Buddhist and non-Buddhist, and from the conviction that the Madhyamaka view must be understood by all those who seek to achieve buddhahood.

GC's title announces that it will consider the "profound key points" of the Madhyamaka. This apparently redundant translation seeks to render two terms. The first "profound" (*zab*) connotes both philosophical profundity, as well as a focus on the doctrine of emptiness. The practices leading to buddhahood are often divided into the profound (*zab mo*) and the vast (*rgyas pa*), with the former concerned with insight into the nature of reality and the latter with the deeds of the bodhisattva motivated by compassion. The use of the term *profound* here suggests that the text will focus upon the former. The term translated as "key points" (*gnad*) suggests that which is most essential or important; the term appears often in tantric literature to refer to the key points in the body where the *cakras* are located. The title announces that the text gathers these key points and unites them into an "essence." The Tibetan term is *snying po*, meaning that which is both most important and most fundamental, and is used in both the literal (*snying* means "heart" and medical treatises speak of the "essences" of various foods) and figurative senses.

This descriptive title is followed by an ornamental one, and it is that title, *Klu sgrub dgongs rgyan*, by which the text is known: *An Adornment for Nāgārjuna's Thought*. Nāgārjuna is an iconic figure in the history of Buddhism, especially in

---

For a translation of Tsong kha pa's most famous exposition of emptiness, his *Great Exposition of Insight* (*Lhag mthong chen mo*), see Joshua W. C. Cutler, ed., *The Great Treatise on the Stages of the Path to Enlightenment*, vol. 3 (Ithaca, NY: Snow Lion Publications, 2002), 105–372; pp. 163–83 are particularly pertinent. For a detailed study of Tsong kha pa's view on the compatibility of emptiness and conventional phenomena, as set forth in *Lhag mthong chen mo*, see Elizabeth Napper, *Dependent Arising and Emptiness* (Boston: Wisdom Publications, 1989).

For a translation of the views of Tsong kha pa's disciple Mkhas grub rje on many of these same issues, see José Ignacio Cabezón, *A Dose of Emptiness: An Annotated Translation of the "sTong thun chen mo" of mKhas grub dGe legs dpal bzang* (Albany: State University of New York Press, 1992).

For discussions of later Dge lugs thinkers, especially 'Jam dbyangs bzhad pa, author of the textbook literature on Madhyamaka at both Bla brang and 'Bras spungs monasteries (where GC studied), see Jeffrey Hopkins, *Meditation on Emptiness* (London: Wisdom Publications, 1983); Jeffrey Hopkins, *Emptiness Yoga* (Ithaca, NY: Snow Lion Publications, 1995); Jeffrey Hopkins, *Maps of the Profound: Jam-yang-shay-ba's Great Exposition of Buddhist and Non-Buddhist Views on the Nature of Reality* (Ithaca, NY: Snow Lion Publications, 2003); Daniel Cozort, *Unique Tenets of the Middle Way Consequence School* (Ithaca, NY: Snow Lion Publications, 1998); and Donald S. Lopez Jr., *A Study of Svātantrika* (Ithaca, NY: Snow Lion Publications, 1987).

Tibet. He was sufficiently well known in India that in several sūtras and tantras
the Buddha prophesies his advent, specifying in one text that he will appear
four hundred years after the Buddha passes into nirvāṇa (GC quotes a prophecy
from the *Laṅkāvatāra Sūtra* at ¶¶141, 161, and 180). According to traditional Tibetan biographies, he lived for six hundred years; modern scholars tend to place
him in the second century CE. A large number of works—philosophical, devotional, tantric—are attributed to him, the most famous (and widely accepted
by modern scholarship as his) being the *Mūlamadhyamakakārikā* or *Madhyamakaśāstra*, the *Treatise on the Middle Way*, the most important text of what
is known in Tibet as his "logical corpus" (*rigs tshogs*). A number of hymns
of praise (*stotra* or *stava*) are also ascribed to Nāgārjuna, and are known in
Tibet as the "devotional corpus" (*bstod tshogs*); some of these seem to present
what might be termed a more "substantialist" view than the famous philosophical works. The apparent discrepancy between these writings gave rise to an
important and long-lasting controversy in Tibet as to which of the two genres of Nāgārjuna's oeuvre should be regarded as his final and definitive position. This came to be known as the *rang stong gzhan stong*, or "self-emptiness,
other emptiness" controversy, that is, whether reality itself is empty of intrinsic
existence (self-emptiness) or whether reality itself is intrinsically existent, but
empty of (that is, lacking) any number of extraneous and polluting qualities
(*gzhan stong*).[2] The Dge lugs were, from the time of Tsong kha pa himself, firm
proponents of the position that Nāgārjuna's highest teachings were contained
in his logical corpus, whereas important Rnying ma and Bka' brgyud thinkers
(as well as the suppressed Jo nang) held that the devotional corpus was supreme.
This question attracted renewed interest in the so-called nonsectarian (*ris med*)
movement, which flourished in Khams and A mdo during the late nineteenth
and early twentieth centuries.[3]

Thus, the phrase "Nāgārjuna's thought" (*dgongs pa*) in GC's title is highly
charged. The term *thought* in Tibetan has a more specific meaning than it does
in English when one speaks of "the life and thought" of a famous philosopher. Here it has the sense of intention, of what Nāgārjuna really had in mind
when he made a particular statement. The term is especially important in Buddhist hermeneutics, where, faced with widely contradictory statements by the
Buddha in a vast range of sūtras, Buddhist scholastics developed strategies for

2. See David Seyfort Ruegg, "The Jo-naṅ-pas, A School of Buddhist Ontologists," *Journal of the
American Oriental Society* 83 (1963): 73–91.

3. See E. Gene Smith, *Among Tibetan Texts: History and Literature of the Himalayan Plateau*
(Boston: Wisdom Publications, 2001), 225–72, 355.

identifying what the Buddha meant, regardless of what he said. Such strategies, of course, are predicated on the claim that it is possible to discern the contents of the mind of the enlightened one, contents that may be quite different from the semantic meaning of his words. As we shall see, GC generally eschews such claims in his text, and thus the presence of the term is noteworthy.

Yet the claim of access to Nāgārjuna's true intention is countered by the fact that the text calls itself an "ornament" (*rgyan*), that is, a mere embellishment, an adornment, an accouterment whose purpose is merely to beautify and highlight the body of Nāgārjuna's mind. In other words, the text claims to offer nothing new, nothing of substance, only an accessory to the substance already present. This is, of course, a common Buddhist trope, for there is no greater transgression in Buddhist thought than innovation (*rang bzo*); all Buddhist discourse must be only the elaboration of what was always present in the Buddha's mind.

In fact, as we shall see, GC's work is only occasionally concerned specifically with Nāgārjuna's philosophy (regardless of where its true manifestation is to be found among his writings), directly quoting only eight passages from four of his works.[4] The presence of Nāgārjuna's name in the title of the work, therefore, is in many ways totemic, signaling that the work is concerned with the most sublime questions in Buddhist philosophy.

Furthermore, for an A mdo author from a Rnying ma family who was trained in the Dge lugs academy to select *Adornment for Nāgārjuna's Thought* as the title for his work is an immediate sign that a polemical text is to follow. And the title was not original to GC. It appears in the title of several earlier works, including one of the most famous polemical writings in Tibetan literature: the *Answer to Kar* (*Kar lan*) by Se ra rje btsun chos kyi rgyal mtshan (1469–1544), an attack on the eighth Karma pa, Mi bskyod rdo rje (1507–44), for criticizing Tsong kha pa. Dge lugs readers of GC's work would bring the same charge against GC.

Before reading past the title, it is important to note its orthography. Tibetan texts that are translations of Indian works will present the Sanskrit title transliterated into Tibetan, followed by the title translated into Tibetan. In some cases, the Sanskrit title will also occur in an Indic script, most often an ornamental script called Lantsha (or Lantsa) in Tibetan. Tibetan authors who

---

4. He cites the *Madhyamakaśāstra* four times, at ¶¶78, 113, 179, and 236. The last of these quotations is mistakenly attributed to Āryadeva, but as will be discussed in the section on authorship, there is evidence that this error was made by Zla ba bzang po and not by GC. In addition, he cites the *Vigrahavyāvartanī* at ¶¶118 and 179 and the *Ratnāvalī* at ¶78. He also cites the *Yuktiṣaṣṭikā* at ¶233, again mistakenly attributed to Āryadeva.

knew Sanskrit would sometimes provide a Sanskrit translation of the title of their work, in transliterated Tibetan. GC's text contains not only the Sanskrit translation of the title of his text, but also the Sanskrit title in Lantsha script, providing the pretense of yet even closer access to Nāgārjuna's thought, since the author knows not only how to read the sacred language of Buddhism, but how to write it.[5]

~~~~~

The 1990 edition of GC's collected works follows the title with the statement "Compiled as notes by Zla ba bzang po according to the oral instructions of Dge 'dun chos 'phel." An interpolation by the editor (it does not appear in the earlier editions of the text), this apparently innocuous statement is in fact highly charged. Furthermore, the name of the author of a Tibetan work traditionally appears not at the beginning of the work but at the very end, in the colophon. It is sufficient at this point simply to note this interpolation. We shall return to the vexed question of authorship and authority at the end, in the discussion of the colophon.

~~~~~

The work opens, as Tibetan texts traditionally do, with a poem called the expression of worship (*mchod brjod*). The verses of praise typically begin with the Buddha and move forward in time through the lineage of master and disciple, ending with the author's own teachers. Accordingly, GC begins with the Buddha:

(1) To the sharp weapons of the demons, you offered delicate flowers in return; When the enraged Devadatta pushed down a boulder [to kill you], you practiced silence; Son of the Śākyas, you are incapable of casting even an angry glance at your enemy; What intelligent person would honor you as a friend to protect him from the great enemy, fearful saṃsāra?

5. The Sanskrit title, as it appears on the title page of the Library of Tibetan Works and Archives edition reads (correcting for obvious orthographic errors), *Nāgārjunacchintālaṃkāra madhyamasya gambhiramarma garbhaḥ piṇḍasya sūktaṃ nāma vijahāra*. For *dgongs pa*, he does not use the more common *sandhi* or *abhisandhi*, but instead *cinta*, "thought," "idea." I have thus translated *dgongs pa* as "thought" rather than "intention," but this is based on the assumption that GC was aware of the connotations of the various terms in Sanskrit. He renders *rgyan* as *ālaṃkāra*, *zab gnad* as *gambhiramarma*, and *snying po* as *garbha*. For *legs bshad*, he does not choose the more standard *subhāṣita* but instead *sūkta*, "well spoken," meaning a wise saying, a beautiful verse, or a hymn of the Veda. The Sanskrit and transliterated Sanskrit titles are omitted from the edition of the text translated here in the collected works of GC edited by Hor khang bsod nams dpal 'bar. See *Dbu ma'i zab gnad snying por dril ba'i legs bshad klu sgrub dgongs rgyan*, in *Dge 'dun chos 'phel gyi gsung rtsom*, vol. 2 (Gangs can rig mdzod 11), ed. Hor Khang bsod nams dpal 'bar (Lhasa, Tibet: Bod ljong bod yig dbe rnying dbe skrun khang gis bskrun, 1990), p. 271.

According to various versions of the life of the Buddha, on the night of his enlightenment he was attacked by Māra, the deity of desire and death, who sought to deter the bodhisattva from his quest for a state beyond desire and death. While the buddha-to-be was seated under the Bodhi tree, Māra led a great army of demons against him. They hurled all manner of weapons at him—swords, spears, tridents, clubs, discuses—but as these approached the bodhisattva, he transformed them into blossoms, which rained harmlessly to the ground. Many years later, the Buddha's cousin Devadatta asked the Buddha, now aged, to turn the leadership of the monastic order over to him. When the Buddha refused, Devadatta made three unsuccessful attempts to murder him. In the second of these, Devadatta himself pushed a great boulder down a mountain as the Buddha walked on the path below. A piece of the boulder grazed the Buddha's toe, causing a small wound (that the Buddha is injured at all is explained as the last karmic result of his having committed fratricide in a previous lifetime). GC thus begins his work in a very traditional way, alluding to well-known events in the biography of the Buddha, events that illustrate the Buddha's great forbearance and kindness in response to those who seek to destroy him. But in the final line of this first stanza, he departs from the conventions of Buddhist piety. One would expect the final line to read: "What intelligent person would *not* honor you as a friend to protect him from the great enemy, fearful saṃsāra?" That is, as Buddhist authors have stated and restated over the millennia, only the Buddha (together with his dharma and his saṅgha) is the true place of refuge, the only reliable protection from the sufferings of the cycle of birth and death. Yet GC says something very different. He asks: in this world, fraught with danger, what intelligent person—the Tibetan term is *shes ldan*, literally, "endowed with consciousness," and having here the sense of "what person in his right mind"—would seek protection from someone who is incapable of even casting a malevolent glance at those who tried to kill him? What manner of protection could such a person provide?

Although GC was criticized by his opponents for what they regarded as a rude and even heretical question, GC appears to signal in the opening lines of this work that he has a different vision of the Buddha. This vision will become more developed as the text proceeds, but one can discern in this single question a different kind of Buddhist piety, one which does not see faith in the omniscient Buddha as something to be established by reasoning. Rather, by asking what intelligent person, what person in his or her right mind, would look to the Buddha for protection, GC is implying nothing about the Buddha, but about the generic "intelligent person." The Buddha is indeed the best of all protectors from the sufferings of saṃsāra, but this conclusion is not the outcome of an intellectual process. Indeed, GC seems to suggest that it is only the person lacking in intelligence, lacking in common sense, a person not in his or her right mind who would seek refuge in the Buddha. It is, indeed, counterintuitive for someone to "honor you as a friend to protect him from the great enemy, fearful saṃsāra." The opening lines of the text, customarily devoted to a traditional expression of piety, begin on a note of irony, or perhaps ironic piety; and irony will provide the dominant mood of the *Adornment*. GC opens his work by using the conventions of textual composition to make an unconventional point, thus signalling what is to follow.

The second stanza says,

(2) You are the eye of the world who displayed precise subtlety unerringly through your *aspiration* to the path of liberation, the source of the ambrosia of excellent *virtue* and soothing peace. The assembled philosophers ever respect you without *waxing* or waning, saying, "This is the lord of the *dharma*, the supreme lion of speakers."

In this four-line stanza, the first syllable in each line has a dot beneath it in the Tibetan text, that is, under the words in italics above: *virtue, aspiration, waxing, dharma*; in Tibetan, *dge 'dun chos 'phel*. It would be unusual even for a poet as unconventional and irreverent as GC to compose a poem around the syllables of his own name, especially in the expression of worship, and the content of the stanza is conventional and unremarkable. One would assume that it was composed not by GC but by Zla ba bzang po, raising the question of whether the person addressed in the stanza is the Buddha or GC. The third line reads,

(3) From the maṇḍala of the sun of your wisdom in the sky of Samantabhadra, in the lotus garden of my heart of meager knowledge, innate or acquired, (274) [grows] the glory of smiling stamen of eloquent explanation, surrounded a thousandfold by the rays of reasoning. May the bees of scholars of the three realms enjoy the sweet honey of the true transmission.

Although the authorship of this stanza is ambiguous (it is attributed by some to Zla ba bzang po), the imagery is familiar. The sunlight of the Buddha's wisdom shines forth from the sky of ultimate reality, here called Samantabhadra, the "All Good" (also the name of the primordial buddha, according to Rnying ma), into the author's heart. His heart is compared to a lotus garden, itself bereft of wisdom, whether naturally occurring or acquired through learning. The sunlight causes a lotus to blossom, and its stamen or filament (*kesara*) emerges. This stamen of "eloquent explanation" (*legs bshad*, the same term that appears in the title of the text) is surrounded by the rays of reasoning. The stanza ends with an invitation to scholars, likened to bees, to partake of the honey that will come from this lotus blossom. This honey is called the "true transmission" (*don brgyud*, literally, "meaning lineage").

After the expression of worship, the *Adornment* is both stylistically and topically divisible into two distinct parts. The first part of the work concludes with a series of four-line stanzas, many ending with the line "tha snyad tshad grub 'jog la blo ma bde" (I am uncomfortable about positing conventional validity). This section is in effect a self-contained work having a clear beginning, middle, and end. It is composed in GC's distinctive prose style, which makes frequent use of colloquialisms. And it deals with one topic, the critique of valid knowledge (*tshad ma*). It makes little mention of Madhyamaka or Nāgārjuna and does not in any specific sense merit the title *Adornment for Nāgārjuna's Thought*. As noted in chapter 1, a close friend of GC's, Bla chung a pho (Shes rab rgya mtsho), reports that after his return to Lhasa in 1946, GC presented him with this portion of what would become the *Adornment*, written in his own hand on an Elephant brand pad of Indian paper.

～～～

¶¶4–8 GC begins with a large question: what is truth? He addresses it within the context of what in Buddhist philosophy is called valid knowledge (*pramāṇa, tshad ma*). Although other schools of Indian philosophy identified several sources for accurate knowledge about the nature of reality (including testimony and the Vedas), the Buddhists were renowned for accepting only two: direct perception (*pratyakṣa*) and inference (*anumāna*). As long as direct perception—through the sense consciousnesses, or yogically, through the mental consciousness—was "undeceived" (a term that elicited considerable commentary in the treatises on logic and epistemology), that perception was regarded as a valid source of knowledge about the world. As long as an inference was based on a "correct reason" (again, a term analyzed at great length), that inference was regarded as providing reliable information.

GC was widely read in the scholastic literature on valid knowledge, one of the five topics of the Dge lugs monastic curriculum, and he could easily have explored the question in a traditional scholastic style, with extensive quotations from Dignāga, Dharmakīrti, and their myriad Indian and Tibetan commentators. Instead, however, he approaches the topic in a conversational style, largely free from technical vocabulary. He begins with a simple declaration: "All of our decisions about what is and is not are just decisions made in accordance with how it appears to our mind; they have no other basis whatsoever." That is, apart from our own opinions, there is no objective standard of truth, at least for unenlightened beings: as he says, "This is the case for all common beings." *Common being* (*pṛthagjana, so so skyes bu*) is a technical term here, referring to any being in the universe who has not directly perceived the ultimate truth of emptiness. Beings who have perceived reality directly are called "noble ones" (*āryan, phags pa*).

As long as there is agreement between two people on a given question, then their shared opinion is the truth; whatever disagrees with that is false. But two people can disagree, requiring that they appeal to a third party for resolution. That third party in many cases is not another person but a text, especially a religious work that the two people agree is authoritative. When GC offers an example, it is not a Buddhist sūtra but the Qur'an. Should we seek yet further evidence of GC's iconoclasm, we have here probably the first text in the history of Tibetan Buddhist literature whose initial textual citation is the Muslim holy book. But his choice is hardly random; he selects a text that Buddhists do not regard as authoritative, and he cites it on a question—the permissibility of eating camel meat—upon which Buddhists have no particular opinion.

Truth would therefore appear to be nothing more than the prevailing opinion of the majority, confirmed if necessary by a scripture deemed authoritative by that same majority. But does universal consensus make something true? Here, GC gives an example of a land in which the entire population suffers from jaundice ("bile disease"), causing everything they see to take on a yellowish tint. In this country, the color of a white conch is yellow. It is noteworthy that GC does not adopt a relativistic position here and concede that in the land of the jaundiced the white conch is yellow. Instead, he offers this as an example of the fallibility of the direct perception of those with tainted vision, even if all members of the community share that perception. The existence of something "is not decided even by the agreement of all the common beings of the three realms." Yet those who agree gain conviction and confidence from their shared belief, to the detriment to those in the minority: "When many hundreds of thousands of common beings to whose minds [things] appear similarly gather together, then the thing that they decide upon becomes firmly grounded and unchangeable, and those who speak in disagreement are proclaimed to be denigrators, nihilists, and so on." GC himself would be so slandered.

When common beings declare that something exists, they are simply declaring that it can appear within their sphere of awareness. When common beings declare that something does not exist, they are simply saying that it is beyond their sphere of awareness. GC notes that ultimate reality, the *dharmatā*, falls into the latter category.

He turns next to a story that appears in Candrakīrti's commentary to Āryadeva's *Four Hundred* (*Catuḥśataka*), in which a king is the only person in his realm who is spared from drinking rainwater that causes madness. When his subjects declare that the king is mad, he sees no other recourse but to drink the same water. GC concludes, "Thus, due to the single great insanity from our having continually drunk the crazing waters of ignorance from time immemorial, there is no confidence whatsoever in our decisions concerning what exists and does not exist, what is and is not." The fallibility of humans, then, is not simply a philosophical problem in GC's view, but the defining characteristic of saṃsāra, the beginningless cycle of birth and death.

GC thus rejects the suggestion that decisions made by the ignorant mind have any objective validity. The opinions of the unenlightened can never be anything more than opinion, that which fits into the narrow confines of the ignorant intellect. They carry no authority. It is important to place GC's claim within its philosophical context. One of the things for which Tsong kha pa is most famous is his attempt to harmonize the topics of *pramāṇa* and *madhyamaka*, that is, to set forth a system that was simultaneously able to posit a basis of valid knowledge while upholding the doctrine of the emptiness of all phenomena. Tsong kha pa is said to have been brought to tears while reading Dharmakīrti, so moved was he by the power of his logic, which Tsong kha pa came to see as the sole gateway to the experience of emptiness. And much of Dharmakīrti's work is devoted to discussing why direct perception and inference, and only those two, provide reliable knowledge about the world. GC will have nothing of this.

¶¶9–19 After this general discussion of the question of an objective standard of knowledge, GC moves to a more specifically Buddhist context as he has a hypothetical opponent raise an objection: "We concede that our decisions are unreliable, but when we follow the decisions of the Buddha, we are infallible." Detailed arguments for the omniscience and infallibility of the Buddha appear throughout Buddhist literature, the most famous in Tibet occurring in the second chapter of Dharmakīrti's *Commentary on Valid Knowledge* (*Pramāṇavārttika*). Again, although familiar with this argument, GC does not allude to it here. Instead, approaching the question in a more direct way, he simply asks, "[W]ho decided that the Buddha is infallible?"

> If you say, "The great scholars and adepts like Nāgārjuna decided that he is infallible," then who decided that Nāgārjuna is infallible? If you say, "The Foremost Lama [Tsong-kha-pa] decided it," then who knows that the Foremost Lama is infallible? If you say, "Our kind and peerless lama, the excellent and great so and so decided," then infallibility, which depends on your excellent lama, is decided by your own mind.

Here, GC satirizes the notion of lineage that is so central to Tibetan Buddhism, according to which one receives teachings from one's teacher, who received them from his teacher, who received them from his teacher, and thus from Tibet back to India, and in India, through a lineage of teachers, back to the Buddha himself. It is this lineage that established authority, authenticity, certainty. But GC disrupts this lineage of authority by bringing it down to the present moment, and the narrow perspective of the unenlightened mind of the current disciple. It is the disciple who declares the infallibility of his own teacher, and so on back in time. Thus, rather than the lineage of teacher and student carrying authenticity forward in time to the present, for GC, it is the ignorance of the present that is injected into the lineage of the past, infecting it with uncertainty and fallibility backward through time across the generations, until it seems to call into question the authority of the Buddha himself. As we shall see below, GC is not challenging the omniscience of the Buddha; he is, rather, calling into question the ability of the unenlightened mind to contain and thus control enlightenment.

In order to make his point painfully clear, he cites a Tibetan proverb, which says that "it is a tiger who vouches for a lion, it is a yak who vouches for a tiger, it is a dog who vouches for a yak, it is a mouse who vouches for a dog, it is an insect who vouches for a mouse. Thus, an insect is made the final voucher for them all." The word clumsily translated here as "voucher" (*dbang po*) has the sense of both a witness and a judge, a person who can certify the claim of another. GC plays on the traditional trope of the Buddha as the lion whose roar of the dharma frightens away the other denizens of the forest, the non-Buddhist philosophers, but then immediately turns the metaphor to his own purpose, with each creature in a descending order of nobility being called upon to judge its superior. Thus, Nāgārjuna is a tiger; Tsong kha pa, the first Tibetan mentioned in the lineage above, is a yak. The lineage deteriorates to a dog, to a mouse, and then to an insect, whose tiny mind becomes the final judge of all those above it.

Having thus dismissed the opinion of the majority and the authority of the enlightened as standards of truth, GC finally introduces the topic of *pramāṇa*, valid knowledge. His hypothetical interlocutor says, "Since the mere agreement of the majority is not sufficient, it must be decided from the point of view of valid knowledge." A consciousness is considered valid if it perceives its object in a nondeceptive way; that is, it must perceive its object correctly. GC notes the circularity of this doctrine: one cannot decide whether the object is perceived correctly until one knows that the perceiving consciousness is valid; one cannot know whether the perceiving consciousness is valid until one knows that the object has been perceived correctly. "Therefore," he asks, "when does one decide?" Seeking to limit the possibility of error by calling in further forms of perception—looking at an object, touching it, asking a friend to look at it—in no way solves the problem, since each of these forms is subject to error. "For two people with bile disease, a yellow conch can be seen with their eyes and touched with their hands, and they both agree that it is yellow."

Having discredited all knowledge of the unenlightened as nothing more than opinion, GC concedes that this is our lot and that there is no alternative. "Therefore, as long as we remain in this land of saṃsāra, it is true that there is no other method than simply making decisions, having placed one's confidence in this mind in which one can have no confidence in any of the decisions that it makes." The objects of our everyday experience are fictions, and we have no choice but to make decisions about them with our ignorant mind, which has created those fictions. What GC seems to find particularly irksome, however, is that the unenlightened are not content to limit their limited mind to the conventional world, but seem compelled to make all manner of grandiose statements about the ultimate, about the nature of reality, to give a name to all manner of supramundane qualities, each of which is beyond expression and beyond imagination.

GC concludes his discussion of the impossibility of valid knowledge by noting the range of opinion on the fundamental question of whether external objects exist apart from consciousness. He notes that the great fifth-century Theravāda master Buddhaghosa—whose works were not translated into Tibetan and which GC encountered during his visit to Sri Lanka—stated that external objects exist. The Yogācāra master Asaṅga said that external objects ("the imaginary") do not exist but that consciousness ("the dependent") does intrinsically exist. The Madhyamakas, however, said that even consciousness does not intrinsically exist. If these great masters could not agree on such a central question, what hope is there for the benighted?

¶¶20–28 GC continues his consideration of the limits, and limitations, of perception, arguing that our world is comprised by what we can perceive, but that it is a mistake to conclude that the universe is ultimately confined to what the ignorant mind can encompass. "[T]o think that the earth, stones, mountains, and rocks that we see now are still to be seen vividly when we are buddhas is very much in error." He upholds the tenet of the Madhyamaka that all beings will eventually achieve buddhahood, but he does so in order to raise a different point: how enlightenment is understood by the unenlightened. And here he focuses not so much on the mind but on the body, on the physical form as the container of consciousness, and how the size and shape and configuration of that container color the experience of the world, or perhaps more precisely, how that container creates the world. One frequently encounters the claim that different types of sentient beings see things differently, that what is water to the human is ambrosia to the god and pus to a ghost. GC does not repeat this point (he alludes to it at ¶231); instead, he describes the unique perceptions of different beings, how for the donkey the taste of grass is sweet, how for the rooster there is the daily intimation of the dawn, and that these perceptions are present only when consciousness inhabits the body of a donkey or a rooster. He is referring here to the process of rebirth, how consciousness gains and loses specific capacities as it migrates from one body to the next. Turning to humans, he notes that our world is defined entirely by our sense organs. If we had more than five senses, our world would be very different; if our eyes were set vertically rather than horizontally on our face, our world would be different. "It is impossible to hear any sound that does not fit within this small hole of the ear." Consciousness is therefore limited because it is embodied. To forget this and assume that the universe is only what can be comprehended by the five senses and the ignorant mind is a grave error. Indeed, if we were able to perceive reality as it is with our present awareness, there would be no need to follow the Buddhist path. "Therefore, the ultimate purpose for cultivating the noble path is in order to newly understand what the mind did not perceive and the eyes did not see before."

Yet for GC the gap between the unenlightened and the enlightened is wide. Mahāyāna sūtras often describe the "buddha fields" of different buddhas—the most famous being the Land of Bliss, Sukhāvatī of the buddha Amitābha—and how they differ from our world. These buddha fields are invariably flat, lacking the various asymmetries and imperfections, the ups and downs, that mar our world. Observing our cosmos, called the Sahā world, a bodhisattva from another buddha field was moved to observe, "Lord, just like priceless beryl gemstones thrown in the mud, Lord, so are those bodhisattvas and mahāsattvas who are reborn in the world-system Sahā to be regarded."[6] The difference is indeed often expressed as that between mud and jewels. And GC himself cautions against thinking that the earth and stones we perceive today will still be perceived when we are buddhas. But the jewels that bedeck the buddha fields are also products of our limited imagination. All the assumptions that we hold about the world of enlightenment, what GC calls "supramundane qualities," are simply concocted from the realm of rebirth, indeed, from the human realm alone. The realm of enlightenment as we imagine it is not utterly different, it is simply a beautified version of the human realm. Akaniṣṭha (referring here not to the highest heaven in the Realm of Form but to the buddha field Ghanavyūha) is adorned with jewels because humans find jewels to be beautiful. The buddhas in the buddha fields in the form of the saṃbhogakāya, the "enjoyment body," are adorned with thirty-two major marks and eighty ancillary marks because humans find these physical attributes to be beautiful.

From one perspective, GC is merely reiterating the familiar doctrine of upāya, skillful methods: the Buddha teaches what is most beneficial to his audience, regardless of whether it is ultimately true. In the opening scene of the Vimalakīrti Sūtra, the Buddha reveals the marvels of the buddha fields to his audience, prompting someone to ask why it is that the fields of other buddhas are so splendid, filled with jeweled lotuses, while the field of Śākyamuni Buddha, that is, our own world, is so ordinary. The Buddha then touches the earth with his toe, and the world is miraculously transformed into a bejeweled paradise. He explains that what he has revealed is the true nature of his land, that he uses his miraculous powers to make it appear squalid in order that his disciples will develop a sense of renunciation and practice the path. It seems in this sūtra, then, that our world, when seen in its true nature, is a paradise.

But GC argues here that even the jewel-encrusted buddha field is a product of our limited imagination. It is limited not simply by the confines of human understanding, but by historical and geographical circumstance as well. That

6. The statement appears in The Dispelling of Ajātaśatru's Remorse (Ajātaśatru-kaukṛtya-vinodanā-sūtra). See Donald S. Lopez ed., Buddhist Scriptures (London: Penguin Classics, 2004), 178.

is, the buddhas and their buddha fields are described as they are in the sūtras because the sūtras were set forth for an audience of humans living in ancient India. The enjoyment body of a buddha, therefore, is bedecked in the raiment of an Indian king. If the Buddha had preached the dharma in China, the enjoyment body would have a long beard and be dressed in a dragon robe. If the Buddha had preached the dharma in Tibet, he would have described the buddha field as flowing with buttered tea. This is not, it must be noted, simply a Tibetan argument for the cultural construction of reality. For GC, each of these appearances was specifically construed by the Buddha in order to appeal most efficiently to the predilections of the limited minds of his audience. As for reality as it is known by the omniscient Buddha, what GC calls "the inconceivable secret," "it is certain that it is not suitable to be spoken in our presence, or that even though it were spoken, it is something that we could not understand." The chasm between the ignorant mind and the enlightened mind appears to be only widening.

The sūtras describe a buddha with skin the color of gold, with the image of wheels on the soles of his feet, with a crown protrusion atop his head. They describe such a buddha seated on a throne of jewels set upon the backs of lions. These are things that the ignorant mind can comprehend. But the contents of the sūtras are not limited to accommodations to human comprehension. The sūtras describe other qualities of a buddha, qualities that the ignorant mind cannot comprehend, and it is to this, the literally inconceivable, that GC next turns. How are we to understand the statement that the Buddha can make an aeon equal to an instant? How can we understand the statement that the Buddha can place a world system inside an atom?

Time and space are the defining categories of the world. An instant is the smallest unit of time, an aeon is the longest; an atom is the smallest unit of space, a universe is the largest. If the Buddha is able to make the same these things that stand at the extremes of difference, what implications does this have for our world, and how do we explain the Buddha's ability? If we attribute it to his magical powers, then a buddha should also be able to take something that is empty of intrinsic existence and endow it with intrinsic existence. He should be able to immediately transform a sentient being into a buddha. But the sūtras do not report such powers. The categories of the conventional—instants and aeons, atoms and universes—define our world and our deeds within it. To deny the existence of these categories is to fall into nihilism. "[C]ould there be a sin more heavy than the Buddha's putting that very nihilism into practice when he actually makes them the same size?"

The Buddha, of course, cannot be charged with nihilism. There must be some solution to the dilemma, some way of harmonizing the ultimate and the conventional. One solution would be to maintain the conventions of time and space and then proclaim that the Buddha's ability to make an atom and a universe equal in size is proof of the immense power of the Buddha to turn what is not into what is. The Buddha's magical transformation, then, would be a special case. GC rejects this perspective that makes the conventional the arbiter of existence. He prefers the ultimate perspective. For the Buddha, large and small are not contradictory, hence he is not turning the unequal into the equal; for his nondual wisdom, they are already equal, they are of one taste. For GC, the magical powers of the Buddha are not at play; it is our own ignorant mind that is the magician. "Therefore, a world not fitting into an atom is a great feat of magic conjured by this very misconception of ours, which we choose to call valid knowledge." In order to illustrate his point, GC gives other examples of the performance of the impossible, selecting as his exemplars two figures most respected in the Dge lugs for their philosophical acuity. Candrakīrti milks a picture of a cow and Atiśa shrinks his body to fit inside a tiny mold.

Thus, the central question that GC confronts here is that of the relationship between the unenlightened state and the enlightened state, and the ability of the unenlightened mind to make valid judgments. He wants rather radically to discredit any conventional knowledge that may be claimed about the state of enlightenment while constantly recalling those wondrous abilities ascribed to the Buddha which are logically impossible. He lampoons the monks who are willing to sacrifice the rhetorical and philosophical impact of such miracles on the altar of dogmatic consistency. He sees in their obsession with consistency a domestication of the rhetoric of enlightenment, until the sūtras serve no other purpose than to validate their plodding logic and the operations of ignorance.

¶¶29–34 Having dispensed with instants and aeons, GC turns next to consider the ultimate of antipodes, existence and nonexistence. In his first sermon, the Buddha described a middle way between the extremes of indulgence and asceticism he had known prior to his enlightenment. For Nāgārjuna and the Madhyamakas, however, a middle way must be found between existence and nonexistence; centuries of commentary, in India and Tibet, have been devoted to that task. Here, GC takes his turn.

He begins by describing existence and nonexistence as yet another of the confining categories of the ignorant mind; that we see them as mutually exclusive and are unable to imagine something that is neither existent nor nonexistent is, again, simply due to the limitations of our awareness. Thus, from this limited perspective, someone who proclaims, as Nāgārjuna does at the beginning of his *Treatise on the Middle Way*, that reality is free from the eight extremes—of cessation, production, annihilation, permanence, coming, going, difference, and sameness—would be condemned as a nihilist.

The diet of the nomads of the Northern Plain (Byang thang) of Tibet is so limited that the only sweet thing they know is the taste of milk. Thus, for them, whatever is sweet must be milk, and whatever is not milk cannot be sweet. The defining categories of sweetness for their palate therefore are milk and nonmilk; it is impossible for them to conceive of something that is sweet but is not milk, and anyone who claimed that there was such a thing would be derided by them. Someone whose experience of the world is sufficiently limited that he only knows two people, one named Rnam rgyal and one named Tshe ring, would conclude that when someone is at home and he knows that Rnam rgyal is elsewhere at the moment, then that person must be Tshe ring. "[O]ur mind continually oscillates between existence and nonexistence. There is no method for abiding in something that is other than those two." Yet the sūtras clearly state that the middle path is between existence and nonexistence. What are we to make of such declarations?

Here, GC turns his sights on his former monastic fellows, the Dge lugs pa geshes of his day. For them, he says, how one understands statements about a middle way between existence and nonexistence depends above all on who makes the statement. If the statement appears in the writings of "an earlier Tibetan scholar," that is, a Rnying ma pa or Bka' brgyud pa before the advent of Tsong kha pa, then that person is to be dismissed as a nihilistic fool. If, however, the statement appears in a sūtra, or in a treatise by Nāgārjuna, then the geshes "patch it with words" so that statements that reality is neither existent nor nonexistent are interpreted to mean that reality is neither ultimately existent nor conventionally nonexistent. "In fact, the only difference is that if they direct refutations at the Buddha, they fear being labeled evil persons with evil views, [whereas] if they are able to refute earlier Tibetans, they are labeled heroic scholars." The more forgiving of these geshes, he notes, will sometimes excuse the errors of the earlier Tibetans because they wrote without the advantage of Tsong kha pa's insights.

GC observes, however, that if one confines oneself to the words themselves, there is no difference between what the Buddha said and what the earlier Tibetans said, yet the Buddha is extolled and the Tibetans are condemned.

Furthermore, the enlightened Buddha saw no need to make the kinds of qualifications of existence and nonexistence that the geshes feel compelled to provide. "Therefore, if the earlier Tibetans and the Buddha are to be refuted, refute them equally. If they are to be affirmed, affirm them equally." GC's contempt for those who focus not on what was said, but on who said it, anticipates much of the debate over the authorship of the *Adornment*.

GC concludes this section of the text by stating again that we must accept that all of our decisions are fabrications of a mind that has no objective foundation. He concedes that such acceptance creates a great fear, the beginning of the fear of emptiness, which must be feared before it can be comprehended. To leave our misconceptions in place, claiming that to call them into question is to fall into nihilism, and then to concoct something called "true establishment" and claim that it is this that must be refuted, "is just the talk of some scholars who are skilled in dry words."

¶¶35–46 In the next section, GC turns to a different, but related, question, that of the conception of self in the unenlightened. Buddhism is of course renowned for the doctrine of no-self (*anātman*), that there is no permanent, partless, independent entity among the impermanent constituents of mind and body. The conception of such a self, indeed, is called the most fundamental form of ignorance; it is the root of all suffering. Yet one person is physically and mentally distinguishable from another; one person's misdeeds do not produce negative karmic consequences for someone else; when one person achieves enlightenment, it is not the case that all beings in the universe also do so. Thus, if Buddhism rejects the idea of "self," it admits the idea of persons. And although Buddhist philosophical treatises are filled with analyses of the "I" and the "self," the Buddha, and other enlightened beings, commonly speak in the first person singular, and virtues like self-reliance and being a light unto oneself are commonly extolled. There would thus seem to be two types of "I," two types of "self," two types of "person": one that does not exist and one that does. The problem is drawing the line that divides them. If the purpose of Buddhist insight is to destroy the conception of self, precisely what that self is must first be identified. This identification is made through a specific process in one of the more famous Dge lugs systems for meditating on emptiness, or no-self, and it is to this process and its assumptions that GC objects. Before coming to his objection, some additional background is required.

According to the Madhyamaka school as interpreted by Tsong kha pa, the belief in self can only be destroyed through recourse to reasoning: the belief in self is an innate conception that besets all sentient beings, but it is incapable of withstanding reasoned analysis. Numerous reasonings, such as the lack of the self's being one or many, are therefore set forth in Madhyamaka texts, each designed to prove that the self does not exist. For Tsong kha pa, *self* refers to an intrinsic existence that is falsely ascribed to persons and to other phenomena. He is fond of citing Candrakīrti's gloss of *self* in his commentary on Āryadeva's *Four Hundred* (*Bodhisattvayogacaryācatuḥśatakaṭīkā*) as "that which does not rely on another" (*gzhan la rag ma las pa*).

Both the self of persons and the self of phenomena must be negated, but the self of persons is usually attacked first because it is more intimate. The first step in a fourfold procedure is therefore the identification of this self, called "the object of negation" (*dgag bya*). Dge lugs authors often quote Śāntideva (at *Bodhicaryāvatāra* IX.140) on this point: "Without contacting the imagined object, its non-existence cannot be apprehended." The first step thus involves a watchful awareness of precisely what the self is like.

The next three steps involve making this self the subject of a logical statement. A Buddhist syllogism has three parts: a subject, a predicate, and a reason. In order for the syllogism to be valid, certain relations must obtain among these three parts. First, there must be pervasion (*khyab pa*), that is, whatever falls under the category of the reason must necessarily fall under the category of the predicate. Second, the reason must be a property of the subject. If both of these relations obtain, then the predicate is a property of the subject and the syllogism is correct. For example, one of the first correct syllogisms learned by Dge lugs monks is, "The subject, the color of a white conch, is a color, because of being white." Here, the subject is the color of a white conch, the predicate is being a color, and the reason is being white. In order for this statement to be correct, it is necessary first for there to be pervasion; that is, that whatever is white is necessarily a color. Second, the reason must be a property of the subject; that is, the color of a white conch must be white. Because both of these relations obtain, the predicate is a property of the subject (the color of a white conch is a color), the syllogism is correct, and the thesis (the subject plus the predicate) is proved.

In meditation on emptiness, the self is made the subject of a syllogism. Any number of reasons may used to prove that the self does not exist. For example, the syllogism could be, "The subject, the self of persons, does not intrinsically exist because of not being either intrinsically the same as or different from the aggregates." Here, "the aggregates" refers to the classic Buddhist division of the constituents of the person into five groups: forms, feelings, discriminations, conditioning factors, and consciousnesses. Since everything in the universe is either the same as or different from one of these constituents, anything that is not either the same as or different from them does not exist. That is, there is pervasion between the reason and the predicate. The second step in the proof of the syllogism would be to establish that the reason is a property of the subject— in this case, that the self is not intrinsically the same as or different from the five aggregates. To establish that this is indeed the case requires a long and detailed investigation, examining each of the aggregates (and their subcategories) in turn in an effort to determine whether any of them is the self. Assuming that such effort fails to result in the identification of the self with one of the aggregates, the next step would be to determine whether the self is intrinsically different from the aggregates. For this to be the case, the self would have to exist entirely apart from the mind and the body. This is a claim that is rejected in Madhyamaka. With it now established that the reason is a property of the subject, one moves automatically to the conclusion that the predicate is a property of the subject, that the self does not exist.

Tsong kha pa calls the identification of the object of negation "perceiving clearly the aspect of the I, the substratum for the innate awareness that thinks, 'I am,' and understanding the essential point of making the I appear."[7] What he means by this phrase is that there is, or more accurately, there appears to be, an I that is the referent of the mind that thinks, "I am." It is this I that must be identified at this point in the meditation. But this I is elusive, and special techniques must be employed to cause it to show itself. Dge lugs texts in genres such as "instructions on the view" (lta khrid) and "stages of the path" (lam rim) provide specific techniques for fabricating the false sense of self. One of the most famous of these is to sit in meditation and imagine being falsely accused of a crime. At that moment, it is said, one will feel righteous indignation: "I did not." The referent of that "I" is the autonomous self that, in reality, is an illusion. The belief in such a self is the "innate conception of self" and the fundamental ignorance, and it is this conception that must be destroyed. This, in brief, would be the standard Dge lugs description of "identifying the object of negation."[8]

---

7. Tsong kha pa, *Dbu ma'i thal 'gyur ba'i zab lam dbu ma'i lta khrid*, in *The Collected Works (gsuṅ 'bum) of the Incomparable Lord Tsoṅ-kha-pa Blo-bzaṅ-grags-pa* (*Khams gsum chos kyi rgyal po shar tsong kha pa chen po'i gsung 'bum*), vol. *tsha* (New Delhi: Mongolian Lama Guru Deva, 1978), 2a5–6 (821 in the Guru Deva edition).

8. For a more detailed discussion, see Donald S. Lopez Jr., "Painting the Target: On the Identification of the Object of Negation (*dgag bya*)," in *Changing Minds: Contributions to the Study of Buddhism and Tibet in Honor of Jeffrey Hopkins*, ed. Guy Newland (Ithaca, NY: Snow Lion Publications, 2001), 63–81.

GC finds this problematic. He first makes note of the Dge lugs assertion that all cases of the thought "I," even among the unenlightened, are not necessarily cases of ignorance; that is, they are not necessarily cases of the innate conception of self, but are instead valid states of consciousness. The standard Dge lugs view is that ordinary sentient beings, including those who ascribe to false philosophical views, have many thoughts of "I" in which the I is *not* either wrongly conceived to be intrinsically existent or correctly conceived to be nominally existent. GC wonders, then, why a stronger form of that same thought should somehow become invalid, should somehow become a case of ignorance, a case of the conception of intrinsic existence or, as he refers to it here, the conception of true existence (*bden 'dzin*).

He then alludes to the standard technique of fabricating the false sense of self by imagining in meditation a case of being falsely accused of being a thief. If this is indeed a sense of false accusation, how can the honest and accurate thought "I am not a thief" be construed as a form of ignorance? If the weak thought "I am" is not a form of ignorance, why should the thought "I am not a thief" be a form of ignorance? If it is a form of ignorance, it would seem that the Dge lugs pas should claim that any veridical statement made in response to an erroneous statement is also a form of error. The difference between thinking "I am" and "I am not a thief" is only one of strength of conviction.

As GC has already made clear, it is his view that there are no valid forms of knowledge among the unenlightened, and therefore all thoughts prior to the realization of emptiness, all thoughts of "I," regardless of their strength, are cases of ignorance.

His second problem with the standard instructions for identifying the object of negation is that they are offered to those who have not yet understood emptiness; otherwise, why would they need the instructions? Yet Tsong kha pa is renowned for his assertion that until one has understood emptiness, it is impossible to distinguish between mere existence or conventional existence (which is true in the sense that it exists) and intrinsic existence or true existence (which is false in the sense that it is utterly nonexistent). If this is the case, how is it possible for someone who has not understood emptiness to identify the object of negation, to pinpoint the I that does not exist in contradistinction from the I that does exist? Because the Prāsaṅgikas deny true existence and the Svātantrikas uphold true existence conventionally, it is impossible for them to engage in a debate in which the subject of the syllogism is commonly understood by both parties. What hope is there for the person undertaking his or her first meditation on emptiness? How could such a person possibly correctly identify the object of negation?

GC would argue, then, that the object of negation as identified by the Dge lugs pas is little more than a scholastic epiphenomenon, a bit of sophistry ultimately designed to validate the operations of ignorance. To identify the object of negation, as defined by the Dge lugs, in meditation on emptiness, one must have already understood emptiness, in which case the meditation would be pointless. The degree of philosophical sophistication required to identify the object of negation is necessarily absent in those for whom the instructions are apparently intended. The solution, for GC, is to identify an object of negation that is more prosaic and quotidian, yet at the same time more fundamental and hence more profound. For him, every thought of "I" is ignorance. "If it is the case that the mind which is the conception of true existence, grown accustomed to from time immemorial, does not occur more than a couple of times a day, then it is most amazing."

The conception of self is twofold: the conception of a self of persons and a conception of a self of phenomena. For the latter, *self* does not mean a subjective sense of an autonomous "I," obviously, but instead a quality of self-sufficiency and independence, what is termed "true existence" (*bden grub*). GC thus turns next to the conception of true existence regarding not the person but the objects of everyday experience—in the language of Tibetan Buddhist epistemology, "pillars and pots." For GC, the conception that objects are truly established is so familiar that it is as if instinctive. In India, if a boy saw a man approaching who was (1) his father, (2) a teacher, and (3) a member of the brahmin caste, his first thought would be not "a brahmin is coming" but "my father is coming," because the man's identity as his father is most familiar, most natural, most intimate to the boy. In the same way, when an unenlightened being sees a pot, the first thought, whether it be conscious or not, is that the pot is truly established. Dge lugs texts speak of the "object of negation by reasoning" (*rigs pa'i dgag bya*), in this case, the falsely existent pot which must be negated, leaving the conventionally existent pot, which is not to be negated by reasoning. For GC, such talk is so much sophistry; "the pot must be negated, the pillar must be negated, existence must be negated, nonexistence must be negated." And he emphasizes that this is not merely the position of scholars of old, of the Rnying ma pa. He quotes a famous line from the distinguished Dge lugs scholar and tutor of the Qianlong emperor, Lcang skya rol pa'i rdo rje (1717–86), who wrote in his *Song of the View* (*Lta ba'i mgur*), "Leaving this vivid appearance where it is, they search for something protruding to refute." That is, the object of negation should be the object itself as it vividly appears to the senses and to the mind; the object of negation is not an appendage.

One may object that such an unrefined approach runs the risk of nihilism, that in refuting the truly existent and falsely conceived object, one may destroy the conventionally existent object as well. But GC dismisses this as a pointless worry. No one would think that the pot that he sees in front of him is utterly nonexistent. Instead, one would think that the pot does not exist as it appears. According to the Dge lugs interpretation of Madhyamaka, objects appear falsely to the senses of all beings other than buddhas. One seeks in meditation to develop a vision of emptiness, the lack of true existence. When one rises from meditation and again perceives the objects of ordinary experience, those objects appear to the senses to truly exist. However, if the vision of emptiness has been powerful, one does not assent to such an appearance; one views objects as like illusions, appearing one way but existing another. This is called the composite of appearance and emptiness. Thus, to perceive objects as truly existent but to know that that perception is false is not nihilism—it is the Madhyamaka view. According to the Dge lugs taxonomies of the path, the "illusionlike *samādhi*" (*sgyu ma lta bu'i ting nge 'dzin*) does not technically occur until an advanced stage of the path to enlightenment. But GC, propounding a kind of populist Madhyamaka here, seeks to grant the awareness of illusion to anyone who is able to conclude that things do not exist as they appear, "even though the yellow hat abbot," that is, the Dge lugs geshe, would object. For GC, the best course is to consign everything to the fire of reasoning; false conceptions will be destroyed, and the illusionlike conventional objects will survive.

¶¶47–55 GC next considers the role of reasoning among the unenlightened. He begins by having his hypothetical opponent ask, "Without asserting that conventions are validly established, how is it that you do not lack confidence in dependent origination?" By "conventions" he means conventional truths (*saṃvṛti satya, kun rdzob bden pa*), all phenomena in the universe other than emptiness, which is the ultimate truth (*paramārtha satya, don dam bden pa*); conventional truths include pillars, pots, the body, consciousness, thoughts, and the Buddha himself. They exist, but they do not exist in the way that they appear to beings other than buddhas. One of the hallmarks of Tsong kha pa's interpretation of Nāgārjuna is that although conventional truths are deceptive in that they appear to intrinsically exist when in fact they do not, they nonetheless are valid from the perspective of functionality: a pillar can support a beam, a pot can hold water. Furthermore, although conventional truths are empty of intrinsic existence, they are nonetheless subject to the laws of cause and effect: a seed produces a sprout; the combination of clay, water, and the efforts of a potter produce a pot. Thus, despite the reality of emptiness, causation, called here "dependent origination," remains valid. Indeed, Tsong kha pa, following Nāgārjuna, argues for the compatibility of emptiness and dependent origination. GC's hypothetical opponent thus asks whether his previous critique of valid knowledge does not carry the danger of denying the conventional viability of the objects of ordinary experience.

GC responds sarcastically that what is referred to as "establishment by valid knowledge" is little more than the pedantic application of syllogistic reasoning ("establishment by reasoning of the three modes") to the obvious functions of everyday life, bringing an unnecessarily minute analysis to the coarse objects of experience, providing thereby levels of differentiation to "the objects of artificial ignorance," that is, the ignorance unique to humans that arises from inculcating false philosophical systems. Dge lugs pa scholars are renowned for describing the functionality of conventional truths with terms such as *trustworthy* and *infallible*, but GC sees this as useless verbiage adding to what everyone, "all six types of transmigrators," instinctively knows from their own experience. A child learns from cruel experience that fire is hot. For the father to then reprimand the child by presenting a syllogism about the effect of fire on human flesh would be superfluous. GC mocks this as an example of what is often extolled as "proving it with the valid knowledge of scripture and reasoning."

Thus, GC does not see any particular danger of nihilism in denying the existence of valid knowledge among the unenlightened. He argues that the objects of ordinary experience—earth, stone, mountains, and rocks—will remain as the constituents of the unenlightened world, whether their existence is logically proved or not. And if mountains remain, there is no reason to fear that the objects of ordinary experience that are central to Buddhism—the three jewels, the law of cause and effect, dependent origination—will not also persist. That is, for GC, the denial of valid knowledge has no negative consequences for the practice of Buddhism. All these appearances will be transformed upon the attainment of enlightenment. If the "good things" such as the three jewels were somehow to disappear first, leaving the rocks behind, then the ultimate nature of reality would not be beneficent or even Buddhist, confirming instead the beliefs of "common beings of base nature who lack religion." In contrast, GC believes that at the moment of enlightenment, all conventionalities will disappear simultaneously, to be replaced by the union of body and mind, the union of the ultimate truth and conventional truth, the union of virtue and sin. The Buddha's omniscient mind is said to have two modes, the knowledge of the multiplicities (*yāvadbhāvikajñāna, ji snyed pa mkhyen pa'i ye shes*), which understands each of the phenomena of the universe in their specificity; and the knowledge of the mode (*yathāvadbhāvikajñāna, ji lta pa mkhyen pa'i ye shes*), which understands the single mode of being of the universe. Imagining the moment of buddhahood, GC writes, "I think that those billions of parts of the knowledge that sees the multiplicities all become the nature of the single knowledge that sees the mode of being."

Among the unenlightened, then, belief is not reasoned conviction in the truth but merely involuntary assent through the force of habit. Everyone knows that what happens in dreams is not real. Yet while dreaming we are doomed to believe in what transpires, responding to it with a range of emotions. If you dream that you have fallen off a cliff, you logically conclude as you fall that you are plunging to your death. Yet you do not die. All manner of illogical and impossible things happen in dreams, things that in the dream seem to be entirely logical. Hence, the presence of logical proof or valid knowledge does not certify something as real. We are compelled to believe by habituation to our circumstances. No accurate conclusions about the nature of reality follow from such belief.

GC next introduces a topic to which he will return repeatedly in the text, that of assertion for oneself (*rang ngo'i khas len*) and assertion for others (*gzhan ngo'i khas len*), translated more literally as "assertion from one's own perspective" and "assertion from the perspective of another." GC will consider these terms in some detail later in the *Adornment*, in the context of whether the Madhyamaka has a thesis. Here, however, he introduces it into his discussion of the enlightened and the unenlightened perspectives.

The unenlightened are so conditioned by ignorance that they must involuntarily believe in, assent to, and even assert the dualistic appearances of the world. A yogin who has understood the highest philosophical view, that of the Prāsaṅgika branch of Madhyamaka, is free from such false beliefs and, from that perspective, has no assertion. Yet if this yogin debates with one of the unenlightened, he must speak in terms of the assertions of the unenlightened. This is called using the "assertion for others."

GC's critique of valid knowledge has serious consequences for the practice of the Buddhist path. If the realm of the unenlightened and the realm of the Buddha are so utterly distinct, if all the objects of the ordinary world utterly disappear in the world of enlightenment, how is it possible to move from one realm to another? What is the path? GC introduces the topic of assertions for oneself and for others to address this crucial question of communication across the chasm. Thus, eschewing the philosophical context of the Madhyamaka for the moment, he says that assertion for oneself is what one truly believes, while assertion for others is what one is compelled by circumstance to concede. After his enlightenment, the Buddha remained seated under the Bodhi tree for a full week without shutting his eyes and without speaking. This was his experience, "his own system," something that is inexpressible and beyond our comprehension. From his own perspective, the Buddha need not speak or make assertions. After his enlightenment, he walked to the Deer Park in Sarnath and there turned the wheel of the doctrine and set forth the four noble truths. From his perspective, there was no need to do this. He spoke, using the terms and categories of the unenlightened out of compassion, in order that others may silently understand what he had recently silently understood. Thus, the Buddha's teaching is an assertion for others. This distinction between the Buddha's own assertions is then both the dilemma and the solution. And how could it be otherwise? "Who would believe in something like all the ways of perception and the ways of explanation of buddhas and sentient beings being wrapped up in one intention and one voice?"

Thus, to truly have no assertion from one's own perspective, to abide in the inexpressible and the inconceivable, is to be enlightened. To try to escape humiliation in the debating courtyard of a Dge lugs monastery by saying "I have no assertion" is to make a mockery of buddhahood and the path to it. It is proper to use the misconceptions of the unenlightened to destroy the misconceptions of the unenlightened. "But when it is used as a tool to damage the view of having no assertion, then there is no method for entering the *dharmadhātu.*"

¶¶56–76 What is often regarded as the first part of the text, the part that many (but not all) believe was composed by GC himself, concludes with a poem in twenty-one stanzas. The first seven stanzas end with the refrain "I am uncomfortable about positing conventional validity" (tha snyad tshad grub 'jog la blo ma bde). Here GC reiterates many of the points that he has made earlier, noting the circularity of assertions of valid knowledge: that objects are deemed true or false depending on whether they appear correctly to a valid consciousness, but the validity of that consciousness is posited based on the accuracy of its perceptions of true and false objects. If the objects of our experience are illusory from the perspective of enlightenment, it is difficult to term any knowledge that we have about the conventional world "valid knowledge."

These complications extend into the realm of reasoning. At ¶60, GC introduces two technical terms familiar from the Dge lugs curriculum on logic, called "types of reasons" (*rtags rigs*). They are *nonobservation of the suitable to appear* (*snang rung ma dmigs pa*) and *nonobservation of the nonappearing* (*mi snang ma dmigs pa*). These are names of two types of reasons used in a syllogism that seeks to prove the absence of something. For example, if one wanted to prove that there was no smoke in the middle of a lake on a dark night, one could do so by proving that there is no fire on the lake. The smoke would not be visible on the lake because of the darkness; hence its presence or absence could not be confirmed by direct perception. However, one could reason that because there was no fire, which would be visible at night, there is no smoke. The absence of the fire would therefore be the nonobservation of the suitable to appear. The other type of reason, called the "nonobservation of the nonappearing," pertains to proofs of phenomena that cannot be directly perceived with the senses, such as the presence of virtue or sin in a person.

In the stanza, GC says that the extreme of existence is negated by the nonobservation of the suitable to appear, and that the extreme of nonexistence is abandoned by the nonobservation of the nonappearing. What he seems to mean is that the extremes of existence and nonexistence are not symmetrical in that they require different kinds of reasons to disprove them. The extreme of existence, generally taken to mean (through "patching it with words") intrinsic existence or true existence, is negated through recourse to various forms of reasoning, such as the reasoning of the lack of being one or many, according to which such things would be intrinsically one or intrinsically many if they did intrinsically exist; being intrinsically one or intrinsically many would be "suitable to appear." The extreme of nonexistence is sometimes taken to mean an utter nonexistence; sometimes it is taken to mean a kind of nihilism, which denies causation, the karmic effects of actions, and the existence of rebirth. Because this extreme of nonexistence is an absence, it would have to be disproved by reason of the nonobservation of the nonappearing. Thus, one kind of reason is used to deny one extreme and another kind of reason is used to deny the other.

GC's concern is one that he has already expressed. The validity of these two forms of reasoning relies on the ability to distinguish between that which is suitable to appear but does not, on the one hand, and that which cannot appear because it does not exist, on the other. But how could an unenlightened being ever perceive what is imperceptible, much less make a valid distinction between what does not appear and what does not exist?

Turning next to the realm of human relations at ¶¶61–62, he notes a fine point that often occurs in Buddhist discussions of desire and hatred, friends and enemies. It is said that one should not feel attachment for friends or hatred for enemies. However, it is noted, this is not a claim that friends and enemies do not exist. There are beings who seek to be helpful, and they are friends. There are beings who seek to be harmful, and they are enemies. The ideal, then, is to acknowledge the existence of these classes of people, but not to respond to their existence with feelings of attachment or aversion. To recognize friends and enemies is thus valid knowledge. To respond to them with desire and hatred is mistaken. Like so many of the distinctions set forth in the treatises, GC finds this one to be entirely hypothetical and abstracted from experience. At ¶63 he concludes the stanzas that end with this refrain by noting the excessively intimate and thus hardly impartial relation between the two forms of valid knowledge: direct perception and inference. Inference draws conclusions from information gathered by the direct perception of the senses, yet inference is used to judge whether such direct perception is accurate. This is like a child testifying for its father. Hence the refrain: "I am uncomfortable about positing conventional validity."

GC continues with his critique of circularity at ¶¶64–65, turning next to the "Great Charioteers" (*shing rta chen mo*), the founders of the philosophical schools, such as Nāgārjuna and Asaṅga. Their authority, it is claimed, can be proved by reasoning. But if one is endowed with the reasoned capacity to judge their authority, what need is there to regard them as authoritative, as persons to be followed? Yet if one lacks the capacity to decide, how does one know whom to follow? Similarly, it is said that one learns how to distinguish between the definitive (*nītārtha, nges don*) and the provisional (*neyārtha, drang don*) among the statements of the Buddha by using the reasoning found in the definitive scriptures. Yet if one already is endowed with the ability to use stainless reasoning, there is no need to rely on the scriptures. And if one cannot distinguish between the definitive and the provisional until one has studied the definitive scriptures, how would one ever identify the definitive scriptures in the first place?

GC alludes at ¶¶66–67 to the famous story of the encounter between the Indian master Asaṅga (regarded in the Dge lugs as the founder of Cittamātra school) and the next buddha, Maitreya. Asaṅga had spent twelve years in meditation, hoping that Maitreya would appear to him and answer his questions. At the end of the twelve years, he found a wounded female dog lying outside his cave. Her wound was filled with maggots, and Asaṅga was at a loss as to how to help the dog without killing the maggots in the process; as a devotee of the Mahāyāna, he was dedicated to the welfare of all beings. He therefore cut off a piece of his own thigh and prepared to transfer the maggots from the dog's wound to his own flesh, using his tongue, when Maitreya magically appeared. Maitreya had been the dog, but Asaṅga had been unable to perceive him in all his splendor because of the impediments in his own mind. Asaṅga's compassion for the plight of the dog had cleared away the impediments that twelve years of meditation could not dislodge. Incredulous that the future buddha could not be seen by others, Asaṅga lifted Maitreya onto his shoulders and carried him into town. Most people saw nothing, although one old woman saw Asaṅga carrying a dog on his back.

If even the ordinary sense perception of Asaṅga and the old woman could be so mistaken, GC finds little reason to have faith in the natural mind. If great scholars of the Madhyamaka view of Nāgārjuna or the Cittamātra view of Asaṅga disagree on all manner of philosophical points, GC finds little reason to have faith in the minds of scholars. Thus, ordinary people, constantly seeking what they think is true, find only the innate conception of true existence, the root cause of all suffering. Scholars, also seeking what they think is true, find only the artificial conception of true existence, that is, the mistaken conception of reality based on false views.

At ¶¶68–74 GC returns to the topics with which he had opened his discussion: that the things we consider valid are the things with which we are familiar; that the truth of the unenlightened is simply the opinion of the majority; that such truths are in fact multiple, changing as one moves from place to place. Such disagreements multiply among the various types of beings who populate the realm of saṃsāra; if even learned philosophers can be mistaken, it is unwise to grant validity to the perceptions of fools. Alluding to his claim that buddha fields are described in the sūtras as filled with jewels simply because humans think that jewels are beautiful, he writes, "Therefore, in the ruins of a magical city in an empty plain, an illusory pile of jewels is often found." These inconstant appearances, both the beautiful and the ugly, will all eventually disappear, upon the achievement of buddhahood.

GC concludes the poem with two stanzas (¶¶75–76) that appear to be even more skeptical than what he had argued earlier. There he had said that providing logical proofs of ordinary experience was unnecessary; when a child touches a flame, the sensation of pain is self-evident. But here he seems even to question this. Does the fact that one's hand touches a needle prove that the needle exists? In the final stanza he writes, "When we plant the seed of truth, we know it to be false. When we taste the fruit of the false, it seems to be true." This is not simply wordplay. As he discussed earlier, when the Buddha teaches the four truths, he is not speaking from his own perspective. He is speaking in the language of the false, of the deceptive, of the unenlightened, in order to bring beings to the state of enlightenment. Yet when we, the unenlightened (like the nomads of the north who think that everything that tastes sweet is milk), experience the false, we think that it is the true.

If the report of GC's friend Bla chung a pho is accurate, this would conclude the portion of the *Adornment* that was actually written in GC's own hand. And it is the case that the text to this point forms something of a self-contained unit, dealing with a single topic, that of the possibility of valid knowledge among the unenlightened. It is written in a distinctive prose style, and it contains verses that appear elsewhere in GC's oeuvre.

If the *Adornment* were the composite of two distinct works, one could expect a clear break to occur here, with a shift in topic and in style. The question of authorship will be taken up in a more sustained way in the discussion of the colophon. However, two points can be made briefly here, in part as an introduction to what will follow.

The remainder of the text is clearly less focused than what we have encountered thus far, with the author returning to a topic that he has dealt with ten pages earlier, often merely paraphrasing what he has already said. Long discussions of a technical topic are interrupted by an aside of one or two sentences on an unrelated issue before the author launches into a new discussion. And while the first part of the text deals consistently with the question of valid knowledge in a way that is accessible to those uninitiated in the fine points of Dge lugs scholasticism, the remaining two-thirds of the book is all over the map—or, more precisely, all over the Madhyamaka map, offering up opinions on a range of topics incomprehensible to those Tibetan readers unfamiliar with the Dge lugs curriculum. Here are some of the things that the author will discuss: *chos can mthun snang ba* (the commonly appearing subject); *don dam pa'i khyad par sbyar ba* (the use of the qualifier *ultimately*); *grub mthas blo bsgyur ba* (the mind influenced by philosophy); *drang nges* (scriptural interpretation); *kun rdzob dpyod pa dang don dam dpyod pa'i skabs* (the contexts for conventional and ultimate analysis); *rigs pas dpyad bzod* (the ability to withstand analysis); *rigs shes pa'i ngor ma snyed pa* (not being discovered by reasoning); *ma snyed dang med pa nges pa* (not being discovered versus being determined not to exist); and *snang rung ma dmigs pa* (the nonobservation of the suitable to appear).

However, it is important to note that this "second part" of the text begins not with a new topic, but just where the "first part" left off: with the discussion of whether the Madhyamaka yogin has an assertion (*dbu ma pa la khas len yod dam med*). Indeed, it is as if the twenty-one stanzas of poetry had been interpolated, interrupting the argument that precedes and follows them.

¶¶77–85 One of Nāgārjuna's most famous and most commented-upon statements is his declaration that he has no thesis (*pratijñā, dam bca'*). It is a pronouncement whose interpretation seems to have been as vexing and controversial among Tibetan scholiasts of the fourteenth century as it has been for modern scholars.[9] The locus classicus of the declaration is found at the twenty-ninth stanza of his *Refutation of Objections* (*Vigrahavyāvartanī*). To very briefly set the scene, in the first *śloka* of the work, the opponent states that if it is true, as Nāgārjuna claims, that all things lack intrinsic nature (*svabhāva*), then Nāgārjuna's own statement must also lack intrinsic nature, in which case the statement cannot deny the intrinsic nature of things. At *Vigrahavyāvartanī* 29, Nāgārjuna responds, "If I had some thesis (*pratijñā*), I would incur that fault; because I have no thesis I am faultless." The autocommentary explains that there can be no thesis when all things are empty, utterly quiescent, and naturally pristine. Therefore, because he has no thesis, no mark of a thesis is entailed by his previous statement that all things lack intrinsic nature.[10]

In Tibet, Nāgārjuna's declaration elicited extensive commentary. There were some who took it quite literally, arguing that the Madhyamakas have no system of their own (*rang lugs*), no thesis (*dam bca'*), and no assertion (*khas len*), even on the conventional level. It is interesting to note that one of those who asserted that the Madhyamakas have no assertions was the young Tsong kha pa; according to his secret biography, Tsong kha pa strove to be such a Madhyamaka, changing his position not through a careful study of the autocommentary to

9. For the standard study of this question, among the Indian Madhyamakas as well as in Tibet (focusing on Tsong kha pa and his contemporaries), see D. Seyfort Ruegg, "On the Thesis and Assertion in the Madhyamaka / dBu ma," in *Contributions on Tibetan and Buddhist Religion and Philosophy*, ed. Ernst Steinkellner and Helmut Tauscher (Wien: Universität Wien, 1983), 205–41. On the views of some Rnying ma pa authors on the question, see Franz-Karl Ehrhard, "Observations on Prāsaṅgika-Madhyamaka in the rÑiṅ-ma-pa School," in *Tibetan Studies: Proceedings of the 4th Seminar of the International Association of Tibetan Studies, Schloss Hohenkammer-Munich 1985*, ed. Helga Uebach and Jampa L. Panglung (München: Kommission für Zentralasiatische Studien Bayerische Akademie der Wissenschaften, 1988), 139–47. Modern declarations that the Madhyamaka has no thesis have been gathered by Elizabeth Napper; see *Dependent-Arising and Emptiness* (Boston: Wisdom Publications, 1989), 700–701n208.

10. See E. H. Johnston and Arnold Kunst, "The *Vigrahavyāvartanī* of Nāgārjuna with the Author's Commentary," *Mélanges chinois et bouddhiques* 9 (1948–51): 29.

the *Vigrahavyāvartanī* but rather after being rather rudely corrected in a vision by Mañjuśrī.[11]

What would come to be regarded as the standard Dge lugs position on the question is set forth at some length by Tsong kha pa's disciple Mkhas grub rje (1385–1483) in his *Great Summary* (*Stong thun chen mo*). Mkhas grub cites a number of statements by Nāgārjuna that affirmatively set forth specific doctrines in order to indicate to his Tibetan opponents that Madhyamakas have doctrines which they both accept and actively expound. Mkhas grub reads *Vigrahavyāvartanī* 29 to say that if the Madhyamaka held that the statement that everything lacks intrinsic nature itself possessed intrinsic nature, then the fault of internal inconsistency would indeed be entailed. However, Nāgārjuna states that he has no thesis, meaning that he has no thesis which itself is intrinsically established (*rang bzhin gyis grub pa*).[12] In addition to countering the claim that the Madhyamaka has no assertions from a perspective that can be termed philosophical, Mkhas grub also considers the negative consequences of such a claim from the perspective of Buddhist practice, arguing that without assenting to and upholding certain statements it would be impossible to go for refuge to the three jewels, to create the aspiration to enlightenment (*bodhicitta*), to take and maintain the monastic vows; in short, it would be impossible to practice the Buddhist path.[13]

As we have seen, for GC the primary referent of the Madhyamaka's having no assertion is the silence of the Buddha; all subsequent speech is merely a compassionate concession to the ignorant world: as he said at ¶52, "That the Tathāgata remained under the Bodhi tree for a week without closing his eyes is his own system, which is without assertions. His turning of the wheel of doctrine of the four truths so that this very view [of reality] could be understood is a presentation of assertions for others, which he entered into through the power of compassion." GC thus has little patience with those who would make the statement "I have no assertion" into a topic of disputation on the debating courtyard, arguing about whether the declaration that one has no assertion is, in fact, itself an assertion. Such disputation makes a mockery of what for GC is one of Nāgārjuna's most powerful statements.

11. See Tsong kha pa, *Rje rin po che'i gsang ba'i rnam thar rgya mtsho lta bu las cha shas nyung ngu zhig yongs su brjod pa'i gtam rin po che'i snye ma*, in *The Collected Works*, vol. *ka*, 2b4–5.

12. See *The Collected Works of the Lord Mkhas-grub rje dge-legs-dpal-bzañ-po*, vol. *ka* (New Delhi: Mongolian Lama Guru Deva, 1980), 150a1–3; and Ruegg, "On the Thesis and Assertion," 219.

13. *Collected Works of the Lord Mkhas-grub*, 151b6–152a6; and Ruegg, "On the Thesis and Assertion," 222–23.

It should not come as a surprise by this point to learn that in the discussion that follows, GC takes a somewhat different approach to the question of the Madhyamaka's assertion than that found in other commentators on Nāgārjuna's famous claim. Rather than "patching" Nāgārjuna's statement that "I have no assertion" with words like "I have no *intrinsically existent* assertion," as one finds in Mkhas grub, GC prefers to consider the possibility that to have no assertion means, from the ultimate perspective, literally to remain silent. He recalls those occasions on which the Buddha said nothing when asked a question. For example, there are the famous fourteen questions, called the "unindicated views" (*avyākṛta*), to which the Buddha remained silent.[14] In the *Scripture on Discipline* (*Vinayāgama*), however, it is said that to remain silent is to concede defeat. Thus, if one wishes to adhere sophistically to the claim that having no assertion is itself an assertion, then one has no choice but to conclude that the Buddha was conceding defeat when he remained silent; as GC says, "[Y]ou should not be proud of the fact that you carry around in your hand this kind of argument that would utterly defeat the Bhagavan." But the Buddha's silence cannot be so simplistically interpreted; Nāgārjuna praises the Buddha in his *Garland of Jewels* (*Ratnāvalī* I. 74) for not teaching those incapable of understanding. And when the Buddha's wealthy patron Anāthapiṇḍada invited the Bhagavan to his grove for the noon meal, the Buddha said nothing, thereby indicating his assent.

Although GC might have recoiled at the suggestion, it is difficult to resist the urge to interpret these silences, each of which seems to have a different meaning. In the passage from the *Ratnāvalī*, Nāgārjuna does not say that the Buddha did not speak, but that he did not teach the profound doctrine to

14. Although there are a number of versions of the list of what Henry Clarke Warren, in his 1896 *Buddhism in Translations*, translated as "Questions which tend not to Edification," one common version is as follows:
1. Is the world eternal?
2. Is the world not eternal?
3. Is the world both eternal and not eternal?
4. Is the world neither eternal nor not eternal?
5. Is the world endless?
6. Is the world not endless?
7. Is the world both endless and not endless?
8. Is the world neither endless nor not endless?
9. Does the Tathāgata exist after death?
10. Does the Tathāgata not exist after death?
11. Does the Tathāgata both exist and not exist after death?
12. Does the Tathāgata neither exist nor not exist after death?
13. Are the soul (*jīvam*) and the body identical?
14. Are the soul and the body not identical?

those who were not suitable vessels for it. And when the Buddha did not reply to Anāthapiṇḍada's invitation, it simply signified his acceptance of the invitation. But the "meanings" of these various silences does not seem to be GC's point here. He appears instead to be offering the reminder that there were occasions when the Buddha did not speak, often with devastating effect; he is suggesting, then, that there is something to be gained in taking quite literally Nāgārjuna's statement that he has no assertion: "If one has understanding, the very fact that he had no assertion will itself be able to create the correct view in one's mind."

But GC is not one to say that the Buddha never spoke, that Candrakīrti, a monk of Nālandā, never said, "This is Nālandā monastery." They clearly did speak. They made declarative statements. The question, then, is the status of their utterances. Here, GC remarks that once one makes their utterances the subject of logical analysis, once one begins to consider whether the statement "I have no thesis" is itself a thesis, then one has entered the realm of conventional analysis. And here, the Madhyamaka's method is provided by the Buddha: "Whatever the world says exists, I also say exists." He likens the Madhyamaka's situation to that of a person who has been captured by a fierce Khams pa chieftain who demands to know, apparently on the threat of losing one's life, whether he (that is, the chieftain) is a "universal monarch" (*cakravartin*). When, upon answering in the affirmative, he demands to know, "Is that what you really believe?" (literally, "Do you assert that as your own system?" khyod kyis rang lugs su khas len pa yin nam), one has no recourse but to say that this is one's own conviction, despite the fact that one does not believe it; "such an assertion is made involuntarily out of fear of Bu long ma [the chieftain]."

This is the situation of the Madhyamaka, who asserts what is necessary only in terms of the assertions of others, despite claiming it to be his own view. In the everyday activities of life, it is simply good manners, when meeting people from another culture, to maintain a distinction between one's thoughts on the one hand and one's words and actions on the other; one should comport oneself in a manner that is not discomfiting to others. If this is the case even in the limited realm of human society, it is not difficult to imagine that there is a difference between what the Buddha understands himself and how he leads his disciples. They are two different spheres, and it is important to recognize, and maintain, their difference. Thus, GC provides two options when it comes to the Madhyamaka view: one can adopt the ultimate perspective, in which case reality is inexpressible, or one adopts the conventional perspective, in which case reality must be classified as either existent or nonexistent. He leaves the choice to the reader.

GC would seem to say, then, that everything which the Madhyamaka asserts is asserted for others, or what he also terms "asserted powerlessly"—that is, asserted without personal conviction. He also suggests, however, that the Madhyamaka must also decide what is and is not to be asserted for others. How is the Madhyamaka to make such a decision? This would seem inevitably to raise the issue of *neyārtha* and *nītārtha*, the provisional and the definitive.

There are those who respond to the declaration that the Madhyamakas have no assertion by noting the existence of many statements attributed to Nāgārjuna and asking, "If they are not the statements of Nāgārjuna, whose statements are they?" GC mocks such people as being no different from fools who say, "There simply are these sūtras which teach that the self exists, and say that external objects and three final vehicles are truly established, and so on. If this is not the statement of the Tathāgata, whose statement is it?" Each of these is a doctrine that the Buddha set forth but which, according to Madhyamaka exegetes, he did not in fact believe. Thus, anyone who would claim that these things are true because the Buddha said them does not understand the difference between the literal and the nonliteral, the definitive and the provisional among the Buddha's many pronouncements. This would imply that GC accepts the existence of criteria for determining which of the Buddha's statements can be accepted literally and which are intentional (*ābhiprāyika, dgongs pa can*). Yet earlier in the *Adornment*, at ¶65, as we recall, he called into question the entire process of scriptural interpretation: "Correct reasoning is found in the definitive scriptures; the provisional and definitive are differentiated by stainless reasoning. If one understands with reasoning, why search for the definitive meaning? If one does not understand with reasoning, how does one find the definitive meaning?" This statement, combined with his general critique of the very notion of valid knowledge for unenlightened beings, would seem to imply that there is no means, short of becoming enlightened oneself (or, at least, reaching the bodhisattva *bhūmi*s), for distinguishing the literal from the nonliteral, for determining what is and is not to be asserted by Madhyamakas for the sake of others, because, in the end, *all* assertions are merely provisional; the Madhyamaka has no assertion.

It is simply impossible for common beings to make such determinations. Every thought that occurs in the mind of a common being is rooted in desire, hatred, or ignorance. If there were just one accurate assumption present in our mind, how pathetic that it has done us so little good over the long course of saṃsāra. As he writes at ¶82,

> All of the thoughts experienced by cats and dogs are expressed within no more than three or four modulations of their feline and canine voices. Apart from that, they have no other method. In the same way, we common beings, relative to bodhisattvas who have attained power [that is, one of the *bhūmis*], do not even reach the level of dogs and cats. How is one able to formulate within the tiny hole of our thoughts [the question of whether] the great sky of the *dharmadhātu*, free from extremes and seen by the knowledge of all aspects, is a nonaffirming negative or an affirming negative?

It is embarrassing, then, for so-called scholars to proclaim that saying that one has no assertion is itself an assertion. He likens those who do so to the same northern nomads who know only the flavors of milk and yogurt: when given sugar for the first time all they can say is that it tastes like milk.

It is clear, then, that GC places little stock in thought (*rtog pa*), that which for the Dge lugs pas provides the invaluable conduit to the direct realization of emptiness. His devaluation of thought is further evinced in his gloss of the Madhyamaka's lack of any assertion. An assertion, for GC, is a verbal statement that the speaker believes; a Madhyamaka has no assertion because he never makes statements derived from his own thoughts (*bsam pa*). As he said at ¶51,

> The fact that a yogin who understands reality (*dharmatā*) does not assert as his own system even one among all objects in the way that they are perceived and conceived by a common being is the meaning of the Prāsaṅgikas not taking their own position. When one opponent who has assertions debates using scripture and reasoning with an opponent without assertions who abides in a state of meditative equipoise, free from verbalization, whatever answers the latter gives all become mere assertions. Thus, there is no place to fit this view of having no assertions within words, sounds, and, particularly, the reasoning of logicians.

Two questions seem to remain for GC. The first is the question of the nature of the passage (once the storied Dge lugs path of reasoning has been rejected) from the conceptual to the nonconceptual, from the unenlightened to the enlightened state. He offers no direct answer to this question in the *Adornment*, although it provides the motif for so much of the text. To gain another perspective on the question, one must also look to his *Treatise on Passion* (*'Dod pa'i bstan bcos*), with its exaltation of the sexual yogas of the *anuttarayoga* tantras as the supreme means of passing into a state beyond thought. The other question, alluded to above, is that of the principles which guide the Madhyamaka's strategy of making assertions for others. What is and what is not to be asserted for others? For an answer to this question, GC refers us, perhaps surprisingly, to Tsong kha pa, who seems once again left with the task of negotiating between the conventional and the ultimate. GC says at ¶81, "[A]lthough it is true that these external capacities [of the four elements] must be asserted powerlessly, one must distinguish them from what one must not assert in one's own system. Since this point is made very clearly in the Foremost Lama [Tsong kha pa]'s answers to Red mda' ba's questions, be honest and look there."

Unfortunately, GC does not provide a more specific reference to Tsong kha pa's answer to his teacher Red mda' ba's questions in this admittedly obscure source (demonstrating GC's impressive familiarity with Tsong kha pa's oeuvre). If we are to judge simply by the titles, there are several works to which he may be referring; a perusal of their contents yields two possibilities, both of which contain an identical passage on the question of the Madhyamaka's thesis.[15] There, Tsong kha pa takes up the question of the assertions of the Prāsaṅgika who has not yet gained direct understanding of emptiness. He explains that for the noble (āryan, 'phag pa) Prāsaṅgika, one who has yogic direct perception of emptiness, all assertions are destroyed in the state of meditative equipoise (samāhita, mnyam gzhag). In the subsequent state (pṛṣṭhalabdha, rjes thob), all dependently arisen phenomena appear like reflections and are not negated. For the common being (pṛthagjana, so so'i skyes bu) Prāsaṅgika, one who has not yet directly perceived the nature of reality, the situation is quite different. Such a person determines, apparently through reasoning, that dependently arisen phenomena lack any intrinsic nature and are like reflections. Having made this determination, the Prāsaṅgika who is a common being must not only accept this as his own system but also assert that this is the case. Although this entails that the Madhyamaka have an assertion, Tsong kha pa declares that possession of an assertion does not become a fault for the time being. This Prāsaṅgika has not yet attained the vision of emptiness in which the reflectionlike appearance of dependently arisen phenomena will be refuted. He must, therefore, uphold it.

15. The first of the two works is entitled *Rje btsun red mda' ba chen pos skyan bzhugs pa'i drung du 'bul ba la rtog ldan byang seng ba grogs mched btad pa'i dus kyi zhu yig* and is located among the miscellaneous works (*thor bu*) in the second volume (*kha*) of the Lhasa edition at 62b4–68b1 (322–34 in the 1978 Guru Deva edition). The second work is entitled *Rje btsun 'jam pa'i dbyangs kyi lam gyi gnad rje red mda' ba la shog dril du phul ba* and occurs in the fourteenth volume (*pha*) of the Lhasa edition at 1–6a1 (671–81 in the 1978 Guru Deva edition). The relevant passage occurs at 65a1–5 in the first work and at 4b3–5a3 in the second.

Tsong kha pa and GC, then, seem to be in agreement on the referent of the statement that the Madhyamaka has no thesis; both say that it is the direct yogic perception of emptiness that constitutes the noble silence from which the Madhyamaka does not speak. They would seem to differ on the technique for reaching that state. But prior to attaining that silence, the Madhyamaka must speak. GC has said that all the assertions made by the Madhyamaka are assertions for others, but the question remains of what precisely is to be asserted. Tsong kha pa also addresses that question in his answers to Red mda' ba.

His point is a familiar one: that the Prāsaṅgika analyzes the ideas of the opponent and then crafts assertions which are the opposite of what the opponent holds, but adapted in such a way that the opponent may perceive his own error. Tsong kha pa thus moves the question of the Madhyamaka's assertions entirely into the sphere of philosophic contestation. He emphasizes that the assertions of the Madhyamaka are not randomly chosen from a survey of the tenets of all philosophical schools, beginning with the Nihilists (rgyang phan). Instead, the assertions are situationally determined. Thus, the opponent's eventually coming to perceive the invalidation of his own assertions and the Madhyamaka's positing of his own system are similar. "Furthermore, until [the Madhyamaka] sees the faults in both positions [his own and those of the opponent], it is said that one must act as if it were one's own position; it is unsuitable to say, 'It is merely an assertion for others; it is not my assertion.'"[16]

It is clear why GC would find Tsong kha pa's statement appealing. It confirms his reading of Nāgārjuna's declaration at Vigrahavyāvartanī 29 as a reference to the silent vision of emptiness. It explains how the assertions of the Madhyamaka who has yet to perceive emptiness directly are derived, that is, in specific opposition to the assertions of the opponent. And, finally, it instructs such a Madhyamaka to act as if the assertions were his own, without claiming that they are made merely for others, much like GC's admonition to tell the threatening chieftain what he wants to hear in order to save one's life. On this point, however, there appears to be a difference in implication between GC and Tsong kha pa, with GC portraying the Madhyamaka's statement as a lie told for a noble purpose: he has no assertion but claims that he does in order to defeat the opponent. Tsong kha pa seems instead to suggest that it is only the ārya Prāsaṅgika who has gained the right to say that he has no assertion; the pṛthagjana Prāsaṅgika is obliged to uphold the reflectionlike appearances

16. Rje btsun red mda' ba chen pos skyan bzhugs pa'i drung du 'bul ba la rtog ldan byang seng ba grogs mched btad pa'i dus kyi zhu yig, 65a5.

of dependently arisen phenomena until the point of gaining the direct vision of emptiness in which all appearances are destroyed.

All of this may suggest a greater affinity between Tsong kha pa and GC, at least on the topic of the Madhyamaka's assertion, than one might imagine—and at least a greater affinity between GC's argument and Tsong kha pa's statements on the topic that occur outside his exegetical writings, in works such as the Written Instructions on the Madhyamaka View (Dbu ma'i lta ba'i khrid yig), where he writes, "Although they make proofs and refutations about what is and is not the meaning of reality (yang dag pa'i don), their own system has no assertions" and "You must understand that for the perception of others, they assert things in accordance with the conventions of the world, but in their own system they do not have to assert even a single thesis."[17] Indeed, the opposition to Tsong kha pa often attributed to the Adornment, although certainly present on several major issues, is by no means thoroughgoing; GC's most vituperative contempt is reserved not for Tsong kha pa but for the complacent scholastics who claim to preserve his legacy.

We find in GC's treatment of the Madhyamaka's thesis certain themes that recur throughout the Adornment, most notably the constant pressure, whatever the issue may be, toward the level of the ultimate (paramārtha). GC seems to long ever for the nonconceptual state, where interpretation is finally obviated. Although frustrated by the constraints of language, he also writes most eloquently about that state and shows a profound appreciation for the rhetorical power of the statements from the sūtras and śāstras that evoke the ultimate, as well as a profound annoyance with the small-minded interpreters who seek only doctrinal consistency. When the Madhyamaka must speak, GC seems quite content to follow the conventions of the world. It is in the intermediary moment, however—when the Madhyamaka must not speak simply of worldly conventions, but must use language to bring others to the silence of emptiness—that we find the crux of GC's dilemma, for as he says later at ¶125, "Without this presentation of assertions for others, how can the opportunity arise for the speaking of one word of dharma between the Buddha who perceives existence as infinite purity, and common beings who perceive everything as impure and contaminated?"

17. Tsong kha pa, Dbu ma lta ba'i khrid yig, in The Collected Works, vol. ba, 20b2 and 22b2–3. For a more detailed discussion of Tsong kha pa's various views on the question of the Madhyamaka thesis, see Donald S. Lopez Jr., "dGe 'dun Chos 'phel's Position on Vigrahavyāvartanī 29," in The Buddhist Forum III, ed. T. Skorupski and U. Pagel, School of Oriental and African Studies (London: University of London, 1994), 161–84.

¶¶86–92 GC begins by saying, as he has already said several times, that "when one arrives at the final rank of turning an instant into an aeon and an atom into a world, and so on, all categories are unified." Prior to this point, however, he has been content to refer to the state of enlightenment as inconceivable; when he discusses the enjoyment body of a buddha and the landscape of a buddha field, he does so simply to show that even they are described in terms accessible to the limited awareness of benighted humans. He returns to the topic of enlightenment here, but for the first time introduces the tantric perspective. Thus, among the pairs that are unified in the state of liberation, he mentions not only existence and nonexistence but the "son clear light" and the "basic clear light." According to the systems of *anuttarayoga* tantra, through the instructions of the guru, one is able to generate in meditation a subtle form of consciousness called "the mind of clear light" and then use that subtle consciousness to understand emptiness. There is a more fundamental mind of clear light that, according to the some tantric systems, manifests only at the moment of death. The first type of mind of clear light that is transformed into the wisdom that realizes the subtle emptiness with spontaneous great bliss is called "the path clear light" or "the son clear light." The fundamental or basic mind of clear light is called "the mother clear light." Through the meeting of the mother clear light and the son clear light, the "truth body" (*dharmakāya*) of a buddha is achieved. GC does not describe such a buddha as appearing in the form of an Indian king, however, but in the body of Vajravarāhī with two faces. Vajravarāhī is the consort of tantric buddha Cakrasaṃvara. Her name means "Diamond Sow" and she has two faces: the face of a beautiful woman and, protruding from behind her right ear, the face of pig—an image that presumably does not derive from a human aesthetic.

For GC, the acceptance of the inconceivable is necessary for all those who follow the Mahāyāna. Otherwise, to engage in the tantric practice of imagining oneself as a multiarmed wrathful buddha brandishing weapons and seated in sexual union with a beautiful consort would be merely to indulge in logical contradictions. To regard a horrific buddha—multiheaded; multiarmed; garlanded with severed heads; brandishing swords, tridents, cleavers, and skull cups; trampling the bodies of enemies; embracing a consort—as simply the "wrathful emanation" of a more familiar and less frightening buddha is to reduce the wrathful deity to a painting, an image to be identified on a thangka. If the two bodies of a buddha—the truth body (*dharmakāya*) and the form body (*rūpakāya*)—and the thirty-two major marks and eighty ancillary marks that adorn the body of a buddha are merely accommodations to the limited sensibility of the ignorant, as GC himself had argued earlier, why, he now asks, do some buddhas, who have equally amassed the collections of merit and wisdom and are equally adorned with the major and ancillary marks, also have the face of a sow or a lion?

The answer: in order to disrupt the conception of the ordinary, to overthrow what we consider "valid knowledge." This, he says, is the purpose of the entire Vajrayāna path, from the initial stages of regarding your lama as a buddha, through to the visualization of yourself as the buddha Vajradhara, to the more advanced visualization in which the multiple deities of the maṇḍala are arrayed throughout one's body. "All of this, such as offering the five meats [beef, elephant flesh, horse flesh, dog flesh, human flesh] and the five ambrosias [feces, urine, semen, blood, brains] to the Buddha, are set forth for the purpose of smashing to dust the conceptions of the ordinary, together with the reasoning of logicians." To do so for any other reason would violate common sense, reason, and propriety. He quotes the famous ordinance of the king Ye shes 'od (whom the text mistakenly calls Zhi ba 'od) who, in the period between the earlier and later disseminations of the dharma in Tibet, bemoaned the degenerate practice of bogus tantric yogins: "Have pity on those who make offerings to the Tathāgata with the mud of filth and [as a result] go to [the hell called] Mud of Corpses." The true purpose of regarding the impure as the pure is to overcome the conception of the ordinary. One should therefore see the earth as the goddess called Buddhalocana, who in the maṇḍala is the embodiment of the earth element; the deities at the periphery of the maṇḍala should change places with those at the center.

¶¶93–99 GC returns to his earlier theme of the conceit whereby the unenlightened describe the conventional and the ultimate, with the ultimate being limited to what they can understand and express in words. Having divided the universe into the existent and the nonexistent, reality as it is understood by the Buddha must fall into the category of the nonexistent, because it is beyond the ken of the unenlightened. What the unenlightened assert must therefore be overturned by reasoning in order to ultimately reach the state of the Buddha, who is without assertions, and the essence of whose dharma cannot be located. He cites Dignāga and Dharmakīrti to support his claim that logic alone is not the path to buddhahood.

He turns next to the use of the adverbs *ultimately* and *conventionally* to qualify existence. Dge lugs discussions of emptiness seek to distinguish clearly between not existing ultimately and being completely nonexistent. Thus, nothing in the universe, including emptiness, exists ultimately, but this does not entail that everything is nonexistent. In fact, everything that exists, exists conventionally. For GC, this is just so much sophistry, once again doing little more than certifying the operations of ignorance. To say that not existing ultimately does not constitute nonexistence is, in fact, to say that the ultimate consciousness, the wisdom consciousness that directly understands emptiness ("the wisdom of a noble being"), has no implications regarding the status of the objects of ordinary experience. It is typically said that the object that is qualified by emptiness is "not found" by the wisdom consciousness. But, GC argues, if this "not finding" does not abrogate the existence of the object, what is its force? The existence of phenomena is therefore once again validated by the conceptions of the unenlightened. To say that something "does not ultimately exist" is thus a vapid statement unless it is used for nonexistent subjects. "Intrinsic existence" (*svabhāvasiddha, rang bzhin gyis grub pa*) and "the horns of a rabbit" can be said to not ultimately exist, because they are utterly nonexistent. But in this case, what purpose does the qualification *ultimately* provide, apart from implying that they exist conventionally? For GC, then, it is not only unnecessary but misleading to say that something does not ultimately exist when it is in fact simply nonexistent. By focusing on "ultimate existence" as the target of Madhyamaka reasoning, "existence" is allowed to persist, and the operations of ignorance are not disrupted. Instead, the target should be the root of ignorance.

GC uses two technical terms here: *object of negation by the path* (*lam gyi dgag bya*) and *object of negation by reasoning* (*rigs pa'i dgag bya*). The objects of negation by the path are the afflictions (*kleśa, nyon mongs*): desire, hatred, and ignorance and the other root and secondary negative states. These are destroyed over the course of the path to enlightenment. The objects of negation by reasoning are the hypothetical referents of the misconceptions of the unenlightened. Thus, a creator deity is an object of negation by reasoning; eternal sound is an object of negation by reasoning; a permanent, partless, and autonomous self is an object of negation by reasoning; intrinsic existence is an object of negation by reasoning. These are hypothetical because they are, in fact, utterly nonexistent. They therefore do not need to be destroyed. What does exist and what does requires destruction is the belief in them, the conception of them; such beliefs and such conceptions, as forms of ignorance, are objects of negation by the path.

According to the taxonomies of the path, when a particular affliction of a particular strength is destroyed by a bodhisattva, that affliction is simultaneously and utterly eliminated with respect to each of the various levels within saṃsāra. There is no need in this case to use the qualification *ultimately*. In the debating courtyard, it is sometimes said that a rabbit does not have long and sharp horns on its head because it has no horns at all. Yet no one would seek to prove that because a rabbit has no horns, it does not have ultimately existing horns. If the qualification *ultimately* is so widely applied in the case of things that supposedly exist, why is it not applied in the standard example of nonexistence, the horns of a rabbit?

GC's larger point is that the purpose of the practice of the Buddhist path is to cultivate new states of awareness that will destroy old and afflicted habits of mind. There is no need to speak here in terms of "ultimate" and "conventional" and no danger in not making such distinctions. Such distinctions are equally meaningless in the realm of reasoning. Otherwise, the conception of true existence, the fundamental form of ignorance, is preserved as some form of conventional existence, and reasoning is used to refute something else, something superfluous. He quotes the same passage from Lcang skya again: "Leaving this vivid appearance where it is, they search for something protruding to refute."

¶¶100–103 GC pauses from his polemic for a moment in order to emphasize the importance of the distinction between the Svātantrika and Prāsaṅgika branches of the Madhyamaka (as understood by Tsong kha pa) on the question of the conventional status of objects. He tells two stories of encounters between famous scholars on what it is that is being pointed to when one identifies an object. For the Svātantrika, on the conventional level, things objectively exist as they appear to a "nondefective" awareness. Thus, there is no fault in saying that a pillar is a pillar and a table is a table. To believe that the square piece of wood on four legs is a table is a valid form of knowledge and thus would be the Svātantrika's own assertion. For the Prāsaṅgika, even on the conventional level, the object does not naturally abide among its parts. Thus, when we point to a table, we are only pointing to the "basis of designation" (*gdags gzhi*) of the table, to which the name "table" is imputed. To believe that the square piece of wood on four legs is a table is a form of ignorance. The Prāsaṅgika could say, "The square piece of wood on four legs is a table," but this would be an assertion for others, not the Prāsaṅgika's own position. The object is never itself but is rather designated to its parts. Thus, for the Prāsaṅgika it would not even be correct to say, "That thing in front of me is the thing in front of me," but rather, "That thing in front of me is the basis of designation of the thing in front of me." This kind of regression from one basis of designation to the next is not merely a philosophical exercise, according to GC. The goal is to continue to the point at which it is impossible to say "this is" about anything. At that point, the positive term for this outcome, *freedom from superimposition*, and the negative term, *nonaffirming negative*, become synonymous. "Therefore, it seems that arriving at this place is the crucial point on the path that severs the root of saṃsāra."

GC returns to his examination of scholastic categories when he next takes up what it means to have one's mind affected by tenets (*grub mthas blo bsgyur ba*). The ignorance that afflicts sentient beings is often divided into the innate (*lhan skyes*) and the artificial (*kun btags*), with the former the result of perpetual misconception over the long course of saṃsāra and the latter the result of studying false philosophical systems. GC finds the distinction between the two difficult to discern, arguing that the philosophically unsophisticated, and even the illiterate, have their own folk wisdom to which they subscribe.

The more interesting question, however, is what the term *tenet* refers to in the phrase "a mind affected by tenets." It is typically taken to mean a false tenet. But as Tsong kha pa points out, the Madhyamakas see the tenet of dependent origination as proof of the emptiness of intrinsic existence, whereas the other Buddhist schools see it as the proof of the presence of intrinsic existence. GC sees no way to distinguish between what is and is not a "tenet" other than to decide that any conclusion that results from inference is a tenet, and any conclusion that results from direct perception is not. In such a case, the ordinary thought "I am" should be regarded as a case of innate ignorance, while a notion of the self as endowed with such "philosophical" attributes as permanence, partlessness, and autonomy would be a case of artificial ignorance. Yet GC concedes that it is sometimes difficult to tell the difference. For example, for the Prāsaṅgikas, the innate ignorance would be the conception of a table existing objectively, without being designated as such by language or thought. Artificial ignorance, deriving from having one's mind affected by the tenets of the Svātantrika master Bhāvaviveka, would be the conception of the table as intrinsically existing but not truly existing. Again, GC finds fault with the fine points of philosophy, especially when they serve as impediments to what he regards as a higher wisdom.

GC concludes this section by again calling into the question the distinction between innate and artificial ignorance, between a mind that has not been, or has been, affected by tenets. One would certainly not claim that the minds of all the human beings in the world have been affected by one of the many Buddhist or non-Buddhist philosophical systems. Yet the beliefs of all beings are culturally conditioned. A child's thinking that it can urinate wherever it wants is an innate mind. That same child's knowledge that it had better not urinate on the carpet is a mind affected by the tenets of the parents. It is difficult to find some "conventional existence" apart from this worldly wisdom. Thus, even the Prāsaṅgikas, the masters of the highest of all philosophical schools, regard the conventional as that which is renowned in the world.

¶¶104–7 GC turns next to the objects of ordinary experience and their ontological status. He approaches the topic from the familiar Buddhist assertion that the same object appears differently to different types of beings: what appears to a human seems undeniable to a human, what appears to a ghost seems undeniable to a ghost, and so on. The standard example is that which appears to humans to be a cup of water. To a god, that liquid would appear as ambrosia; to a fish, it would appear as an abode; to a ghost, it would appear as pus; to a denizen of hell, it would appear as molten bronze. This example is put forth by Asaṅga as proof that there are, in fact, no external objects; all experiences are only projections of the mind.

When Tibetan doxographies catalog the assertions of the various non-Buddhist and Buddhist philosophical schools of India, one of the topics commonly considered is the status of external objects. The Cittamātra ("mind only") school of Asaṅga is the only Buddhist school to deny the existence of external objects. Yet all of the Buddhist schools would agree that when a god, a human, a fish, a ghost, and a denizen of hell look at what for the human is a cup of water, they each see something different. Those schools that assert the existence of external objects must therefore account for what is "really there."

According to the Dge lugs, the highest of the philosophical schools—that is, the school that represents the Buddha's understanding—is the Prāsaṅgika branch of Madhyamaka, which, it is said, upholds the existence of external objects, but asserts that each object is a mere designation. In the case of the differing perceptions of liquid by the different types of beings, the Dge lugs would argue that each of those perceptions is a valid form of knowledge, partly because the nature of ambrosia, water, and pus are each present in the liquid; it is simply that different beings perceive different natures, and none perceive them all.[18] They would say, therefore, that a house seen by a human and a house seen by a ghost, although appearing differently to them, would each be established by conventional valid knowledge. They would also say, however, that the external object—what is "really there"—the basis of the different perceptions by the human and the ghost, is not in fact seen by either of them in its entirety.

18. For a discussion of Dge lugs interpretations of this famous example and their position on the status of external objects, see Daniel Cozort, *Unique Tenets of the Middle Way Consequence School* (Ithaca, NY: Snow Lion Publications, 1998),107–52 (esp. pp. 113–23), 299–313, 455–58.

GC is not particularly taken with this explanation. He disparages it as being no different from the position of the non-Buddhist Sāṃkhyas, who hold that the fundamental nature of all matter, called principle (*pradhāna*), pervades all manifestations of the material world, but itself remains invisible and unmanifest. The Prāsaṅgika position is similar to the Cittamātra position, in that both would say that the object perceived by each type of being is valid for that being. The Cittamātra (or Yogācāra—GC uses the terms as synonyms) does not claim that "the something" that each of the beings perceives differently is a cup of water. Instead, they hold that these various appearances arise through the activation of certain potencies (*vāsanā, bag chags*) that abide in the foundational consciousness (*ālayavijñāna, kun gzhi rnam shes*) of each being. GC seems to approve of this position because it accounts for the wide variation of experience without positing a common object of experience. He concludes with a poem in which he says that it is not only the case that the six types of beings see six different things; even among humans, who have six sense organs (eye, ear, nose, tongue, body, mind), things can appear in six different ways without there being a common object.

The question, then, is what the Buddha sees. This leads GC to the topic of the two obstructions: the afflictive obstructions (*kleśāvaraṇa, nyon mongs kyi sgrib pa*) and the obstructions to omniscience (*jñeyāvaraṇa, shes bya'i sgrib pa*). Although variously defined, the afflictive obstructions are the afflictions of desire, hatred, and ignorance, which must be destroyed in order to achieve liberation from rebirth; they are therefore abandoned by the arhat. The obstructions to omniscience are more subtle and insidious, consisting of the predispositions of ignorance that prevent the simultaneous understanding of all phenomena in the universe. These obstructions, together with the afflictive obstructions, must be abandoned by the bodhisattva in order to achieve buddhahood. The Prāsaṅgika interpretation of the two obstructions, as presented in Dge lugs, is that upon the destruction of the afflictive obstructions (which begins at the first bodhisattva *bhūmi* and concludes at the eighth), the conception of intrinsic existence is utterly destroyed. However, objects continue to falsely appear to intrinsically exist to the sense consciousnesses until the destruction of the obstructions of omniscience, which finally occurs only with the attainment of buddhahood. It is therefore only a buddha who is not subject to false appearance.

Bringing this topic to the question of ontological status of objects, GC states that all of the things that appear so solidly and irrefutably to the unenlightened are obstructions to omniscience. This is the case even if we use Madhyamaka reasoning, such as the famous sevenfold reasoning of Candrakīrti that proves that a chariot is not to be found among its parts. Such reasoning may undercut our misconception that things exist as they appear, but it will have no effect on our sense experience, where things will continue to appear to be intrinsically existent until the achievement of buddhahood. It is because the Buddha has utterly destroyed the obstructions to omniscience that he can see through walls; it is because we have not destroyed them that we cannot. Things appear to intrinsically exist. To assent to that appearance is an afflictive obstruction; to merely perceive such appearance is an obstruction to omniscience. Śāntideva compares it to a magic show. The magician conjures the illusion of a beautiful woman. The members of the audience see her and think that she is real. The magician sees her and knows that she is not. The response of the audience is like that of a person with the afflictive obstructions; the response of the magician is like that of a person who has abandoned the afflictive obstructions, but still has the obstructions of omniscience.

¶108 In a passage that does not seem to immediately follow what precedes or follows it, GC pays homage to the Buddha (glossing the opening stanza of Dharmakīrti's *Pramāṇavārttika*) as one who has unified all apparent contradictions, yet who compassionately speaks the dharma to disciples, regardless of their capacities.

¶¶109–11 How things appear to those who have and those who have not understood emptiness leads to the topic of the commonly appearing subject (*chos can mthun snang ba*), raising in turn the question of the very possibility of communication. GC is not referring here to the difference in perception between the Buddha and a sentient being, but that between a Prāsaṅgika and a non-Prāsaṅgika. Even something as apparently simple as a stone would not be understood in the same way. For the non-Prāsaṅgika, the stone would not exist if it were not intrinsically existent. For the Prāsaṅgika, it can only exist because it is not intrinsically existent. Thus, the word *stone* would communicate something very different to the two persons.

Extending this philosophical distinction into the realm of the ordinary, as is his wont, GC notes that the problem of reference is not limited to Prāsaṅgikas and those who are not Prāsaṅgikas. When an Indian and a Chinese say "Long live the king," they each have their own conception of who this king is and what he looks like. (GC is unclear here as to whether the Indian and the Chinese are speaking the same language.) Yet something is communicated between them because they have little at stake in their statement, or in its referent.

GC returns to the topic of assertions for oneself and assertions for others, and offers a new definition for each. An assertion for oneself is an assertion about things that exist as they appear according to one's philosophical position. An assertion for others is an assertion about things that do not exist as they appear according to one's philosophical position. From the Prāsaṅgika perspective, the only thing that exists as it appears is emptiness. Thus, assertions about anything other than emptiness would be an assertion for others. Such an interpretation entails the apparently disquieting consequence that many of the assertions most central to Buddhist practice, such as those concerning the four truths and the five paths, are assertions about things that appear mistakenly, and thus are assertions for others. GC's position recalls the standard Dge lugs identification of definitive (*nītārtha, nges don*) and provisional (*neyārtha, drang don*) scriptures according to the Madhyamaka, where the definitive is emptiness, the defining nature of phenomena; hence definitive scriptures are those that set forth emptiness. All other statements, regardless of whether they are to be taken literally or nonliterally, are provisional. GC's point here is also consistent with his earlier argument that the Buddha has no position, so all of his statements are assertions for others. And GC is able to find scriptural support, in the famous statement from the *Dhammapada* (which he had translated from Pāli into Tibetan when he was in Sri Lanka) that the dharma is like a raft, to be left behind upon reaching the other shore. He also cites Śāntideva, who says (in GC's reading) at *Bodhicaryāvatāra* IX.76 that one must maintain one's delusions about the state of enlightenment in order to achieve enlightenment. The path is therefore like a ladder: progress depends on each rung, yet each rung is left behind as one ascends higher and higher. As one grows older, one sets aside childish things. How can one proceed to buddhahood without leaving behind the misconceptions of the unenlightened?

¶¶112–14 From time to time throughout the text, GC compares the position of modern-day Dge lugs pas with that of "earlier scholars," always finding fault with the former and favoring the latter. One of the standard objections to the doctrine of emptiness, expressed by hypothetical opponents going back to the works of Nāgārjuna, is that if everything were empty of intrinsic existence, causation would be impossible. The standard response to this objection is that emptiness is not nothingness; that things lack intrinsic existence does not mean that they are utterly nonexistent. The earlier answer to the objection, and one that GC seems to find preferable, is that the Prāsaṅgikas have no assertions regarding existence or nonexistence. GC has said earlier that when one debates with others, one has no choice but to use their categories, to make "assertions for others." Yet he seems to admire the scholars of old who saw no point in engaging in debates about existence and nonexistence, retaining the perspective of enlightenment in which all opposites are unified.

The Madhyamakas are renowned for their reasoning and for their demolition of the positions of others. Yet the purpose of their reasoning is unique. When others use reasoning, negation of one thing entails the affirmation of its opposite. By disproving the position of the opponent, one's own position is proved. In contrast, the Prāsaṅgikas use reasoning to refute the positions of others but then turn that reasoning on their own positions. GC takes an example from the opening stanza of the second chapter of Nāgārjuna's *Treatise on the Middle Way*. In seeking to identify what motion (or "going") is, Nāgārjuna states that going is not to be found on the part of the path that has already been traversed, "the gone over." It is not to be found on the part of the path that has not yet been traversed, "the not-yet-gone-over." If going is not to found on the gone over or the not-yet-gone-over, going is not to be found. Thus, rather than refuting one possibility in order to prove another, Nāgārjuna refutes all possibilities.

But GC seeks always to take the focus away from the debating courtyard, where he seems to have so excelled, to meditative experience. He therefore introduces two terms from the taxonomies of the path, *meditative equipoise* (*samāhita, mnyam gzhag*) and *subsequent attainment* (*pṛṣṭhalabdha, rjes thob*). The former is the vision of emptiness during which nothing appears except the absence of intrinsic existence. The latter is the state that occurs at the conclusion of this vision, when conventional phenomena again appear. It is these two profound experiences, rather than words mouthed in the debating courtyard, that provide the meaning of the statement that nothing exists ultimately and everything exists conventionally.

¶¶115–17 Continuing in his praise of the "earlier Tibetans," GC turns next to the two types of selflessness: the selflessness of persons (*pudgalanairātmya, gang zag gi bdag med*) and the selflessness of phenomena (*dharmanairātmya, chos kyi bdag med*). It is the position of Tsong kha pa and his followers that the two types of nonself differ only with respect to what it is that lacks self: persons or phenomena other than the person. Otherwise, the two are equally the absence of intrinsic existence and the two are equally subtle. The earlier Tibetans had a different understanding of the two terms: they differed both in their nature and in their subtlety. Thus, the selflessness of the person was the absence of intrinsic existence of the person (just as the Dge lugs would say). However, the selflessness of phenomena was freedom from the elaborations of existence, nonexistence, both existence and nonexistence, and neither existence nor nonexistence. Moreover, the two types of nonself differed in subtlety and hence in their place on the path. To understand the selflessness of the person was to overturn the misconception of self of ordinary beings, who naturally regard the self as an autonomous entity. This insight, however, was ultimate in name only; in fact, it remained on the level of the conventional, because it was simply the understanding of the nonexistence of what the ignorant hold to exist. This wisdom, therefore, however profound, did not pass beyond the four extremes of existence, nonexistence, both, and neither. The more subtle insight was to be free of the four extremes of elaboration.

GC provides some quotations from Śantideva, most notably the famous second stanza of the ninth chapter of his *Bodhicaryāvatāra*, in support of the view of the earlier Tibetans: "The ultimate is not within the mind's sphere; the mind is said to be the conventional." GC praises the Buddha as being unique among all teachers because his teaching does not abide in the domain of existence or nonexistence. Other teachers propound doctrines that merely adorn the innate ignorance with scripture and reasoning. To support his view, GC quotes Tsong kha pa's *Praise of Dependent Origination* (*Rten 'brel bstod pa*). Again, GC finds fault not with Tsong kha pa but his descendants.

These contemporary Dge lugs pas feel that they are displaying their philosophical acuity when they say, for example, that the term *inexpressible* is itself an expression. But they are like two jaundice sufferers debating about a yellow conch; they are like a person who dreams that he is dreaming and recognizes the dream within a dream (but not the dream itself) as a dream. As long as the debaters are not cured of jaundice and as long as the dreamer is not awakened, they remain enmeshed in categories of truth and falsity within the realm of illusion. This is something that GC has already said several times. But he concludes his point by saying, "One must know that this is both a fault of ignorance and a quality of dependent origination." It is, of course, a fault of ignorance. But GC's statement that it is also a quality of dependent origination places him at odds with Tsong kha pa's famous claim, following Nāgārjuna, for the compatibility of emptiness and dependent origination: because phenomena are dependently arisen, they are empty of intrinsic existence; because phenomena are empty, they are dependently arisen. For Tsong kha pa, this mutual implication of emptiness and dependent origination provides the essential relation between the conventional and the ultimate. For GC, as we have seen, the conventional and the ultimate are two very different realms, and dependent origination—with its categories of cause and effect, whole and part, basis of designation and designated object—is, at least in some way, responsible for the duality that confines consciousness.

¶118 GC returns to what it means for the Madhyamaka to have no assertion. He begins with the kinds of pedantic arguments that are made about the topic in the debating courtyard, such as the statement that having no assertion is itself an assertion. These arguments, GC concludes, are inevitable whenever a Prāsaṅgika debates with a proponent of true existence because of the disparity in their perspectives; for the latter, even the term *absence of intrinsic existence* intrinsically exists. Thus, he returns to the hypothetical opponent who opens Nāgārjuna's *Refutation of Objections* (*Vigrahavyāvartanī*) with the objection, "If nothing intrinsically exists, then your words also do not intrinsically exist." GC then adds his own verses, in the same meter and style of the citation from the Indian text, having the opponent continue by saying, "If you have no assertion, then why is having no assertion not an assertion?" This objection does not occur in Nāgārjuna's text, and thus Nāgārjuna does not respond to it. So GC does so for him, again writing in verse, "That I have no assertion is just your assertion; that a white conch is yellow is just your assertion." GC put his own example of the color of the conch in the land of the jaundiced into the mouth of Nāgārjuna in order to make a point that he assumes is also Nāgārjuna's: the entire topic of what is and is not an assertion is a controversy confined to the realm of ignorance. In this way, GC provides an adornment for Nāgārjuna's thought. If one wishes to define an assertion as a statement that someone believes in from the depths of his heart, then there is no possibility of the Buddha teaching the dharma in accordance with the limited understanding of sentient beings. If things exist as they appear and are described as they exist, then there is no purpose in pursuing the Buddhist path; the discrepancy between the mode of appearance and the mode of being must be maintained.

¶119 The discussion of what is asserted for the sake of others is interrupted by a brief paean to the Buddha that describes him as valid person (*pramāṇabhūta, tshad ma'i skyes bu*).[19] GC explains that non-Buddhists seek to establish the

---

19. On this term, see Ernst Steinkellner, "*Tshad ma'i skyes bu*: Meaning and Significance of the Term," in *Proceedings of the Csoma de Körös Symposium, held at Velm-Vienna, Austria, 13—19 September, 1981*, ed. Ernst Steinkellner and Helmut Tauscher (Wien: Arbeitskreis für Tibetische und Buddhistische Studien, Universität Wien, 1983), 275–84; and Eli Franco, *Dharmakīrti on Compassion and Rebirth* (Wien: Arbeitskreis für Tibetische und Buddhistische Studien, Universität Wien, 1997), 1–43.

authority of their teacher first, and then follow his scriptures. Buddhists, on the other hand, first establish that the Buddha's teachings are valid and then follow him on this basis. This, GC says, is the method of Dharmakīrti, and indeed the second chapter of Dharmakīrti's *Pramāṇavārttika* is devoted to this proof. According to a standard Dge lugs presentation, the phenomena of the universe may be divided into three categories: the manifest, the slightly hidden, and the very hidden. The manifest are the objects of the senses, and their existence is determined by direct perception. The slightly hidden are those phenomena that cannot be directly perceived in ordinary sense experience, but whose existence can be established through inference. Examples of the slightly hidden include subtle impermanence, the law of karma, rebirth, and emptiness. The very hidden are those things that can be known only by a buddha, such as the circumstances of someone's lifetime in the distant past or the far future, or what particular karmic conditions produced the individual colors in the feathers of a peacock's tail.

Because the manifest and the slightly hidden are accessible to direct perception and inference, respectively, the statements of the Buddha need to be taken on faith only when he speaks of the very hidden. And GC cites the famous statement from Āryadeva that because the Buddha is correct about emptiness, one can assume that he is also accurate with regard to lesser matters. GC endorses this view and declares that one can follow whatever the Buddha says without the slightest fear of harm. We recall, of course, that GC has repeatedly said that the Buddha must adapt his teachings to the limited capacities of his disciples, such that what he says may not, and, from GC's perspective, cannot be the ultimate truth. GC compares the situation to that of a mother and child. The mother may keep the child from going outside by saying that there is a tiger on the prowl (when there is not) and discourage the child from wandering far by threatening to cut off his or her ears (when she will not). Although these statements are not true, they are for the benefit of the child. In the same way, one can confidently follow whatever the Buddha says without needing to consider whether what he is saying in a particular instance is provisional or definitive. Those who have argued that GC was somehow not a Buddhist might read this paragraph.

¶¶120–25 Yet the Buddha did adapt his teachings to the circumstances of time and place, employing skillful methods to both the minutiae of monastic discipline and the final nature of reality. As an example of the former, GC recounts that, in response to complaints of laymen, the Buddha had his monks raise the hem of their lower robe. Later, a group of six immodest monks went swimming, revealing enough of their bodies that the laymen complained to the Buddha.[20] The Buddha therefore issued another rule, this time lowering the hem of the robe. The Buddha's pronouncements on this point were obviously made entirely to please his patrons; he had no opinion on the matter. GC concludes that all of the statements of the Buddha were made to accord with the three realms of saṃsāra.

GC next returns to a point that he had also made earlier: there is little to be gained in engaging in refutations and proofs about the constituents of the conventional world. No matter how far one has advanced on the bodhisattva path, the conventional world will continue to be perceived as ordinary beings see it: false appearances, created by the obstructions to omniscience, persist until buddhahood. Thus, within the conventional realm, even someone who has seen emptiness directly "must involuntarily assert whatever was asserted earlier." Even to proclaim that nothing exists has no effect on ordinary habits of mind. "Therefore, I see no reason why the pair, refutation and proof, need to be taken so seriously." The Madhyamaka who has no assertions continues to use language to name the components of the conventional world.

GC provides an example, however, that casts the question of assertion for others in a somewhat different light. A magician casts a spell on an audience that makes them see an elephant. When the audience asks the magician whether the elephant is real, he says that it is. "That is the magician's assertion of the elephant for others." However, such an assertion is not simply a matter of accommodating those who are at present incapable of understanding the truth. The magician has created the illusion and is in a position to disillusion the audience, yet he allows its credulity to continue. GC does not explain the metaphor. In the standard reading, the audience, which sees the elephant as real, represents sentient beings who have not understood emptiness. The magician, who sees the elephant but knows that it is not real, represents the bodhisattva who has understood emptiness but to whom conventional phenomena continue to appear as if they were intrinsically existent; the bodhisattva perceives objects to intrinsically exist, but does not assent to that false appearance. The person who arrives at the performance after the spell has been cast does not see an elephant at all; this person is like the Buddha, who has destroyed both the misconception and the misperception of phenomena.

20. GC is apparently referring here to the story of King Pasenadi and his queen Mallikā observing monks playing in the water, recounted in the Pāli Vinaya IV.112. For an English rendering, see Nyanaponika Thera and Hellmuth Hecker, *Great Disciples of the Buddha* (Somerville, MA: Wisdom Publications, 1997), 259–60.

The latecomer never arrives in GC's version, and the audience does not simply believe that the elephant is real; it has sufficient doubt to ask the magician, who lies to them, although to tell the audience the truth would seem only to enhance his reputation as an illusionist. The magician therefore is not compelled to "powerlessly assert" what is not true. His agency recalls the opening passage in the *Vimalakīrti Sūtra* mentioned above. After the Buddha touches the earth with his toe and transforms our world into a bejewelled garden, he explains that what he has revealed is the true nature of his land, that he uses his miraculous powers to make it appear squalid so his disciples will develop a sense of renunciation and practice the path. This suggests that the impermanence and suffering so central to the basic doctrines of Buddhism, which are set forth as the reason saṃsāra must be abandoned, are presented here simply as instantiations of the Buddha's powers, of his skillful methods to bring others to enlightenment.

And GC indeed turns next to the question of the interpretation of scripture, and its relation to the question of assertions for oneself and for others. Those who claim that Nāgārjuna indeed had assertions can point to his most famous work, the *Treatise on the Middle Way*, asking why he would compose such a text if he had no system and no assertions of his own. Again, in GC's view, this is missing the point, for it is clear that the Buddha himself taught many sūtras that do not represent his final view, at least as that view is understood by the Madhyamakas. For example, in two famous sūtras, the *Saṃdhinirmocana* and the *Laṅkāvatāra*, the Buddha explains that there is a foundational consciousness (*ālayavijñāna, kun gzhi rnam shes*), external objects do not exist, and the ultimate reality is the nonduality of subject and object. Each of these assertions is central to the Yogācāra, and each is rejected by the Madhyamaka, who explain that the Buddha set forth these doctrines to those who were temporarily unsuited for the higher Madhyamaka teachings. For the Madhyamakas, the Buddha's proclamations of the emptiness of intrinsic existence are the definitive meaning and the Buddha's own system; his elaborations of all other doctrines are his assertions for others. GC seems to imply the standard Dge lugs view here; gone, at least for the moment, is his contention that anything and everything that the Buddha speaks, by the mere fact that it is expressed in human speech, is an assertion for others. The Buddha's "own system" is silence. GC returns to this position (after repeating the story about the Khams pa chieftain) when he says, "Without this presentation of assertions for others, how can the opportunity arise for the speaking of one word of the dharma between the Buddha who perceives existence as infinite purity, and common beings who perceive everything as impure and contaminated?"

¶¶126–31 GC then turns to the topic of the meaning of the terms *conventional analysis* and *ultimate analysis*. In the standard Dge lugs reading of the term, conventional analysis deals with the operation of conventional truths, while ultimate analysis examines conventional truths to determine their true nature; furthermore, ultimate analysis in the true sense of the term is reserved for the Madhyamaka, with all other schools engaged in conventional analysis. Once again, GC finds this unnecessarily pedantic and seeks to redefine the terms in more ordinary words. Thus, any reflection that considers whether something is real, whether it exists as it appears, is ultimate analysis. Any reflection that regards things as mere appearances is conventional analysis. From this perspective, not only are non-Madhyamakas engaged in ultimate analysis; the term applies equally to untutored beings who strike gold. They do not regard the gold as like an illusion; the gold that they discover exists most objectively. Indeed, they subject it to ultimate analysis, seeking its final mode of being. And they find it. It is because they find the gold to be real that they are attached to it. This is why the Buddha explained that ignorance is the root of the other two poisons, desire and hatred.

Continuing his assault on the Dge lugs vocabulary, GC criticizes those who would say that "assertion for oneself" and "assertion for others" are the same. He appears to be alluding here to terms that are central to Candrakīrti's critique of Bhāvaviveka: inference known to oneself (*svasiddhānumāna, rang grags kyi rjes dpag*) and inference known to the other (*parasiddhānumāna, gzhan grags kyi rjes dpag*). In this context, the terms refer to a Madhyamaka's use of the opponent's own assertions to defeat him in debate. The terms are indeed synonyms: the "oneself" in the first phrase is used from the opponent's own perspective, the "other" in the second phrase is used from the Madhyamaka's perspective. GC presumably knows this, but it provides him with an opportunity to again remind us of the ontological and epistemological chasm that exists between ignorant sentient beings and the Buddha. He mentions a story in the *Pile of Jewels* (*Ratnakūṭa*) in which the bodhisattva Vegadhārin sought to use his supernormal powers to see the top of the Buddha's *uṣṇīṣa*, the crown protrusion on the Buddha's head, one of the thirty-two marks of a superman. He went first to the summit of Mount Meru, the central mountain in the Buddhist universe, then to the heaven of Brahmā, and finally completely beyond this universe to the world of the buddha Padmaśrīsārarāja in an effort to gain sufficient height, but he was never able to see it.

If one has conviction in the dharma—that is, if one is a Buddhist—one must have conviction in the inconceivable. To assume that anything that cannot be imagined by the small human mind does not therefore exist is to become a nihilist, who assumes that that which cannot be perceived with the senses does not exist. GC gives as an example the standard syllogism about smoke and fire: where there is smoke, there must be fire; where there is fire, there must be smoke. The presence of one can be inferred from the presence of the other, because neither has ever been perceived without the other. GC calls this inserting the final mode of being of all phenomena inside a single hair-pore of reasoning. And he identifies a fire that has no smoke as "a thousand transformations of happiness and suffering, good and bad, which radiate as a hundred thousand rays of the white and red light of Samantabhadra."

GC exercises his exegetical skills on a passage from Candrakīrti's commentary on his own *Entrance to the Middle Way* (*Madhyamakāvatāra*), in which he says, "It takes great hardship to overcome the conventional." According to GC, Tsong kha pa, in a passage that GC does not identify, then comments on the statement, explaining that it is not necessary to engage in ascetic practices in order to overcome the conventional. GC creatively interprets this to mean that because it is not necessary to practice asceticism to overcome the conventional, those who do engage in the ascetic practice of following the path would certainly do so. Because it is therefore so difficult to overcome the conventional, until one has undergone the great hardship of doing so, one has no choice but to affirm the conventions of ordinary experience. For prior to the achievement of buddhahood, the innate ignorance continues to cause the objects of experience to falsely appear to be intrinsically existent. These appearances occur without any conscious decision on the part of the subject; they arise involuntarily. At that point, as a result of the artificial ignorance that develops from inculcating false philosophies (and, as we have seen, GC interprets this term very broadly), one must describe these false appearances of phenomena with terms like *good* and *bad*, and *existent* and *nonexistent*. As a consequence, one must remain against one's will in saṃsāra until the conventional is overcome. This need to assert the conventions of the world involuntarily is a reason for sorrow. GC again cites Candrakīrti, again out of context (the passage occurs in his critique of Cittamātra in the sixth chapter of the *Madhyamakāvatāra*), to say that anyone who undergoes great hardship to reach a stage where he is unharmed by the world is worthy of praise.

¶¶132–34 In this section, GC addresses the topic of invalidation by reasoning (*rigs pas gnod pa*). It derives from the common assumption in Buddhist thought that wisdom can destroy ignorance because wisdom is an understanding of the truth, while ignorance is a misunderstanding of the truth. In the realm of logic, it is held that any conclusions drawn from reasoning that analyzes the conventional are superseded by conclusions drawn from reasoning that analyzes the ultimate. Conclusions drawn from inference can in turn be superseded by the vision of yogic direct perception. GC again finds this all rather hypothetical, noting that there is no power greater than ignorance in the minds of the unenlightened. If "invalidation by reasoning" refers simply to a more powerful form of consciousness overcoming the less powerful, and the validity of the more powerful consciousness is simply a function of its power, then the misconceptions of ignorance would be valid. But "invalidation by reasoning" cannot mean that; GC quotes Śāntideva, who said that if invalidation were merely a matter of power, then it would be impossible to convince anyone that a woman is unclean. He is referring here to the standard Buddhist arguments for nonattachment, which seek to quell male lust by describing the female body as a bag of filth. Śāntideva's point, apparently, is that there is no more powerful emotion than lust; if invalidation consisted merely in the strong overcoming the weak, it would be impossible to overcome the world's conception of the female body as clean and hence desirable. Because that conception has been successfully destroyed by Buddhist monks, invalidation must mean something more nuanced.

Invalidation by reasoning would therefore seem to derive not from the strength of the consciousness in a crude sense, but in the precision of its analysis. Yet who sets the standards for such precision? GC notes that the Cittamātra employs reasoning to prove that external objects do not exist. But from the perspective of the Madhyamaka, who holds that external objects do exist, this is not a case of negating the existence of external objects. Rather, the reasoning of the Cittamātra is too weak to discern the existence of external objects. Thus, it is not the case that the Cittamātra has found external objects to be nonexistent; it is simply that they have been unable to find them. Yet the Madhyamaka would say that when they use their own reasonings to seek intrinsic existence, they do not discover it, and this "not finding" proves that intrinsic existence does not exist. GC finds this to be amazing. He considers the case of "other emptiness" (*gzhan stong*) asserted by the Jo nang pa, that reality is empty not of intrinsic existence but of all negative qualities. The Dge lugs consider this doctrine heretical, an "extreme position." If "invalidation by reasoning" is something defined by one's opponent, then even this profound Jo nang doctrine would be consigned to the conventional. In fact, because the category of "invalidation by reasoning" operates entirely within the realm of worldly conceptions of existence and nonexistence, its conclusion that something does not exist carries no weight. As GC has already stated, to conclude that because something does not fit inside the tiny mind of the unenlightened, it therefore does not exist, is the height of folly. "If one believes that this very nonfinding is the final meaning of not existing, then there is no opportunity whatsoever for entering into the mode of being of phenomena."

¶135 GC returns to a concept that he introduced in his long poem at ¶60: the nonobservation of the suitable to appear (*snang rung ma dmigs pa*). In Buddhist logic, this is one of the standard reasons that something does not exist. If there were smoke on a lake at night, one would see fire. Because fire, which is "suitable to appear," is not observed, one can conclude that there is no smoke. The nonobservation of the suitable to appear is one of two types of nonobservation signs (*ma dmigs pa'i rtags*). The other is the nonobservation of the nonappearing (*mi snang ba ma dmigs pa*), which is used to prove the absence of something that is not perceivable by ordinary consciousness; the standard example is a kind of invisible ghost called a flesh eater (*sha za*). Because a flesh eater is not observed in a particular place by someone who has the psychic powers to see it, one can conclude that the flesh eater is absent there. In his ongoing crusade to call into question the categories of the debating courtyard, GC asks how one draws the line between the suitable to appear and the nonappearing. As he notes, many types of superknowledge (*abhijñā, mngon shes*) are described in Buddhist texts. Some people can see ghosts, but some bodhisattvas can perceive billions of sentient beings in a handful of sand. Thus, what is and is not suitable to appear depends entirely on the level of attainment of the observer. Pointing yet again to the highly circumscribed perspective of ignorant sentient beings, to whom so little is "suitable to appear," he says, "The nonobservation of the suitable to appear that is agreed upon with one voice by many millions of vulgar common beings is just a portion of the nonobservation of the suitable to appear. Therefore, one must understand that the nonexistence which they prove is just one side of nonexistence."

¶136 GC returns to the topic of affixing some qualification to the object of negation. According to the standard Dge lugs description of the two branches of Madhyamaka, the Svātantrikas refute the "true establishment" (*bden par grub pa*) of objects, but they do not refute their "intrinsic existence" (*rang bzhin gyi grub pa*). The Prāsaṅgikas, however, refute both their true establishment and their intrinsic existence. It is also commonly said that what is being refuted by the Madhyamaka is not existence but truly established existence, that to refute existence would be nihilistic. GC mocks this assertion, as he has before, saying that if this is the case, then one really should pile on even more qualifications, that what should be negated is not "existence," or "truly established existence," but "intrinsically existent truly established existence." To affix all these qualifications to the object of negation does not sharpen the focus on the target of wisdom, it changes the target. We have become well accustomed to both the perception and conception of falsely appearing objects over the long course of rebirth in saṃsāra. A pot for us is indistinguishable from a "truly established pot." There is no need to specify it so precisely.

¶¶137–38 GC repeats the common Madhyamaka assertion that nothing exists ultimately, even ultimate truths. Emptiness is empty. Everything that exists, exists conventionally. That is, nothing exists objectively; everything exists as a mere designation by consciousness. What kind of consciousness is qualified to designate existence, however, is the subject of considerable discussion, with the Dge lugs concluding that it would be a "faultless mind that is not affected by adventitious causes of error." Given everything that he has said to this point, one would conclude that this phrase would prove irresistible to GC. But he does not pounce, apparently content to point out that all the great scholars of India and Tibet, of both earlier and later times, agree that the entire conventional world is something that is posited by "this mere thing."

¶¶139–44 GC returns to his argument that despite what is refuted by their reasoning, Prāsaṅgikas must continue to make assertions about the world. As he has said repeatedly, reasoning will refute what does not exist and will leave the rest; there is no need to fear logical overkill. All reasoning takes the measure of what it is capable of refuting. Thus, one need not worry that proving that a rabbit has no horns may lead one to think that a rabbit has no head.

All philosophical schools are, in one sense or another, concerned with the disjunction of appearance and reality. They do not merely describe the way things appear; they seek to identify a reality that is not apparent. The value of a philosophical system is therefore to be found not in the degree of its internal consistency but in its ability to accommodate contradiction. Thus, the Sāṃkhya asserts that effects are already present in their causes, but they are not yet manifest. The Cittamātra asserts that an object and the consciousness that perceives it are of the same entity, yet there seems to be an external world. The Madhyamaka says that things which exist for an ordinary consciousness are found not to exist under analysis. If the value of a philosophical system resides in its absence of contradiction between the way things appear and the way things are, then these various assertions are so much noise. Indeed, the Madhyamaka is filled with apparent contradictions. Because they refute the four extremes—of existence, nonexistence, both existence and nonexistence, and neither existence nor nonexistence—one commonly finds statements like "If it is not the case that it does not exist, it does not follow that it is existent" and "If it is not the case that it exists, it does not follow that is nonexistent." That is, the negation of one element of a dichotomy does not imply the affirmation of its opposite, even though this lack of implication appears contradictory. GC describes this as "two things that are appropriately contradictory are put together in the same place harmoniously." From the worldly perspective, even the Madhyamaka has to admit that these are contradictions, but saying so is yet another case of an "assertion for others."

¶¶140–45 GC returns to the topic of what is, and is not, negated by reasoning by stating the position of Tsong kha pa: sense objects appear to exist in and of themselves, but in fact they do not exist in that way. Thus, such an essence— that things exist as they appear in sense experience—does not exist even conventionally. GC thus endorses the understanding of nonexistence gained by a "reasoning consciousness" (*rigs shes*), a meditative awareness that sets out to investigate the final mode of being of an object and discovers in the end that the object cannot be found. He contrasts this with the understanding of nonexistence gained through a form of reasoning whose sole aim at the outset is to refute the existence of something.

In contrast with the standard Dge lugs distinction between the lack of intrinsic existence on the one hand and utter nonexistence on the other, GC declares that the reasoning consciousness, which at the end of its investigation concludes that the lack of intrinsic existence means utter nonexistence, has in fact understood the nonexistence of the category of nonexistence. Because such a person has recognized nonexistence for what it is, there is no danger of falling into nihilism, the standard Dge lugs warning to those who identify the object of negation too broadly. On the other hand, someone who sets out specifically to deny utterly the existence of specific constituents of conventional reality, like cause and effect and dependent origination, will find a way to do so. This selective refutation of certain of the elements of the conventional world leads to nihilism; the insight into the universal absence of both existence and nonexistence does not. The error, GC explains, is to define the world as the existent and then regard nonexistence as its otherworldly nemesis. Instead, one should regard both existence and nonexistence as constituents of the conventional. Then, upon understanding that all phenomena of the universe are free from the elaborations of the four extremes (existence, nonexistence, both, neither), even nonexistence will be free from the extreme of nonexistence. This is the teaching of Nāgārjuna, and the Buddha prophesied his coming in the *Laṅkāvatara Sūtra* in order to encourage those in the future to follow him.

GC continues his praise of nonexistence by noting that sentient beings fail to achieve enlightenment not because they believe too strongly in existence, but because they lack sufficient faith in nonexistence. The ultimate happiness that all beings seek is not to be found among the existent things of this world; it is to be found among the nonexistent. The myriad qualities of buddhahood are all beyond our conception of what exists, and thus "seem to exist within this nonexistence of ours."

Indeed, the world of existence is confined by nonexistence, and therefore the refutation of the extreme of nonexistence (among the four extremes) is the most subtle of all reasonings, because the mode of being of everything in the universe is nonexistence, in the sense of the "not finding" of any true nature. The end of the investigation of all the appearances of the world and the end of the process of reasoning is this absence. As long as one has not achieved buddhahood, this nonexistence stands at the limit of what can be understood; the other shore that the Buddha reached after aeons on the bodhisattva path is indeed far beyond.

GC interrupts this rather lyrical passage to find fault with another scholar. This time, it is not a Dge lugs pa but the famous Sa skya scholar Go rams pa bsod nams seng ge (1429–89). Go rams pa, it seems, described the afflictive obstructions as the conception of true existence, and the obstructions to omniscience as the conception of the four extremes. Therefore, if one wishes to achieve liberation from rebirth as an arhat, one need only understand the absence of true existence. If one wishes to achieve buddhahood, however, one must gain freedom from the four extremes of elaboration, including the conception that true existence is either existent or nonexistent. Elsewhere in his writings, however, Go rams pa had identified the assertion of the absence of true existence as a form of nihilism. GC wonders, then, how anyone could become an arhat by holding a nihilistic view. It is universally accepted, he explains, that one abandons the afflictive obstructions through the "view," that is, the understanding that there is no self, and that one abandons the obstructions to omniscience through method, that is, by empowering the wisdom consciousness through the accumulation of merit until it is able to overcome those obstructions. (This is the Dge lugs view.) Only a confused person would differentiate the two obstructions from the perspective of how own apprehends the nature of reality.

¶¶145–46 GC returns to the topic of assertions for oneself and assertions for others, this time citing the common tenet that although the Buddha has destroyed all imperfections, he nonetheless sees everything that sentient beings see. How could this possibly be so, GC asks, given the great chasm that divides their perception, unless one is able to distinguish between what is seen for oneself and what is seen for others? He provides an example.

The first topic that young monks in the Dge lugs monastery learn to debate about is colors, and one of the first consequences they learn is, "It follows that the subject, the color of a white conch, is white, because of being a color." In order for this statement to be correct, three things must be true. First, the reason, "being a color," must be a property of the subject, "the color of a white conch" (which it is). Second, there must be pervasion between the reason, "being a color" and the predicate, "being white." That is, the category of being a color must be pervaded by the category of being white, such that whatever is a color is necessarily white (which it is not). Third, there must be reverse pervasion between the predicate and the reason. That is, whatever is not a color must necessarily be not white (which it is). Because the second criterion is not fulfilled, the statement is not correct. It would be correct, however, to say, "It follows that the subject, the color of a white conch, is a color, because of being white," because the color of a white conch is a color and because whatever is white is necessarily a color. GC seems to take some delight in now demonstrating how even the color of a conch, the most elementary of topics, debated by shaven-headed children, can illustrate a most profound problem in Madhyamaka philosophy.

He asks us to imagine that a debate about the color of a conch takes place between someone with clear sight and someone suffering from jaundice. The person with clear sight states his position: the color of a conch is white, not yellow. The person with jaundice responds with a consequence: "It follows that the subject, the color that I see in front of me, is not the color of a conch, because of not being yellow." This is what is called a contradictory consequence, a statement that the person with jaundice does not believe, but in which the reason and the pervasion are accepted by the opponent.[21] A contradictory consequence

---

21. There is an apparent problem here. The syllogism that the person with jaundice wishes to imply would be, "The subject, the color which I see in front of me, is yellow because of being the color of the conch," which derives from taking the opposite of the reason and making that the

carries with it an implied syllogism. That syllogism is the "correct" position, in this case a veridical statement, from the perspective of the person with jaundice. This implied syllogism is extracted from the contradictory consequence by taking the opposite of the reason and turning that into the predicate, and taking the opposite of the predicate and turning that into the reason. Therefore, "It follows that the subject, the color that I see in front of me, is not the color of a conch, because of not being yellow" becomes "The subject, the color that I see in front of me, is yellow, because of being the color of a conch." This is a correct syllogism for the person with jaundice because it fulfills the three criteria: the reason is a property of the subject, that is, the color that he sees in front of him is the color of a conch; there is pervasion, that is, whatever is the color of a conch is necessarily yellow; and there is reverse pervasion, that is, whatever is not yellow is necessarily not the color of a conch.

The purpose of debate is to use the opponent's own assertions to demonstrate the fallacy of his position. Thus, the person who holds the correct view does not simply state that view, but seeks to lead the opponent to it via the opponent's own assumptions. Thus, if the person with clear sight is going to engage in a debate with the person with jaundice, a certain number of assumptions must be shared. Specifically, he must concede that from the perspective of the jaundiced opponent, what he sees before him is yellow; whatever is the color of a conch is necessarily yellow; and whatever is not yellow is necessarily not the color of a conch. Without accepting these, at least for the sake of argument, there can be no debate.

From a Buddhist perspective, the color of the conch is not as important as its other qualities: that it is impermanent, that it lacks true existence, that it is like an illusion. And all this can be conveyed, via debate, by the clear-eyed opponent, without his jaundiced adversary doubting for a moment that a conch is yellow. That is, communication is possible concerning the nature of the conch without there being agreement about something as basic as its color. This, for GC, is an analogy of the Buddha's teaching of the dharma to the unenlightened.

¶¶147–61 GC begins ¶147 with a paraphrase of a statement he had made above. Someone who continues to insist that Prāsaṅgikas have a system of their own

---

predicate, and taking the opposite of the predicate and making that the reason. However, in order for the implied syllogism to be acceptable, the opponent (the person with clear vision) has to accept the presence of the reason in the subject and the pervasion of the consequence. The opponent would accept the presence of the reason in the subject, that the color that he sees in front of him is not yellow. However, he would not accept the pervasion, that whatever is not yellow is necessarily not the color of a conch.

because Nāgārjuna made many statements need only remember that on different occasions the Buddha said that the self exists, that external objects are real, and that there are three final vehicles (such that not all beings will achieve buddhahood). No proponent of the Madhyamaka would assume for a moment that any of these assertions represented the Buddha's "own system." This, once again, is the meaning of "assertion for others."

This statement seems to serve as a conclusion to the preceding paragraph, after which (in the middle of ¶147) GC embarks on a lengthy discussion of what remains at the end of the process of analysis. He begins, "It is stated with very great clarity that even the negation of truth in the ultimate sense is at the level of the conventional. Therefore, even the negation of production from the four extremes must be done conventionally." The first sentence means simply that true existence, the false reality that ignorant beings imagine phenomena to possess, is utterly nonexistent, and thus does not exist even conventionally. GC concludes from this that production from the four extremes takes place at the level of the conventional. This is something of a point of contention, even within Dge lugs.

The refutation of the four extremes of production derives from the first chapter of Nāgārjuna's *Treatise on the Middle Way*, where it is stated that things are not produced from the four extremes of production: self, other, both self and other, or neither self nor other. There is no disagreement among Tibetan interpreters of Madhyamaka that the production from the four extremes is refuted ultimately. And there is no disagreement that production from three of the four extremes is also refuted conventionally. The question centers on production from other. The doctrine of dependent origination would seem to imply that effects arise from causes that are other, that is, different from themselves, on the conventional level; a sprout is different from a seed, a pot is different from clay. Yet GC, with other Tibetan interpreters—both Dge lugs and non-Dge lugs—holds that all four extremes of production are refuted both ultimately and conventionally. He does not argue here for the refutation of production from other conventionally; he simply declares it in order to make his own point: that in order to refute the conception that things are true ultimately, one must first refute "all of these subtle ideas that conceive things to be true conventionally." GC is clearly playing with the technical vocabulary here: the conception of true existence (*bden par 'dzin pa*) is generally taken as a synonym for the conception of ultimate existence (*don dam par 'dzin pa*); to understand that things exist conventionally is to understand that things do not exist truly or ultimately. But here GC seeks to distinguish between the conception that things truly exist ultimately and the conception that things truly exist conventionally. One may assume that he means by the former some kind of hypostatized status imagined by deluded philosophers. And one may assume that he means by the latter the ordinary ignorance of the world, which assumes things exist in the way that they appear. However, given what has come before and what will come after, GC seems to be taking "these subtle ideas that conceive things to be true conventionally" to mean what for the Dge lugs is the correct Madhyamaka view: although nothing is true ultimately, everything is true conventionally. That is, phenomena exist conventionally and are true in the sense that effects predictably follow from causes, and objects viably perform functions. GC is arguing, then, that this ordinary sense of existence must be called into question before any further misconceptions that rest upon it can be refuted.

He thus takes aim at the technical term *mere production* (*skye ba tsam*). It is commonly said that things are not produced from self or other, and are instead merely produced; that is, production is imputed to them without that production residing in the cause or the effect. The assertion of such mere production is one of the hallmarks of Madhyamaka, especially in its Dge lugs interpretation. But GC finds little purchase in the term *mere*, asking sarcastically why the Madhyamaka—renowned for refuting that things are truly established because they are neither the same as nor different from their parts—could not assert the existence of "mere" true establishment. GC finds it astounding that the Dge lugs will claim that a pillar cannot withstand analysis from the reasoning of the four extremes—that is, it can be shown neither to exist, not exist, both exist and not exist, nor neither exist nor not exist—yet claim that a pillar conventionally exists and merely exists. GC is obviously troubled by this term *mere*, seeing it as yet another of the masks of ignorance.

This leads GC to another term, *withstanding analysis by reasoning* (*rigs pas dpyad bzod*). Its common Dge lugs usage is found in the claim that reasoning refutes what does not exist, such as intrinsic existence, but does not refute what does exist, such as mere existence. Thus, when one analyzes a pillar, for example, the pillar is not able to withstand reasoning in the sense that an intrinsically existent pillar is refuted; the merely existent pillar remains at the end of the process of analysis.

But how, GC asks, should one distinguish between what is and is not able to withstand reasoning? Each philosophical school draws the line at a different location. A permanent self is able to withstand reasoning by the Sāṃkhya, who asserts that such a self exists. In this case, it becomes difficult to claim that something withstands the reasoning of one school but not another, as occurs when the Madhyamaka claims, against the Yogācāra, that external objects exist, and claim, also against the Yogācāra, that the foundational consciousness (*ālayavijñāna*) does not.

GC returns to his criticism of the Dge lugs affirmation of "conventional establishment" that is able to withstand analysis, asking for whom it could possibly be intended. The term makes no sense to those who have not studied philosophy ("the old men of the world whose minds have not been affected by tenets"), and it would not be accepted by the non-Madhyamaka schools, who have their own ideas about what does and does not withstand analysis by reasoning.

This leads GC into yet another discussion of what it means for the mind to be affected by tenets. And he concludes, once again, that the minds of everyone, with the possible exception of cats and dogs, have been affected by tenets. Indeed, any thought that anyone has, apart from the knowledge that one was born and someday will die, is the product of some kind of philosophy, in the broad sense of the term. GC's reiteration of this point seems to interrupt the critique of mere existence, yet it is not unrelated. The topic of the mind being affected by tenets, or not, is central to the notions of artificial and innate ignorance, with the former resulting from studying false philosophical systems. GC's implication is that the Dge lugs insistence on mere existence, far from being an accurate description of the nature of reality that counters the innate ignorance, is in fact yet another false tenet (albeit less false than the assertions of the non-Madhyamaka schools) confirming the conceptions of the innate ignorance.

As long as mere production is asserted, the refutation of the four extremes of production would seem to carry little force. Nāgārjuna's purpose in enumerating the four extremes was to identity all possible forms of production and then to demonstrate that each is untenable. If mere production is some fifth possibility, what purpose was there in refuting the other four? Indeed, what purpose does the adjective *mere* serve? Why not refute truly established true establishment and affirm mere true establishment? If mere production is not to be refuted, then the mere afflictive obstructions and the mere obstructions to omniscience certainly should not be. "Therefore, it is seen that among the thoughts of ordinary worldlings there is not found even the slightest thing to be refuted."

Thus, the Dge lugs interpret Candrakīrti's question, "Which of your productions is it?" to refute the four extremes of production but to imply the existence of mere production. His statement, therefore, would pertain only to rival philosophical schools who actively uphold one of the four extremes, and would be wholly irrelevant to the innate conception of some real production shared by all of the unenlightened. In this case, Madhyamaka reasoning is reduced to a difference of opinion among philosophers: each has his own perspective, and reasoning can do no real damage to ordinary, and more deeply ingrained, false opinion. If the criterion of truth is the ability to see at night, then human sight is "invalidated by reason," because the night vision of an owl is superior.

This has important implications for the practice of the Buddhist path. If wisdom is merely a matter of opinion, then there would be no final view; the various assertions of the Buddhist (and non-Buddhist) philosophical schools would simply be a variety of ideas that bore little relation to one another. They would disagree, but that disagreement would have no weight because none would be able to refute the other. Without refutation, there can be no proof. Far from being the relativist that he is sometimes portrayed to be, GC implies quite clearly here that there is a single reality, and in order to be free forever from the sufferings of this world, this reality must be known. He shares the Buddhist view that insight into reality has salvific power, that wisdom destroys ignorance and the afflictions it engenders. If there is no single reality to be understood, then there can be no path of vision (*darśanamārga, mthong lam*), the moment marking the beginning of the ten bodhisattva stages, in which emptiness is perceived directly for the first time in an experience in which the mind and emptiness seem mixed indistinguishably, like water poured into water. From that point on, over the course of the path of meditation (*bhāvanāmārga, sgom lam*), the bodhisattva abandons more and more subtle afflictions over nine levels. None of this would be possible if there were not a higher form of awareness that can overcome the lower. Otherwise, "It would be entirely acceptable to make whatever presentations one wished." Indeed, if simply not finding something (as opposed to finding it not to exist) was considered the sign of wisdom, then rocks would be buddhas. And a wrong consciousness that infers wrongly that where there is smoke there is no fire would not be inferring that there was no fire; it simply would not have found it.

A hypothetical opponent objects that one must differentiate clearly between different types of objects for different levels of awareness. The reasoning analyzing the ultimate searches for ultimate existence, and does not find it. The reasoning analyzing the conventional searches for mere existence, and finds it. Ultimate existence and conventional existence are two different things; different reasonings are used to analyze them, and the conclusions of one form of reasoning are not relevant for the other. Thus, to find that ultimate existence does not exist has no implications for conventional existence.

GC responds that if the domains of reasoning are isolated from each other in this way, such that what one reasoning does not find in one domain can do no damage to what another reasoning finds in another, then it would seem to be the case that the most common form of reasoning, the reasoning of ignorance that finds truly established phenomena everywhere, would be immune from any other form of reasoning. GC finds it incredible that the objects of everyday experience, "the things found by the six collections of consciousness," although these consciousnesses have been polluted by ignorance over the long course of saṃsāra, are somehow considered existent, while true existence, the object found by ignorance itself, is proclaimed as nonexistent. The former are "not found"; the latter is "found not to exist." GC finds this distinction to be dangerous, preventing the possibility of the negation of intrinsic existence being a nonaffirming negative, implying nothing else in its place. As long as the process of reasoning results only in "not finding," ignorance can never be destroyed; it simply shifts into another domain. As long as one holds that different types of consciousness find different kinds of objects, "what is found by one is not found by the other. How is it possible that one has even the slightest capacity to invalidate the other?"

GC is obviously disquieted by the Dge lugs concern with the maintenance of objects of ordinary experience as "mere appearances" and the contention that such objects persist on the conventional level. He wishes that Nāgārjuna were still alive so that we could ask him whether there is any difference between believing in conventional truths and believing in true existence. His implication, of course, is that Nāgārjuna's answer would be no. The desire and hatred that we feel in relation to food and drink come from the belief that food and drink are real, from the misconception of these objects of our everyday experience, and from nowhere else. To claim that "conventional existence" is something other than the way we ordinarily misconceive the world and is instead some kind of veridical status perceived by the Buddha himself is to place one's faith in ignorance.

GC is once again chastising those who are simply certifying the operations of ignorance by granting them the status of conventional. And he is once again pointing to the chasm that separates the unenlightened from the enlightened. However, he is in no way suggesting that enlightenment is therefore impossible. He alludes to the *tāntrika*s who hold that just this human body—made of the four elements of earth, water, fire, and wind—is the foundation for progressing on the path to buddhahood. Such an assertion does not preclude the possibility of the human body also serving as cause for desire, hatred, and ignorance. One must in fact understand that this body, this earth, is at once the sole foundation for wisdom and the sole foundation for the afflictions. Anyone who does not understand this is "very far away indeed from the system of the Buddhist Madhyamakas." GC repeats the Buddha's prophecy of Nāgārjuna, that he will destroy the positions of existence and nonexistence. Those who patch this with words and interpret it to mean that he will destroy the positions of true existence and ultimate nonexistence are simply affirming the worldly categories of existence and nonexistence. "I don't know whether this destroys the essence of Nāgārjuna's teaching or upholds it."

¶¶162–66 Because the Svātantrikas assert that objects intrinsically exist conventionally in the sense that they are naturally objects of the consciousnesses that observe them, the Svātantrikas believe slightly in the operations of the ordinary mind. The Prāsaṅgikas, however, destroy everything that it is believed by that mind. This is why in the perfection of wisdom sūtras, the Buddha goes down the list of the phenomena in the universe, the 108 categories of the afflicted and the pure. Beginning with form (*rūpa, gzugs*) and ending with the omniscient consciousness of a buddha (*sarvākarajñāna, rnam pa thams cad mkhyen pa*), he says of each, "does not exist." As GC will explain later in the *Adornment*, it can be said that the Svātantrikas have their own assertions because they insist on the use of autonomous syllogisms (*svatantrānumāna, rang rgyud kyi sbyor ba*); Bhāvaviveka criticized Buddhapālita for not stating the syllogism that was implied by his consequence.[22] Because they differ on the status of the conventional, the two branches of Madhyamaka also differ on what constitutes the union of the conventional and the ultimate. For the Svātantrikas, that phenomena exist ultimately but are empty of true existence would constitute the union. For the Prāsaṅgikas, everything lacks true existence and ultimate existence (which, for them, are synonyms), such that conventional truths are like illusions: appearing to be real but lacking reality. This illusionlike nature of the conventional extends even to the constituents of enlightenment, such as the ten bodhisattva stages and the five things that are certain about the enjoyment body (*saṃbhogakāya*): the body (adorned with the major and ancillary marks); the abode (the highest buddha field); the doctrine (the Mahāyāna); the

---

22. On Candrakīrti's criticism of Bhāvaviveka, see David Seyfort Ruegg, *Two Prolegomena to Madhyamaka Philosophy: Candrakīrti's "Prasannapadā Madhyamakavṛttiḥ" on Madhyamakakārikā I.1 and Tsoṅ kha pa blo bzaṅ grags pa / Rgyal tshab dar ma rin chen's "Dka' gnad / Gnas rgyad kyi zin bris," Annotated Translations*, Studies in Indian and Tibetan Madhyamaka Thought, pt. 2 (Wien: Arbeitskreis für Tibetische und Buddhistische Studien Universität Wien, 2002), 3–135; and Jeffrey Hopkins, *Meditation on Emptiness* (London: Wisdom Publications, 1983), 441–530.

audience (only bodhisattvas who have achieved at least the first *bhūmi*); and the duration of the teaching (until saṃsāra is empty). When even these exalted things are analyzed, they are found ultimately to be untenable. Conceding that the stages of the path and the qualities of enlightenment must be set forth, GC concludes, "Yet there are contexts when these are also upheld."

However, as long as one imagines the enlightened state as something that can be explained by worldly reasoning, there is no hope of finding that enlightened state. GC quotes the same passage from the *Samādhirāja Sūtra* for the third time before concluding that the six collections of consciousness have been present throughout the long course of saṃsāra and have defined the categories of our experience. If one somehow imagines that these same categories will lead to liberation from saṃsāra, "what is the purpose of an interest in emptiness?"

¶¶167–73 There is considerable discussion in Dge lugs texts on Madhyamaka regarding the dangers of defining the object of negation too broadly (*khyab che ba*), such that in refuting what does not exist, those things that do exist may be refuted in the process. GC finds this a ridiculous worry. The Dge lugs seem obsessed with differentiating between (1) those elements with mere existence that are not negated by reasoning, such as the objects of sense experience and (2) the intrinsic existence imagined by (in GC's terms, "the referent object of") ignorance. Yet all the things that appear to the sense consciousnesses of the unenlightened are ultimately the products of ignorance. The danger, then, is not in defining the object of negation too broadly, but too narrowly. If one is concerned above all to preserve the appearances of those things that merely exist, one will in the end only validate the misconceptions of ignorance. GC is not concerned here with the bodhisattva who has achieved the yogic direct perception of emptiness; it is entirely suitable for such a person to differentiate between what is and is not negated in the vision of emptiness and its aftermath. But such persons are exceedingly rare. How could someone for whom the ideas of true existence and existence are inextricable ever pretend to claim that they discern the line between what is to be negated and what is not? This would be like being confronted with the illusion of an elephant and concluding that the legs are not real, but the trunk is.

There are those who say that the analysis which investigates whether an object ultimately exists is conventional analysis, not ultimate analysis. Such a state depends on defining *ultimate* in two different ways. When it is stated that something does not ultimately exist, *ultimately* is a synonym for *intrinsically, truly, objectively*, and so on. When one says that the analysis of such existence is not ultimate, *ultimate* refers to the ultimate consciousness, the direct realization of emptiness. Such a realization does not engage in analysis. In that sense, analysis is conventional. GC would accept such an explanation, but he also sees dangers in it. The situation that he described before of rejecting the four extremes of production (from self, other, both, and neither) would therefore be carried out conventionally, as would the assertion of a fifth type of production, called mere production; it would be found conventionally, but would not be found ultimately—not because it was searched for from the ultimate perspective and not found, but because it had not been sought from the ultimate perspective at all. This would lead one to conclude that no matter how much one searched for production and did not find it, that would still not qualify as not finding production, because a fifth possibility of production, mere production, would emerge at the conclusion of the search. Only not finding an object ultimately would constitute its not being found. GC concludes that "[t]hese ideas are a case of believing that genuine presentations of the ultimate are only conventional truths." That is, it is yet another case of certifying the objects of ignorance if one limits the powerful notion of searching for something and not finding it to the realm of the ultimate, while claiming that the negation of the four types of production entails not the emptiness of production of the four extremes but rather a fifth type of production. The entire point of the analysis of the four types of production is to first delimit all possibilities of production and then demonstrate that each is untenable. If these are simply being refuted from the conventional perspective, why bother to refute them?

GC is again ready to admit that someone who has already understood emptiness directly would know that there is no difference between describing reality in positive terms as freedom from the elaborations of the four extremes of existence, nonexistence, both, and neither, on the one hand, and describing reality in negative terms as the lack of intrinsic existence. For such a person, these two phrases are simply different descriptions of emptiness, and thus the failure to differentiate between them is immaterial; there is no danger that some conventional phenomenon will be implied. But such persons are not GC's worry. Those who are just beginning to understand emptiness do not, and cannot, differentiate between the absence of true existence and the absence of existence (an inability that GC finds salubrious). However, if one continues to assert that there are "factors of appearance," such as the "mere pot," that persist in the face of the understanding of emptiness, then the beginner who has understood the nonexistence of the pot would perceive that pot in the very next moment. This denigrates the exalted state of meditative equipoise, described as the vision of the absence of all conventional appearances. The union of the two truths is often described as the wisdom that, having perceived emptiness directly, subsequently sees all objects as like illusions. If one is intent on upholding the existence of mere appearances as conventionally valid, then the conventional will appear in the vision of the ultimate. "If that is the meaning of the union of the two truths, how sad."

GC returns, then, to a point that he has already made repeatedly: the object of negation is nothing more or less than what the unenlightened believe to be true. He sees great danger in delineating fine distinctions between true existence and mere existence: the danger is that one will concoct elaborate systems of objects of negation, each philosophically nuanced, and leave utterly untouched the desire, hatred, and ignorance that define saṃsāra. If one asserts that the idea that "a pot exists" is a valid form of knowledge, one must certainly also assert that the idea that "the absence of intrinsic existence exists" is also valid. Yet if one is intent on distinguishing between the conception of a pot and the conception of a truly existing pot, one should equally distinguish between the conception of emptiness and the conception of a truly existing emptiness. GC has already noted that the unenlightened are utterly incapable of distinguishing between existence and true existence among the objects of their ordinary experience. Making a distinction regarding emptiness, with which the unenlightened are entirely unfamiliar, is all the more ludicrous. Furthermore, the person who has perceived emptiness directly perceived only an absence; emptiness is a nonaffirming negative that implies nothing. Even such a person is not able to say whether emptiness merely exists or whether it truly exists. It is therefore not simply ludicrous, but in fact impossible for those with no experience of emptiness to distinguish between existence and intrinsic existence, whether it be of a pillar or of emptiness itself.

Everything in the universe, including emptiness, is empty. Nāgārjuna (at *Madhyamakakārikā* XIII.7) asks, "If there is nothing that is not empty, how could the empty be so?" GC paraphrases this as "[B]ecause even the emptiness of intrinsic existence does not exist at all, there does not exist anything that is not empty of intrinsic existence." That is, emptiness, the final nature of reality, does not exist (or, to patch it with words, does not intrinsically exist). If this is the case even for emptiness, then there can be nothing in the universe which exists intrinsically. But such statements, GC says, cause laughter among the unenlightened. The unenlightened of ancient China, for example, would be equally amused by the claims that the emperor of China is not the king of the world and that his queen is unclean. Yet both statements are true. The purpose of the Buddhist path is to overturn the misconceptions of the world, not uphold them. And that there are those who have successfully completed the path proves that these misconceptions can be overturned. GC quotes Śāntideva once again: "Otherwise, the determination that a woman is unclean would be invalidated by the world."

If one is limited in one's assertions to those things that are not challenged by the perceptions of the world of the unenlightened, then one must uphold the conception of true existence, since this is the fundamental perception of the world. Yet this would reduce one to simply proclaiming the existence of ordinary sense objects. What good does that do? GC thus compares the various slogans of the Dge lugs, such as "conventional truths are not invalidated by a reasoning consciousness," to the statement that a fool's claim that the water in a mirage is real cannot be invalidated by a wise man's claim that it is a mirage. The purpose of reasoning would thus be reduced to simply certifying how things appear.

At ¶171, GC summarizes, rather cryptically, much of the foregoing discussion. He says that Candrakīrti destroyed all assertions about the world when he set forth the meaning of emptiness. Yet when he set forth the conventional world, he did not mention emptiness; he simply resorted to the worldly arguments that were most powerful. The dilemma for GC throughout has been to portray the chasm that separates the unenlightened from the enlightened in the starkest possible terms, while at the same time to chart the passageway across it. In many ways, this is the most traditional of Buddhist themes, embodied in the four truths, said to be the Buddha's first teaching after his enlightenment: there is a world of suffering; there is a cause of that suffering; there is a state beyond the world of suffering; there is a path to that state. For GC, those who continue to ignore the chasm that yawns before them are doomed to remain on this side. As long as they insist on claiming that the appearances of the world are somehow immune from the Madhyamaka critique, they do nothing more than authorize the operations of ignorance. GC therefore returns again and again to his ridicule of the Dge lugs vocabulary and his insistence on the utter devastation of the world that emptiness entails; hence his attack on the notion of "valid knowledge" and his repeated citation "If these senses were valid, what could the noble path do for anyone?" And yet, at the same time, there must be a path, there must be communication between the Buddha and sentient beings. Thus, GC quotes the vexing statement from the *Saṃyuttanikāya* in which the

Buddha says that he has no quarrel with the world.²³ In addition, he returns again and again to the question of assertions for oneself and assertions for others, concluding that the Buddha has no assertions for himself (at least in terms of human speech); everything that he says is an assertion for others.

Candrakīrti destroyed the conventional with his proclamation of emptiness. The chasm yawns. Yet he also set forth the ten stages of the bodhisattva path in great detail in his *Entrance to the Middle Way* (*Madhyamakāvatāra*), and he wrote a treatise on the three jewels. He argued against the Yogācāra that external objects exist. When he set forth the conventional in this way, he set emptiness aside and used the conventions of the world to present the most persuasive argument possible. This, for GC, is the model. What he finds irksome is seeking to use the reasonings of the world to explain what is beyond the world. If such a thing were possible, "why should one seek the middle path?"

The middle path to which he refers is that between the two extremes of existence and nonexistence. The Dge lugs pas claim to avoid the extreme of nonexistence with the assertion that everything exists conventionally and claim to avoid the extreme of existence with the assertion that nothing exists ultimately. It would seem, then, that for the Dge lugs the two extremes to be avoided are not nonexistence and existence but the extremes of not existing conventionally and not being nonexistent ultimately. GC compares this to understanding that a cooking pot is not unbroken yet understanding that it is not nonexistent; such understanding is presumably as useful as the knowledge that the pot is broken. "It is in very strong agreement with worldly appearance."

GC sees all such assertions as futile attempts to reconcile the understanding of someone who has directly understood emptiness with the ignorance of the world. If there were some possibility of such reconciliation, it would have occurred sometime over the long history of saṃsāra. That it has not suggests that these two perspectives are quite incompatible.

¶¶174–81 Returning to the question of invalidation by reasoning, GC notes that according to the Madhyamaka, the Yogācāra (called here Vijñaptika) does not find external objects but does not find that they do not exist, because according to the Madhyamaka, external objects exist and thus cannot be found to be

---

23. The passage occurs in the *Khandhasaṃyutta* of the *Khandhavagga* (*Saṃyuttanikāya* III.138). For an English translation, see Bhikkhu Bodhi, trans., *The Connected Discourses of the Buddha* (Boston: Wisdom Publications, 2000), 1:949. Candrakīrti alludes to the statement at *Madhyamakāvatāra* VI:166 and cites the passage twice in his autocommentary at Derge *dbu ma, 'a*, 276a2–3 (commenting on VI.81) and at Derge *dbu ma,'a*, 309a2 (commenting on VI.166), identifying it only as "from *āgama*." GC presumably cited the passage from Candrakīrti rather than from the *Saṃyuttanikāya*, although he may have encountered the latter in Sri Lanka.

nonexistent. Yet the Madhyamakas claim that they not only do not find true existence, but also find that it does not exist. As a Madhyamaka, GC endorses this claim, one that can be made because the Madhyamakas use superior reasoning to destroy the assumptions of ordinary experience. Yet there are those who conclude on the one hand that true existence does not exist because it cannot be found by reasoning, but who also claim on the other hand that mere existence is not contravened by reasoning. The problem is that ignorant beings cannot distinguish between true existence and mere existence, despite what they claim. He compares such people to a man who has lost a needle and concludes, after duly searching, that the needle does not exist. Some time later, the man finds the needle. Those who hold that Madhyamaka reasoning negates ultimate existence but does not negate conventional existence do so on the basis of the claim that ultimate reasoning has one object, namely ultimate existence, while conventional reasoning has a different object, conventional existence. To GC, this is akin to saying that the subsequent discovery of the needle has no implications for the previous conclusion that the needle did not exist, because the two conclusions (that the needle does not and does exist) have different objects (the nonexistence and existence of the needle). In this case, all possibilities of the existence of the needle could be contained between two categories, the occasionally existent and the occasionally nonexistent. One could conveniently draw the same conclusion about true existence and dispense with trying to negate it through other categories such as the four extremes (of existence, nonexistence, both, and neither) and the four alternatives (*mu bzhi*, one of the versions of which is the production of one effect from one cause, of one effect from many causes, of many effects from one cause, and of many effects from many causes).

The conception of true existence and the understanding of its absence are very different states of mind, with very different objects. Why should one assume that one should have any consequences for the other? It is sometimes said that wisdom displaces ignorance because wisdom is stronger than ignorance, but GC notes that there is no mental state stronger than sexual desire, yet the sexual desire of a male who lusts for the body of a woman does not overcome the understanding of an arhat that the body of a woman is unclean. But such measures of the strength of a given state of mind are based entirely on worldly experience. GC thus advises that one follow Candrakīrti's course. As discussed above, Candrakīrti set emptiness aside when setting forth the conventional, where one must use the most effective worldly reasonings to decide what exists (and thus to uphold as one's own system) and what does not exist (and thus to regard as the system of others). And this pertains to all objects of desire, all objects of hatred, and all objects of ignorance. From the perspective of the world, objects of knowledge are understood in terms of mutually exclusive opposites: light and dark, fire and water, hot and cold. If this is the case for the ordinary objects of the world of the unenlightened, then if one cannot see ultimate truths and conventional truths as contradictory, "what opportunity for liberation is there"? When views change so radically over the course of a single person's life, how could the understanding of someone who has directly perceived emptiness and the understanding of an ordinary person not be contradictory? If this distinction is not maintained, one is doomed to remain in the abode of the conceivable.

How could it be that all of the philosophical systems of the world are somehow threatening to the ideas of ordinary beings, yet the highest of all philosophical systems, the Prāsaṅgika, in no way challenges their patterns of mind? With typical irony, GC presents the view of someone who imagines such a thing: The conventional and the ultimate are indeed different, but the presence of one need not displace the other. No two things are more different than stone and water, yet they occur together without one changing the nature of the other. A stone remains hard at the bottom of a lake, rainwater remains wet when it rolls off a stone. Thus, the ignorance of sentient beings and the wisdom of the Buddha together pervade the universe without contradicting each other.

From this perspective, the Prāsaṅgika reasonings seem to have no other purpose than to exalt one to a transcendent state above the conventional objects perceived by the senses. The Prāsaṅgika would therefore be agnostic about the operations of ordinary consciousness; the point is to achieve a state beyond consciousness. The conventional and the ultimate would be two unrelated domains, such that a conventional consciousness could indeed be called a valid form of knowledge. All opinions and all perceptions—whether they be of humans, animals, insects, or ghosts—would therefore be equally valid and worthy of respect. They are all conventional truths. Yet because their perspectives are so different, GC wonders what purpose there is in calling them conventional truths when what is true for one is not true for the other. If what appears to a human does not contravene what appears to a ghost, then what appears to a buddha does not contravene what appears to any sentient being. "Therefore, all this impure appearance would remain where it is forever."

Both the space that he devotes to the topic and the tone of his argument suggest that GC is most serious in his critique of the separation of the ultimate and conventional realms. Yet in one sense it seems at odds with things that he has said previously. He has emphasized again and again the great difference that exists between the unenlightened and the enlightened states, and has reminded us that the realm of the Buddha is utterly beyond the confines of our small mind. Here he wants to maintain that separation from one perspective but collapse it from another. The very purpose of the Buddha's teaching is to disrupt our ordinary conceptions and lead us to the inconceivable state. The great hindrance to that transformation seems, ironically, to be the assumption that the world of the Buddha is utterly different from ours. GC seems to want us to come to this conclusion, but not too quickly.

At ¶179, GC provides three examples from the works of Nāgārjuna of statements that are not the Madhyamaka's own view. The first, already encountered above (from *Vigrahavyāvartanī* 1), states that because words do not intrinsically exist, they are unable to refute intrinsic existence. The second (from *Vigrahavyāvartanī* 26) states that if one reverses, that is, refutes, the absence of intrinsic existence, the presence of intrinsic existence is proved. The third (from *Madhyamakakārikā* XIII.7) states that if there were anything that was not empty, there would also exist something that is empty. None of these represent Nāgārjuna's own view. They are instead either statements made by a hypothetical opponent or consequences stated to the opponent that present his own views back to him. In each case, the opponent believes that there must be a consistency in the ontological status of what is negated and what negates it: if the object of negation exists, then the emptiness which is the absence of that object as well as the reasoning that negates that object must exist. If the object of negation is truly established, the reasoning that refutes it must also be. If one is merely existent, the other must be; if one is nonexistent, the other must be. GC's point here is that each of these quotations from Nāgārjuna represent the opponent's position, and thus are wrong. Those who would hold that what is true for the ultimate is the ultimate and what is true for the conventional is the conventional and that ultimate reasoning does not impinge upon the conventional realm are in fact not Madhyamakas but their opponents. Yet they somehow imagine that their understanding of the ultimate and the conventional represents the Madhyamaka view. Thus, GC says scornfully, "This seems to establish the tenets of the Madhyamaka system."

Rather than seeking consistency between the object of negation and what negates it, there is no choice but to destroy the positions of existence and nonexistence. And to support this, GC quotes the Buddha's prophecy of Nāgārjuna for a third time. He chastises those who, rather than destroying existence and nonexistence, seek not only to preserve both but to place them in a position of noncontradiction. Such people would use as their analogy of the union of the two truths the statement that there is no earth in gold, but there is earth in earth. In the same way, there is no appearance of the conventional in the vision of the ultimate, but there are conventional appearances in conventional experience. This, GC says, is not a union of the two truths, the conventional and the ultimate, but actually the union of two ultimates: "the ideas of a vulgar worldling who is the ultimate of fools, and the wisdom of the Buddha, the ultimate of the wise." Simply because the understanding of one thing leads to the understanding of its opposite, like light and darkness, this does not entail some union of opposites.

¶¶182–86 Thus, when the unenlightened speak to each other about "truth" and "existence," they think that they understand something, but this is based on nothing more than the fact that they share the same limited perspective. When the Buddha says that things do not ultimately exist, yet they nonetheless exist, there is no possibility that the unenlightened will have the slightest understanding of what he means. Even if an unenlightened person who has come to some understanding of Prāsaṅgika were to say the same thing to a common worldling, that being would still not understand anything. The "philosophy" of such common worldlings, which simply validates their own limited experience, cannot even account for the world of the unenlightened, because it fails to take into account the perspectives of animals, children, and fools, who do not understand language. Thus, this validation of the conventional, far from being a description of reality, pertains only to a limited population of humans, that which falls between the categories of the very learned and the very stupid.

  GC returns to a point he has made before concerning the state of meditative equipoise on emptiness. This state is defined as a direct perception of emptiness, without the appearance of conventional phenomena and without the presence of discursive thought. Thus, no reasoned refutation of intrinsic existence takes place during this meditative state. It would take place instead in the state subsequent to meditative equipoise, when conventional objects once again appear. However, if one holds to the position that Nāgārjuna criticized in the passages above, that is, the position that the negation of true existence must itself truly exist, then it would follow that one would perceive the absence of true existence in the state of meditative equipoise and would perceive the true existence of that absence in the state subsequent to that. There would thus seem to be little benefit in gaining the direct perception of emptiness in the first place. As long as one remains in the world of the conventional, words must be understood in terms of their opposites; contradiction is fundamental to the categories of experience, hence the good is what is not bad. Those who seek to maintain the validity of the conventional would seem to want to define the good as the conception that the truth itself is truly established and the bad as the conception that true establishment is like an illusion, appearing one way and existing another. This is precisely the opposite of what for GC is the correct view: conceiving the truth to be truly established is bad, while conceiving true establishment to be like a magician's illusion, appearing to be present but in fact absent, is good. Seeing no contradiction between the ultimate truth and the conventional truth leads to such profound misunderstanding; it is "the system of those who hold that no ideas, from those of the Buddha to those of sentient beings, are contradictory."

Tsong kha pa argued that in Prāsaṅgika, one would not use phrases such as "these are assertions of my own system," because he saw the term *own system* (*rang lugs*) to itself imply true existence. For Tsong kha pa, the words *own* and *other* in the phrases "my own system" and "the system of others" did not refer to persons but to the status of objects. Thus, anything asserted as one's own system would exist on its own. The Svātantrikas, who insist upon the use of autonomous syllogisms, thus assert that objects are endowed with their own independent mode of existence, whereas the Prāsaṅgikas assert that they lack such independence. From this perspective, the Prāsaṅgikas do not have their own system.

As long as one does not understand this, all discussion about one's own system and the system of others is just a quarrel among the unenlightened; when they come to some agreement, they somehow assume that this unanimity serves as the foundation for the presentation of the nature of reality. This, of course, leads nowhere. One must instead adopt a position that does not agree with the thought and speech of the world and move to the noble place, the state of one who has directly realized emptiness. Having done so, one will no longer need to resort to assertions of one's own system or the system of others, apart from recognizing that the thoughts of the noble are superior and the thoughts of sentient beings are inferior.

Indeed, there is no greater conceit than to imagine that the nature of reality can be described in the language of the unenlightened. The Buddha uses such language simply because there is no other way to communicate with sentient beings. The unenlightened are like barbarians who know no other language than their own; if one wishes to communicate with them, one must speak the language of barbarians. The Buddha therefore compassionately speaks to sentient beings using the categories of their world—the world that he has himself transcended—in order to lead them beyond the world. If he were to speak in a way that entirely called that world into question, there could be no communication. Thus, the Buddha uses the language of the world, even when he describes his own passage beyond it.

We see GC's pendulum—which has been swinging toward the realm of the contradiction of the ultimate and the conventional and the discontinuity and even disjunction of the perspectives of the Buddha and the world—pausing for at least a moment to remind us that although it is ridiculous to imagine that the world exists as the unenlightened describe it, the possibility of communication between the Buddha and sentient beings remains, if only because the Buddha compassionately deigns to speak our language.

¶¶187–200 GC returns to the topic of the commonly appearing subject. He begins with a straightforward Dge lugs description of the differences between syllogisms (*prayoga, sbyor ba*) and consequences (*prasaṅga, thal 'gyur*), noting that in a syllogism, the reason, the predicate, and the object (that is, the subject or basis of the debate) must be upheld by the person who states the syllogism. A consequence, however, uses the assertions of the opponent to defeat the opponent, without the person who states the consequence needing to accept them. A consequence is thus known as a "reason that is renowned to others." Hence, in order for a Prāsaṅgika to defeat an opponent, there is no need for a commonly appearing subject, that is, an object about whose status the two parties in the debate agree; the Prāsaṅgika is able to refute the position of the opponent by using the opponent's own assertions against him. As explained earlier, to state an autonomous syllogism is to imply the autonomy of the constituents of that syllogism. From the perspective of the Prāsaṅgika, there can be no autonomous syllogisms, because nothing exists autonomously. Candrakīrti therefore eschews their use and is immune from all refutation by them. The Prāsaṅgika does not uphold the opposite of what the opponent asserts and is thus the true follower of the middle way, because he avoids the extremes of existence and nonexistence.

GC continues to explore the notion of no commonly appearing subject, that there is absolutely nothing that a Prāsaṅgika and a worldling hold in common. From one perspective, this seems ridiculous: a Prāsaṅgika obviously sees the pillars and pots that others see. But to make such a claim is to identify the appearances of the world as conventional truths, and for GC this is the source of all error. In fact, no appearances are mere appearances. All appearances are appearances of true existence, and all thoughts are conceptions of true existence.

The world accepts these, the Prāsaṅgika refutes them. This is the reason there is no commonly appearing subject. Reasoning identifies the object of negation and then refutes it; the conception of true existence could not be identified by another consciousness that itself conceives of true existence. Thus, reiterating what he said about Candrakīrti in ¶171, GC explains that the Prāsaṅgikas offer two, and only two, perspectives on the conventional status of a pillar. The first is the perspective of the yogic direct perception of emptiness in which the pillar is utterly nonexistent. The second is the perspective of the period subsequent to meditative equipoise, in which the pillar appears in accordance with the conventions of the world as something that performs the function of supporting the roof beam, yet without assenting to its false appearance, caused by the obstructions of omniscience, as something that truly exists.

If ignorance were not the conception of ultimate or true existence and were instead just the conception of mere existence, then we would not be wandering in saṃsāra. Any other qualifications that we could make concerning the object of negation simply add artificial objects of negation and provide no assistance in uprooting the innate ignorance.

GC remains skeptical about the possibility of the unenlightened distinguishing between true existence and mere existence, seeing an unbroken continuity in the sequence of thoughts that begins with "Form exists" and "Truly established form exists." The innate conception of the object must therefore be the target of the negation, not something else. Whatever the unenlightened call "the reasoning that investigates the mode of being" are simply variations on ignorance.

He is especially critical of those who want to call themselves Madhyamakas by asserting that a pot is not to found by reasoning, yet who also want to claim that a pot exists. No system of logic accepts some mode of existence that lacks a mode of being. Those who would insist on such have no need for the Madhyamaka view. The purpose of Nāgārjuna's critique was to eliminate all possibilities of existence. GC thus again quotes the opening stanza of the second chapter of the *Treatise on the Middle Way*, which declares that motion does not occur on the gone over or the not-yet-gone-over. To claim to understand this argument while also claiming that motion nonetheless exists "squanders all the reasonings of the father Nāgārjuna and his sons."

Such insistence on simultaneously claiming nonexistence and existence is particularly discouraging because even benighted sentient beings are capable of understanding what it means to refute the way that something is or something is not. What benighted beings cannot do is to see even the tiniest fraction of what the Buddha sees. The Buddha thus adopts the system of the Prāsaṅgikas and uses our own conventions to teach the dharma, as he did when he spoke with Cūḍapanthaka (or Cūlapanthaka), a monk so stupid that he was unable to memorize a single stanza in four months (but who went on to become an arhat and one of the sixteen *sthaviras*, renowned for his ability to create emanations).

GC reiterates what he takes to be Candrakīrti's understanding of no commonly appearing subject, in which the subject of the debate does not appear commonly to the two parties because the subject is not validly established from one's own perspective, and one does not accept the opponent's interpretation of what constitutes valid establishment. If there can be no agreement on the status of the subject under debate, the other constituents of the syllogism—the sign, the predicate, and the probandum—cannot be validly established. But, alluding possibly to Tsong kha pa, GC mentions some "latter-day scholars" who have bracketed the real meaning of no commonly appearing subject and concocted a different one. He presumably has in mind the argument that "no commonly appearing subject" refers to the difference in what constitutes valid knowledge when two people debate. There is, however, a commonly appearing subject in the sense that the subject is validly established, and hence "commonly appearing" from the respective perspectives of the two parties. This is a dangerous position, according to GC, for two reasons. First, to concede any degree of common appearance is to run the risk of simply certifying the ignorance of those who think that conventional truths are ultimate truths. Therefore, as GC has concluded before, making overly fine distinctions about the various ways in which the subject can and cannot be said to commonly appear is counterproductive, because it leads to the conceit that the unenlightened and the enlightened perceive the same things. Second, to concede any degree of common appearance is to imply that the diligent study of the great Madhyamaka texts leads only to a validation of the mentality of both fools and the exponents of false philosophies.

¶¶201–14 GC returns to the direct perception of emptiness when he distinguishes between two nonaffirming negatives: the nonaffirming negative which is the absence of a pot and the nonaffirming negative which is the absence of all phenomena. A nonaffirming negative is a negation that implies nothing positive in its place. The nonexistence of a pot should be such a negative, but GC notes that it is difficult for something else not to appear to the mind, such as the place in which the pot is absent. The nonexistence of all phenomena (and it is noteworthy that GC speaks only of their nonexistence, apparently eschewing the more precise descriptions of the Dge lugs, which would speak of the absence of intrinsic existence in all phenomena) implies nothing in its place, because existence and nonexistence encompass all possibilities of conventional awareness. GC describes the mind that understands this nonaffirming negative as "directed toward the peace of liberation." He provides quotations from Śāntideva, Candrakīrti, and the Second Dalai Lama, each of which seem to be making a somewhat different point. First, he quotes Śāntideva (at *Bodhicaryāvatāra* IX.34) in a statement GC has just paraphrased: "When the real and the unreal do not remain before the mind, then, because there is no other possibility, being without an object, it is completely calmed." The mind that is calmed, he says, is conventional awareness, and he quotes the controversial second stanza of the ninth chapter of the same text: "[The ultimate is not within the mind's sphere.] The mind is asserted to be the conventional." GC next quotes Candrakīrti, who provides an etymology of the term *saṃvṛti*, generally translated as "conventional" but more literally meaning "concealer." He said (at *Madhyamakāvatāra* VI.28), "Because delusion obscures the nature, it is a concealer. Its fabrications, perceived to be true, were said by the Muni to be 'conventional truths' [literally, 'truths for a concealer']." Ignorance is therefore a concealer of reality, and the fabrications by ignorance, taken to be true by the unenlightened, are called "truths for a concealer," the term more commonly translated as "conventional truths." GC then offers another quotation, this time from the Second Dalai Lama and this time not about the nature of the conventional but about the nonaffirming negative, described as freedom for the elaborations of assertion. This is a statement that fits quite well into GC's call to move beyond the constraints of the categories of existence and nonexistence.

In considering the series of quotations presented by GC, it is not immediately evident that the mind that Śāntideva says is pacified when the real and the unreal no longer remain before it is the awareness that he calls conventional. And it is unclear whether that awareness is the obscuration that Candrakīrti calls a concealer. An argument could presumably be made to connect the three statements, but GC does not make it. He simply declares that it is the case, and in apparent reference to the great volume of commentary that these passages, especially *Bodhicaryāvatāra* IX.2, have elicited over the centuries, he suggests that it should be self-evident, "if one does not manipulate the statements of such great masters," that the passages mean "that *concealer* is the name of the mind, and that what is true for that is called *truth for a concealer.*"

One of the conceits of this mind is the assumption that valid knowledge exists among the unenlightened. With this assumption in place, one has no choice but to accept the viewpoint of the unenlightened as one's own system. The decision to use a consequence rather than an autonomous syllogism thus has implications far beyond the mechanics of debate. Using consequences entails no submission to the ideas of others; it instead provides the means of demonstrating their fallacies. In setting forth the nature of reality, this is the technique not only of the Prāsaṅgikas but of the Buddha himself.

This is not to imply that the term *own system* can never be used when describing the Prāsaṅgikas, or the Buddha. Yet it is important to distinguish between the occasional use of the term here and the technical sense of the term as the perspective of those who are constrained by the obstructions of omniscience into believing in the false appearances of the world and who then involuntarily make all manner of false claims about them. Systems of logic derived from such claims are not to be taken seriously.

In the *Saṃyuttanikāya*, the Buddha declares, "I do not dispute with the world, the world disputes with me." GC glosses this provocative statement at ¶203. When worldlings debate with the Buddha, they somehow assume that the perceptions of the world are shared by the Buddha, that there is some commonly appearing subject. When the Buddha teaches the dharma, he does not challenge the modes of thinking of the world, but sets forth the path in its terms. His teaching is therefore an "assertion for others." If all the appearances of the world were valid, there would be no point in the Buddha teaching the path or for others to strive to follow it.

GC then returns to the question of the distinction between not finding something and finding it not to exist. He cites Tsong kha pa's statement: "Although the eye consciousness does not find sounds, it does not find that sound does not exist." Drawing a parallel between this statement and ultimate analysis, when the mind analyzing the ultimate seeks the final nature of a pillar, for example, it does not find the pillar, yet it does not find the pillar to be nonexistent. GC sees great danger in the distinction between not finding and finding not to exist, because it provides an opportunity to affirm the appearances of the world by making them exempt from ultimate analysis. By making the statement, Tsong kha pa is "assisting the process." But GC also wants to challenge the analogy. Sound is indeed not found by the eye consciousness. But no one would claim that it could be; obviously, such a search would be futile from the outset. However, if a suitable consciousness is assigned to the task, not finding something should constitute finding that it does not exist. Ultimate analysis is not performed by an ultimate consciousness, that is, by yogic direct perception of emptiness. It is performed by a conventional consciousness, as Tsong kha pa himself asserts. It is therefore difficult to claim that the ultimate and the conventional are separate domains such that what is found, or not found, in one does not impinge upon the other. Those who assert otherwise do not believe in freedom from the elaborations of the four extremes and continue tiresomely to insist that having no assertion is itself an assertion, and that existence persists when ultimate existence is refuted. Those who have found freedom from elaborations are indifferent to the reasonings of the world. Madhyamaka reasoning surpasses such reasoning because it is not founded upon the duality of existence and nonexistence. As long as one places one's trust in reasoning based on duality, the final mode of being of the universe will remain elusive. Indeed, the understanding of emptiness begins with a sense of despair over all the reasonings, terms, and conceptions of the world.

Those who remain in the various stages of misconception will never understand emptiness, which GC calls the "final object of the empty class." Indeed, they will not even understand the conventional phenomena associated with enlightenment. As GC argued earlier in the text, attachment to the logic of the world prevents entry into the inconceivable, such as the invisibility of the Buddha's crown protrusion and the fact that the enjoyment body of a buddha, the *saṃbhogakāya*, is newly born upon the achievement of buddhahood, yet never dies. For the canons of worldly logic, these are merely contradictions. But GC does not limit his examples to the inconceivable powers of the Buddha; here he mentions two of his disciples whose deeds defy reason. The Buddha's attendant, Ānanda, burned a lamp at night, although moths flew into the flame and were killed. The famous mass murderer, Aṅgulimāla, killed 999 people, cut off their little fingers, and made a necklace for himself. Yet he became a monk and then an arhat, destroying the twenty forms of the view that there is a real person (*satkāyadṛṣṭi, 'jig tshogs la lta ba*). (These are four wrong views about the self for each of the five aggregates; for example, that the self is form, that the self is endowed with form, that the self owns form, and that the self abides in form.) The logical systems of vulgar beings would simply reject these as impossible. When the six types of sentient beings—gods, demigods, humans, animals, ghosts, hell beings—see a cup of liquid, they each see something different; according to the Dge lugs, they do so because the natures of six different kinds of liquid (ambrosia, water, pus, and so on) are simultaneously present. Why would one then assume that a Buddha and a sentient being see a pot in the same way?

Thus, there can be no commonly appearing subject in a debate between a Madhyamaka and a non-Madhyamaka. As a result of the obstructions to omniscience, phenomena appear to be truly established to the sense consciousnesses of all beings except buddhas. Those who have understood emptiness still suffer from this misperception until the attainment of buddhahood, although they do not believe in it, just as a magician does not believe in the illusion he has created. But for someone who has not understood emptiness, form is both perceived and conceived to be truly established, and there is no other understanding of form that is possible. If one does not see truly established form, one does not see form; it is impossible to distinguish between them. Thus, any syllogisms that such a person could state with form as the subject, such as "The subject, form, does not truly exist, because of being dependently arisen," would have no effect. For the Madhyamaka who has understood emptiness, the form that is imagined by the person who has not understood emptiness does not exist, and thus cannot serve as the subject of a syllogism. There is, therefore, no commonly appearing subject.

GC likens conversation between worldlings and "the noble," those with direct realization of emptiness, to conversation between the insane and the wise: what is the case for one is not the case for the other. Communication is sometimes possible on the purely verbal level, with no agreement in substance. "[T]he presentation of the conventional is posited from the viewpoint of just words—and the presentation of the insane is posited by the insane." And the differing perspectives of the wise and the insane are not merely matters of opinion, because one is true and the other is false. What the insane think is gold is in fact just a stone. We are the insane; "[t]hus, it is possible that what exists for us does not exist for noble beings." GC therefore sees no reason to pay deference to the perceptions of the world. Instead, one should seek to free oneself from the power of the reified objects of experience. The obstructions to omniscience grow weaker and weaker until the achievement of buddhahood, "the body of union," in which one's omniscient consciousness eternally and simultaneously perceives all phenomena in the universe, like water poured into water. This is the state of buddhahood, so different from our own. If one imagines that the bodhisattva amasses the collections of merit and wisdom over the course of three periods of countless aeons so that he can share the perceptions of common beings, then there is no need to undertake that path. It would be better to invest in gold.

The goal of the Buddhist path, therefore, is to destroy the obstructions to omniscience. In Sanskrit (*jñeyāvaraṇa*) and Tibetan (*shes bya'i sgrib pa*) this term literally means "obstructions to objects of knowledge." GC plays on that meaning here, noting that the purification of the afflictive obstructions of desire, hatred, and ignorance results in a purification of consciousness; the conception of true existence is destroyed. Yet this subjective purification has no visible effect on the objects of experience, which continue to appear as if they were truly existent. In GC's terms, the "curtain of objects of knowledge" remains drawn. Returning again to his corporeal conception of enlightenment, GC endorses the view of the fifteenth-century Sa skya translator Stag tshangs shes rab rin chen, who argued that obstructions also take physical form, and that these must also be purified if one is to destroy the obstructions to omniscience.

GC comes finally to what appears to be his answer to the question that he raised many pages ago: what does it mean when it is said that the Madhyamaka has no assertion? And he answers without citing an Indian text or ridiculing a Dge lugs geshe. He answers in simple and direct language, unencumbered by technical vocabulary: "[T]he statement that if one is a Madhyamaka, it is not suitable to have one's own system means that if one is a Madhyamaka, it is not suitable to have a mode of assertion based on one's own thoughts." Being a Madhyamaka therefore is not contingent upon professing a particular set of tenets. Nor is it a rank gained by ascending to a particular level of the path. Being a Madhyamaka involves instead a recognition of the limitations of one's own thoughts, an acknowledgement of one's own ignorance. To have no assertion, therefore, does not so much mean that one deftly crafts consequences from the opponent's position, but rather that one resists the powerful compulsion to make assumptions about the nature of reality based upon what goes on in one's own mind. Like the psychotic who finally stops listening to the voices inside his head, the Madhyamaka recognizes his own delusions, and does not submit to them.

What, then, is the process of destroying that delusion? What is the path? Having previously scorned the various "artificial" conceptions of true existence— those gained by studying false tenets—as so many sand castles on the bedrock of the fundamental ignorance, the belief in self, GC here finds some value in them. Because the ordinary conception of self is so engrained as to be virtually unrecognizable to the ordinary being, it is not going to be accessible to reasoned analysis. As GC notes, "[T]he way of thinking about the self at the time of being an ordinary being seems to be a door leading elsewhere" (and he will identify that "elsewhere" shortly). Yet the artificial conceptions of self—that the self is permanent, partless, and independent; that objects do not ultimately exist but intrinsically exist—are reified forms of the fundamental ignorance and thus more accessible to scrutiny and analysis. Thus, even to hold such views provides the beginning of insight into their negation. "Therefore, I wonder whether all of these so-called artificial conceptions of true existence are not something like the lower rungs of the ladder leading to the path of liberation."

The goal, or at least the short-term goal, then, is to become a Madhyamaka. To do so, one must stop believing in one's own thoughts. But this is not merely a matter of will, it is a matter of insight. And to gain that insight, one must first believe various assertions about the nature of the self, assertions that are not instincts but ideas. These ideas can then be rejected, the assertions refuted, until one has no assertions of one's own.

¶¶215–16 Having mentioned the lower rungs of the path to liberation, GC turns to the upper rungs, and the question of the conception of self in tantric practice. He again alludes to the passage from Tsong kha pa's *Praise of Dependent Origination*: "Those who oppose your teaching, no matter how long and how hard they try, are like those who repeatedly summon misfortune, because they rely on the view of self." GC paraphrases the passage (which he had cited approvingly before) for his own purpose, saying not that those who oppose the Buddha's teaching rely on the view of self, but that their view of self becomes more stable. GC takes this as an opportunity to consider the problem of self in tantric practice, specifically the form called deity yoga (*lha'i rnal 'byor*). In this practice, considered by Tsong kha pa the defining constituent of the tantric path, the meditator imagines himself or herself to be a fully enlightened buddha (in this case Vajrasattva), adorned in the raiments of a *saṃbhogakāya* and seated on a thousand-petaled lotus blossom. Imagining oneself in this way is called the practice of "divine pride" (*lha'i nga rgyal*). At that time, one repeats the mantra "oṃ svabhāvaśuddhāḥ sarvadharmāḥ svabhāvaśuddho 'haṃ" (Oṃ, naturally pure are all phenomena, naturally pure am I). Does not such a proclamation strengthen rather than weaken the conception of self? GC concedes that it reinforces the view of selfhood, yet this is the path to buddhahood. In the previous paragraph he had said, "[T]he way of thinking about the self at the time of being an ordinary being seems to be a door leading elsewhere." This "elsewhere" is the state of Vajrasattva. The ordinary view of self is therefore not to be identified, analyzed, and uprooted; it is simply to be replaced. As is clear from his earlier comments, GC recognizes the value of artificial conceptions of self as lower rungs on the path. But tantric practice seems to be the essential key for destroying the most fundamental ignorance, the belief in self. That self is not merely to be eliminated, leaving only its absence, a nonaffirming negative; it is to be replaced by another conception of self. "Therefore, by grasping a self that is different from the self of one's earlier ordinary ways of thinking, from that point onward I would think that the door is open to meet the pervasive lord [Vajrasattva] face to face." Indeed, as Tsong kha pa himself says, the divine pride of oneself as Vajrasattva should take as its model the ordinary conception of self.

¶¶217–23 Returning to his critique of worldly wisdom, GC notes that the so-called reasoning of the three modes (the presence of the reason in the subject or *phyogs chos*, the pervasion or *rjes khyab*, and the reverse pervasion or *ldog khyab*) exalted in the debating courtyards is nothing more than worldly inference—if this is this, it must be that—used by hunters when they are tracking the animals that they want to kill. That something like this would be identified as valid knowledge analyzing the conventional is unseemly in the extreme. One must therefore come to a decision about the status of the valid knowledge of the unenlightened. If one is going to accept it, then one must also accept that things truly exist and that (and GC uses this example yet again; his repeated allusion to it should be read in light of his *Treatise on Passion*) a woman is clean. In short, one must accept the powerful appearances to which the mind has become accustomed over the long course of saṃsāra. If one rejects those appearances, however, one must also reject the logical systems based upon them. This is why the earlier translators of the Sanskrit sūtras and śāstras into Tibetan translated the Sanskrit *saṃvṛti* as *kun rdzob*, literally, "completely obscured" or "completely obscuring." To call the objects of ordinary experience "completely obscuring truths" means that they hide reality, they are confusing, they are mistaken.

The standard Dge lugs claim, however, is that it is impossible to come to a direct realization of emptiness without first gaining an inferential understanding of emptiness, developed through the use of reasoning, such as Candrakīrti's sevenfold reasoning, which searches for a chariot among its parts. Thus, it would seem that one cannot destroy the obstructions to omniscience without recourse to reasoning.

GC is clearly not a critic of Candrakīrti; he has quoted him to support his arguments throughout the text. The issue, then, is not Candrakīrti or his reasoning, but how it is used and the claims that are made on its behalf. For GC, the Dge lugs invest excessively in the ability of reasoning to dislodge the most fundamental ignorance. The danger, as always, is that reasoning will identify some hypostatized "ultimate existence" and refute that, leaving the operations of ordinary ignorance unscathed. "[U]ltimately existent delusion is an object of abandonment, but delusion is not an object of abandonment."

Everything, whether it can be seen by the mind or not, is included within the two truths, the ultimate truth and the conventional truth. Yet even the term *conventional truth* is misunderstood to mean the objects of everyday experience. Once again quoting Candrakīrti, GC notes that conventional truths are in fact fabrications by ignorance which are taken to be true by the unenlightened. The "valid knowledge" and the "reasoning" of which the Dge lugs are so enamored, therefore, are not essential stepping-stones on the path to enlightenment, but faint moments of understanding that briefly interrupt the ongoing flow of ignorance.

It is commonly stated in the Dge lugs that because things do not ultimately exist, this does not mean that they are utterly nonexistent; because they are conventionally existent, they in fact exist. Thus, what is being negated is not existence but ultimate existence, with *ultimate* here being a synonym for *intrinsic, autonomous,* and *true.* And as we have repeatedly seen, GC is unhappy with this claim. He therefore does not think it would contradict this assertion to also say that what exists in the face of the reasoning consciousness of a noble person, that is, someone who directly realizes emptiness, does not qualify as existent; it is only emptiness, the mere absence of the object. The reasoning consciousness of a noble person is also called the ultimate consciousness, because it has emptiness, the ultimate truth, as its object. Thus, the statement that "because things do not ultimately exist, they do not qualify as nonexistent"— with "ultimately exist" being read not as "intrinsically exist" but as "exist for an ultimate consciousness"—risks denying the force of the realization by the ultimate consciousness that things do not ultimately exist: it demeans the emptiness perceived by a noble being and upholds the deluding objects perceived by the vulgar. GC then provides a correlate to that statement: "Because things conventionally exist, they qualify as existent." This statement in fact simply certifies the assumptions of the benighted. It would seem appropriate, then, to also say, "Because it does not exist for the mistaken perceptions of the world, it qualifies as nonexistent." That is, if the fabrications of ignorance are to be regarded as constituents of conventional existence, then what is not perceived by ignorant sentient beings must be nonexistent. The Dge lugs statement that "because things do not ultimately exist, they do not qualify as nonexistent, and because things conventionally exist, they qualify as existent" is akin to saying, "Because the wise do not find that an illusory horse and elephant are a horse and an elephant, they do not qualify as nonexistent, but because they are found by fools, they qualify as existent." The insistence on the validity of "mere appearance" denies the power of wisdom and exalts the power of ignorance.

¶¶224–26 GC next takes up the term *multiplicity* or *variety* (*ji snyed pa*), meaning literally "as much as there is." The term appears in describing a buddha's
omniscience, which is said to have two aspects, the knowledge of the mode (*ji
lta ba'i mkhyen pa*) and the knowledge of the multiplicities (*ji snyed pa'i mkhyen
pa*). GC notes that the term appears to mean merely the objects discerned by
the limited awareness of unenlightened sentient beings—that is, whatever is to
be found in the space defined vertically by the Peak of Existence, the highest
level of the Formless Realm above and the lowest of the hells below, and defined horizontally by the eastern peak and the western peak in the ring of iron
mountains encircling our world. This would mean that the Buddha's "wisdom
of the multiplicities," one of the two aspects of his omniscience, would be limited to those things found by the minds of vulgar beings. But because one finds
something, it does not mean that one understands it. GC compares it to finding gold under the hearthstone of the kitchen: one may not know that it is gold
until it is identified as such by a knowledgeable person. In the same way, the
Buddha identifies the varieties of phenomena as being free from elaboration.
This is called "seeing the mode," referring to the other aspect of the Buddha's
omniscience. He therefore advises us to place a little faith in the Rnying ma pa
explanation of the primordially enlightened buddha, Samantabhadra: the final
nature is always present; it need only be identified.

¶¶227–33 GC once again compares syllogisms and consequences. In a brief and
rather cryptic passage, he reinterprets four types of reasoning enumerated by
Tsong kha pa in his *Great Exposition of Insight* (*Lhag mthong chen mo*).[24] GC
calls autonomous inferences, which rely for their veracity on the autonomous
connections between the subject, predicate, and reason, "reasoning of dependence," and he calls consequences "reasoning of functionality" and "effective
reasoning." Investigation using commonly appearing signs and predicates is
"reasoning of tenability." The "reasoning of reality" (*chos nyid*) is discovery
through reasoning which is not that of logic.

Returning to a point he had made early on in the *Adornment*, GC notes
that what we mean by the term *everything* is merely everything that we can
imagine. To say that nothing exists means that the things that we can imagine,
"the objects of the mind," do not exist. Nihilism is commonly described as the

24. For an English translation with reference to the Tibetan text, see Joshua W. C. Cutler, ed.,
The Great Treatise on the Stages of the Path to Enlightenment (Ithaca, NY: Snow Lion Publications,
2002), 3:329. See also Jeffrey Hopkins, *Maps of the Profound: Jam-yang-shay-ba's Great Exposition
of Buddhist and Non-Buddhist Views on the Nature of Reality* (Ithaca, NY: Snow Lion Publications,
2003), 318–19.

denigration of phenomena, and GC notes that this would include both objects and subjects, such that saying that nothing exists would mean that neither our mind nor its objects are real. Such a conclusion, in fact, is the goal of the Buddhist path. One accumulates merit over the course of many aeons in order to understand that the dharma has no location, at which point there would seem to be little danger of nihilism.

The process of the path, however, is not merely the negation of the mind and its objects but their gradual transformation until one reaches the rank of a buddha. But such transformation is impossible if one is consumed by calculating how much dirt, stones, and rocks there are in the world, as well as quantifying women, meat, and beer. The features of saṃsāra should be familiar enough to those who have resided here from time immemorial, without the need for logical proofs of them.

These proofs, furthermore, called the "reasoning of the three modes," are of the most limited applicability. Humans and tigers do not desire the same thing because their thought processes, or "reasoning of the three modes," are different. It is quite odd, therefore, that something that is not shared by humans and animals should be claimed to provide accurate conclusions about everything in the universe, from the buddha field of Akaniṣṭha to the most torturous hot hell of Avīci.

Yet birth in each of the various realms of saṃsāra brings with it its own experiences, such that a cup of liquid appears as fire to a hell being and ambrosia to a god. And as sentient beings are born into each of these different realms, they do not bring their past perceptions with them, but perceive the liquid as what it is for a being of that realm, without having to inquire as to what it is; their perceptions change from lifetime to lifetime. One thing that does not change over the long course of saṃsāra, however, is the innate ignorance, the conception of true existence: what this ignorance imagines to be real—that is, the intrinsic existence of the various phenomena of the universe—"has accompanied the mind beginninglessly, without ever changing." It therefore seems quite odd that it requires so much effort to precisely identify "the object of negation." In fact, there is nothing more engrained in the mind than the conception of true existence. When this conception, or "the subject," is so familiar, one need not expend much effort to find its object. Indeed, if nihilism is a view that is contrary to appearances that are widely known in the world, then holding that true establishment does not exist—though it appears to all six types of sentient beings—would be the ultimate form of nihilism.

¶¶234–36 GC turns next to some of the claims made about what can and cannot properly be said to be empty. It is sometimes said that emptiness is only the final nature of things that exist, not of things that do not exist. It would therefore be inaccurate to say that the horns of a rabbit are empty of intrinsic existence. Yet GC notes that intrinsic existence is ascribed to many things that do not exist, such as the principle (*pradhāna*) asserted by the Sāṃkhya and the nonexistence of rebirth asserted by the Carvāka. Insisting that emptiness pertains only to things that exist requires that one first decide what exists and what does not exist, and then establish emptiness for the former. "In that case, it is impossible to understand emptiness until one has attained buddhahood," because only a buddha understands the categories of existence and nonexistence. The skill to prove emptiness must be acquired first, at which point it can be used anywhere, just as someone who knows how to pour water into a pot retains that skill whether there happens to be a pot present or not.

GC cannot leave this point without one more comment about the horns of a rabbit. When someone asserts, "There is no point on the horn of a rabbit," this statement does not qualify as a nonaffirming negative (implying nothing positive in its place), because the basis of the negative statement, the horn of a rabbit, does not exist. However, when someone says, "There is no point on the horn of a yak," this statement is a nonaffirming negative, because yak horns and their points exist. Thus, GC notes that making this distinction puts one in the difficult position of turning something that does not exist into something that does exist (because the statement about the horns of a rabbit is not a nonaffirming negative and thus must imply something positive), while turning something that does exist into something that does not exist (by making the absence of a tip on the horn of a yak a nonaffirming negative). Having sought to avoid the charge of nihilism throughout, GC is able to make it here, quoting Nāgārjuna (misidentified in the text as Āryadeva) to the effect that nihilism is regarding something that once existed to be now nonexistent.

In Dge lugs discussions of emptiness, a distinction is drawn between the object of negation (*dgag bya*) and the basis of negation (*dgag gzhi*). The object of negation is what is to be negated by reasoning; in this case, it is true existence or intrinsic existence. The object of negation does not exist, but it is imagined to exist by ignorance. The basis of negation is the object that is empty of true existence or intrinsic existence. It is therefore also called "the basis which is empty" (*stong gzhi*). The basis of negation exists and is not refuted in the process of reasoning. This is yet another of the Dge lugs distinctions that GC finds dangerously sophisticated. He therefore asks what would be wrong with redefining the terms slightly, making true existence the basis of negation and making its nonexistence to be emptiness. The nonexistence or absence of true existence is already the meaning of emptiness, so the only real change would be to make true existence the basis of negation, that is, the basis which is empty. Since true existence does not exist even conventionally, such a shift would remove the possibility of some kind of conventionally existent basis of negation being left behind at the end of the process of reasoning; there would be only the absence of the object of negation. Such a shift would have the further advantage that it would not depend, as the standard Dge lugs distinction does, on unenlightened beings having to differentiate between conventional existence and true existence, which they are incapable of doing. As long as one continues to insist that there be a distinction between the object of negation and the basis of negation, GC says, then one is simply washing the stains of true establishment off a pot with the water of Nāgārjuna's six texts on Madhyamaka reasoning. This image is important here. True establishment is represented as something superficial to the pot rather than something inseparable from it; true establishment can thus be washed away, leaving the pot intact, just as the object of negation can be refuted, leaving the basis of negation unscathed. All of this is wishful thinking for GC. It is not like washing the stains off a pot, but like washing the face of a beautiful woman: the more you wash her face, the more beautiful she becomes. Thus, the more one attempts to distinguish between true establishment and conventional existence, the stronger the appearance of true establishment will become. "The conception of true existence that has existed beginninglessly, and true establishment that has been nonexistent beginninglessly—these two would be joined in union facing each other. How could this be?"

¶¶237–38 Tibetan doxographies distinguish between Mahāyāna and Hīnayāna in terms of both path and tenet. To be a Mahāyānist by path means to aspire to buddhahood on the bodhisattva path. To be a Hīnayānist by path means to aspire to the state of an arhat on the path of either a *śrāvaka* or a *pratyeka-buddha*. The distinction by tenet places the two Indian Buddhist schools of Madhyamaka and Yogācāra under the Mahāyāna heading and the two schools of Sautrāntika and Vaibhāṣika under the Hīnayāna. This distinction is made generally on the basis of whether or not these schools accept the Mahāyāna sūtras as the word of the Buddha.

It is also the case that each of the four Indian schools provides (from its perspective) a complete presentation of the various paths to liberation, setting forth the path of the *śrāvaka*, *pratyekabuddha*, and bodhisattva. From this perspective, it is possible to make a distinction between path and tenet. Thus, if one aspired to the rank of an arhat but held the Madhyamaka view that the emptiness of intrinsic existence was the meaning of selflessness, one would be a Hīnayānist by path and a Mahāyānist by tenet. Indeed, according to Tsong kha pa (with strong support from Candrakīrti), anyone who achieves liberation as an arhat must understand Nāgārjuna's emptiness. Thus, for Tsong kha pa, there has never been an arhat who was not a Mahāyānist by tenet. It is also the case that the Vaibhāṣikas and Sautrāntikas set forth the path of the bodhisattva to buddhahood, although their presentation of the nature of buddhahood is very different from that found in the Mahāyāna schools. Thus, a follower of the Vaibhāṣika who aspired to buddhahood could be called a Hīnayānist by tenet and a Mahāyānist by path.

This is yet another of the Dge lugs distinctions to which GC most vigorously objects. He has no apparent problems with someone making the distinction between Mahāyānist by path and Mahāyānist by tenet; he does not deny the existence of arhats, and he accepts that one must understand emptiness in order to abandon the afflictive obstructions. But he rejects the suggestion that it follows from such a distinction that a Vaibhāṣika who aspires to buddhahood could be called a bodhisattva. A bodhisattva is someone who aspires to buddhahood, and this buddhahood and the path to it are set forth fully only in the Mahāyāna sūtras and treatises. Thus, the bodhisattva must ascend through the ten stages (*bhūmi*), which are not described by the Hīnayāna schools, in order to achieve the three bodies of a buddha (the *dharmakāya*, *saṃbhogakāya*, and *nirmāṇakāya*), endowed with the five wisdoms: the mirror-like wisdom (*ādarśajñāna, me long lta bu'i yes shes*), the wisdom of equality (*samatājñāna, mnyam nyid ye shes*), the wisdom of specific understanding (*pratyavekṣanajñāna, so sor rtogs pa'i ye shes*), the wisdom of accomplishing activities (*kṛtyānuṣṭhānajñāna, bya ba sgrub pa'i ye shes*), and the wisdom of the sphere of reality (*dharmadhātujñāna, chos dbying ye shes*). None of these is presented in the Hīnayāna tenet systems.

Compassion is not a unique quality of Buddhists. Even followers of non-Buddhist schools, like the Sāṃkhyas, wish to help others. But it is ridiculous to suggest that they therefore embark on a bodhisattva path. A Vaibhāṣika bodhisattva would hold all the views of the Vaibhāṣikas, such as there being three final vehicles (and, therefore, that not all beings will one day become buddhas), and when arhats and buddhas attain nirvāṇa, they enter a state of cessation in which mind and body are utterly extinguished. The buddhahood sought by such a bodhisattva would not be genuine buddhahood. "Therefore, how is it possible that a person on an erroneous path from the start could have a hope for the final fruition which is not false?"

GC is once again finding danger in what he regards as the sophistry of the doxographers, who spend their time laying out all possible combinations and permutations of the path, rather than simply following it.

¶¶239–40 One of the most famous analogies in Indian philosophy, and one employed in Madhyamaka, is the rope snake. A coiled rope in a darkened corner can be easily mistaken for a snake; based on that mistake, all manner of fear, and deeds motivated by fear, can occur. In the same way, it is said, the ordinary objects of our existence, which merely exist conventionally, are imagined to ultimately exist. And based on that simple misconception, all of the desire and hatred that drive the engine of saṃsāra arise. By shining a light into the corner, one can easily see that there is no snake there, only a rope, and the fear is dispelled. By shining the light of wisdom on the objects of our experience, they can be seen to lack ultimate existence, and desire and hatred dissipate.

We should not be surprised at this point to find the GC has a different idea about ropes and snakes. He says that merely saying to a frightened person, "It is not a snake" is not entirely effective, because the appearance of the snake and the attendant fear continue for that person. Moreover, there are stories of skilled artists being frightened by their own paintings of wrathful deities. And Śāntideva said that when a magician conjures a beautiful woman, he still feels lust for her, even though he knows she is not real. One can assume from this that when the magician conjures a tiger, he feels afraid. Thus, GC suggests that rather than picking up the rope and saying, "This is not a snake," the true hero picks up the rope and throws it out the door. "Thereby, both the basis of error, the coiled rope, and the appearance of error, the snake, are gone without a trace." His point should be familiar by now. There is a danger in making too fine a distinction between the object of negation (the snake) and the basis of negation (the rope), negating one while leaving the other in place. Since they are so difficult to distinguish, the better course is to eliminate both.

GC offers a final caution about the commonly appearing subject. At the end of his *Great Exposition of Insight* (*Lhag mthong chen mo*), Tsong kha pa notes that one of the results of achieving deep states of concentration is that objects begin to appear wispy and insubstantial, like rainbows.[25] He cautions that such an experience is not to be mistaken for the illusionlike *samādhi*, which results from reasoned analysis of the object of negation. Yet in the Dge lugs statements of Madhyamaka reasonings, a rainbow is often provided as an example, as in "The subject, a pillar, is like an illusion, because of being dependently arisen like, for example, a rainbow." This strikes GC as pointless, because giving a rainbow as an example in an autonomous syllogism stated to a follower of a philosophical school that asserts that all phenomena truly exist would have very little effect—and would in no way convey the meaning of phenomena being like illusions, as Nāgārjuna uses the term.

¶241 The *Adornment* concludes with some advice on the practice of the path, but not, of course, without irony. Throughout the text, GC has spoken about the path as a process of transforming the mind—of replacing the earth and stones of the world of the unenlightened not simply with the gold and jewels of the pure lands, but with the inconceivable abode of the Buddha. He has alluded often to the way that the mind of a single individual changes over the course of a life, using this as proof that one should not place too much stake in one's own opinions, nor consider them as constituting some form of "valid knowledge." He speaks here of maturation, of how one's interests change as one grows older. Thus, when one no longer takes pleasure in playing in the ashes of the hearth, the mind of childhood is growing weaker. When one begins to lose interest in sex, the mind of the prime of life is growing weaker. When one finds no pleasure in property and wealth, the mind of maturity is growing weaker. But rather than portraying this as a movement from naiveté to wisdom, GC says about each of the passing stages, "Therefore, one must strive to create it." He is being facetious.

The standard taxonomy describes five paths to enlightenment, beginning with the path of accumulation, then the path of preparation, the path of vision, the path of meditation, and finally the path of no further learning, which is buddhahood itself. The bodhisattva path is also described in terms of the ten stages. The first begins with the initial direct perception of emptiness. On the eighth, one abandons the afflictive obstructions. GC explains here that when one has achieved the second of the five paths, one should strive for the first; when one has achieved the eighth bodhisattva stage, one should strive for the first stage; when one has achieved buddhahood, one should strive for the

25. For an English translation with reference to the Tibetan text, see Cutler, *The Great Treatise*, p. 355.

path of accumulation, which marks the very beginning of the path to buddhahood. He calls this the "taking of the entire teaching as the practice in a single sitting, in one human lifetime." Indeed, "one should practice the entire teaching on the single lotus throne of the Densely Adorned Realm." This is the pure land of Akaniṣṭha, special abode for the *saṃbhogakayas* of the buddhas.

GC is gently mocking the approach to the path counseled by Atiśa and Tsong kha pa. There is the famous story (recounted, among other places, in the *Blue Annals*, which GC translated with George Roerich) of Atiśa's meeting with the great Tibetan translator Rin chen bzang po (958–1055) in which Atiśa praised the elder Tibetan for his great learning, saying that if there are such learned men in Tibet already, there was no need for Atiśa to come from India to teach the dharma. Atiśa then asked Rin chen bzang po how he practiced tantra, and he explained that he practiced each of the tantras separately. Atiśa replied, "Rotten translator. There was indeed a purpose in my coming to Tibet."[26] Atiśa famously advocated the practice of sūtra and tantra, and of the individual tantras, together, "in a single sitting," and he sets forth such an approach in his most famous work, the *Lamp for the Path to Enlightenment* (*Bodhipathapradīpa*).

This work, in turn, was said to have inspired Tsong kha pa's most famous volume, the *Great Exposition of the Stages of the Path to Enlightenment* (*Byang chub lam rim chen mo*). In this work, Tsong kha pa does not set forth all the practices of Hīnayāna, Mahāyāna (or, more technically, Pāramitāyāna), and Vajrayāna, but instead only those teachings that are essential to the path to buddhahood. Thus, for example, one must first develop a sense of repulsion for saṃsāra, set forth in the Hīnayāna, before one can develop the extraordinary compassion of the Mahāyāna. But as one moves through the teachings common to the path of enlightenment, there is great value in returning to earlier stages to revivify one's practice—to meditate on death and impermanence (Hīnayāna teachings), for example—even at higher stages of the path. The path is thus very much a continuum, where much is to be gained by moving not only forward but back.

As we have seen, GC's model of the path is not so much one of gradual stages, but rather a ladder that takes one higher and higher in a vertical ascent until one arrives at a raft. One rides the raft to the other shore and then leaves it, and the perceptions and conceptions of the world behind, as one achieves the state of buddhahood, never to go back.

26. See George N. Roerich, *The Blue Annals* (Delhi: Motilal Banarsidass, 1979), 249.

¶¶242–48 The text concludes with a prayer, one that includes the standard elements of gratitude to the teacher, the request for forgiveness for any faults in the text, the wish that the text be pleasing to scholars, the entreaty to be cared for by the lama in lifetime after lifetime, and a dedication of merit.

The first stanza reads:

> The wisdom that is beyond existence and nonexistence is the essential point of the profound thought of Nāgārjuna, the father, and his sons. This eloquent explanation distills into one the traditions of the forefathers, the best of the new and ancient schools of the snowy land.

This is clearly a gloss on the title of the text while making reference to the best of the new (the *gsar ma* schools, including Dge lugs) and the ancient (the Rnying ma). According to his friend and disciple, Rak ra rin po che, this stanza may or may not have been composed by GC. However, he states that the final four stanzas of the poem are definitely GC's work. The reference there to "lama Mañjunātha," "protected by Mañjuśri," a standard epithet of Tsong kha pa, suggests that GC did not regard the *Adornment* as an anti-Dge lugs tract, as so many would see it.

chapter

4

THE AUTHOR

In a recent Tibetan study of the life of GC, we read: "In the world today, the proportion of those who have faith in Buddhism or do research on Buddhism has been growing; there are few who do not know about the *Adornment for Nāgārjuna's Thought*. More and more researchers are also appearing who are raising questions about the identity of the author."[1]

Although this estimation of the *Adornment*'s fame may be somewhat overstated, the question of its authorship certainly remains an active topic of discussion and debate. It is a question that is central to GC's legacy amid the fraught sectarian politics that have persisted in Tibetan Buddhism since the Chinese invasion of 1950.

It is perhaps not surprising that a work offering such a thoroughgoing critique of philosophical authority should be regarded, at least by its critics, as a work of questionable authorship. And, like so many other elements of GC's life, a number of questions must be considered, even before the sectarian battle lines are drawn.

Among the various evidence to be taken into account, the first is to be found in the colophon to the *Adornment* itself, where we read the following at ¶249:

> Born into a family of *mantrikas* in the land of A mdo, unattached to and unhindered by any doctrine, non-Buddhist or Buddhist, new or ancient, he attained learning and achievement. If one has reason to speak his name, he is the *mahāpandita* Dge 'dun chos 'phel. At the time when the kind instructions on Madhyamaka had been received by me from his lips, he asked to look over all the scattered notes. Having done this, together with offering a verse of prayer [before] an image of Nāgārjuna, he said that all the notes should be gathered together in one place. While this final testament of the

---

1. Hor gtsang 'jigs med, *Drang bden gyis bslus pa'i slong mo ba* (Dharamsala, India: Youtse Publications, 1999), 119.

lord himself at the hour of his death was held in my heart, Bdud 'joms rin po che gave the paper on which it was to be written and said, "You must write it in the way [he told you to]." Not bearing to turn away from his exhortation, that lord's stupid student and servant, called Zla ba bzang po of eastern Nyag, performed this task on the auspicious day of the waxing moon of the twelfth month of the Iron Hare year of the sixteenth cycle. May this serve as a cause for all these biased appearances of myself and others to be liberated into mind-expanse of the unbiased pervasive lord Vajradhara.

Composed by GC's Rnying ma pa disciple, Zla ba bzang po (1916–58), this colophon is in many ways quite traditional; in other ways it raises a number of interesting questions concerning the authorship of the *Adornment*. GC is identified as coming from a lineage of *māntrika*s in A mdo, which is, of course, correct. But there is no mention of his education in the Dge lugs academy. Instead, he is described as being "unattached to and unhindered by any doctrine, non-Buddhist or Buddhist, new or ancient," with the term *new* evoking the three "new translation" sects of Bka' brgyud, Sa skya, and Dge lugs (but here especially referring to Dge lugs), and "old" meaning Rnying ma. This description is debatable, even given GC's contempt for debate—but it is not inappropriate in a colophon, where hyperbole reigns. Next, in keeping with GC's assertion of the inexpressible nature of reality, as well as with the pious conventions of the colophon, Zla ba bzang po implies that it is ultimately impossible to describe his teacher in words, but if one must do so, he is "the *mahāpaṇḍita* GC." Notably, Zla ba bzang po does not use the standard Tibetan translation for the Sanskrit term *mahāpaṇḍita* (which is *paṇ chen*) but instead transliterates the Sanskrit term into Tibetan, to suggest his teacher's mastery of the sacred language of India.

What follows is the only direct testimony we have about how the *Adornment* text was composed. Zla ba bzang po says that GC asked to see the "scattered notes" of his instructions on Madhyamaka. These are presumably Zla ba bzang po's own notes, made over time: we have reports from others that GC began teaching Madhyamaka to Zla ba bzang po shortly after his return to Lhasa, and the implication here is that GC asked for these notes to be gathered shortly before his death. It is unclear whether GC continued these teachings until his final days, or whether the notes represented yet another of the many projects he left unfinished after his release from prison. Zla pa bzang po reports that GC looked over the notes, offered prayers to a statue of Nāgārjuna, and then instructed Zla ba bzang po to compile them. This is represented as one of GC's final deeds, "this final testament of the lord himself at the hour of his death."

Zla ba bzang po apparently sought advice from the prominent Rnying ma lama Bdud 'joms rin po che, who encouraged him to compile the notes and publish them; Bdud 'joms himself sponsored the publication, serving as its patron. Zla ba bzang po implies that although he felt unequal to the task, he followed Bdud 'joms rin po che's exhortation to fulfill GC's final wish. Calling himself "that lord's stupid student and servant," Zla ba bzang po reports that he completed the work in the twelfth month of the Iron Hare year. The Iron Hare year was 1951; because Tibetans follow a lunar calendar, the twelfth month would have occurred in February 1952, just four months after GC's death.

Before considering Zla ba bzang po's statement further, let us look briefly at the patron's poem (¶¶250–52) provided by Bdud 'joms rin po che that concludes the text. He describes GC as the second Nāgārjuna, "a new moon who is the wondrous second lord of nāgas," whose white light shines "in the midst of thick darkness of the time of evil views." This latter characterization is something of a stock phrase, yet seems also to pertain particularly to the moment, when strong anti–Rnying ma views prevailed among much of the Dge lugs hierarchy, and Communist views, in the form of the People's Liberation Army, had already entered Lhasa. Recognizing the originality of GC's ideas ("the eloquent explanation, which did not exist before"), he nonetheless claims their affinity with the Rnying ma ("revivifies and uplifts the tenets of an earlier time"). Finally, he calls GC's teachings *ring bsrel*, a term often translated as "relics" but which refers often to the tiny pearl-like beads said to remain among the ashes after the cremation of an enlightened being. Such relics are highly treasured and are said to have magical powers. Describing GC's text in this way ascribes great value to both the teacher and his teachings.

The colophon, then, intends (among more traditional purposes) to establish that GC is the author of the *Adornment*—and that Zla ba bzang po is not. The circumstances surrounding the compilation of the text are detailed, in which the notes are assembled at the instruction of GC, who then reviews and presumably approves them as an accurate record of his teaching. He then directs his disciple to have the notes published; this instruction is part of his final testament, made before a statue of Nāgārjuna. Zla ba bzang po feels unqualified for the task, calling himself "stupid," but acts out of devotion to his teacher, and completes the work very quickly after GC's passing.

All of this seems perfectly plausible. That the text was not written in GC's own hand certainly poses no difficulty: there is an entire genre of Tibetan literature known as "notes" (*zin bris*), often made by a disciple. And even when not so designated, it was common for a disciple to write down what a teacher said and then present it for his correction and approval prior to publication.[2] Thus, although Zla ba bzang po's confession of his stupidity is in some ways a literary convention, it nonetheless is meant to suggest his inability to understand GC teachings fully, so he could not possibly have been the author of the *Adornment*.

At the same time, however, the colophon could be regarded as evidence of GC's absence. It was widely reported that GC drank heavily after his release from prison and was in very poor health before his death. Consequently, the authority of his approval of the notes and of his final wishes could be questioned. But most vexing for those who question the authenticity of the *Adornment* is that GC, a product of the Dge lugs academy, would entrust the compilation of his final work to a Rnying ma pa, and that its publication would then be urged and sponsored by a prominent Rnying ma lama. For GC's many Dge lugs friends, and foes, this was unimaginable. And it is this circumstance, more than any particular element among the contents of the *Adornment*, that has led to its authenticity being called into question.

There is no doubt, however, concerning the existence of the text. Instead, the questions focus on when, and whether, GC gave the teachings that constitute the *Adornment*. There are two contradictory reports from two of GC's close friends and disciples, one Rnying ma pa, the other Dge lugs pa.

As discussed in chapter 1, Bla chung a pho (also known as Shes rab rgya mtsho) met GC upon GC's return to Lhasa in 1946. He received instructions from him on a number of topics, including, he reports, Madhyamaka, and remained devoted to GC until his death. He was with GC the day before he died and participated in the funeral. In his biography of GC, written in 1972, he says that GC came to visit him when he was recovering from a serious illness: "One day, when I was somewhat more lucid, he gave me a small book of Elephant brand paper in which were written the words, beginning with, 'All of our decisions about what is and is not' and ending with the verse, 'I am uncomfortable about positing conventional validity.' He said, 'Look at this, it will keep you from sleeping.' It was a great help to me."[3] He reports that he and Zla ba bzang

---

2. See José Ignacio Cabezón, "Authorship and Literary Production in Classical Buddhist Tibet," in *Changing Minds: Contributions to the Study of Buddhism and Tibet in Honor of Jeffrey Hopkins*, ed. Guy Newland (Ithaca, NY: Snow Lion Publications, 2001), 233–63.

3. See Shes rab rgya mtsho, "Dge 'dun chos 'phel," in *Biographical Dictionary of Tibet and Tibetan Buddhism*, vol. 4, *The Rñiṅ-ma-pa Tradition (Part Two)*, ed. Khetsun Sangpo (Dharamsala, India: Library of Tibetan Works and Archives, 1973), 644. See also Irmgard Mengele, *dGe-'dun-chos-'phel: A Biography of the 20th Century Tibetan Scholar* (Dharamsala, India: Library of Tibetan Works and Archives, 1999), 33, 62.

po later received instruction in Sanskrit poetics from GC, as well as in Madhyamaka philosophy:

> Then he gave Zla ba bzang po instruction in Madhyamaka. He had him take
> notes to supplement the small book he had given to me earlier. . . . At the
> end, when it had been completed and printing blocks had been carved by
> [the sponsorship of] Ka shod pa, he said to Zla ba bzang po, "Later, there
> is going to be controversy about this. The controversy will not occur until
> after I am already dead. If it occurs, it is all right. You must be careful. Do not
> forget the essential points I explained."
>
> He also said, "In order for human birth to have real meaning in this world,
> one must leave some imprint. In my own opinion, I thought that I must draw
> out some of the distinctive features of Madhyamaka and Pramāṇa. Now, I
> have done what is appropriate to suffice for Madhyamaka."[4]

Several important points are made here. Bla chung a pho reports that approximately the first fourth of the text (¶¶4–63) was written by GC in his own
hand prior to his imprisonment. In addition, the instructions on Madhyamaka
were given before GC's imprisonment. And finally, the blocks were carved and
the text published before GC died. It must also be noted, however, that Bla
chung wrote this biography two decades after GC's death, and his memory of
a number of details has proved to be inaccurate.

The Library of Tibetan Works and Archives has in its possession a block-
print edition of the *Adornment* with the date "sixteenth Iron Hare year" written on the back. GC died in the eighth month of that year. Zla ba bzang po
reports that he completed his task in the twelfth month, but whether this refers
to the transcription of the notes or the publication of the book is unclear. The
sponsor of the block print, Ka shod pa, was a prominent government minister
and a friend and patron of GC's; but according to some reports, he was also
instrumental in GC's arrest and imprisonment.

One of GC's closest friends was the Dge lugs incarnate lama Rak ra rin po
che (Bkras mthong thub bstan chos dar [1925–]). He became GC's friend and
student before GC departure from India and resumed the relationship after

4. Shes rab rgya mtsho, "Dge 'dun chos 'phel," 647–48. See also Mengele, *dGe-'dun-chos-'phel*,
36–37, 65–66. On p. 65, Mengele translates the statement "sngar kho bo la gnang ba'i deb chung de'i
'phro nas zin bris 'bri bcug song" as "He made [me] set down in writing his remarks in connection
with notes about the small book [he] had given me earlier." That is, she reads the passage to say
that Bla chung a pho, rather than Zla ba bzang po, took the notes. It is impossible to decide from
the Tibetan, but I have taken the referent to be Zla ba bzang po, in part because he is mentioned
in the previous sentence.

GC's return to Tibet in 1946. Rak ra rin po che went to India in 1949 and thus was not in Tibet during the final two years of GC's life. He published his reminiscences of GC in 1980.[5]

Rak ra rin po che is emphatic that virtually all of the *Adornment* is not the work of GC, and that Zla ba bzang po incurred great sin by claiming it to be. Rak ra carefully cites all the passages that are, in his view, authentic. These consist entirely of poetry: the opening verse of praise to the Buddha, the long section of verses in the middle (¶¶56–76), and a portion of the concluding verses (¶¶244–48); he concedes that the two previous verses (¶¶242 and 243) may have been written by GC as well.[6]

But the rest, he maintains—the remainder of the poetry and all of the prose —was fabricated by Zla ba bzang po (he does not address the close relationship between the content of the poetry and the prose, especially in the first part of the text). Part of his evidence is textual. Rak ra asks how someone could so boldly declare his confident understanding of the Madhyamaka view and then conclude the work on a note of such humility. In other words, how could GC criticize Tsong kha pa in the body of the text and express his reverence for him at the end?

¶244 It is due to my past karma that I hold in my heart the essence of the intentions of all the conquerors in space and time, the refined, cut, and polished jewel of scripture, reasoning, and instructions, the gold of the inconceivable *dharmadhātu*.

¶245 Yet if in all the water in the mouth of the lama Mañjunātha [Tsong kha pa], the ocean of eloquence turning the wheel of the dharma, there is a part muddied by the swamp of my ignorance, I confess it from the heart to the assembly of the impartial.

Rak ra's other evidence is circumstantial. He reports that after GC was released from prison, he had complained to Rak ra that someone named Zla ba bzang po was coming to his house requesting teachings, and that GC had beaten him and thrown him out on several occasions. He also reports that Zla ba bzang po later claimed that GC's harsh treatment of him was similar to the way that Mar pa treated Mi la ras pa, but Rak ra says that GC's antipathy toward Zla ba bzang po bore no similarity whatsoever to this famous story. He maintains that

5. Bkras mthong thub bstan chos dar, *Dge 'dun chos 'phel gyi lo rgyus* (Dharamsala, India: Library of Tibetan Works and Archives, 1980).

6. See ibid., 193–98, 216.

after his release from prison, GC abandoned all of his projects and was deeply depressed.[7] However, he does not offer any philosophical arguments against the attribution of the text to GC. Rather, he seems unwilling to accept that his friend and teacher could have written a work that has caused such contention in the Tibetan community.

Rak ra knew GC well, so what he says must be taken very seriously. At the same time, such statements allow the Dge lugs to retain GC as one of their own (especially in his current incarnation since the Tibetan diaspora as a prescient culture hero) while dismissing what is perhaps his most important work—it need not even be read, as if *who* makes a particular philosophical point is more important than *what* is said. Of course, the *Adornment* addresses this issue directly in ¶32:

> [W]hen scholars these days hear a scripture that refers to neither existence nor nonexistence, they first seek out the identity of the speaker of the scripture. If the scripture is a statement of an earlier Tibetan scholar, they dismiss it [saying]: "The one who says something like that is a nihilistic fool." If the scripture is identified as a statement of the Buddha, Nāgārjuna, and so on, they patch it with words like "The statement 'does not exist' means 'does not truly exist'" and "'Is not nonexistent' means 'is not conventionally nonexistent,'" so that it fits with their own desires. In fact, the only difference is that if they direct refutations at the Buddha, they fear being labeled evil persons with evil views, [whereas] if they are able to refute earlier Tibetans, they are labeled heroic scholars.

This statement, however, does little to settle the question of authorship, apart from suggesting that value ought to be assessed based upon an evaluation of text's contents, not its attribution. When evaluating these claims, we must bear in mind that the book is both stylistically and thematically divided into two distinct parts. The first part of the work concludes with a series of four-line stanzas, many ending with the line "tha snyad tshad grub 'jog la blo ma bde" (I am uncomfortable about positing conventional validity). As noted in chapter 3, this section, were it to be extracted from the rest of the text, could be a self-contained work. It has a clear beginning, middle, and end. It is composed in GC's distinctive prose style. And it deals with a single topic, the critique of valid knowledge (*tshad ma*). Yet, it makes little mention of Madhyamaka or

7. See ibid., 190–91, 250–51. He also reports that the image of Nāgārjuna that Zla ba bzang po mentions in the colophon had disappeared while GC was in prison, and thus GC could not have made the prayer in the manner that Zla ba bzang po reports. See p. 191.

Nāgārjuna and does not merit the title *Adornment for Nāgārjuna's Thought*. As discussed above, Bla chung a pho reports that after his return to Lhasa in 1946, GC presented him with this portion of what would become the *Adornment*, written in his own hand. Thus, if we accept the testimony of Bla chung a pho, we have a reliable piece of external evidence demonstrating that the first part of the text is the work of GC.

The remainder of the work seems more problematic. It is less organized and more repetitious, with the same citations from Indian texts appearing more than once. The vocabulary here is much more scholastic. And it is this portion of the text that deals directly with Madhyamaka.

As one reads through this section of the *Adornment*, one keeps imagining that GC has finally arrived at the conclusion of his argument on this or that point, that he has now moved on to something else. Yet he will then suddenly play on a phrase that he had used several paragraphs before, drawing a conclusion about a topic that he seemed to have left behind. At times in this section, the *Adornment* becomes more epigrammatic, sometimes also cryptic, and GC's words take the form of declarations rather than arguments; his allusions range more widely, and he begins to use the vocabulary of tantra. It is also in the second part of the text that most of the misattributions of passages from Indian texts occur. This apparently chaotic conversation would, on the surface, seem to serve as evidence of something other than GC's direct control over this section of the *Adornment*.

The hypothesis that the text is composed of two parts—the first consisting of the self-contained work, written in GC's own hand and presented to Bla chung a pho, and the second consisting of the assembled notes of Zla ba bzang po—is supported by the original Lhasa block print. The first part of the text is continuous, with only one section break provided (at ¶47).[8] Beginning after the poem (where Bla chung a pho reports that the text given to him by GC ended), sections that are roughly topical are indicated by a blank space in the block, marked with a symbol.

But the two parts are not entirely distinct. The question of whether the Madhyamaka has an assertion is not introduced in the second part of the text, but in the first, at ¶51. Indeed, as noted earlier, if one were to extract the long

---

8. The mark occurs at the question "Without asserting that conventions are validly established, how is it that you do not lack confidence in dependent origination?" In his biography of GC, Bla chung a pho reports that this question (phrased somewhat differently" "If one does not assert that conventions are validly established, how do you present cause and effect?") was posed to GC by the abbot of Smin grol gling monastery. See Shes rab rgya mtsho, "Dge 'dun chos 'phel," 647. See also Mengele, *dGe-'dun-chos-'phel*, 36, 65.

poem about "I am uncomfortable about positing conventional validity," the apparent first part flows seamlessly into the second. And if we regard the text as a unified work rather than two independent pieces stitched together, then it is not difficult to discern a single theme that unifies the text: that of the gap between the unenlightened and the enlightened, and how it might be possible for the former to become the latter.

Yet we have no external evidence for the authenticity of this second section of the text, apart from the statements by some that GC was giving teachings on Madhyamaka to Zla ba bzang po upon his return to Lhasa; and it is unclear whether these teachings constitute what would become the first part of the *Adornment*, the second part, both, or neither.

One could reasonably argue, however, that the very fact that Zla ba bzang po is so roundly excoriated as a fool by critics of GC, such as Dze smad rin po che and Shes rab rgya mtsho (as discussed in chapter 5), suggests that perhaps even they would have to concede that Zla ba bzang po would have been incapable of discoursing, even erroneously, on the fine points of "the commonly appearing subject" (*chos can mthun snang pa*). This section of the text would have to have been written by someone who knew his Tsong kha pa well, even if he had later gone astray. And a friend of GC's recalled in an interview in 1981 that Zla ba bzang po knew neither the number of chapters nor even the subject matter of Nāgārjuna's most famous work, the *Treatise on the Middle Way* (*Madhyamakaśāstra*). How could he have possibly composed an adornment for Nāgārjuna's thought?[9]

Even so, there is the problem of the many errors in the text. Paraphrases are presented as quotations, and quotations are misattributed, with statements by Nāgārjuna mistakenly ascribed to Āryadeva. And many passages are either very difficult to translate or simply nonsensical.[10] How could the great GC have made these glaring mistakes?

9. See Kirti rin po che Blo bzang bstan 'dzin, *Dge 'dun chos 'phel gyi rab byed zhabs btags ma* (Dharamsala, India: Kirti byes pa grwa tshang, 2003), 256.

10. On page 345 of the Hor khang edition, we find "mig ldan mig ldan gyi sa na ldan / long ba long ba'i sa na ldan." On page 348, we find "kun rdzob kun rdzob kyi sa na ldan / don dam don dam gyi sa na ldan." Both phrases are difficult to translate. On page 330, the standard phrase *'phral gyi khrul rgyu* (adventitious causes of error), a phrase that twelve-year-old Dge lugs monks learn in their lessons on *blo rigs*, becomes instead *'phral rgyu khrul rgyu*. On page 302, a citation from *Madhyamakakārikā* XI.1ab reads in the Derge edition "sngon mtha' mngon nam zhes zhus tshe" (When asked whether the beginning could be known [the great sage remained silent]). But in the *Adornment* we read "sngon mtha' sngon rnams zhus pa'i tshe." On page 334, one finds the following strange passage, "ming btags pa'i sna rgol gyis dung gi kha dog dkar po yin gyi ser bo min par khas blangs pa la," which would mean something like "an opponent who imputes names asserts that the color of a conch is white and not yellow."

It is possible that GC did not make the errors, yet is nonetheless the author of the *Adornment*. Indeed, the fact that he did not make the errors could serve as proof of his authorship. All the mistakes enumerated in note 10 are the products of the notorious homophony of the Tibetan language. The statement about the sighted and the blind ("mig ldan mig ldan gyi sa na ldan | long ba long ba'i sa na ldan") becomes immediately comprehensible when we substitute the final possession indicator *ldan* with *bden*, meaning "true," so that the statement reads, reflecting perfectly GC's storied skepticism, "Being sighted is true for the sighted, being blind is true for the blind." Someone who had not studied the basic textbooks on epistemology (*blo rigs*) could easily hear *'phral gyi khrul rgyu* as *'phral rgyu khrul rgyu*.

GC will sometimes tamper with a quotation in order to make it say what he wants it to.[11] But he does not misidentify an author. How, then, could Nāgārjuna (Klu sgrub) be mistaken for Āryadeva ('Phags pa lha)? There is no homophone here. But, in fact, there is. Dge lugs monks often refer to Nāgārjuna in speech with the affectionate nickname Phags pa klu, pronounced *pak ba lu*, very similar to the Tibetan name for Āryadeva, pronounced *pak ba lha*. For each of these errors, we might imagine a late-night dictation session in which the student is trying desperately to write down everything his teacher says even though he understands little, that the teacher is from A mdo and has never lost his strong accent, and that the teacher is, on occasion, also drunk.

So perhaps Zla ba bzang po was telling the truth in the colophon: that he was in fact not capable of compiling the *Adornment* but that he also wrote down everything his teacher said—or, at least, what he heard him say. Perhaps it is true that Zla ba bzang po could honestly say, like another somewhat slow-witted disciple, Ānanda, "Thus did I hear."

---

11. As in the quotation from *Madhyamakakārikā* on page 302, this is another case of mishearing, replacing *mngon nam* with the homophonic *sngon rnams*. See ¶78 of the translation. Regarding the passage on page 334 about the former opponent who imputes names, when we read on in the paragraph, we find that the *ming btags pa'i snga rgol* is having a debate about the color of a conch with a *mkhris nad can gyi phyi rgol*, an opponent who has bile disease, causing everything to seem yellow. It is therefore possible that the student wrote down *ming btags pa'i snga rgol* when the teacher simply said *mig dwangs* (or perhaps *mig dag*) *pa'i snga rgol*, an opponent with clear vision.

THE CRITICS

There is a long history of polemical debate in Tibetan Buddhism, going back to the legendary confrontation of the Indian monk Kamalaśila and the Chan monk Moheyan at the end of the eighth century. That tradition of polemic extended into the twentieth century and on into the exile period, where the *Adornment* has earned further fame as the subject of particular controversy. Responses to the work have been extreme. It has been praised by some (typically non–Dge lugs) scholars and excoriated by others. A thorough study of the refutations of the *Adornment* would require a separate and lengthy volume. Here, I will attempt only to give some sense of the tone of these texts.

The first response to appear was written by a young Dge lugs incarnate lama of Dga' ldan monastery named Dze smad rin po che (Blo bzang dpal ldan bstan 'dzin yar rgyas [1927–96]). A close disciple of the Dalai Lama's junior tutor, Khri byang rin po che, he was a brilliant scholar and poet who, after escaping to India, would play a key role in the Shugs ldan controversy (described below). But as a young scholar of only twenty-eight years, in 1955, two years after receiving his geshe degree and only three years after the publication of the *Adornment*, he published a detailed refutation longer than the text he was attacking. His attitude toward the *Adornment* is evident from the title of his work: *The Magical Wheel of Slashing Swords Mincing to Dust the Evil Adversary with Words to Delight Mañjuśrī* (*'Jam dpal dgyes pa'i gtam gyis rgol ngan phye mar 'thag pa reg gcod ral gri'i 'phrul 'khor*). A vicious attack on GC, the work gushes with acid invective. At the same time, it is clearly the product of a very learned scholar. It deserves a separate study as a fascinating exemplar of the concerns of Dge lugs scholasticism in 1955, four years after the People's Liberation Army entered Lhasa, four years before the Dalai Lama departed.

Dze smad rin po che constantly refers to GC as a madman (*dge chos smyon pa*) and punctuates his arguments with "alas" (*kye hud*). When he cites passages from the *Adornment*, he never gives the title of the text, but writes instead, "it says in the mistaken explanation (*log bshad*)." And the explanation is not simply mistaken, but evil:

> As the protector Nāgārjuna said, "Those who seek the sinful are without virtue, yet pretend to be virtuous." The invisible lord [Māra], in order to destroy the teaching of the sage [the Buddha], has incarnated as the so-called "Dge 'dun chos 'phel," who mixed this wrong explanation, having a nature of poison, with his tongue of envy and then spit it out of his mouth.[1]

Dze smad rin po che does not limit himself to countering the arguments in the *Adornment*. He attacks GC personally, chastising him repeatedly for his drunkenness (supported with quotations from Nāgārjuna himself). For Dze smad rin po che, GC is a disgrace to the Dge lugs:

> Initially, he stayed at the monastery of Bkra shis 'khyil in Mdo smad, where he entered the course of study and reflection. However, because he was bereft of merit and aspirations to goodness, his studies came to be accompanied by the afflictions. Because he put his effort into some modes of reasoning that are directed outside [Buddhism], all the proponents of reasoning who were living there shouted with a great roar, condemning him as a "materialist." As a result, he came to central Tibet. He stayed at 'Bras spungs for a while, but it was his nature to devote himself only to stringing together words. He came to be a demon of the dharma, a learned person bound in slavery to desire, hatred, and ignorance. As it is said, "A bird who slips out of a trap, a woman who roams to three husbands, a monk who has disgust for the dharma; among the types of deceit, these three are the worst." Living at a special abode like the glorious 'Bras spungs, dwelling place of ten million scholars and adepts, he had opportunities, both great and small, for hearing, thinking, and meditation, but, serving as an example of "the butter bag is not permeated by butter," he set off for foreign lands. At the end, he was left with no faith in the three supreme ones. He lost his *pratimokṣa* vow, casting it aside like a stone and kept company with women. Because of engaging in some evil deeds, in the end, by breaking the royal laws, he had the courage to wander all the way to prison. Because he drank beer and liquor without restraint, he engaged in some insane behavior. (12.2–13.1)

1. Dze smad blo bzang dpal ldan bstan 'dzin yar rgyas, *'Jam dpal dgyes pa'i gtam gyis rgol ngan phye mar 'thag pa reg gcod ral gri'i 'phrul 'khor*. The front cover of the text reads *Dbu ma klu sgrub dgongs rgyan gyi dgag pa* (Delhi: D. Gyaltsan and K. Legshay, 1972), 11.5–12.1.

He mounts his attack from a number of perspectives, often sarcastically rephrasing the words of the text itself. Thus, regarding Zla ba bzang po's verse of praise of GC that opens the text (¶2), he writes,

> In praising his lama GC [Dge chos], the disciple Zla bzang wrote, "The assembled philosophers always respect you without waxing or waning, saying, 'This is the lord of the dharma, the supreme lion of speakers.'" To determine whether or not this is just a lie meant to change the perceptions of others, if you can still gather together the inmates who were in prison with GC, ask them, and it will be clear. Therefore, Zla bzang, it would be good if after that you would write, "The assembled prisoners always reproach you without waxing or waning, saying, 'This is the lord of old dogs, who speaks what is not the dharma.'" (14.4–5)

At ¶23, GC had argued that the state of enlightenment is utterly beyond human conception. Thus, the accounts of the pure lands that appear in the sūtras are not descriptions of the pure lands as they really are, but rather are depicted in terms that would be appealing to the audience of the day. Because the Buddha taught the dharma in India, the sūtras describe things that the people of ancient India would find most beautiful, such as gold and jewels. If the Buddha had set forth the sūtras in Tibet, the pure lands would have been described differently. Here is Dze smad's comment:

> How could the supramundane qualities asserted by us Buddhists—the marvelous abandonments and the marvelous realizations—be fabricated, modeled on this world and the human realm? Because you morons like beer, liquor, and cigarettes, is it said [in the sūtras] that in Akaniṣṭha there are cigarettes to smoke? Must it be said that if someone is a discile to whom the dharma is spoken by an actual body of the Buddha, then what exists in Akaniṣṭha must be in accordance with whatever that disciple likes? If it is someone who likes to eat meat, does it say [in the sūtras] that in the land of Akaniṣṭha yaks are slaughtered? (55.3–6)

Later in the text, he offers a point-by-point parody of each of the twenty-one verses on valid knowledge (¶¶56–76). These are the first three:

> Having seen that the object of knowledge posited to exist by the mind and the valid knowledge which is undeceived with respect to the object is a case of the former being established as the object of the latter, I am most comfortable about positing conventional validity.

Having seen that the conventional, which merely appears to the mind, and being empty of entity in fact, proceed with one helping the other, I am most comfortable about positing conventional validity.

Having seen that GC, who conceals the mountain of his own faults, and Zla bzang, who searches for the faults of others with a needle, take turns at one being stupider than the other, I am most comfortable about positing conventional validity. (101.5–102.2)

Beneath all the invective, however, are many valid points that result from careful scholarship. Dze smad rin po che notes, for example, that the conversation between Sangs rgyas rgya mtsho and 'Jam dbyangs bzhad pa (described at ¶100) could not have occurred, because the former died before the latter was born (118–19). He notes a number of cases in which passages from Indian texts cited to support a particular point are taken out of context. For example, at ¶21, GC cites the *King of Meditations* (*Samādhirāja*): "The eye, the ear, the nose are not valid; the tongue, the body, the mind are not valid. If these senses were valid, what could the noble path do for anyone?" Dze smad points out that the passage continues, "These senses are not valid because their nature is neutral matter" (51.1–2). That is, the passage is referring to the physical sense organs—the eye, the ear, the nose, the tongue, the body—and stating that they are not valid forms of knowledge because they are physical; the passage is not referring to the sense consciousnesses, as GC implies. Dze smad offers several such examples.[2] He even provides a list of misspellings (194.4–6).

Dze smad rin po che takes particular delight in noting the numerous misattributions of quotations, the places where, for example, a statement that GC identifies as being from Āryadeva is in fact a statement from Nāgārjuna; GC does not even seem to recognize the words of the person whose thought he claims to adorn. Dze smad writes,

If you, the madman GC and your retinue, do not even know who the authors of these texts are, it is frightening that you would comment on the meaning of the profound reality [*dharmatā*]. It is frightening that you would refute the lama Mañjunātha [Tsong kha pa], king of dharma. It is frightening that you would compose a treatise to serve as an adornment for the thought of the noble Nāgārjuna. Although madmen know nothing, do you

---

2. For example, he explains that the story about the king drinking the crazing waters (¶7) recounted by Candrakīrti is somewhat different from GC's retelling (see ibid., pp. 25–27). He provides the context for the quotation from Candrakīrti at ¶23 (see p. 55). He explains that at ¶¶23–26, GC has misunderstood the statement that the Buddha can make an atom equal to a world (see p. 59).

not now see that the fault of lying about the most basic knowledge, described at length, has been revealed? These great waves of insanity, making mistakes about everything, starting from the author of a text, are reason for pity. (170.1–3)

Dze smad rin po che's refutation is not devoted entirely to dismissive ridicule of GC. He seems to find GC's positions genuinely dangerous. Among his many errors and transgressions, GC has committed the sin of defining the object of negation too broadly, opening the door to what for Dze smad is a nihilistic relativism. For example, at ¶¶35–40, GC had criticized what he took to be the overly fine distinction made by the Dge lugs between the ordinary thought of "I" and the conception of self. Dze smad rin po che argues that this distinction must be upheld. Otherwise, "all of the thoughts of ordinary common beings would become objects of negation by the path; whatever conceptions they had of virtue and sin would be objects of negation. Therefore, you [GC] should seek refuge in the meditation of Hwa shang who said, 'For example, it does not matter whether a white or black cloud blocks the sky. Thus, do not reflect on anything, do not contemplate anything'" (82.5–6). Here Dze smad identifies GC with the views of the Heshang (rendered in Tibetan as Hwa shang) Moheyan, the Chinese master who brought Chan to the Tibetan court in the late eighth century and who was, at least according to legend, defeated in debate by the Indian master Kamalaśīla, who represented the Madhyamaka view. Moheyan was banished by the king, but he is said to have left one shoe behind, meaning that remnants of his dangerous view would remain. A standard trope of polemical literature in Tibet has been to identify one's opponent with what are regarded as the antinomian position of the Chan master.[3] Here, we see this trope persisting even to 1955, when the Chinese and their dangerous views have returned to Lhasa in the form of the People's Liberation Army.

The other lengthy refutation of the *Adornment* is by GC's own teacher, Rdo sbis dge bshes Shes rab rgya mtsho (1884–1968). Shes rab rgya mtsho is regarded as one of the most brilliant Tibetan scholars of twentieth century, and was highly regarded by the Thirteenth Dalai Lama.[4] He came to Lhasa from

3. See Donald S. Lopez Jr., "Polemical Literature (dGag lan)," in *Tibetan Literature: Studies in Genre*, ed. Roger Jackson and José Cabezón (Ithaca, NY: Snow Lion Publications, 1995), 217–28.
4. The following biographical information is drawn from Heather Stoddard, "The Long Life of rDo-sbis dGe-bśes Śes-rab rGya-mcho (1884–1968)," in *Tibetan Studies: Proceedings of the 4th*

Bla brang monastery (as GC would) in 1905, and became a monk of Klu 'bum House in Sgo mang College of 'Bras spungs monastery (as GC would). The Thirteenth Dalai Lama assigned him with the task of assisting in the editing of the collected works of Bu ston. In 1921, he was entrusted by the Dalai Lama with the exalted position of editor of a new edition of the *bka' 'gyur,* the translation of the word of the Buddha, which he worked on for twelve years. It was during this period that GC came to Lhasa and attended Shes rab rgya mtsho's lectures at Sgo mang. They are said to have regularly engaged in shouting matches, with Shes rab rgya mtsho referring to GC as "the madman."

Shes rab rgya mtsho apparently held unusually progressive political views for a Dge lugs monk of his day. Rahul Sankrityayan reports in his diary that in a conversation with him in 1934, Shes rab rgya mtsho expressed his sympathy for Mao.[5] In 1936, and after the death of the Dalai Lama, Shes rab rgya mtsho left Lhasa, never to return. He held several positions in the Kuomintang (KMT) government, and translated Sun Yatsen's *Three Principles of the People* (*Sanminzhiyi*) into Tibetan. He attempted to return to Tibet in an official capacity in 1944 but was refused entry by the Tibetan government.

Shes rab rgya mtsho served as vice-chairman of the important Mongolian and Tibetan Affairs Commission of the KMT from 1947–49, and remained on the mainland after the overthrow of the KMT. He accepted numerous appointments from the Communist government, including those of vice-governor of the newly formed Qinghai Province (which included much of A mdo) and chairman of the Chinese Buddhist Association. He died in 1968 after being vilified and beaten by Red Guards during the Cultural Revolution.

Published incomplete, Shes rab rgya mtsho's response to the *Adornment* runs to 246 pages, more than twice the length of GC's work. Although highly critical, it is less vicious than Dze smad's text, as is evident beginning with the title, *Analysis of the So-Called "Adornment of Nāgārjuna's Thought," Roar of the Fearless Lion* (*Klu sgrub dgongs rgyan la che long du brtags pa mi 'jigs sengge nga ro*). The tone is less one of all-out attack than of a slightly more good-natured chiding and correction, as perhaps is fitting for the teacher of a wayward student. It is not the work of a young and contentious scholar, but of an old man; Shes rab rgya mtsho seems to have composed his response when he was in his

Seminar of the International Association of Tibetan Studies, Schloss Hohenkammer-Munich 1985, ed. Helga Uebach and Jampa L. Panglung (München: Kommission für Zentralasiatische Studien Bayerische Akademie der Wissenschaften, 1988), 465–71.

5. Ibid., 467.

late seventies.[6] Yet it is hardly avuncular; it is both highly patronizing and highly sarcastic. Here is how he begins:

> Alas, GC. Squatting, with your palms joined at your heart, say, "Kind precious teacher, with a mind of regret for the sins that I have done, like poison inside me, I seek protection in any way I can from my deed of abandoning the dharma." Listen well and bear this in mind, as it says in the sūtras. I am going to instruct you with great and overwhelming love in the splendid beauty of the path of reasoning of the three modes of consequences and syllogisms. My refutation of this recently appearing *Adornment for Nāgārjuna's Thought* has two parts: a refutation of the title and the refutation of the text.
>
> The first [the refutation of the title]. At the outset, calling it "profound key points of the middle way" is incorrect because that which is a profound key point of the middle way is simply what you decide it to be, and you have no reliability whatsoever. This follows because you yourself said [at ¶8] that you are a great madman who has been drinking and drinking the crazing waters of ignorance from time immemorial. You accept the reason and the pervasion. When you add Zla ba bzang po of Nyag rong as your friend, it follows that it no way makes you stronger because you are just piling one madman on top of a madman and error on top of error.[7]

Like Dze smad, Shes rab rgya mtsho mocks both GC and Zla ba bzang po, but he often targets the latter for particular scorn, describing the two with the phrase "Zla bzang yab sras," "Zla ba bzang po and his [spiritual] son [GC]," and suggesting that the text might more properly be entitled *Adornment for the Thought of Zla ba bzang po* (see 3:163, 233). Also like Dze smad, She rab rgya mtsho offers his own verse-by-verse rebuttal of the twenty-one stanzas on valid knowledge, beginning as follows:

6. Because Shes rab rgya mtsho's work is incomplete, it lacks a colophon, where the date of composition would be provided. However, one can infer from a biography by Lha rams pa Skal bzang rgya mtsho that it was written sometime between his seventy-fifth and seventy-seventh year. If these dates are based on the traditional Tibetan reckoning in which a child is considered one year of age during the first year (and hence is always one year older than European reckoning), the response would have been composed between 1958 and 1961. See Lha ram pa Skal bzang rgya mtsho, "Rje btsun bla ma dam pa, Pra dznya sa ra'i rnam par thar pa phun tshogs legs lam gyi rtse mo," in *Rje btsun shes rab rgya mtsho 'jam dpal dgyes pa'i blo gros kyi gsung rtsom* (Xining, China: Mtsho sngon mi rigs dpe skrun khang, 1984), 3:658–60. Further specification can be found in a letter from Shes rab rgya mtsho to Khri byang rin po che, suggesting that the response was completed after Khri byang rin po che had arrived in India, that is, sometime in 1959 at the earliest. See the letter "Rgyal ba'i yongs 'dzin khri byang rin po cher gnang ba," 3:574–75.

7. Shes rab rgya msho, *Klu sgrub dgongs rgyan la che long du brtags pa mi 'jigs sengge nga ro*, in *Rje btsun shes rab rgya mtsho 'jam dpal dgyes pa'i blo gros kyi gsung rtsom*, 3:2.

The object of comprehension and the comprehending valid knowledge are mutually non-deceptive. Thus, by what power is conventional valid knowledge not posited? Your discomfort is a fault of your mistaken mind.

The unanalyzed world and philosophical tenets serve as ornaments to justify each other. Thus, by what power is conventional valid knowledge not posited? Your discomfort is a fault of your mistaken mind. (3:118)

Shes rab rgya mtsho's various arguments are too lengthy even to summarize here. But one theme can be noted. One of the most consistent reasons that Shes rab rgya mtsho offers for rejecting a particular statement in the *Adornment* is that it is, for want of a better word, original; that is, it has no precedent in the tradition of Buddhist philosophy in India or Tibet: "Yet this was not said by the Buddha. It did not exist in India. It did not appear in Tibet in the past" (3:163). Referring to a set of three statements, he writes, "You must search for the three people who assert this. There is not even one such person among the Prāsaṅgikas and Svātantrikas. There is no one in all of the Dge lugs monasteries, great and small, like Se ra, 'Bras spungs, and Dga' ldan. Where are they even among the multitude of logicians who are scholars and adepts of Sa skya, Rnying ma, and Bka' brgyud?" (3:238) Elsewhere he writes,

> This [claim] that the Prāsaṅgikas have no assertion is the most secret of the profound and pure instructions discovered by Dge of A mdo and Zla of Nyag in the middle of the darkest night through the enormous power of their merit. It was unknown to all of the Prāsaṅgikas of the Land of the Noble, such as the masters Buddhapālita and Candrakīrti and was [not known] by even one of the Svātantrikas of India, such as the masters Bhāvaviveka and Śāntarakṣita. (3:170)

Shes rab rgya mtsho's charge, however, is not simply that GC is guilty of the crime of innovation, but that the positions GC sets forth destroy any possibility of progress on the path to enlightenment. Playing on the statement (cited repeatedly by GC) from the *Samādhirāja Sūtra* that if the senses were valid, the noble path would have no purpose, Shes rab rgya mtsho declares, "The children who debate about colors will come to attack you and pull out your beard. GC, from your position which does not accord with that of anyone in the world, not a single person would be able to proceed on the noble path" (3:230)

Although the responses of Dze smad and Shes rab rgya mtsho were written independently (and the latter composed after its author had left Lhasa), they are linked by the personal connection of each of the authors to the important monk and scholar Khri byang rin po che (1901–81), a staunch defender of the Dge lugs.

In the first decades of the twentieth century, the Thirteenth Dalai Lama (1875–1933) made preliminary attempts at modernizing the Tibetan government (often without the support of the powerful Dge lugs monasteries). About this time, the worship of the wrathful deity Rdo rje shugs ldan ("Powerful Thunderbolt") experienced a revival. This deity had first come to prominence at the time of the Fifth Dalai Lama in the seventeenth century, when he was worshipped as a protector of the Dge lugs sect, especially against incursions by the Rnying ma. During the reign of the Thirteenth Dalai Lama, a Shugs ldan revival was led by the influential Dge lugs monk Pha bong kha pa (1878–1943). The Dalai Lama responded by issuing a ban on many mediums (including mediums of Shugs ldan) who, possessed by a protector, would predict the future. Monks of the Dge lugs monasteries of Lhasa were warned against propitiating him. But the Dalai Lama died in 1933, and the worship of Shugs ldan continued.[8]

Pha bong kha pa was the guru of many of the most important Dge lugs monks of the twentieth century (both in terms of scholastic and political influence), most prominently Khri byang rin po che, who was the junior tutor of the current Dalai Lama and thus one of the most influential Dge lugs monks in Lhasa in the 1950s and in the diaspora until his death in 1981. Khri byang rin po che was himself a strong proponent of Shugs ldan.

One of Shugs ldan's particular functions has been to protect the Dge lugs sect from the influence of the Rnying ma, cautioning adherents of the Dge lugs against even touching a Rnying ma text; he is said to punish those who attempt to practice a mixture of the two sects. One can imagine, then, that the Powerful Thunderbolt would not have smiled upon the *Adornment*, given both its content (with its criticism of contemporary Dge lugs scholasticism) and the circumstances of its production (teachings given by a former Dge lugs monk to a Rnying ma disciple and published by a prominent Rnying ma lama).

Although GC seems to have been a favorite of Pha bong kha pa prior to his departure for India in 1934 and a friend of Khri byang's after his return to Tibet in 1946 (he was en route home from Khri byang's house on the night

8. On the origins of Shugs ldan worship, see Georges Dreyfus, "The Shuk-den Affair: History and Nature of a Quarrel," *Journal of the International Association of Buddhist Studies* 21, no. 2 (1998): 227–70.

of his arrest), Khri byang rin po che apparently encouraged the writing of the responses of both Dze smad and Shes rab rgya mtsho.[9]

The influence of Shugs ldan extended into exile. In 1975, a work was privately published in the Tibetan refugee community under the title *Sacred Words of the Able Father* (*Pha rgod bla ma'i zhal lung,* better known as "The Yellow Book"). Written by Dze smad rin po che, the book recounts stories, told to him by Khri byang rin po che, about the calamities, disasters, and other sad fates that had befallen twenty-three prominent figures (including two Paṇ chen lamas) who over the course of the centuries had invoked the wrath of Rdo rje shugs ldan, especially those followers of the Dge lugs who had engaged in the practices of the Rnying ma. GC was not among them.

By the 1980s, GC, so misunderstood and unacknowledged in life (at least in his view), had ascended to the rank of cultural hero, both in Tibet and among the refugee community. His biography (by Bla chung a pho) had been included in the *Biographical Dictionary of Tibet and Tibetan Buddhism,* published by the Library of Tibetan Works and Archives in Dharamsala in 1973—in, it should be noted, a volume about the Rnying ma pa.[10] In 1980, the library published Rak ra rin po che's memoir about GC, followed by Kirti sprul sku's volume of interviews in 1983. In the same year in Tibet, Hor khang published an essay about his old friend. And in 1990, Hor khang published his three-volume edition of

9. Dze smad rin po che was Khri byang rin po che's close disciple, and they were members of the same monastic college, Dga' ldan shar rtse. It is difficult to imagine that Dze smad would have written the text without his teacher's approval. Shes rab rgya mtsho had permanently departed from Lhasa before GC's death and the publication of the *Adornment.* However, it appears that a request from Khri byang rin po che was conveyed to him, perhaps in 1959 or 1960, to compose a refutation of the *Adornment.* In a letter to Khri byang rin po che, Shes rab rgya mtsho describes his composition of the work and promises to keep Khri byang rin po che's request secret, but says that if it were not kept secret there would be no harm ("skul ba por thugs dgongs ltar sbed pa yin smod I ma sbas na'ang ci skyon"). See the letter "Rgyal ba'i yongs 'dzin khri byang rin po cher gnang ba," in *Rje btsun shes rab rgya mtsho 'jam dpal dgyes pa'i blo gros kyi gsung rtsom,* 3:574–77. The quotation above appears in 3:577. See also 3:572–73, 578–79, and 584. These references to the *Adornment* seem to have been first noticed by Hor gtsang 'jigs med in his *Drang bden gyis bslus pa'i slong mo ba* (Dharamsala, India: Youtse Publication, 1999), 131–34, although some of the page references are mistaken.

Both the circumstances of Khri byang rin po che's request and his wish that it remain secret require further investigation. Since Dze smad rin po che's lengthy refutation had already been published, there would seem to be little reason for another one, apart from the authority that a refutation from Shes rab rgya mtsho, as GC's former teacher, would carry. One could also speculate that Shes rab rgya mtsho was asked to keep the request secret because of his association with the Communist government.

10. In *Masters of the Nyingma Lineage* (Crystal Mirror II) published in Berkeley by Dharma Publishing in 1995, GC is listed on page 394 among "Additional rNying-ma Authors."

GC's collected works (with a slightly different edition appearing in Dharamsala in 1991), thus bringing GC's words to a new audience.

This occurred at a time of liberalized Chinese policies in Tibet, a result of which was an explosion in Tibetan-language publications, especially in GC's home region of A mdo, where his memory was preserved with especial pride. Among the works that appeared there was one entitled *Scripture and Reasoning Incinerating the Thicket of the Proponent of Error, a Vajra Tongue of Fire* (*Log smra'i tshang tshing sreg pa'i lung rigs rdo rje me lce*). It was an edited volume of essays by four Dge lugs scholars, each largely devoted to the refutation of the *Adornment*.

Given the hundreds of pages of refutation that had already appeared from Dze smad rin po che and Shes rab rgya mtsho, the very existence of this work is perhaps as important as its content. The attitude of the authors is not one of reverence toward a compatriot. In the foreword, GC is condemned for his lack of faith in Buddhism and for propounding a philosophical view so relativistic that it would permit the destruction of the Buddha's teachings. The criticism of GC is not limited to the *Adornment* (whose authorship is acknowledged as controversial), but extends to his originality in any domain.

> If it is said that GC was unrivalled from the perspective of his original views, regarding his views on the dharma, the things that appear in the *Adornment for Nāgārjuna's Thought* are merely imitations of the apparent refutations that oppose the views of the Foremost Lama by the followers of earlier Tibetans, such as Go, Shag, and the translator Stag. Apart from that, there is not a single new argument that is suitable to be put forward. If one considers his history and pilgrimage guide, one time he made a collection of old writings and one time he printed the notes of what he saw and heard when he went to India. Apart from that, what does he provide through his research that was new and that did not exist before? Furthermore, in his history, there are many mistakes in years, verses, and place names. There are those who say that he had a new perspective. When people from a small remote land who do not understand the ways of foreign science see a motion picture for the first time, they are amazed. But, these things are unable to generate wonder even in a student at a mediocre school who has studied modern science today. In short, from whatever perspective, whether it be that of the dharma or science, there is not a single wondrous imprint to be counted. Therefore, raising him up as a *mahāpaṇḍita* of surpassing knowledge would

seem to be an example of getting an ant in your eye and thinking it is a huge black bug.[11]

It would require additional volumes to consider the specific refutations of the *Adornment* in any detail. One small observation might be made here, however. As noted above, Shes rab rgya mtsho repeatedly remarks that the statements that appear in the *Adornment*, whether they derive from GC or from Zla ba bzang po, have no foundation, either in Indian Buddhism or in any of the sects of Tibetan Buddhism. One might initially fail to identify why this is a fault. But in Buddhist scholasticism, there is no more damaging charge that can be leveled at an opponent than that of innovation. As a tradition that derives authority from lineage, all doctrines, regardless of their actual originality, must trace their authority back through the past, ideally to the words of the Buddha himself. And because those words are so vast and diverse, each doctrine must be placed in a particular tradition of interpretation. Not to do so is to be guilty of innovation; the Tibetan term is *rang bzo*, which has the sense of fabrication, of concoction, of something made up.

In Tibetan Buddhism, which looks ever back to India, the Land of the Noble (*'phags yul*), as the unadulterated source of its Buddhism, precedent is thus of

11. Chu skyes bsam gtan, ed., *Log smra'i tshang tshing sreg pa'i lung rigs rdo rje me lce* (Lan kro'u, China: Kan su'u mi rigs dpe skrun khang, 1977), 9–10.

Another contemporary Dge lugs scholar from A mdo is also quite critical. Yon tan rgya mtsho (1933–2002) devotes ten pages of his 1977 *Gdong lan lung rigs thog mda'* to a refutation of some of the arguments in the *Adornment*. He begins by acknowledging the controversy over the authorship and the claims by some that GC was himself a Rnying ma pa. He notes, however, that from a young age, GC had studied at the great Dge lugs monasteries, making it difficult to claim that GC's renowned learning did not derive from the Dge lugs. Yet he finds the arguments in the *Adornment* simplistic in the extreme: "Specifically, even a fool like me can establish from his own experience that all of the reasonings that are set forth in the *Adornment* derive merely from shifting the meanings of words that are as familiar as the wind even to a beginning student of elementary logic at the monastery." Thus, although the *Adornment* may seem profound to someone unfamiliar with the word of the Buddha and the works of Nāgārjuna, anyone who has studied these texts will see that it is nothing more than instructions to an audience of fools. Whether or not it represents GC's own views, it is mass of contradictions. See Mdo smad pa Yon tan rgya mtsho, *Gdong lan lung rigs thog mda'* (Paris: n.p., 1977), 178–79.

As Hor gtsang 'jigs med correctly notes in his *Drang bden gyis bslus pa'i slong mo ba*, p. 131, GC's position is stated and attacked, without mentioning his name or the *Adornment*, by Sgo mang dge bshes Tshul khrims rgya mtsho, a lecturer at the Central Institute for Higher Tibetan Studies in Sarnath, in his *Dka' gnad kyi don gsal bar byed pa dus kyi me long* (Delhi: Mongolian Lama Guru Deva, 1983). The relevant sections occur at pp. 158–86 and 202–21.

One should not assume, however, that all recent responses have been negative. For an appreciative essay by a Rnying ma monk from GC's boyhood monastery of G.ya ma bkra shis 'khyil, see Ngag dbang chos grags, "Dbu ma klu sgrub dgongs rgyan dang 'brel ba'i gzhung gi don gnad 'ga' la rags tsam dpyad pa," *Bod ljong zhib 'jug* 3 (1997): 61–69.

primary importance. Each sect traces its doctrines back through the period of transmission of Buddhism from India to Tibet and back further to a lineage of Indian masters: the visits to Tibet by Padmasambhava and Vimalamitra for the Rnying ma; the tutelage of 'Brog mi under Virūpa for the Sa skya; the three visits to India by Mar pa the Translator, where he studied under Maitrīpa and Nāropa, for the Bka' brgyud. Even for the Dge lugs, the only major sect without a direct historical link to India (although their appellation as the "new Bka' gdams" implies an appropriation of Atiśa), lineage is of vital importance. The Dge lugs lineage is established not through travel between India and Tibet, however, but through certain visionary experiences of Tsong kha pa, in which Nāgārjuna and his chief commentators appeared to indicate to him that it is the interpretation of Buddhapālita and, by extension, Candrakīrti that contains the true meaning of the middle way. Thus, to say that the positions in the *Adornment* bear no relation to this lineage of interpretation, despite ample citation of these founding figures, is considered particularly damning: GC (and Zla ba bzang po) made it all up.

The editor of the 1997 volume of refutations of the *Adornment*, although clearly deferential to Shes rab rgya mtsho, makes a very different point. As cited above, he writes, "the things that appear in the *Adornment for Nāgārjuna's Thought* are merely imitations of the apparent refutations that oppose the views of the Foremost Lama by the followers of earlier Tibetans, such as Go, Shag, and the translator Stag." "Go" is Go rams pa bsod nams seng ge (1429–89), "Shag" is Shākya mchog ldan (1428–1507), and "the translator Stag" is Stag tshang lo tsā ba shes rab rin chen (born 1405). These three eminent scholars of the Sa skya sect, writing in the generation after that of "the Foremost Lama," Tsong kha pa, are renowned in the Dge lugs for having the temerity to dispute the views of Tsong kha pa (although Stag tshang famously later recanted). For long periods in Tibetan history, this was all that Dge lugs monks knew of these three scholars, because the printing of their works had been banned.[12] In the *Adornment*, Stag tshang and Go rams pa are mentioned by name; the former with approval, the latter with disapproval.[13]

12. See E. Gene Smith, "Banned Books in the Tibetan Speaking Lands," in *21st Century Tibet Issue: Symposium on Contemporary Tibetan Studies, Collected Papers* (Taipei: Mongolian and Tibetan Affairs Commission, 2004), 364–81.

13. See ¶¶213 and 143. In his biography of GC, Bla chung a pho describes a conversation in which GC expressed his admiration for Go rams pa's *Lta ba'i shan 'byed*. See Shes rab rgya mtsho, "Dge 'dun chos 'phel," in *Biographical Dictionary of Tibet and Tibetan Buddhism*, vol. 4, *The Rñiṅ-ma-pa Tradition (Part Two)*, ed. Khetsun Sangpo (Dharamsala, India: Library of Tibetan Works and Archives, 1973), 648. See also Mengele, *dGe-'dun-chos-'phel*, 37–38, 66.

The larger point is that Shes rab rgya mtsho condemns the *Adornment* because everything in it was new. The editor of the 1997 collection, Chu skyes bsam gtan, condemns the *Adornment* because nothing is new. This polarity of positions among the opponents of the text suggests that the compulsion to condemn the text sometimes overwhelms serious engagement with its arguments. The possibility that an admittedly brilliant scholar such as GC, trained in the Dge lugs academy, would compose a work highly critical of the foundations of Dge lugs scholasticism, going so far as to question the authority of Tsong kha pa (although, as we have seen, such criticisms are far fewer than one might be led to believe by reading the refutations), and then that such a work would be published by a prominent Rnying ma lama, seems to have been unbearable.

The precedents for GC's views among previous Tibetan authors, as well as the question of their direct and indirect influence on the *Adornment*, merit a separate study, but some preliminary observations are appropriate here. GC's central theme in the first part of the *Adornment* is that conventional valid knowledge (*tha snyad tshad ma*) is impossible for the unenlightened, and what the ignorant regard as "valid knowledge" thus bears no relation whatsoever to the Buddha's understanding of either the ultimate or the conventional. This position is not unique to GC, having been set forth most famously (or infamously, from the Dge lugs perspective) by the Sa skya scholar Stag tshang lo tsā ba shes rab rin chen (born 1405) in his *Grub mtha' kun shes*. For example, he writes (in a statement that would fit seamlessly into the *Adornment*), "To take the valid knowledge [of ordinary beings] that analyzes conventional truths to be the Buddha's wisdom that understands the multiplicities (*ji snyed pa mkhyen pa'i ye shes*) is the root of a host of contradictions." See Stag tshang lo tsā ba shes rab rin chen, *Grub mtha' kun shes nas mtha' bral sgrub pa zhes bya ba'i bstan bcos rnam par bshad pa legs pa bshad kyi rgya mtsho* (Thimphu, Bhutan, 1976), 109a6 (215). On Stag tshang's critique, see Helmut Tauscher, "Controversies in Tibetan Madhyamaka Exegesis: Stag Tshaṅ Lotsāba's Critique of Tsoṅ kha pa's Assertion of Validly Established Phenomena," *Asiatische Studien / Études Asiatiques* 44, no. 1 (1992): 411–36.

Like that of GC, Stag tshang's critique elicited vociferous polemical responses from generations of Dge lugs scholars; 'Jam dbyangs bzhad pa's famous *Grub mtha' chen mo* is in one sense a lengthy response to Stag tshang (and borrows heavily from him). For a study of a critique of Stag tshang by the otherwise more ecumenical First Paṇ chen Lama, see José Cabezón, "On the *sGra pa Shes rab rin chen pa'i rtsod lan* of Paṇ chen bLo bzang chos rgyan," *Asiatische Studien / Études Asiatiques* 49, no. 4 (1995): 643–69. Stag tshang is quoted unapprovingly by Dze smad rin po che at 43.1.

Given his wide reading, one must assume that GC was aware of Stag tshang's position, certainly from reading 'Jam dbyangs bzhad pa (the author of the *yig cha* literature of the Dge lugs monasteries where he studied) and probably from reading Stag tshang himself.

GC is also accused of being influenced by two other famous Sa skya scholars, Go rams pa bsod nams seng ge (1429–89) and Shākya mchog ldan (1428–1507), both of whom wrote extensively on Madhyamaka and on the questions of valid knowledge, the Madhyamaka thesis, and the commonly appearing subject. For Go rams pa, see, for example, his *Rgyal ba thams cad kyi thugs kyi dgongs pa zab mo dbu ma'i de kho na nyid spyi'i ngag gis ston pa nges don rab gsal* (also known as *Dbu ma'i spyi don*), in *The Collected Works of Kun-mkhyen Go-rams pa Bsod-nams-seng-ge (Kun mkhyen go bo rab 'byams pa bsod nams seng ge'i bka' 'bum)*, vol 5 (*ca*) (Dehra-dun, India: Sakya College, 1979), 95b2–105b1. For Shākya mchog ldan, see, for example, his *Theg pa chen po dbu ma rnam par nges pa'i bang mdzod lung rigs rgya mtsho* (also known as *Dbu ma'i rnam nges*) in *The Complete Writings of Gser-mdog Paṇ-chen Śākya-mchog-ldan (Gser mdog Paṇ chen Shākya mchog ldan gyi gsung 'bum legs bshad gser gyi bdud rtsi)*, vol. 14 (*ba*) (Thimphu, Bhutan: Kunzang Tobgey, 1975–78), 31a4–32a7.

Regardless of the philosophical problems raised by the text, one must conclude that much of the response that the *Adornment* has and continues to elicit derives directly from the sectarian politics so rife in Tibetan Buddhism in the twentieth century. And so the *Adornment* became anathema for the Dge lugs. If it could be shown that GC was not the author, he could be spared. If GC was the author, he must be condemned.

I am grateful to Georges Dreyfus for these references. On antecedents to Go rams pa and Shākya mchog ldan, see Paul Williams, "Rma bya pa byang chub bstson 'grus on Madhyamaka Method," *Journal of Indian Philosophy* 13, no. 3 (September 1985): 205–25.

Regardless of what influence the work of these earlier scholars may have had on GC's thought on these various issues, GC's way of formulating and expressing them is very much his own.

chapter

6

THE QUESTION OF
MODERNITY

What can be said with certainty about the *Adornment* and its author? First, it seems certain, upon the evaluation of the available evidence, that GC is the author of the *Adornment*, that the *Adornment* is the final work of the most innovative Tibetan author of the twentieth century. But as we have seen in chapter 5, innovation is classified as a crime in Tibetan Buddhism, a crime with which GC was charged and for which he was punished. Yet regardless of how GC would have characterized his other works, it is highly doubtful that he would have regarded the *Adornment* as in any way innovative, in any way modern. It is therefore necessary to consider the vexed question of modernity in the *Adornment*, in some ways the most traditional work produced by the most modern of Tibetan authors.

If there is a single theme that runs through the work, it is that GC seems to be objecting (although he does not mention the story) to the command delivered by Mañjuśrī, the bodhisattva of wisdom, when he appeared in a vision to Tsong kha pa. Mañjuśrī told Tsong kha pa to guard the conventional, to preserve the appearances of the world. It is this concern to uphold the validity of the conventional—understood primarily as the cause and effect of actions—in the face of the ultimate emptiness of all phenomena that seems to motivate much of Tsong kha pa's work. It is a concern with strong ethical implications, serving as a check against the antinomianism that the doctrine of emptiness might inspire, an antinomianism to which, some would argue, GC himself succumbed. At the same time, the strong emphasis on the viability and hence value of conventional truths provides a fitting ideological basis for the Dge lugs, a sect whose leaders, beginning in the seventeenth century, had set out and succeeded to rule Tibet, acquiring vast wealth and power for themselves in the process. This was a power that GC sought to challenge, even from his days in the debating courtyard; so it is in some ways not surprising that he took the scholastic vocabulary of the Dge lugs pas and turned it against them, using it to undercut their most cherished foundation, perhaps imagining that to defeat them in the *Adornment* could somehow lead to their defeat in the Potala. Instead, he was imprisoned in the dungeon below it.

Judging from the polemical responses it elicited, the *Adornment* clearly was regarded as subversive by the Dge lugs orthodoxy. Part of the perceived subversion may be traced to GC's concerted attempt to wrest certainty, and hence the control of enlightenment, away from its traditional scholastic moorings. But he did not merely seek to set it adrift. His point, reiterated again and again, is that emptiness completely contradicts the world and, therefore, that one of the hallmarks of Tsong kha pa's thought, the compatibility of the two truths, is a gross error. There is no commonality whatsoever between the way things are perceived by the ignorant mind and the way they are perceived by the enlightened mind. The statements in the sūtras that we cannot conceptually understand should not be taken as an opportunity for exegesis, but rather should serve as an indication that enlightenment completely contravenes the world. Referring to the Dge lugs, he writes at ¶196, "Here, the path of the noncontradictory union of the two truths appears in brief to be a system in which the understandings of the Buddha and sentient beings are mixed as one without contradiction. If one believes in such a thing, there is no opportunity for believing even in the words *saṃsāra nirvāṇa*." Indeed, GC sees in the Dge lugs obsession with consistency an evisceration of Nāgārjuna's critique, a domestication of the rhetoric of enlightenment, until it does nothing more than validate the operations of ignorance.

His position, however, is not simply one of radical skepticism. Rather, it is a pious skepticism that seeks, however vaguely, to define a path to enlightenment. GC's reverence for the Buddha, for Nāgārjuna, for Candrakīrti, is clear. He is seeking to shift the focus away from the elaborations of the Dge lugs scholastics and bring it (back) to the Buddha. This is, of course, a common trope in the history of Buddhist thought. But GC deploys it in his own way, arguing against interpretation in order to portray both enlightenment and unenlightenment in the starkest terms. The Dge lugs interpretation of the statements of the Buddha and of Nāgārjuna, especially with regard to the nature of reality, are for GC excessively subtle, refined to the point of obscurity. To seek logical consistency above all else, as GC claims the Dge lugs do, is to forget those beings at both ends of the continuum of consciousness: benighted sentient beings on one side, and the Buddha on the other. GC thus proclaims a kind of populist Madhyamaka, in which the simple declarations of existence and nonexistence are to be taken quite literally—without the mediation of interpretation by those learned in logic—and their implications felt with their full force.

In the first part of the *Adornment*, therefore, GC seeks to demonstrate that all claims made by the unenlightened are merely opinion, and that any attempts by them to describe the nature of reality are so much conceit and folly. He continues this point in the second part of the text, but returns again and again to the tension between the need for communication between the enlightened and the unenlightened and the need to utterly destroy the conceptions of the unenlightened. As he says at ¶171,

> The master Candrakīrti destroyed all presentations of the conventional when he explained the ultimate. When he explained the conventional he disregarded the ultimate truth and merely followed whatever were the most powerful worldly reasonings. But if one is able to determine all the presentations of the objects and subjects that are beyond the world through including them in the reasoning of the world, then why should one seek the middle path?

The ultimate is thus beyond the purview of the unenlightened, and the failure to acknowledge this is a fatal obstacle to progress on the path. At the same time, we must speak, and so in the realm of the conventional one should simply concede the categories of the world without imagining that their domain of efficacy extends into the ultimate.

The apparently unbridgeable chasm between the conventional and the ultimate, between the unenlightened and the enlightened, is spanned only by the compassionate Buddha, who makes use of his skillful methods to lead the suffering to salvation. This most traditional Buddhist view is also that of GC. He seeks to emphasize, however, the Buddha's skillful use of language, how the Buddha employs the language of the world to somehow lead sentient beings beyond the world. His words, therefore, carry a great power, and thus GC objects most strenuously to attempts to paraphrase and reinterpret them so that they conform to the categories of the unenlightened mind.

GC's differences with the Dge lugs geshes are particularly vivid on this point. As he says in the *Adornment* at ¶20, "[T]o think that the earth, stones, mountains, and rocks that we see now are still to be seen vividly when we are buddhas is very much in error." Here is Dze smad rin po che's attempt to refute this claim:

> It follows that the subject, these earth, stones, mountains, and rocks that we perceive today, do not appear to a noble buddha, because what you wrote about this due to your mistaken ideas is correct. If you accept that, then it follows that the subject, the teacher Śākyamuni, did not see any earth, stones,

mountains, or rocks, because of your assertion. If you accept that, then it follows that that subject [the teacher Śākyamuni], did not even see the Bodhi tree at Vajrāsana in India, because of your previous assertion.[1]

Using the standard debate format, Dze smad takes GC's assertion that the ordinary objects of the world do not appear to a buddha and draws from it the conclusion that Śākyamuni Buddha did not see earth, stones, mountains, or rocks during the years of his life following his attainment of buddhahood. It would absurdly follow from GC's statement, therefore, that the Buddha did not see the Bodhi tree in Bodh Gayā (Vajrāsana), beneath which he sat for forty-nine days after his enlightenment. One can see Dze smad rin po che's point here; if the implications of GC's statement are drawn out, they very quickly violate common sense. However, it must also be said that Dze smad seems to miss entirely the evocative quality of GC's statement, the rhetorical quality that is its strength, and hence the poetics of enlightenment that GC is seeking to restore. GC's point is that enlightenment violates common sense and as long as one seeks to understand it within such limitations, all possibility of enlightenment is destroyed. GC offers his own exegesis of Nāgārjuna, but one that calls for evocation over exegesis. Indeed, one might conclude that in his polemical response to the *Adornment,* Dze smad rin po che seems to instantiate the pedantic scholasticism that GC scorns. The vicious nature of the attacks on the *Adornment* may in fact derive as much from the content of the text as from the circumstances of its production.

But is GC's insistence on what one might term the poetics of enlightenment somehow modern? There are many ways in which he might be regarded as a modernist. He was an avant-garde intellectual who explored new forms (from the Tibetan perspective) in his prose, in his poetry, in his painting. He associated with social and political revolutionaries during his years in South Asia, and he constantly called upon Tibetans to break with the past. He borrowed from the methods of British colonial archaeology.[2] And he also may be the first

---

1. Dze smad Blo bzang dpal ldan bstan 'dzin yar rgyas, *'Jam dpal dgyes pa'i gtam gyis rgol ngan phye mar 'thag pa reg gcod ral gri'i 'phrul 'khor* (Delhi: D. Gyaltsan and K. Legshay, 1972), 47.6–48.2.

2. See Toni Huber, "Colonial Archaeology, International Missionary Buddhism and the First Example of Modern Tibetan Literature," in *Bauddhavidyāsudhākaraḥ: Studies in Honour of Heinz Bechert on His 65th Birthday,* ed. Petra Kieffer-Pülz and Jes-Uwe Hartmann, Indica et Tibetica 30 (Swisttal-Odendorf: Indica et Tibetica Verlag, 1997): 297–318. GC's time in South Asia might be compared to that of another Tibetan traveler. See Per Kvaerne, "Khyung-sprul 'Jigs-med nam-mkha'i rdo-rje (1897–1955): An Early Twentieth-Century Tibetan Pilgrim in India," in *Pilgrimage in Tibet,* ed. Alex McKay (London: Curzon, 1998), 71–84.

Tibetan to be counted as a Buddhist modernist. This is a term that itself requires exegesis.

The "scientific" study of Buddhism began in Europe in the early nineteenth century as an offshoot of the new science of philology. From that point the academic discipline of Buddhist studies developed in the wake of the projects of European (and later Japanese) colonialism. Also in the nineteenth century, in apparent response to Christian missions, Asian elites (often monks) across their continent created what scholars have recently begun to refer to as modern Buddhism.[3]

This Buddhism rejects many of the ritual and magical elements of previous forms of the tradition, emphasizing equality over hierarchy and the universal over the local, and it often exalts the individual above the community. Yet modern Buddhism does not see itself as the culmination of a long process of evolution, but rather as a return to the origin, to the Buddhism of the Buddha himself. It seeks to distance itself most from those forms of Buddhism that immediately precede it, that are even contemporary with it. It is ancient Buddhism, and especially the enlightenment of the Buddha twenty-five hundred years ago, that is seen as most modern, as most compatible with the ideals of the European Enlightenment.

3. The conjunction of the terms *Buddhism* and *modern* has a long history. In 1871, Henry Alabaster, Interpreter of Her Majesty's Consulate General in Siam, published *The Wheel of the Law*. The book included a long section called "The Modern Buddhist; Being the Views of a Siamese Minister of State on his Own and Other Religions," a record of Alabaster's conversations with the foreign minister of King Rama IV, devoted largely to comparisons of Buddhism and Christianity. In 1911, Alexandra David-Neel, long before she found magic and mystery in Tibet, and when she was simply Alexandra David, published *Le modernisme Bouddhiste et le Bouddhisme du Bouddha*. For her, Buddhist modernism and the Buddhism of the Buddha were the same. She called for a return to the Pāli scriptures and a rejection of the ritual and sacerdotalism that had infected the tradition since the Buddha entered nirvāṇa.

The academic recognition of a phenomenon called Buddhist modernism began in 1966, when Heinz Bechert, in *Buddhismus, Staat und Gesellschaft in der Ländern des Theravāda-Buddhismus*, used the term to describe tendencies that began in the late nineteenth century, when monastic elites in Sri Lanka and Southeast Asia sought to counter the negative portrayal of Buddhism by colonial officials and Christian missionaries. See Heinz Bechert, *Buddhismus, Staat und Gesellschaft in der Ländern des Theravāda-Buddhismus* (Frankfurt/Berlin: Metzner, 1966). In 1970, Gananath Obeyesekere coined the term *Protestant Buddhism*, also to describe Sri Lanka. He argued that local Buddhists had adopted elements of Protestant Christianity in response to colonial and missionary authority. See Gananath Obeyesekere, "Religious Symbolism and Political Change in Ceylon," *Modern Ceylon Studies* 1, no. 1 (1970): 43–63. In the introduction to a recent anthology, I argued that modern Buddhism is a global phenomenon and has, in effect, developed into an autonomous Buddhist school, with its own sacred canon (including works such as Jack Kerouac's *The Dharma Bums*) and saints (like D. T. Suzuki). See Donald S. Lopez Jr., *A Modern Buddhist Bible: Essential Readings from East and West* (Boston: Beacon Press, 2002;. published in the United Kingdom as *Modern Buddhism: Readings for the Unenlightened* [London: Penguin, 2002]).

Modern Buddhism did not come to Tibet. There were no movements to ordain women, no publication of Buddhist magazines, no formation of lay Buddhist societies, no establishment of orphanages, no liberal critique of Buddhism as contrary to scientific progress, no Tibetan delegates to the 1893 World's Parliament of Religions in Chicago, no efforts by Tibetans to found world Buddhist organizations.[4] Tibet remained relatively isolated from the forces of modern Buddhism, in part because it had never become a European colony. Christian missionaries never were a significant presence, Buddhist monks were not educated in European languages, European educational institutions were not established, the printing press was not introduced. Indeed, due in part to its relative isolation from Europe, many, in both Asia and the West, considered Tibet a pure abode of Buddhism, unspoiled by the forces of modernity.

GC encountered Buddhist modernism during his sojourn in South Asia. While there he espoused the cause of the Maha Bodhi Society of wresting control of Bodh Gayā from the Hindus and restoring it to the Buddhists. He found a certain solidarity with his fellow Buddhists in Sri Lanka. He accepted the claims of modern science and noted their compatibility with Buddhist doctrine, arguing in his essay in *Melong* that the Buddha knew that the world was round. But, like almost everything else with GC, his stance regarding the standard elements of Buddhist modernism was not entirely unambiguous. He cautioned against triumphantly proclaiming the compatibility of Buddhism and science in all domains; he argued that the international solidarity of Buddhists must be tempered by a recognition of doctrinal and cultural difference; he claimed that far from having disappeared from India, authentic Buddhist practice was still to be found there in the middle of the twentieth century. Yet he remained committed to many of the ideals of the Buddhist modernism of the day, going so far as to include in his pilgrimage guide to India a form that Tibetans could fill out and send to India (with their dues) in order to join the Maha Bodhi Society.

Nor would one identify GC's many projects in India as particularly avant garde. He made translations from Tibetan into English, but he does not seem to have translated from English into Tibetan (although information copied from encyclopedias appears in essays such as "'Dzam ling rgyas bshad" ["Extensive Description of the World"]). We find in his collected works no translations into

4. Tibet and Tibetan Buddhism were included in the plans of several important Chinese modern Buddhists, including Taixu (1890–1947). On these efforts see Gray Tuttle, *Tibetan Buddhism in the Making of Modern China* (New York: Columbia University Press, 2005). See also Holmes Welch, *The Buddhist Revival in China*, Harvard East Asian Series 33 (Cambridge, MA: Harvard University Press, 1968). On Taixu, see Don A. Pittman, *Toward a Modern Chinese Buddhism: Taixu's Reforms* (Honolulu: University of Hawai'i Press, 2001).

Tibetan of Hume, Nietzsche, or Marx, although he was said to read English well. Instead, he translated the classics of the orientalist modern (and the European construction of classical India): the *Bhagavad Gītā*, which had been translated into English by Charles Wilkins in 1785; *Śakuntala*, translated into English by Sir William Jones in 1789; and the *Dhammapada*, translated into German by Albrecht Weber in 1860.

Just as Tibet had been surrounded by Buddhist cultures in the early seventh century but did not know Buddhism (at least according to the traditional histories), so was it surrounded by modern Buddhist movements in the early twentieth century, in India and in China, but did not know Buddhist modernism. Following a practice dating to the seventh century, Tibetans had to go to India to learn the latest forms of Buddhism and bring them back to Tibet. And so, like Thon mi sambhoṭa and Rin chen bzang po before him, GC went to India. But unlike them, he was not dispatched as a royal emissary, and he did not return as a hero; he was thrown into prison. Right before or perhaps right after his imprisonment, GC gave teachings on Madhyamaka. How would his encounter with modernity manifest itself in his final work, the *Adornment*?

It is noteworthy that we find in the *Adornment* almost no overt evidence of GC's remarkable encounter with the modern world during his twelve years outside Tibet. He mentions the Qur'an, but there was a Muslim community in Lhasa and in his home region of A mdo, where he might have learned something about the text. The only direct evidence in the text of his travels is his brief mention of the great fifth-century Theravāda scholar Buddhaghosa, whose works had not been translated into Tibetan, and whom GC presumably studied in Sri Lanka. In discussing what is visible and invisible to the unenlightened, he certainly could have mentioned microscopes, telescopes, and X rays (all of which he discusses in his travel journals), but he does not. Indeed, what is striking about the *Adornment* is that a scholar who had such a strong interest in history and historical research, who sought out editions of texts and hunted through archives for materials which would allow him to write an accurate history of Tibet, seems to have so little use for history here, presenting a transhistorical and transrational vision of enlightenment that seems rather radical even in Buddhist terms, especially because it appears to be grounded in no conventional practice.

The standard view of much Buddhist modernism, both in South Asia and Europe, was that the Buddha was not a supernatural being but an extraordinary man. Here among the dizzying divinities of India was a man with just one head and two arms. He had rejected the myths of ancient India that organized society into an oppressive caste system, that had placed all power in the hands of priests who performed elaborate sacrifices in which they muttered unintelligible chants. The Buddha found the truth through his own efforts and then made it accessible to all, describing a universe in which there was no god, in which the transcendent unity of the *Upaniṣads* was replaced by the inexorable law of cause and effect. His life had certainly been embellished by legends over the centuries, but European scholars, reading the most ancient scriptures, had been able to strip away these mythic accretions to reveal the man who taught above all a system of ethics, who preached no dogma, who was born a man and died a man. It was with the rise of the Mahāyāna that he had become a deity, and it was with the rise of tantra that he had become debauched. The Buddha known to the Tibetans, then, was the Buddha most remote from his true nature, as understood by so many Buddhist modernists.

GC ascribed to none of this. He held the Mahāyāna sūtras and the tantras to be the word of the Buddha, and as is clear in the *Adornment*, the world of the Buddha is literally inconceivable by the unenlightened; GC is not a modernist who exalts the mundane over the transcendent.

Like so many Buddhist modernists, GC argues powerfully in the *Adornment* for a return to the Buddha, but his is a very different Buddha. He sounds unmistakably modern at ¶23, where he argues that the various qualities of the pure lands described in the Buddhist sūtras are merely reflections of local human tastes; if the sūtras had been spoken in Tibet rather than India, the pure lands would have been described differently. But far from being the cultural relativist that he is often accused of being, one might note that GC never questions for a moment that the Buddha spoke the sūtras, and the tantras. And the pure lands are described in these terms simply because these are the only terms that humans can comprehend; the true nature of the buddha fields is very different. As GC writes at ¶90, "If the two form bodies are displayed for the welfare of others, and the major and ancillary marks are fundamentally only for the sake of creating serenity in the minds of others, how is it possible that a body, with the complete major and ancillary marks established as the final imprint of the two collections, has the face of a sow, or the face of a lion, and so on?" There is no disenchantment of his world.

The *Adornment* may be judged a modernist work from the perspective of its style: it is a collage of elements drawn from disparate sources, its tone vacillating between pious poetry and biting satire. In its content, however, it is highly traditional. GC does not wish to distinguish himself from the past but to identify with it. It is from his contemporary Dge lugs scholars that he wants to distance himself. And despite their condemnation of him as a nihilist, it seems clear that GC regarded himself as a more authentic Buddhist than they. He may have been a skeptic and an iconoclast, but he seems to have seen these guises as completely compatible with the role of a devout Buddhist, who never doubted for a moment the omniscience of the Buddha and his myriad miraculous powers.

But should the lack of overt modernism in the *Adornment* give us reason to pause? We recall that GC seemed always somehow in disguise. When he was in the monastery in A mdo, he would assume the philosophical guise of a Jaina in order to uphold the non-Buddhist position that plants have consciousness. At the monastery in Lhasa, he would disguise himself as an illiterate *ldab ldob* and go to the debating courtyard to defeat the most brilliant scholar-monks. In India, although a distinguished scholar, he traveled unrecognized, seen only as a simple beggar. As a writer on the page, he was a master of genre. As an actor in the world, he excelled at playing the part. Yet he longed for recognition for who he truly was.

When GC was in Sri Lanka, he completed his travel journal, *The Golden Surface*, the work that he believed would form whatever legacy he would have in Tibet. He assembled the various chapters and sent them to a friend in Tibet, describing their contents in case anything was lost as the package made its way north, and asking that any misspellings be corrected. In the course of his requests and instructions, he offers an assessment of his work.

> All the people who are born in this world are given, through their past actions, the work that is appropriate for them. This is the work set for me. Thus, I have wandered through the realm, expending my human life on learning. The fruit of that is left in the form of a book. I think that it would be difficult for me to either hope or expect to benefit others in this life through such things as teaching and learning.[5]

The term translated as "teaching and learning" (*'chad nyan*) literally means "explaining and listening," and refers to the traditional Buddhist forms of monastic education in Tibet: a teacher explains a text, a student listens to that explanation. GC clearly had little patience with listening while he was a monk in Tibet, and no one had asked him to explain the dharma. Instead it was his lot, his karmic fate, to wander and to learn, and to record what he had learned in a book.

5. Dge 'dun chos 'phel, *Rgyal khams rig pas bskor ba'i gtam rgyud gser gyi thang ma (smad cha)*. In *Dge 'dun chos 'phel gyi gsung rtsom*, vol. 2 (Gangs can rig mdzod 11) (Lhasa, Tibet:·Bod ljongs bod yig dpe rnying dpe skrun khang, 1990), 187.

As he wrote these words in Sri Lanka, probably in 1941, GC had no idea that when he finally returned to Tibet five years later, he would be asked to explain the dharma, and that there would be those who not only listened, but recorded what he said, even if they did not always understand it. It seemed that GC had found respect at long last, at least by some, as a lama, as he had once been identified, before his birth. A lama before he came into the world, he played the role of a lama just before he left it. And so in the *Adornment* he spoke as a lama, reciting passages from the sūtras and śāstras from memory, with his words recorded by his disciple. Yet those words have garnered little respect for GC as a lama, at least among the monks of his sometime Dge lugs sect. Reading the work fifty years later, it is not so much the specific ideas that are so bold—the possibility of valid knowledge among the unenlightened had been debated for centuries in Tibet—but how they are expressed. The *Adornment*, an apparent fusion of trenchant essay and brilliant musings, is at once straightforward and ironic, conversational and poetic, confident and introverted. Yet it is not simply a matter of style. GC manipulates, often with great subtlety, the foundational categories of Buddhist philosophy so that the aesthetics of enlightenment might triumph over the philosophical certainty derived from reason. It is perhaps in this sense that the *Adornment* might best be regarded as a modernist work. Along the way, GC allows the reader to discern the outlines of the universe—not of all possible discourse, but of possible Buddhist discourse—and to mark the boundary between the orthodox and heretical. His critics charged that he crossed that line; instead, perhaps he traveled far to touch it. At the same time, GC offers a glimpse of the elusive boundary between the universe of things that can be stated and the universe which cannot be spoken because it cannot be thought, the inexpressible realm about which he wrote so eloquently.

The *Adornment* was not intended to be GC's final word. It became so only because of his untimely death, a death dealt not by foreign invader but by his own Buddhist government. Yet since we can only imagine what else he might have said had he been allowed to live, GC should have the last word here:

> If [what I have written] somehow enters the door of a wise person,
>> intent on learning,
>> Then the fruit of my labor will have been achieved.
>> For the smiles of the stupid and the approval of the rich,
>> I have never yearned even in my dreams.